Evidence in Literary Scholarship

ESSAYS IN MEMORY OF
JAMES MARSHALL OSBO

James Marshall Osborn, 1906–1976. From the bronze relief by William McVey.

Evidence in Literary Scholarship

ESSAYS IN MEMORY OF
JAMES MARSHALL OSBORN

Edited by

René Wellek
and
Alvaro Ribeiro

CLARENDON PRESS · OXFORD
1979

Oxford University Press, Walton Street, Oxford OX2 6DP

OXFORD LONDON GLASGOW
NEW YORK TORONTO MELBOURNE WELLINGTON
IBADAN NAIROBI DAR ES SALAAM CAPE TOWN
KUALA LUMPUR SINGAPORE JAKARTA HONG KONG TOKYO
DELHI BOMBAY CALCUTTA MADRAS KARACHI

© *Oxford University Press 1979*

British Library Cataloguing in Publication Data
Evidence in literary scholarship.
1. Criticism—Addresses, essays, lectures
I. Wellek, René   II. Ribeiro, Alvaro   III. Osborn,
James
807   PN85   78-40240
ISBN 0-19-812612-3

*Printed in Great Britain by
Western Printing Services Ltd, Bristol*

James Marshall Osborn
1906-1976

RENÉ WELLEK

FRIENDS, COLLEAGUES, and former research assistants who became
friends have united here in honouring the memory of James
Marshall Osborn, collector of manuscripts, bibliographer, editor,
biographer, and literary historian. A short memoir of his life and
work seems an appropriate introduction.

Jim, as he was known to all his friends, was born on 22 April
1906, the son of Clare Marshall and Mildred Sleeper Osborn in
Cleveland, Ohio. Both the Osborn and the Sleeper families came
to the United States from England. In 1643 Thomas Osborn
arrived in New Haven, Connecticut, where he became a tanner.
During the mass migration from the New England states to what
was then the Western Reserve, about 1810, six Osborn brothers
settled in a location on Lake Erie just west of Cleveland, which was
later known as Bay Village. Jim's grandfather, Reuben Osborn, was
the first Mayor of Bay Village. His father studied civil engineering at the Case School of Applied Science in Cleveland and then
did private engineering work 'including building electric factory
docks, shipyards and similar projects' until 1908, when he became
the City Engineer in Lorain, Ohio. In 1918 he was appointed
City Manager of East Cleveland, Ohio. He was one of the first
City Managers in the country, an important innovation which
took the administration of many American cities out of the hands
of political appointees. All his life Jim honoured the memory of
his father by taking an active interest in the National Municipal
League. He served as a member of the governing Council from
1954 to 1973. He was a member of the Executive Committee from
1962 to 1966. In 1966 he received the Distinguished Citizen
Award from the League. Some time in the fifties Jim donated a
conference room to the headquarters of the Municipal League in

New York in memory of his father, and it has been used for small conferences, workshops, and seminars ever since.

Jim's father later became the City Manager in Kenosha, Wisconsin. Thus, following the migrations of his father, Jim attended public schools in Lorain, Ohio, East Cleveland, Ohio, and Kenosha, Wisconsin. In 1924 he went to Wesleyan University, Middletown, Connecticut, where he received his B.A. in 1928. He was, I am told, an avid football player and edited the local student humorous magazine, *The Wesleyan Wasp*. Still, in these undergraduate years, which did not foretell a scholarly career, he became interested in English literature of the seventeenth and eighteenth centuries. One of his teachers was Homer E. Woodbridge, who later produced a thoroughly documented monograph on *Sir William Temple* (1940). Jim preserved a lifelong loyalty to his Alma Mater. He served as President of the Class of 1928 and gave generously to its fund.

After graduation Jim went to work with the Guaranty Trust Company in New York, in the investment advisory department. In New York he met Marie-Louise Montgomery, the daughter of John Flournoy Montgomery, who later served as United States Minister to Hungary from 1933 to 1942. Mr. Montgomery related some of his experiences in his book *Hungary, the Unwilling Satellite* (1947). In these years the Osborns visited him in Budapest. Jim had married Miss Montgomery in 1929, and two sons were born to the couple: Marshall, now a Professor of Mathematics at the University of Wisconsin, Madison, Wisconsin, and Thomas, a freelance conductor of symphony orchestras in the Los Angeles area. One day, so the story goes, Jim came back from the bank, bored and disgusted with his work, and told his wife then and there that he was quitting and going to study English literature. They could afford to live on their income, and there was no point in wasting one's life in an uncongenial occupation. Marie-Louise concurred loyally and enthusiastically, helping him in every way until her death at Christmas 1968.

In the fall of 1932 Jim enrolled as a graduate student in the English department of Columbia University and attended, as his fellow student James L. Clifford informs me, a large lecture course on the eighteenth century given by Ernest Hunter Wright (1882–1968) who later published *The Meaning of Rousseau*, and also a course by Samuel Lee Woolff on Dryden, Defoe, and Swift.

Clifford calls Woolff 'the dullest teacher I ever had in my life. But he sold us on Dryden and Swift' (letter of 9 January 1977). Jim also did work on the Victorians with Emery Neff (born 1892), well known mainly for his work on Carlyle, and with Hoxie Neale Fairchild (1894–1973), who had just published his *Romantic Quest*. In the spring of 1934 Jim wrote an M.A. thesis called 'A Study of the Literature of Travels in Greece as Known in England from 1700 to 1850', largely under the direction of Fairchild. The topic was far from being romantic or even pre-romantic. It was, to judge from a later reworking as 'Travel Literature and the Rise of Neo-Hellenism in England', *Bulletin of the New York Public Library*, lxvii (May 1963), 279–300, rather the reverse. Instead of looking at the interest in Greece as heralding romanticism, as Harry Levin did in his undergraduate essay *The Broken Column*, or as preparation for political Philhellenism, as Terence Spencer did in *Fair Greece, Sad Republic* (1956), Jim regarded the revival of interest in Greece as largely the antiquarian concern of the early travellers: a phase he calls 'archeographical'. The published essay traces English travel books from Sir George Wheler's *Journey into Greece* (1682) to Thackeray's burlesque *Notes of a Journey from Cornhill to Grand Cairo* (1846), clearly distinguishing the stages in the English interest in Greece.

In 1934 Jim took his family to Oxford to study for a B.Litt., mainly under David Nichol Smith and Brett-Smith. Nichol Smith's course on the History of English Studies determined the direction of Jim's future research. Faced with the riches of the Bodleian Library, he began to devote himself to what proved to be one of the main themes of his life-work: the early history of English scholarship. He compiled then for F. W. Bateson's *Cambridge Bibliography of English Literature* the invaluable first-hand bibliography of 'Literary Historians and Antiquaries' which lists (ii. 892–932) hundreds of rare items, often for the first time, allowing an accurate survey of the writings of such antiquaries as William Oldys, Edmond Malone, and Joseph Ritson in their entirety. In the Bodleian Jim was able to examine the papers of Edmond Malone. They sent him to Dryden, to Malone's biography of Dryden and the manuscript additions in Malone's copy for a second edition which never materialized. Even at that time Jim conceived the idea of a monograph on Edmond Malone, which, alas, was never finished. Still, an edition of the Boswell–Malone

correspondence is ready for publication as part of the Yale edition
of the Boswell papers, and there are, among others, very substantial
papers on 'Edmond Malone: Scholar-Collector' in *The Library*, 5th
ser., xix (1964), 11–37, 'Edmond Malone and Dr. Johnson' in
Mary M. Lascelles *et al.*, ed., *Johnson, Boswell and Their Circle:
Essays Presented to Lawrence Fitzroy Powell in Honour of His
Eighty-Fourth Birthday* (Oxford, 1965, 1–20), and 'Edmond
Malone and Oxford' in W. H. Bond, ed., *Eighteenth-Century
Studies in Honor of Donald F. Hyde* (New York, 1970, 323–38).

To be a scholar–collector was his own ambition, one he began
to cultivate in his Oxford years, of which we have a tantalizing
glimpse in the reminiscences by David Daiches included in this
volume. Jim himself tells of his first visit, in October 1934, to
Sotheby's.

It proved to be an episode so hilarious in its naïveté that only time has
lessened the embarrassment with which I recall it. My wife accompanied
me, and we arrived at the sale room so early that it was almost empty.
The U-shaped table covered with green baize below the auctioneer's
podium was deserted. Ignorant of the hallowed custom which reserved
each seat at the table for veteran members of the book trade, Mr. Maggs,
Mr. Quaritch, Mr. Dobell, Mr. Myers, and others, my wife and I sat
there and proceeded to bid in about twenty lots. Only later did I learn
how outrageously naïve our intrusion had been. In the eyes of the
bookmen we must have seemed as green as the cloth on the table before
us. (From 'The Osborn Collection, 1934–1974' in *Yale University
Library Gazette* (Oct. 1974).)

The research on Dryden became his thesis for the Oxford
B.Litt. in 1937 and the nucleus of his first book, *John Dryden:
Some Biographical Facts and Problems* (New York: Columbia
University Press, 1940). Its first half is a history of Dryden biography. 'Every biography of Dryden, long or short, is examined
carefully as to its contribution to our knowledge of Dryden's life
and for its peculiarities of method.' (See my review in *Modern
Philology*, xl (1942), 104–7.) Something like a miniature history of
literary biography in England emerges. Johnson's, Malone's,
Scott's, and Saintsbury's lives in particular are analysed to bring
out the distinctions of purpose and temperament, method and
technique, with great clarity. The second half of the book is made
up of miscellaneous studies contributing to Dryden's biography,

often on minor points, shedding light on obscure details in Dryden's career or some personal or literary associations. Material, much of it unpublished, was gathered here for a new life of Dryden, which Jim knew Charles E. Ward was then preparing with an edition of Dryden's letters (1942) and which he accomplished with a *Life* in 1961. Jim arranged for a new revised edition of his Dryden book in 1965, adding a welcome chapter surveying the new biographical scholarship.

Out of the Dryden book came an elaborate review of Hugh Macdonald's *Bibliography of John Dryden* in *Modern Philology* (1941), which offered many corrections and additional information. When George R. Noyes brought out his revised one-volume edition of Dryden's *Poetical Works* (1950), he could, in the Preface, acknowledge Jim's help. In 1961 Jim had the good luck to acquire a portrait of Dryden originally owned by a kinsman of Dryden. He gave an account in 'A Lost Portrait of John Dryden', *Huntington Library Quarterly*, xxxvi (Aug. 1973), reproducing the two preserved versions.

In 1938 Jim returned to the United States, and, recommended to Professor Chauncey B. Tinker by George Sherburn, the Pope scholar then at Harvard University, Jim settled in New Haven, in an association with Yale University which proved a commitment for the rest of his life. He became a Research Associate in the English department, without pay and without teaching duties. He was at first absorbed in preparing the book on Dryden for print and began at the same time his enormous activity for the organization of English literary scholarship. He was early engaged in the newly founded English Institute. At the first meeting (28 August– 9 September 1939) he read a paper entitled 'The Search for English Literary Documents', printed in *The English Institute Annual, 1939* (Columbia University Press, 1940), pp. 31–55, in which he gave sensible concrete advice about archival research, about dealing with dealers and collectors, about ferreting out scattered letters from private owners or public collections. The lecture begins with Jim's creed that 'finding literary documents is the foundation of literary research upon which interpretive criticism must rest' (p. 31). In 1939–40 he commuted to his old Alma Mater, Wesleyan University, to give a course in 'Methods of Literary Research'.

Jim believed in the community of scholars and in the necessity of communication between them. He was shocked by the needless duplications in literary research and conceived the idea of an annual *Work in Progress in the Modern Humanities*, which he edited from 1938 to 1942. This enterprise, theoretically excellent, was discontinued, partly because of the difficulties of assembling materials after the outbreak of the War but also because of criticisms which raised the questions of whether the listing of a project does not sometimes suggest an invidiously rival enterprise and of whether the listing itself may not be an attempt to stake out a claim without any solid basis in actual work.

The same concern lay behind the less ambitious but more practical idea of a newsletter for scholars working in the same field. Jim suggested the founding of a *Johnsonian Newsletter* to his friend James L. Clifford in 1940, and when its success became apparent he started *The Seventeenth Century Newsletter* in 1942 and edited it for five years. Since then newsletters have spawned in such proliferation that it is impossible to keep up with them.

Another enterprise was the founding of the Index Society, which was to print research tools. It began with Carlton Brown and Rossel Hope Robbins's, *The Index of Middle English Verse* in 1942, and subsequently published Thomas Copeland's *Checklist of Edmund Burke's Letters* (1955) and the important *Short-title Catalogue, 1641–1700* (3 vols., 1945–51) by Donald Wing.

The War brought many interruptions. Jim joined the staff of the Connecticut State Defense Council as Assistant Director of Air Raid Warden Schools, which necessitated absences four days a week in Hartford and countless speeches. In 1940 he acquired the Whirlwind Farm in Wallingford and began breeding Holstein cattle.

The manuscript collection, which had started with the purchase of a manuscript by William Morris in Jim's student days and had developed in Oxford in earnest with the purchase of seventeenth- and eighteenth-century materials from Percy Dobell in 1937, was enriched in February 1938 with a new treasure. Jim bought the papers of Joseph Spence from the Duke of Newcastle. Here was important work to do, for the papers included many more anecdotes about Pope and his contemporaries than appeared in Singer's edition of 1820. For years Jim struggled to disentangle these materials and to discover a rational method of arranging and editing them. It was 1966 before the two volumes of Joseph

Spence's *Observations, Anecdotes, and Characters of Books and Men* were published by the Clarendon Press. The introduction sketches the history of anecdotes as a literary genre and examines Spence's qualifications and reliability as a reporter. The incredibly intricate textual problems raised by the many overlapping manuscripts which had to be used are lucidly set forth and tabulated, and the whole mass of materials is arranged chronologically by subject matter and fully annotated. Jim's edition is a model of editorial care, a masterpiece of craftsmanship which helped him to earn the coveted Oxford D.Litt. in 1968. He was, I believe, the first American to *earn* this degree. As a by-product of the Spence edition we must not forget the printing of Spence's manuscript, in French, of a sketchy 'History of English Poetry' (see *Pope and His Contemporaries: Essays Presented to George Sherburn*, ed. James L. Clifford and Louis Landa (Oxford, 1949)). Oddly enough this was the very first narrative history of English poetry ever written, though its information even for 1732 was extremely perfunctory. Jim gives a lucid sketch of English literary historiography, an interest I shared with him and which was the subject of our correspondence in the forties. He read and helped with the manuscript of my *Rise of English Literary History* (University of North Carolina Press, 1941). He also encouraged his former research assistant Slava Klima to edit Spence's *Letters from the Grand Tour* (mainly from Italy) preserved in his collection (Montreal: McGill University Press, 1975).

Before the edition of Spence could come out, in 1955, a lucky purchase provided the stimulus for another edition. Jim bought the manuscript of the autobiography of Thomas Whythorne composed in 1576, and edited it for the Clarendon Press in 1961. He could not incorporate it into his collection, for it was declared a national treasure. He was happy to present it to the Bodleian Library, with which he had old associations. Later he could proudly point to his name: 'Jacobus M. Osborn' on the tablet listing the principal benefactors of the Library at the top of the staircase leading to Duke Humphrey's Library. Whythorne was a madrigalist and his memoirs are the first English autobiography, a remarkable social document, the life of a musician who was also a poet who composed what C. S. Lewis would have called 'drab' verse. The manuscript is also of interest to linguists, for it is written in a curiously phonetic orthography which yields new information on

sixteenth-century pronunciation. Jim did a superb job of editing
the manuscript (supplying, later, an edition in modernized spelling)
and wrote a lengthy introduction giving all the needed background
information and characterizing the man and his story. The
publication of the book was preceded by a lecture (8 August 1959),
'The Beginnings of Autobiography in England' (Los Angeles, 1960),
which gave a preliminary account of his find. It disputes the claim
that the fifteenth-century *Book of Margery Kempe* is a proper
autobiography. The introduction glances at the two Italian auto-
biographies that were almost contemporary with Whythorne's
(though also published much later), Cardano's and Benvenuto
Cellini's.

In 1967 Jim acquired a collection of seventy-six letters (in
Latin) addressed to Philip Sidney during his years on the Continent by many often eminent scholars, statesmen, and agents of
the time. It allowed him to write his most sustained narrative:
Young Philip Sidney, 1572–1577 (Yale University Press, 1972).
With great expository and narrative skill and in strictly chronological order Jim succeeded in reconstructing the Continental
career of the young English nobleman, showing concretely for the
first time that Protestant circles on the Continent hoped that he
would become the leader of the Protestant League against the
growing might of the Counter-Reformation. The book has nothing
to say on the poet who developed only later but tells a superb story
in which the St. Bartholomew's Night, the court of the Emperor in
Vienna and Prague, the pageantry of Elizabeth's progress, and
negotiations with William the Silent figure prominently. Jim's
interest in the Elizabethan age is further demonstrated by the
edition of *The Quenes Maiesties Passage* (1960) and his co-editing
of a facsimile of Shakespeare's *Poems* (1964).

The Sidney book was Jim's last major finished accomplishment.
In his last years he returned to his old love, Edmond Malone, and
prepared his edition of Malone's correspondence with Boswell
already mentioned. He compiled a monograph on 'The Club': a
careful chronological account of the circle around Dr. Johnson. I
am told that he reached the year 1799 before his death. He wrote
three pages on the morning before his fatal stroke on 17 October
1976. The materials are all assembled, and thus the book can be
finished by another hand.

I have given this account of his books and main articles (there are many more listed in Alvaro Ribeiro's full bibliography) because a scholar's life will survive in his printed work. We may protest against the injustice of an ungrateful posterity to brilliant talkers and walking encyclopedias, but the old saying that *scripta*—and only *scripta*—*manent* is still true. Jim left a legacy in his books and articles which embodies his ideal to present new evidence for the history of English literature in model editions and to reflect on his texts with scrupulous regard for evidence. He achieved what he wanted to perfection. In everything he did (as Mr. Charles Stroh, who knew him only as a cattle-breeder, said truthfully in his remarks at a commemorative meeting) he wanted to have things 'just right'.

Besides his books and articles he left his collection, which will be preserved and be accessible to future generations and should grow with new acquisitions. It is a treasure trove whose like is not found elsewhere except in the largest institutions. I am told it contains at least 47,000 separate items. Its contents, ranging from medieval manuscripts to correspondence of T. S. Eliot, cannot be properly described here. He did so himself in a report, 'The Osborn Collection, 1934–1974', *Yale University Library Gazette* (Oct. 1974) and in a lively lecture *Neo-Philobiblon: Ruminations on Manuscript Collecting* (Austin, Texas, 1973). There is an earlier detailed report by Laurence Witten in the *Book Collector* (Winter 1959). Fortunately Jim's successor as Curator of his collection, Stephen Parks, has been publishing full and careful reports in the *Yale University Library Gazette*, xliv (1970), xlvi (1972), xlviii (1974), l (1976), and lii (1978). These can be supplemented by *The Osborn Collection 1934–1974, a Catalogue of the Manuscripts exhibited in the Beinecke Rare Book and Manuscript Library October 1974–February 1975*, also compiled by Stephen Parks.

In connection with his scholarly activities, Jim received many honours and fulfilled many functions. At Oxford, he became in 1967 an honorary Fellow of St. Catherine's College, with which he had been associated as a graduate student. In 1963 he received an honorary D.H.L. from Kenyon College, in 1973 an honorary Doctorate of Letters from McGill University in Montreal, and in 1976 from St. John's University in Jamaica, New York. At Yale, he was a Fellow of Silliman College, faithfully attending the Monday evening Fellows' meetings, since 1955, and he was a member of the Yale University Library Associates, of which he became Chairman in the year of his death, and since 1954 Adviser on Seventeenth-Century Manuscripts to the Library. He was President of the Elizabethan Club from 1959 to 1961.

But the impression that Jim devoted all his life and energies to his scholarly pursuits is quite mistaken. I have alluded to his interest in the Municipal League. But his civic activities were far more extensive. He was particularly concerned with the New Haven Free Public Library. He was a member of the Board of Library Directors for a one-year term in 1948-9 and then continuously from 1 January 1954 until his death. He was a Treasurer of the Board from 1954 to 1958 and Vice-President from 1959 to 1975, the last year and a half as Acting President. Most of his term as Board member he was Chairman of the Finance Committee and supervised the investment of endowment funds for the Library. He was Vice-President and Chairman of the Finance Committee of the New Haven Symphony Orchestra, which, with the help of the Ford Foundation Matching Fund, managed to become the first symphony orchestra in the nation without a deficit. He was also Vice-President of the New Haven Kiwanis Club and incorporator of the New Haven Preservation Trust.

But his main 'extra-curricular' activity was the management of a farm he bought in Wallingford, Connecticut, in 1940. He bred Holstein bulls very successfully. Many of them won prizes, and one bull has progeny numbering some 20,000. He put his literary skill to benefit the cattle-breeding industry and edited the *New England Holstein Bulletin* from 1944 to 1946. In 1947 he published a *Holstein Handbook*.

All this factual information will suggest something of the breadth of Jim's interests and associations: he was not only a superb specialist but also a man of wide cultivation, an avid traveller in early years at least, not only to the obvious countries of Europe but also to the Middle East: to Turkey, Syria, Jordan, and Egypt, a man with whom one could talk on any subject under the sun, a lover of music and the arts. All those who knew him will cherish his memory as a generous, helpful, social, witty, good-humoured, upright man. He led a full, satisfying life which, with the exception of the last two years of his illness and the blow caused by the loss of his wife, was a singularly happy one. He achieved an equanimity and serenity which did not desert him even in the last days of his life.

On 7 April 1975 Jim called on me and in unusually solemn tones asked me to edit this volume, to write a brief memoir, and to invite the participation of a list of scholars he himself suggested. Some of them were prevented by other obligations or illness from contributing, but the majority submitted papers which reflect Jim's interest and concern for primary evidence remarkably well. I have arranged them in the chronological order of the subjects treated, which range from Shakespeare to Byron with emphasis, in Jim's spirit, on the Restoration period and the eighteenth century.

It remains for me to thank those who have supplied me with information: Jim's sister Hazel Osborn, Stephen Parks, the late James L. Clifford, Richard Leighton Greene, Meredith Bloss, and William N. Cassella, Jr.

Jim Osborn: Some Personal Notes

DAVID DAICHES

WHEN I was invited to contribute to Jim's Festschrift I thought I would do something on nationalism and antiquarianism in eighteenth-century Scotland, because eighteenth-century Scotland has long been a central interest of mine and I knew of Jim's passionate interest in eighteenth-century antiquaries. But time went by, the deadline drew nearer, and I found myself unable to find opportunities to do the necessary reading and thinking. Then I heard the sad news of Jim's death, and I thought vividly of those years in Oxford, many years ago, when Jim and I were fellow research students. I realized that I knew Jim at a time when few of his later colleagues and admirers knew him, and that perhaps the most appropriate contribution I could now make to a volume that was conceived as a Festschrift but which has, alas, turned into a memorial, would be to set down some of my recollections.

It was in October 1934 that I found myself sitting next to Jim at the first of Nichol Smith's series of lectures for research students on the History of English Studies. I had come to Oxford from Edinburgh University where I had studied under H. J. C. Grierson, and Jim had come from New York to re-enter the academic world at Oxford after several years in the world of banking. We got talking as we left the Old Schools, where the lectures were held, and I was struck at once by Jim's immense enthusiasm for Oxford, for Nichol Smith, for scholarship, and his excitement at his now being at the threshold of a career of scholarship. He was some six years older than I and already married, with two young children. I thought what an unusual person he was for me to meet at my first lecture in Oxford. In some ways he seemed very mature, very assured, very much a man of the world, but in others he seemed engagingly childlike. As we walked along the High in the autumn sunshine I soon learned about his major interests and enthusiasms. He talked about philhellenism in early nineteenth-century England, and mentioned Harry Levin's book *The Broken Column*.

He talked about music, in which I soon learned he also had both a keen interest and considerable knowledge. And he preached his own brand of vigorous atheism.

I was about to leave him in Broad Street to go to my college, Balliol, when he suggested that I come along and have lunch with his wife and himself at his place in north Oxford. I readily accepted his invitation, and we continued our walk together, turning into Cornmarket Street and St. Giles ('the Corn' and 'the Giler' as we had both already learned to call them) and then proceeding up Banbury Road. He paused outside a large and prosperous-looking house in Banbury Road and said with a smile, 'How would you like to live here?' I looked at its fine garden, its opulent air, its suggestion of solid nineteenth-century upper-middle-class prosperity, and observed that it must belong to one of the surviving dons who still had substantial private income. Still smiling, Jim said quietly: 'Well, we're only living here temporarily.' I had had no idea that this was the place to which he was taking me, and of course he knew that I had had no idea of this when he made the remark. It was, as I realized later, a characteristic example of his special brand of humorous mischief. He expected me to make some derogatory remark so that he could laugh good-naturedly at my embarrassment when I learnt that, temporarily at least, it was his house.

In the course of our conversation up to this point I had formed the impression that, having left the world of business to enter the world of scholarship, he must have saved up enough to keep himself and his family during his years of graduate study and that this would mean going rather carefully. I thought that as he was entering the academic world relatively late, he would be bound to be behind in the race for promotion and would probably have to be content with starting at a very junior post with people of his own age all senior to him. Having myself come to Oxford on a scholarship from Edinburgh University that provided barely adequate means of living in what seemed to be the inordinately expensive Oxford setting, I was prepared to be sympathetic with the economic problem of someone who actually had a family to maintain while studying. And now I suddenly realized that my new friend was a rich man.

I do not remember what we had for lunch. But I remember meeting Marie-Louise and being impressed by the quietly authoritative way in which she asked the maid to lay another place at table. I remember this lunch primarily as a kind of introduction to the more splendid meals, in much more splendid surroundings, that I enjoyed with the Osborns after they rented the country house of Shotover Cleve some distance from Oxford. Jim really enjoyed living the life of an English country gentleman. He hired as a butler a man who had recently left the service of an English peer and who was a veritable Jeeves. His name was Carter and he undertook to instruct the Osborns in the various niceties of English country-house life; he found Jim a ready pupil. Jim acquired a car especially for Carter to drive, and when I was invited to dine at Shotover Cleve Carter would come for me and drive me out there, duly delivering me back to Balliol late in the evening. Often I would be accompanied by Herbert Keyes, a fellow research student from Wales. Keyes was the son of a miner and I think his scholarship was somewhat less in value than mine, so that he had to be even more careful with his finance. For both of us the opportunity to have a relaxed and elegant evening with the Osborns was something to be relished.

We relished it not only for the good food and drink we got. There was always good conversation, and masses of antiquarian books bought by Jim almost weekly to be displayed and discussed. He also built up a wine cellar. Carter undertook to instruct him here, and he found an apt pupil. (A man who later taught himself brilliantly how to breed dairy-cattle would have had no difficulty in mastering the principles of wine selection.) Once, when Marie-Louise had gone to New York to visit her dentist (yes, she really used to go to New York, on the *Queen Mary*, to visit her dentist, for she did not trust any other), Jim invited Herbert Keyes and myself to a dinner the chief object of which was to sample some newly acquired wine. We had a different wine with each course, each reverently brought in by Carter, while Jim, who behaved like a schoolboy on a holiday treat, chuckled appreciatively. I remember that this was the first occasion on which I drank Châteauneuf-du-Pape—the first Rhône wine I had ever drunk and I think the best. I remember its flavour with absolute clarity, and all my life since then I have been looking in vain for a Châteauneuf with precisely that kind of subtle fruitiness.

My most vivid memory of Carter is of a formal dinner party he gave for me and my fiancée (as she then was) when she came down

from Scotland for the Balliol Commem Ball. We were called for
by Carter in his car in the usual way, and on entering the hall of
Shotover Cleve Carter rapidly changed his role from chauffeur
to butler. As we sat down to dinner my fiancée remarked on the
prettiness of the flowers that decorated the table. She asked
Marie-Louise what they were, but neither she nor Jim could tell
her. Carter was summoned, and the question put. 'Campanula,
madam,' he said, grandly and simply, and then left the room. Pure
Jeeves. I don't know how many times in subsequent years Jim and
I would recall with relish that 'Campanula, madam'.

But of course it was English scholarship that absorbed most of
Jim's interest and attention in those years. I don't think I have
ever met a man who responded with so much enthusiasm to
receiving information about seventeenth- and eighteenth-century
scholars and antiquaries. Not that he was solemn about it. He
would parody Nichol Smith's dramatic way of emphasizing a point.
'William Oldys was a—VERY—GREAT—man.' 'Humphrey Wanley
was (pause) the GREATEST of ALL our CATALOGUERS.' He would
imitate Nichol Smith quoting with relish Oldys's marginal notes
in his copy of Langbaine; 'A woeful critic art thou, Gerard
Langbaine.' (Am I remembering this right?) All these old scholars
and antiquaries took on a lively existence in Jim's imagination, and
he would talk about them and joke about them as though they were
humorously eccentric contemporaries of ours. The three pioneer-
ing Johns—John Leland, John Bale, and John Pits—were the
subject of many jocular references. Hickes's *Thesaurus* figured in
several esoteric jokes that only those who had attended Nichol
Smith's lectures could understand. In the forty years after we
attended these lectures whenever Jim and I met, as we did intermittently on one side of the Atlantic or the other, he would
suddenly chuckle and, as a sort of secret sign of old friendship,
quote something about Oldys or Wanley or William Winstanley or
Edmond Malone.

Jim enjoyed one great advantage over the rest of us: he could
afford to buy early (often first) editions of the works of these old
scholars who figured in the lectures we heard. He would disappear
to London and emerge some days later with marvellous trophies
from a sale-room. He would go to auctions and buy old libraries.
It was marvellous to watch his library build up week by week,
month by month, and to see on each visit to Shotover Cleve newly

acquired copies of the works of all the principals in Nichol Smith's course in the History of English Studies. The rest of us had to read them in the Bodleian. Jim, lucky man, steadily acquired his own copies. Of course he used the Bodleian as well, and acquired a deep love for it, which bore fruit in his later gifts. We all liked Strickland Gibson of the Bodleian, who lectured to research students on bibliography and finished up the course by actually treating his students to an elaborate Elizabethan refreshment. Jim developed a special fondness for Gibson, and spoke of him with great affection. Indeed, one of the most remarkable things about Jim in those early Oxford days was his ability to move from interest in scholarly matters to warm friendship with living scholars. And of course it was in those days that his lifelong love-affair with Oxford began.

I went to America from Oxford in September 1937 to teach at the University of Chicago, and Jim stayed with us at our apartment in Chicago for a few days in the summer of 1938; we talked a lot about Oxford and its characters. It was entirely as a result of Jim's activities that I ever went to Chicago. Ronald Crane, who was head of the English department there, was either a cousin or second-cousin of Jim's, and Jim once wrote to him about me. As a result of this letter, Robert M. Hutchins, then President of the University of Chicago, came to see me when he was visiting Oxford, I think in the spring of 1937. I was then a Research Fellow of Balliol, and Hutchins visited me in my rooms in College. I had just read his book on *The Higher Learning in America* and we had a long and fascinating talk about universities and their function. The upshot was that Hutchins mentioned me favourably to Crane, and Crane invited me to join the Chicago faculty. The invitation came to me by cable in August 1937 when I was in France on my honeymoon.

The most extraordinary time I ever spent with Jim was on the evening of 12 September 1940, when we visited the New York World's Fair together. I was in New York to attend the meetings of the English Institute, where I had given a lecture on T. E. Hulme that same afternoon. (The previous day I had heard René Wellek's lecture on 'Literary Movements and Periods', after which we had had a long talk on critical matters followed by lunch with him and Rudolf Kirk at the Columbia Men's Faculty Club. It is all in my diary.) About 6 p.m. on Thursday 12 September Jim and I went out to the World's Fair where we moved from exhibit to exhibit, consuming inordinate quantities of beer at different places of refreshment in the course of our journeying. Fairly late in the proceedings we found ourselves at a newspaper-printing exhibit where for a small sum you could have a front-page newspaper printed with headlines of your own choice. Jim and I, for some reason, thought that it would be wonderful to have a newspaper with the headline COPS WITH LIVE RATS CHASE DAICHES, OSBORN. We accordingly got two copies printed (I still have mine) and left in a state of high merriment. Every time after that when Jim and I met he would whisper to me, 'Cops with live rats'.

Of course, Jim was not always in merry mood. He was often serious, even solemn, even appearing at times to those who did not know him well to be rather pompous. When he gave advice on the practical matters of life, as he did to me quite often, and always usefully, he spoke with quiet solemnity, but nearly always, as soon as he had finished, he broke into a nervous smile, as though to reassure you that he wasn't taking himself too seriously. This nervous smile of his was one of his most endearing characteristics: it seemed to me to suggest a certain vulnerability beneath the outward assurance.

His American friends and colleagues will know more about Jim's later career as scholar and benefactor of scholarship than I do, as they will know about his wartime career as cattle breeder and the marvellous sale catalogue he produced when he sold his herd. (He and I used to describe it as the first and only bibliography of cows ever published. I said that it threw a new light on the book-sellers' description, 'bound in half-calf'.) What I have set down here are some memories of Jim in the earliest phase of his academic life. I still look back on these years with nostalgia and on my friendship with Jim at Oxford as one of the most rewarding of my Oxford experiences.

Contents

Plates

Hamlet's Skimmington

RICHARD LEIGHTON GREENE

NO ONE questions the importance to the tragedy of *Hamlet* of the play-within-the-play. It is the principal turning-point of the plot, the point where Hamlet undergoes a spectacular change from an inhibited melancholiac to a determined scourge and avenger. Though his full revenge is still to be postponed by delays of his own and others' making, this is his point of no return. We should expect Shakespeare to mark such a moment with clear and forceful speech and dramatic action. Yet many editors and interpreters show some embarrassment at the presence in the text of seemingly incongruous details, and few scenes have taxed more heavily the ingenuity of actors and directors. Not only is there the strange business of the crude dumb-show to be managed and the over-long doggerel dialogue of the spoken play to be endured or cut, but there is the puzzle of Hamlet's first utterances after the breaking-off: the shouted or sung quatrain about the stricken deer and the hart ungalled, and the exultant claim to a fellowship in a *cry* of players. Then, immediately after Horatio agrees that Claudius has publicly betrayed his guilt, Hamlet surprisingly calls for music, another apparent irrelevancy that leads into the byplay with the recorder.

The dumb-show which precedes the spoken play of the murder of Gonzago has generated a formidable body of discussion, much of it certainly misguided and unprofitable. Some producers have found it to be such a problem that they have omitted it altogether. One long-current theory, now discredited by the work of Dieter Mehl, explains the dumb-show as an 'archaism', used by Shakespeare to emphasize the difference between the clumsy and old-fashioned performance of the strolling players and the subtlety and sophistication of his own composition. Mehl shows that pantomimes of this general kind were by no means completely out of fashion at the time of the first showing of *Hamlet*.[1] But this

[1] *The Elizabethan Dumb Show* (Cambridge, Mass., 1966), p. 113; see also

dumb-show is unique in English drama in being a silent acting-out of the content of the spoken play which follows. It has the function, important though sometimes overlooked, of showing what the forever-unacted ending of that play would have been. It is well to have these circumstances understood, but they still do not completely account for Hamlet's speech and action when the breaking-off of the play assures the success of his exploit. In particular, no critic has given a satisfying explanation of his choosing the imagery of a hunted male deer and of a pack of pursuing hounds.

This imagery, usually ignored or treated as random incoherence, may actually contain the clue to an aspect of the whole scene which would almost inevitably suggest itself to many of Shakespeare's audience, familiar as they were with much folk-custom known to few modern auditors or readers. An Elizabethan playgoer, particularly one from the Midlands or the West Country, could hardly miss the resemblance of the dumb-show to the ancient and widespread custom of a primitive dramatic performance designed to shock and to shame into repentance an individual or a couple presumed guilty of sexual sin or even serious indecorum. This is the humiliating pageant best known in England by the name of 'skimmington'.

As with most folk-customs, there are wide variations in nomenclature and in details of procedure. The noun itself is recorded by the *English Dialect Dictionary* as *skymington, skimelton, skimitin, skimiting, skimity, skimmenton, skimmerton, skimmety, skimmiting, skimmity, skiverton,* and *skymaton.*[2] This list is followed by a series of citations which amounts to a useful compendium of descriptive details. All types of skimmington are public shows; in England they are usually dumb-shows with the victims paraded in effigy or impersonated by live actors, often set back-to-back on a horse or donkey and escorted by a noisily derisive crowd.[3]

B. R. Pearn, 'Dumb-Show in Elizabethan Drama', *Review of English Studies*, xi (1935), 403. The dumb-show in *A Midsummer Night's Dream* differs from that in *Hamlet* in having spoken exposition by the Prologue during its action.

[2] (London, 1904), s.v. 'Skimmington'.

[3] Two important and learned articles on the skimmington in continental Europe as well as in England give the subject its most comprehensive treatment: Violet Alford, 'Rough Music or Charivari', *Folklore*, lxx (1959), 505–18, and Natalie Zemon Davis, 'The Reasons of Misrule: Youth Groups and Charivaris in Sixteenth-Century France', *Past and Present*, No. 50 (1971), 41–75. 'Charivari' is the most important synonym for 'skimmington'; it migrates from France

A more strenuous and more interesting kind of skimmington is that which is organized as a mock hunt with hounds. It is this sort which forms a central incident in two novels of West Country life, one famous and the other almost forgotten, both published in the mid 1880s and both laid a half-century earlier. In Thomas Hardy's *The Mayor of Casterbridge* the stag-hunt results in the emotional agony, miscarriage, and death of a principal female character. In Sabine Baring-Gould's *Red Spider* a skimmington planned as a hare-hunt ends in the serious injury of a male participant. Better than any factual accounts these passages of fiction convey to the reader the power of the skimmington to alarm and stun a community. From the abundant but scattered literature dealing with the custom perhaps no better short account can be found than one given in an item in the *Somerset County Gazette* for 8 July 1882 and reprinted in the *Folk-Lore Record* for 1882:[4]

A curious case was heard last week before the magistrates of the division of Hatherleigh; arising out of the old Devonshire custom of 'mock stag-hunting' or 'skimiting riding.' . . . [It] is carried on in the following manner:—The villagers assemble in large numbers and select one of themselves to act the part of the hunted stag, the remainder of the party, some on horseback wearing hunting and other costumes and with horns, being the huntsmen and the hounds. The stag, being previously disguised with antlers and other paraphernalia, is given a few yards start, and forthwith runs, pursued by the huntsmen and the hounds, up and down the village, in and out of the courts and passages, and is eventually pulled down at or near to the house of the offending person, where there is much blowing of horns, shouting, and spilling of blood (which has been got ready for the purpose in bladders), to render the scene more realistic.

Another detailed and spirited account of a particular skimmington stag-hunt is a reminiscence of such an event in 1875 narrated by Richard Kelly, a famous strong man of Okehampton, Devon, who viewed it when a small boy. His narrative was written down

to the United States in the form 'shivaree'. The term 'rough music' is a kind of synecdoche for the whole proceeding.

At the very end of the Davis article the author asks: '. . . is Hamlet perhaps a charivari of the young against a grotesque and unseemly remarriage, a charivari where the effigy of the dead spouse returns, the vicious action is replayed?' (p. 75). It was before I had seen this article that I presented the essential argument of the present paper to an informal seminar of the English department of Wesleyan University and in conversation to the late Rosalie L. Colie.

[4] v. 166–7.

in 1950 by Mrs. L. H. Wreford and published by Theo Brown in an excellent article which briefly records several similar episodes.[5] Mrs. Wreford's opening sentences are significant and deserve quotation:

The 'stag' hunt was a kind of rough justice and public censure for a certain moral lapse. It was regarded as an enjoyment and welcomed in the town, where in those days, as we know, entertainment was very limited. The 'stag' hunt could be held only when *two married* people were known to be guilty. Other such lapses were talked about and the parties given the 'cold shoulder' but no 'stag' hunt for them.

The stag in this hunt was a fleet-footed gardener with deer's antlers tied to his head and a face painted red and brown. He was pursued by a mounted huntsman and the 'hounds', young men 'who were also dressed up and making a sort of barking noise'.

In addition to the adultery so gently referred to by Mrs. Wreford the skimmington was used to publicize and punish unsuitable marriages, particularly (1) second marriages too early in the widowhood of the woman to be socially acceptable, even when not forbidden by ecclesiastical or civil law; (2) marriages regarded as incestuous, i.e. within the forbidden degrees of relationship; (3) marriages of partners strikingly unequal in age, usually second or third marriages of the elder spouse; (4) marriages of women already regarded as of bad character because of previous adultery or fornication. This kind of skimmington, regularly including deer's horns among its properties, is always concerned with some breach of sexual or marital *mores*.

Though the Falstaff of *The Merry Wives of Windsor* only intends and does not achieve adultery, his curious and elaborate punishment at the end of the play has more than a touch of the skimmington about it. He is persuaded to impersonate the spectral Herne the Hunter, 'Disguis'd like Herne with huge horns on his head'.[6] When he appears as planned in Windsor Great Park at midnight, he wears a deer's antlers and makes much of his horned condition in his speeches; he thinks of himself more as a rutting male animal than as Herne: 'For me, I am here a Windsor stag; and the fattest, I think, i' the forest.'[7] The pinching and burning

---

[5] 'The "Stag-Hunt" in Devon', *Folklore*, lxiii (1952), 104–5.

[6] IV. iv. 43. Quotations and line-numbers are from the Oxford edition, 3 vols. (London, 1924–5).

[7] V. v. 13.

of Falstaff by the children disguised as fairies, though done while
they dance in a ring, is followed by 'a noise of hunting', and it
suggests the harrying of the simulated stag which constitutes the
orthodox skimmington.[8] There can be no doubt that the custom
of the skimmington was well known to Shakespeare, and no other
source is known for this idea of a staged pageant as the means of
revenge by a community on a would-be seducer. That a sexual
offender might appropriately be represented as a stag to be hunted
would not have seemed a strange idea at all to a play-going subject
of Elizabeth or James.[9]

A skimmington, however crude and uncomplicated it may be,
is nevertheless conceived as true drama: it is a representation of
one or more real persons in circumstances that are real or postu-
lated as real by those who produce the show. Unlike most drama,
however, it is directed at a dual audience that is unequally divided
between an established group of spectators well acquainted with
each other and one or two members of that community who are
being set off as candidates for ostracism. These members are
expected to recognize themselves in the personages being presented
with disapproval and derision. The effect of the skimmington is to
create publicly a hostility between the audience at large and the
auditors who are also *dramatis personae* more serious than any
hostility that has been recognized before, a hostility usually made
irremediable by the mumming itself. As Baring-Gould puts it in
Red Spider: 'There is no defence and no appeal from the court.
The infliction of the sentence confers an indelible stain, and
generally drives those who have been thus branded out of the
neighbourhood.'[10]

Just such a dual audience is that to which Hamlet's dumb-show
and spoken play are offered. Claudius and Gertrude are the chief
auditors and also the prototypes of two of the three characters
presented. The rest of the audience is the royal court, members of
a community well acquainted with the principals and with each

---

[8] v. v, stage direction after 105.

[9] Compare the 'hunting' of Caliban, Stephano, and Trinculo in *The Tempest*,
IV. i, stage direction after 255: 'A noise of hunters heard. Enter divers Spirits,
in shape of hounds, and hunt them about; Prospero and Ariel setting them on.'
Here some of the hounds are called by name: Mountain, Silver, Fury, and
Tyrant. It should be noted that the ugly trio are bent on sexual violence towards
Miranda as well as rebellion against Prospero.

[10] (London, 1887), ii. 79–80.

other. The hostility to his stepfather which Hamlet now declares becomes indeed an indelible stain. Gertrude's first words to her son at their next meeting are 'Hamlet, thou hast thy father much offended'.[11] The verb she uses echoes Claudius's anxious query during the play of Gonzago: 'Have you heard the argument? Is there no offence in't?' Shakespeare does not show on the stage the immediate effect of the sensational episode on the attitude of the inner circle of courtiers, but later speeches and actions clearly imply that knowledge of the King's confusion and alarm has spread beyond the court to the common people and there worked to Hamlet's advantage. Claudius acknowledges as much in his surprisingly frank speech to unnamed 'attendants', whom Granville-Barker takes to be members of his council:

> How dangerous is it that this man goes loose!
> Yet must not we put the strong law on him:
> He's lov'd of the distracted multitude,
> Who like not in their judgment, but their eyes.[12]

The purpose of the traditional skimmington, over and beyond its function as an outlet for pent-up enmity mixed with real moral outrage, is to stir the culprits who are its target to such remorse and shame that they administer self-punishment: flight from the community or, at the very least, acceptance of dishonourable status. Though Shakespeare makes no explicit mention of flight or abdication as a response by Claudius, it can hardly be doubted that Hamlet would have welcomed with relief either of these resolutions of the situation. Abdication and flight combined would at once satisfy his honour and release him from the repugnant duty of killing a fellow-being, who is, after all, a blood-relation, and in the medieval view of uncle and nephew, a very close one. It should be remembered that the ghost of King Hamlet does not explicitly prescribe the slaying of Claudius as the form that his son's revenge must take. The solemn injunction of the ghost against the use of violence upon Gertrude and the command to let her conscience be her punishment are immediately preceded by the line 'But, howsoever thou pursuest this act'.[13] Surprisingly, perhaps, the ghost does not insist on homicide as the form of revenge.

It is important to notice just here a most significant likeness between the humble institution of the skimmington and the more

---

[11] III. iv. 9.   [12] IV. iii. 2–5.   [13] I. v. 84.

aristocratic code of private revenge. They are both accepted,
where they are accepted, as unwritten, extra-legal, primeval, and
inalienable rights, older and more deeply rooted in the collective
mind of a society than any civil statutes. The skimmington is
everywhere regarded as a remedy for wrongdoing which the official
law of a state or city has failed to move against because of indifference or corruption. In Hamlet's Denmark the civil power is
completely controlled by the chief culprit himself. There is no
free speech, and a free press is centuries away. Hamlet can hardly
entrust his message to the town crier, and he does not think much
of town criers anyway. He is a prince and the heir to a throne, but
his frustration is much like that of a knot of shocked villagers, and
perhaps, like theirs, not wholly unlaced with malice.[14] Hamlet's
dumb-show and play have the same purpose as the homely custom
of the skimmington: to 'catch the conscience' of 'guilty creatures'.

If, then, at the moment when Hamlet realizes the success of his
combined mumming and spoken play, he also recognizes that he
has accomplished the same end as that of a skimmington conceived
as the hunting-down of a stag with hounds, the verse that he
chants is not the 'light and inconsequent lyric' that Granville-
Barker calls it,[15] but a quatrain that refers to Claudius as the deer
that has been wounded in this chase:

> Why, let the stricken deer go weep,
>   The hart ungalled play;
> For some must watch, while some must sleep:
>   So runs the world away.

It refers to Hamlet himself as well, a creature unhurt, with an echo
of the word 'galled' that was spoken in his sarcastic 'reassurance'
just as the player-poisoner entered the action: '. . . let the galled
jade wince, our withers are unwrung.'[16] Likewise his exultant
question, 'Would not this, sir . . . get me a fellowship in a cry of
players, sir?' is seen to be more than 'ironically fanciful', as it is
called by Granville-Barker. The use of the word 'cry' for a troupe
of actors has no parallel elsewhere in Shakespeare. Its regular
meaning, 'a pack of hounds', is of course a figurative transference

[14] Harley Granville-Barker, in commenting on the jesting with Ophelia
before the play, mentions Hamlet's 'cruelty; that flaw in a nature sensitive even
to weakness' (*Preface to 'Hamlet'*, New York, 1957, p. 92).

[15] Ibid., p. 99.   [16] III. ii. 245.

from the yelping of the animals when on a scent, or 'in full cry'. Shakespeare uses it thus in *Othello*, where Roderigo says, 'I do follow here in the chase, not like a hound that hunts, but one that fills up the cry.'[17] In *A Midsummer Night's Dream* Theseus boasts of his hounds, 'A cry more tuneable/Was never holla'd to, nor cheer'd with horn.'[18] The word is applied to a collection of human beings only in *Coriolanus*, and there to express the hero's contemptuous comparison of a plebeian mob to a pack of harrying dogs. He calls the citizens 'You common cry of curs', and Menenius, when the estranged general is threatening the city, shouts to them, 'You have made Good work, you and your cry!'[19] But Hamlet is far from being contemptuous of professional players as such; rather, they are his old and valued acquaintances. His use of the term 'cry' gains a full and satisfying meaning only if we recognize that Hamlet regards the actors on this unique occasion as being the 'hounds' in a skimmington-like 'stag-hunt' of which the object is to flush and publicly pursue an offender against sexual morals. His question to Horatio implies, 'Am I not qualified to join with actors who assume the function of a pack of hounds in a punitive pageant?' Surely Shakespeare has a more positive dramatic purpose in his use of these particular images at this highly emotional moment than a random insertion of 'fantasy and banter . . . to relieve the strain of what has gone before'.[20]

Even Hamlet's sudden call for music, generally regarded as a somewhat awkward device for getting the recorders on stage, may well result from his being in what may be called a skimmington frame of mind, for some kind of music is almost invariably associated with the custom. These recorders must be instruments belonging to the players, although the stage direction calls for hautboys to sound before the dumb-show, and it makes better dramatic sense to have them summoned as part of Hamlet's relish of the successful mumming than to have them appear as 'planted' by him so that he can presently use one of them in a witty comparison addressed to Rosencrantz and Guildenstern.[21]

Finally, what of the couplet spoken by Hamlet just before his call for music:

[17] II. iii. 360.   [18] IV. i. 126.
[19] III. iii. 118; IV. vi. 147–8.
[20] Granville-Barker, *Preface*, p. 100.
[21] Ibid., p. 100 n. 24. The Second Quarto has 'The Trumpets sounds'.

> For if the king like not the comedy,
> Why then, belike, he likes it not, perdy.[22]

The players have been called by Rosencrantz 'the tragedians of
the city'. Neither the dumb-show nor the spoken play has hitherto been regarded as anything but a tragedy. The play is termed a
tragedy by its Prologue, and its content, taken literally, is entirely
tragic. But satirical pageants such as skimmingtons are a province
of comedy, and Hamlet's change of the word, apparently spontaneous, may be a last expression of his attitude toward his own
dramatic exploit.

If Hamlet can be thought of as having in mind the likeness of his
project to a skimmington, his bitter speech to Ophelia immediately
before the dumb-show takes on an implication which has not been
noticed. He speaks a sarcastic condemnation of the disrespect shown
to his dead father, affecting to regard it as forgetfulness: 'Then
there's hope a great man's memory may outlive his life half a
year; but, by'r lady, he must build churches then, or else shall he
suffer not thinking on, with the hobby-horse, whose epitaph is,
"For, O! for, O! the hobby-horse is forgot".'[23] This line of verse,
presumably originating in a folksong context no longer preserved,
was one of the most widely quoted catch-phrases in Elizabethan
and Jacobean literature. It is interjected by the pert youngster
Moth in *Love's Labour's Lost* when Armado stammers, 'But
O—But O—'.[24] It is worked into an ayre of Thomas Weelkes
which recalls the marathon dance or 'nine days' wonder' of the
comedian Will Kempe:

> Since Robin Hood, Maid Marian,
> And Little John are gone-a,
> The hobby horse was quite forgot,
> When Kemp did dance alone-a.[25]

Commentators have tended to dismiss Hamlet's quotation with a
reference to the Puritan dislike of the hobby-horse as a feature of
fairs or May games or morris dances or to assume that he is merely
using a figurative expression for that which is obsolete. But it is

[22] III. ii. 296–7. In the First Quarto the word is 'tragedy' here.
[23] III. ii. 132–8.   [24] III. i. 28–9.
[25] *Ayeres Or Phantasticke Spirites for three voices*, 1608, No. xx, reprinted in
E. H. Fellowes, *English Madrigal Verse 1588–1632*, 3rd edn. (Oxford, 1967), p.
302; noted in connection with this passage by William Ringler, *Shakespeare
Quarterly*, iv (1953), 485.

well to remember that some hobby-horses had a sinister and punitive side and that the kind called 'hooset' or 'wooset' was closely related to the beasts of skimmingtons.[26] It is well to remember also that Shakespeare usually has a reason for his selection of what may seem to be a random snatch of verse. A better reading of the speech than that usually offered by editors and critics would be: 'Alas, that the folk-custom of the hobby-horse or hooset as a scourge of sexual misconduct is no longer kept up.'

The skimmington, charivari, or 'rough music' has taken a wide diversity of forms and procedures in different times and different regions, but it is recognized and defined by its *purpose*: by a dramatic representation to bring to public obloquy and possibly to personal repentance an offender or pair of offenders against the sexual, and particularly the marital, *mores* of a community—the unwritten laws which are older and stronger than civil and ecclesiastical codes. This is exactly the purpose of Hamlet in arranging the dual performance of pantomime and play in dialogue, the former, of course, showing the nearer kinship to the simple folk-drama. We do not know what term Shakespeare might have used to designate a skimmington, but he must certainly have been well acquainted with the custom. There are aspects of the play-scene which are

[26] *The English Dialect Dictionary* equates 'hooset' with the skimmington in its definition 2: 'A serenade of rough music, got up to express public disapproval of flagrant immorality, or of marriages where there is a great disparity of age.' Under 'Wooseting' a few lines farther on it gives a telling citation from *Notes and Queries* (4th ser., xi (1873), 225): 'The ceremony of "wooseting" is the same as in a "skimmeting", and expresses popular disapproval of adultery.' Some hobby-horses had movable jaws to be snapped and clacked, for example, at Minehead, Somerset, Padstow, Cornwall, and Combe Martin, Devon (Herbert W. Kille, 'West Country Hobby-Horses and Cognate Customs', *Proceedings of the Somersetshire Archaeological and Natural History Society*, lxxvii (1932), 69, 70, 72). The 'old hoss' of the much-publicized Padstow May dance kept at least until 1932, when I saw him in action, some remnants of his power of threatening women: the terror of the girls whom he swooped toward was not entirely affected or conventional. 'Hobby-horse' was also a term of contempt for an immoral woman, as used by Leontes in *The Winter's Tale* (1. ii. 276) and by Bianca in *Othello* (IV. i. 155).

Dr. Theodore Lidz makes an interesting comment on the hobby-horse speech in *Hamlet's Enemy* (New York, 1975), p. 154: 'It is possible that the "dumb-show" may have originated as an elaboration of a folk play or folk dance. The hobbyhorse is a basic character in these ritual performances along with the Man-Woman, the Fool, and the Captain or King.' Dr. Lidz does not mention any performance resembling a skimmington, but he recognizes a certain relationship to dramatic folk-custom.

far more sophisticated than the rowdy rough justice of the country-side, but when the emotional resistance of the guilty king collapses, Hamlet exclaims, in effect: 'We have caught this "stag", I and my fellow-hounds, these players.'

The Murder of Falstaff, David Jones, and the 'Disciplines of War'

JOHN BARNARD

THE ACCIDENTAL re-reading of David Jones's *In Parenthesis* while preparing to write an undergraduate lecture on *Henry V* provoked a quite unexpected view of the play. It also forced a closer attention to the workings of Jones's imagination in a work still too little read and admired. The difficulty about *Henry V* for a modern audience is whether, after the First World War, a drama turning on the patriotic heroism of a warrior-king can have any powerful meaning without being subverted by disbelief. (Is Henry at Agincourt merely another example of territorial aggression disguised as honourable war?) A standard defence offered by Tillyard, Dover Wilson, and J. H. Walter, which elevates *Henry V* into a national 'epic' drama, is convincing at the level of intention and the history of ideas.[1] Yet the play's structure is curiously clumsy in some areas, and the final dramatic effect remains two-dimensional. However, *In Parenthesis* forced a reconsideration of the temptation to ascribe *Henry V*'s failure simply to unpalatable military jingoism. Anti-war sentiment over-simplifies Shakespeare's play retrospectively, and, conversely, the comparative neglect of Jones's 'writing' (his preferred description), when set against the popularity of Wilfred Owen's poetry or Graves's *Goodbye to All That*, is probably as much due to its celebration of heroism as to its difficulty and obscurity. If *In Parenthesis* encouraged a more sympathetic understanding of *Henry V*, at the same time it revealed Shakespeare's drama as an intriguing failure, the root cause of which lies in its inability to maintain the heroi-comical mode of *1–2 Henry IV*.

Originally the lecture was intended to express serious misgivings about *Henry V*, but with care taken to outline the conventional

---

[1] See E. M. W. Tillyard, *Shakespeare's History Plays* (1944), *Henry V*, ed. J. Dover Wilson (1947), and the Introduction to the Arden edition of *Henry V*, ed. J. H. Walter (1954; rptd. 1970). All references are to the Arden, hereafter referred to as 'Walter'.

case for the play, along with a warning against allowing its in-
genuousness as a whole to disguise the real complexities present.
For one thing, neither Shakespeare nor Henry is ignorant of the
violence of war. The prime example is probably Henry's threat to
the besieged citizens of Harfleur, a chillingly accurate description
of the actualities of raping and looting by Renaissance soldiery
(III. iii. 10–41). Henry does not glory in his power, but offers the
city its last chance of quarter. As J. H. Walter notes, 'Henry's
conduct of the siege is in accordance with military law', citing
Gentili's *De Iure Belli* (1612) in support, along with references
to the appalling sack of Bovaigne and Stanley's surrender of
Deventer in 1587. Henry, the good general, knows what war
involves and how it should be conducted.

Moreover, the epic dimension is there, provided by the Choruses,
and Henry embodies the virtues of the epic hero. As Tillyard and
Walter maintain, Henry is meant to partake of the virtue with which
Virgil endows his hero in the *Aeneid*'s much more sophisticated
epic strain. Both Henry and Aeneas give themselves up to become
the instrument of their nation's destiny, embodying their culture's
supreme ethical values. In presenting his model Christian King,
Shakespeare drew upon the Renaissance notions of this ideal as set
out by Chelidonius and Erasmus. The danger is that Henry will
degenerate into a Morality figure. Certainly the Archbishop of
Canterbury's description of Prince Hal's conversion is heavily
typological (I. i. 27–31).

The play makes considerable efforts to prevent Henry becoming
a cut-out figure. Immediately before Agincourt he shows himself
aware (briefly) that Heaven, for all its revelation of grace, may not
have forgiven his father's sin (IV. i. 298–303). This moment of
uncertainty reflects back to Henry's insistence on gaining the
Archbishop's unqualified support (I. ii). The recovery of his
French title must be an act justified before God: only then can the
good man as king and the effective ruler as politician be united in
the same person for the first time in the tetralogy. Care is also taken
to demonstrate the sharp and uncomfortable isolation forced upon
Henry the man by kingship. His famous debate with Williams and
Bates convincingly asserts the continuity between king and com-
moner while stressing the necessary impersonality demanded of a
ruler (IV. i. 100–13). As Derek Traversi has observed, Henry's
knowledge of the gap between individual and public function

approaches the tragic—'The universality of the argument . . .
transcends the royal situation.' And when, shortly afterwards,
Henry questions 'ceremony', his words forecast Lear's disbelief
in appearances—

> O be sick, great greatness,
> And bid thy ceremony give thee cure!
> Think'st thou the fiery fever will go out
> With titles blown from adulation?
> Will it give place to flexure and low-bending?
> Canst thou, when thou command'st the beggar's knee,
> Command the health of it?
>
> (IV. i. 257–63)

Such an analysis succeeds in making the play and the king more
complex, but the dramatic and thematic difficulties remain: the
treatment of war, though harsher and less romantic than has sometimes been thought, is nevertheless primarily geared to the
spectacle of patriotic valour.

Interestingly, the much shorter Quarto version, probably
prepared for a reduced cast in the provinces, demonstrates that for
one Elizabethan audience *Henry V*'s realism and grander proportions were irrelevant. Prologue, Epilogue, and Choruses are
excised, destroying the epic frame, Henry's stark warning to
Harfleur is cut, along with his speech on ceremony, his character
is deprived of its little inwardness, and the relationship between the
good king and the good Christian edited out.[2] What remains is a
simple patriotic play, retaining the antics of Pistol, Bardolph, and
Nym. Its audience did not want Henry's lineaments at Agincourt
obscured. Rather than castigate their philistinism, the evidence of
the Quarto provides one contemporary verdict on the fuller play
—*Henry V* is an adventure story masquerading as something more
complicated.

Henry is furthest from the modern reader in his moments of
militaristic patriotism. It is not altogether surprising that his 'Once
more into the breach' peroration concludes by picturing his troops
as a pack of hounds at a hunt—

> I see you stand like greyhounds in the slips,
> Straining upon the start. The game's afoot:

---

[2] For a summary of the cuts, see Walter, p. 169.

Follow your spirit; and upon this charge
Cry, 'God for Harry, England, and Saint George!'
(III. i. 31–4)

War is a test of the hunter's instinct with Henry as Master of
Hounds. A note of patriotic endeavour, an elated gaiety of spirit,
marks the play.[3] Of course, it answered the outburst of public
feeling which greeted Essex's departure for Ireland in 1599, and
the Chorus of Act v reflects that excitement, comparing Henry's
return from Agincourt with the imagined triumphant return of
Essex—

Were now the general of our gracious empress,
As in good time he may, from Ireland coming,
Bringing rebellion broached upon his sword,
How many would the peaceful city quit
To welcome him!

(ll. 30–5)

The feeling of gaiety sticks most ironically in our minds, but it is
one clearly reflected in a contemporary description of the forces
gathered for Ireland—'They were young gentlemen, yeomen, and
yeomen's sons and artificers of the most brave sort, such as did
disdain to pilfer and steal, but went as voluntary to serve of a
gaiety and joyalty of mind, all which kind of people are the force
and flower of a kingdom.'[4] Henry V catches the mood of London
in 1599, and faced with many of Henry's set speeches we are likely
to feel ourselves on the other side of a great divide. He belongs with
the naïveté of Rupert Brooke. The horrors of the First World War
have taught Europe differently, undercutting the basis of traditional epic and heroic views.

Yet reading In Parenthesis alongside Henry V led to an uneasy
sense that neither the play's epic pretensions nor the popular pot-
boiler represented by the Quarto did justice to the awkwardnesses or
the potential of Shakespeare's play. This unease finally crystallized
round Jones's use of Fluellen's phrase, 'the disciplines of war'.
Organized war is a specifically human invention, a communal

[3] On Henry's 'modest "gaiety" ' see Charles Williams's essay on the play,
cited Walter, pp. xiii–iv.
[4] Cited Walter, p. xxvi, from P. Alexander, Shakespeare's Punctuation
(1945), p. 1, which gives no reference.

activity indeed, with its own codes and demands, of which martial vigour and group spirit are only the most obvious manifestations. With very different results the two works explore the necessities of war. The success of *In Parenthesis* may reveal the essential thinness of *Henry V*, yet Jones's sympathetic response intimates the ghostly presence of a third *Henry V*, which is neither a swaggering rodomontade nor a queasy mixture of a morality drama with a history play. But to say this entails a closer look at David Jones's 'writing'.

In Parenthesis, whose 'importance and permanence as a work of art' has been affirmed by T. S. Eliot,[5] is a prose poem first published in 1937. Jones fought in the trenches of the First World War as a ranker, and while deeply aware of the phantasmagoric horrors of that appalling waste, bears witness to an epic dimension in what he and his companions suffered. *In Parenthesis* catches that quality by setting actual events and personal experiences within a network of allusions to earlier history (Romano-British and Welsh as well as English) and to British heroic poetry—Anglo-Saxon, Welsh, Malory's Arthurian legend, and Shakespeare's *Henry V*. Its collocations are surprising but vividly particular—

No one . . . could see infantry in tin-hats, with ground-sheets over their shoulders, with sharpened pine-stakes in their hands, and not recall
> '. . . or may we cram,
> Within this wooden O . . .'
> (p. xi)

The whole structure, depending on fragments, allusions, and disrupted patterns, has strong affinities with the work of Joyce, Eliot, and Pound. It is an epic lament for the soldiers on both sides of the front line, a record of a spirit of war no longer available to the modern world—

It is not easy in considering a trench-mortar barrage to give praise for the action proper to chemicals—full though it may be of beauty. We feel a rubicon has been passed between striking with a hand weapon as men used to do and loosing poison from the sky as we do ourselves. We doubt the decency of our own inventions, and are certainly in terror of their possibilities.

> (p. xiv)

---

[5] *In Parenthesis*, introd. T. S. Eliot (1963). All references are to this text.

Yet, knowing this, Jones could still write—

> Some of us ask ourselves if Mr. X adjusting his box-respirator can be equated with what the poet envisaged, in
>   'I saw young Harry with his beaver on.'
> We are in no doubt at all but what Bardolph's marching kiss for Pistol's 'quondam Quickly' is an experience substantially the same as you and I suffered on Victoria platform. For the old authors there appears to have been no such dilemma—for them the embrace of battle seemed one with the embrace of lovers. For us it is different. There is no need to labour the point, nor enquire into the causes here. I only wish to record that for me such a dilemma exists, and that I have been particularly conscious of it during the making of this writing.

(pp. xiv–v)

It is important to observe that *In Parenthesis* restricts itself to the first part of the war—

> This writing has to do with some things I saw, felt, & was part of. The period covered begins early in December 1915 and ends early in July 1916. The first date corresponds to my going to France. The latter roughly marks a change in the character of our lives in the Infantry on the West Front. From then onward things hardened into a more relentless, mechanical affair, took on a more sinister aspect. The wholesale slaughter of the later years, the conscripted levies filling the gaps in every file of four, knocked the bottom out of the intimate, continuing, domestic life of small contingents of men, within whose structure Roland could find, and, for a reasonable while, enjoy, his Oliver.

(p. ix)

Jones's writing records the point at which our culture's attitude to war changed irreversibly: for that short period the continuity of his war with earlier epic struggles remained.

In Parenthesis asserts what we might expect to have seemed outdated notions of soldierly community and valour. The remarkable description of the troops rising from the temporary safety of a declivity ('the Nullah') to advance into enemy fire has something of the elation which marks Henry V's exhortations to his men—

> Every one of these, stood, separate, upright, above ground,
> blinkt to the broad light
> risen dry mouthed from the chalk
> vivified from the Nullah without commotion
> and to distinctly said words,

> moved in open order and keeping admirable formation
> and at the high-port position
> walking in the morning on the flat roof of the world
> and some walked delicately
> sensible of their particular judgment.
>
> (p. 162)

Jones isolates the moment of commitment to action, the loss of self to the impersonal forces of battle, and the clearing-away of all details but the single fact of the instant, with the men moving in rapt clarity towards death itself, 'walking in the morning on the flat roof of the world'.

A single passage from *In Parenthesis* will not convince the reader of the quality of the work without its steady amassing of felt detail, and its interpenetration by references to earlier epics. Those to *Henry V* focus attention not on Henry himself, but on the common soldiers and their officers—Fluellen, Gower, Pistol, Nym, and Bardolph. This is partly because Jones's own company was a mixture of Welshmen and Londoners. More deeply it is because this area of Shakespeare's play catches the mingling of brutality and nobility under the 'disciplines of war'. The phrase is, of course, Fluellen's catch-phrase, and is used by Shakespeare to comic effect. But Fluellen is also a brave soldier, and, as Jones perceives, his pedantic book learning is a foil for his practical knowledge of those disciplines.[6] *In Parenthesis* characteristically employs the phrase when the company is moving into position for the first time, and is under fire. If the lonely terror of each man is stressed, so too is a sense of their community in fear and physical proximity

> With his [the enemy's] first traversing each newly scrutinised his neighbour; this voice of his Jubjub gains each David his Jonathan; his ordeal runs like acid to explore your fine feelings; his near presence at break against, at beat on, their convenient hierarchy.
>
> Lance-Corporal Lewis sings where he walks, yet in a low voice, because of the Disciplines of the Wars. He sings of the hills about Jerusalem, and of David of the White Stone.
>
> (p. 42)

The reference is half-humorous, but Jones's note reads, 'Cf., as in other places, Shakespeare's *Henry V*. Trench life brought that

---

[6] So too, Fluellen's constant references to the 'pristine wars of the Romans' provides a parallel to *In Parenthesis*'s repeated allusions to Roman Britain, and the mythical foundation of Troy Novaunt by Aeneas' son, Brute.

work constantly to the mind.' The allusions built round Lance-
Corporal Lewis, quietly singing a Welsh Methodist hymn and the
song 'Dafydd y Careg Wen' ('David of the White Stone'), echo
through the writing. Lewis, alone in the company, is imbued with
a knowledge of the epic Welsh past (p. 89)—he 'worshipped his
ancestors like a Chink' (p. 155)—and his Christian name, Aneirin,
is that of the supposed author of the sixth-century *Y Gododdin*,
whose account of the defeat of a small Welsh force, provides
Jones's main structural parallel. After his death during an attack
upon German positions in a wood, Lewis is further associated with
Wales's 'last ruler', Llywelyn, killed in the forest of Buelt, and the
spirit, the Queen of the Woods, pays a last rite which brings
together Welsh myth and *Henry V*—

She carries to Aneirin-in-the-nullah a rowan sprig, for the glory of
Guenedota [north-west Wales]. You couldn't hear what she said to
him, because she was careful for the Disciplines of the Wars.

(p. 186)

The 'disciplines of war' take on a power stemming from necessity.
As the attack begins to crumble, the troops, with neither officers
nor N.C.O.s left to lead them, begin to retreat, but—

Captain Cadwaladr is come to the breach full of familiar blasphemies. He
wants the senior private—the front is half-right and what whore's
bastard gave the retire and: Through on the flank my arse.
    Captain Cadwaladr restores
the Excellent Disciplines of the Wars.

(p. 181)

The reference equates Captain Cadwaladr with Fluellen's act in
forcing Nym, Bardolph, and Pistol to the attack (III. ii), a serio-
comic scene sandwiched with ironic point between Henry's famous
exhortation and his parley with Harfleur.

These allusions create a Fluellen more central than is the case in
Shakespeare's *Henry V*, and are part of Jones's transformation of
the balance between serious and comic. Fluellen's dismay at the
insufficiency of Captain Macmorris's efforts to mine the walls—

For look you, the mines is not according to the disciplines of the war;
the concavities of it is not sufficient; for, look you, th' athversary, you
may discuss unto the duke, look you, is digt himself four yard under

the countermines. By Cheshu, I think a' will plow up all if there is not better directions—

(III. ii. 62–8)

leads in *Henry V* to a comic argument between Welshman and Irishman. Jones, however, repeats Fluellen with terrible irony: the German mining of Duck's Bill, a front-line salient, has been only too efficient—

. . . when they relieve you in Duck's Bill, where his concavities is sufficient; and some of you come alive from the unquiet hill whose eruptions smoulder under each cold lip of clay; and conflagrations change the shape of the sky; and in the morning that mountain is removed that he may work his evils easily in your immediate rear; and last night's demonstration brings him so near, you can hear his sentries breathe.

(p. 116)

An awesome lyricism informs this description of a man-made cataclysm.

It will be clear that Jones handles his allusions to previous heroic literature differently from most twentieth-century writers. Owen, for instance, uses earlier conventions for ironic diminution. *Strange Meeting* is an off-key, internalized fragment of epic, under-cutting the notions of heroism which are the basis of the genre. The examples cited show Jones using a side of Fluellen minimized by Shakespeare, to stress the functional role of discipline and *esprit de corps* in a battle, and to discover a grandeur in his own war. But if Shakespeare's comedy is in this instance aggrandized, Jones also asserts another kind of continuity. Henry V, king and patriot, is excluded from *In Parenthesis*, and his place taken by the common soldier. Bardolph, Nym, and Pistol are as much the heroes as Fluellen. If Jones's Welsh privates 'were before Caractacus was', his Englishmen are 'the children of Doll Tearsheet' (p. x). The common man, and common experience, which includes fear, boredom, fatigue, and extreme discomfort, offering death but little reward in fame or power, is celebrated in its squalor and humanity. Again, the Shakespearian model is changed. Although Jones finds a place for the cowardly and lazy (a behind-the-lines café offers beer, coffee and 'EGG CHIP 3 FRANC' where 'Corporal Bardolph stays and stays' (p. 92)), Part 2, which culminates in the company's first experience of shelling, is entitled, 'Chambers go

off, Corporals stay'. The reference is to the firing of ordnance
which follows Henry's cry, 'God for Harry, England, and Saint
George!' (III. i), and Nym's plea before the breach, 'Pray thee,
corporal, stay; the knocks are too hot. . . .' (III. ii. 3). But where the
'irregulars' try to avoid the fighting, Jones's soldiers 'stay' in the
sense of enduring the bombardment. Their endurance, impatience
of 'base-wallahs', blasphemy, and Cockney wit are marvellously
caught. Given his issue of Trumpeter cigarettes, one soldier
remarks—'Heave that bull-shit to Jerry, tin and all, for a happy
Christmas—it'll gas the sod' (p. 72). As Jones notes, 'as Latin is to
the Church, so is Cockney to the Army' (p. xii). The soldiers' argot
and their impulse towards self-preservation provide a comparison
with a difference to the verbal exuberance and self-serving
scoundrelism of Falstaff's followers, for the troops' motives are
founded on group loyalty and the need to carry on in the face of
common danger. In the process of uncovering the epic dignity of
the common soldier, Jones ennobles *Henry V*'s humorists, and
turns Fluellen into a figure of order. Fluellen is Henry's true
double, and *In Parenthesis* includes Bardolph, Pistol, and Nym
within a community forged by the stresses of war. Joseph Heller's
Catch 22, in a typically modern way, makes the comic figure
protagonist and norm: Falstaff becomes the hero, for Misrule is
the only answer to the madness of war. What places Jones apart is
his ability to set the comic figures at the centre, but to praise and
elegize their deeds within the disciplines of war, without senti-
mentality or betrayal. *In Parenthesis*'s perspective is a tragic one:
these soldiers are bound by a mutual fate to their enemies, against
whom they fight 'by misadventure'. Their friendship and fellow-
feeling are given no easy patriotic context: among the texts that
stand as a memorial at the book's end is one from Leviticus, 'The
goat on which the lot fell let him go for a scapegoat into the
wilderness.' Like Geoffrey Hill's sternly moving poem on the Wars
of the Roses in *King Log*, *In Parenthesis* realizes in war 'a florid
grim music broken by grunts and shrieks'.[7] (The linking of Jones
with Hill is more than fortuitous: both share a sense of the immediate presence of Britain's past.) Jones's harsh mixture of tragedy
and comedy is typified by his picture of soldiers, sodden after a

---

[7] 'Funeral Music', *King Log* (1968), pp. 23–32. The phrase is taken from Hill's
essay on the sequence, p. 67.

night in the trenches, being woken by morning's light—'With unfathomed passion—this stark stir and waking—contort the comic mask of these tragic japers' (p. 60).

Clearly the allusions, both structural and local, to *Henry V* tell a good deal about *In Parenthesis*. At first its reading of Shakespeare's play seems eccentric and anachronistic. The heroi-comical division is there in *Henry V*, and particularly forcefully in III. i–iv, Jones's main source, but it hardly adds up to anything coherent when set against the careful development of Henry as King. Yet *In Parenthesis* adds a dimension to the play. The 'gaiety' of Henry and his men falls into place, and so too does Fluellen's role. The 'disciplines of war' clearly help with Henry's threat to the citizens of Harfleur—both sides are involved in a war whose rules they understand. Just as for the soldiers of *In Parenthesis*, there is no exit but through battle and the circumscriptions of war. On the negative side, it highlights the failure to allot Falstaff and his mock soldiers a properly worked-out role in the play's structure.

Unease at the conventional 'epic' reading as a satisfactory response, and feeling that *In Parenthesis* contained a valuable critical *aperçu*, surprisingly came together when the state of the Folio text was taken into account. J. H. Walter's Arden edition argues, on the basis of several inconsistencies, that Falstaff was not originally meant to die off-stage in Act II, but intended to go to France, and to be present at Agincourt. Believing in the play's integrity, Walter thinks the alteration was for the better (p. xxiv). But an alternative is possible. The change of direction which led to the death of Falstaff resulted in a botched play. What Jones perceives is a side of *II Henry V* meant to balance Henry's idealism while showing the essential need for his kingly perfection.

A brief outline of the Folio's evidence will clarify the situation.[8] It has long been observed that *Henry V* does not tally with the promise made at the end of the Epilogue to *2 Henry IV*, where we are told that the story will be continued 'with Sir John in it', that Henry V will court Katherine, and that there, 'for anything I know, Falstaff shall die of a sweat . . .'. That this promise was initially to be fulfilled is suggested by the Chorus before Act II. This says that the scene is now moved to Southampton, and will

---

[8] For a fuller account, see Walter, pp. xxxiv–ix.

go from there to France, and finally back to England (ll. 35–8). The final couplet, however, adds that the action will not reach Southampton 'till the king come forth'. It appears that Act II was originally made up of three scenes (Southampton, France, London), and that the final couplet was added in an attempt to bring the Chorus into line with the extant play (an attempt which fails). Much later in the play, Pistol threatens revenge on Fluellen and Gower after the leek-eating scene, but suddenly cringes and complains,

> Doth Fortune play the huswife with me now?
> News have I that my Doll is dead i' the spital
> Of malady of France;
> And there my rendezvous is quite cut off.
> Old I do wax, and from my weary limbs
> Honour is cudgelled.
>
> (v. i. 84–9)

As Walter observes, Doll had indeed gone to the spital (II. i. 74–7), but she was 'meat' for Falstaff, and Pistol is married to Nell. Nor has Pistol previously been called 'old'. 'The one person in whose mouth this speech would be appropriate is Sir John Falstaff' (p. xxxviii).

If at one point Falstaff was alive in France and cudgelled (presumably by Fluellen), then the original final scene of Act II must have shown Falstaff and his fellows bidding goodbye to their women. The evidence indicates that these alterations came late in the play's composition, after the Falstaff under-plot was already worked out and, in part, drafted. There are also clues pointing to a good deal of revising round Fluellen's part (at III. ii. 20 his appearance is unannounced, and the exchange between him, Macmorris, and Jamy at III. ii. 58–143 may be an addition to fill the gap created by the loss of Falstaff). There are two further points not noted by Walter. In IV. vi Henry orders all prisoners killed, apparently because the French will not accept defeat. This is immediately followed by the scene in which Fluellen's first words are, 'Kill the poys and the luggage! 'tis expressly against the law of arms . . .' (IV. vii), so providing a reason for Henry's earlier order, though when the king again gives the same order (l. 65) he is angry for an unspecified reason. The cause of the confusion may lie in Holinshed, who gives no motive for Henry's act, and

Fluellen's speech looks like a late change seeking to explain the decision. The killing of the 'poys' raises the further question of the fate of the Boy, who otherwise disappears from the play with no explanation. Lastly, the Quarto order of IV. iv–v makes better sense than that in the Folio. There Pistol takes M. Le Fer prisoner, while the French prepare for battle in the following scene, which is surely the wrong way round. If the scenes are put in the Quarto order, the French prepare for battle, Pistol then takes his prisoner (after the first stage of the fighting), and immediately after, in scene vi, Henry sees the enemy regrouping, and orders the prisoners killed.

Like Walter, I think that Falstaff was alive at this stage, that he (not Pistol) took M. Le Fer prisoner, and that immediately after he is ordered (like everyone else) to kill his prisoner, but does not do so, and that he is later humiliated by Fluellen. This would have given a direct reflection of the Gadshill episode in *1 Henry IV* and of Falstaff's attempt to lug off Hotspur's body in Part 2. Thus Fluellen, the representative of the 'disciplines of war' is called upon to reduce the Lord of Misrule to order. Hence Falstaff and Fluellen were to provide a pair of opposing figures to reflect on Henry. There are other possibilities. Was a 'marriage' between Doll and Falstaff to provide a comic counterpart to Henry's wooing? Was the Boy (presumably the 'page' given to Falstaff by Prince Hal) meant to turn against his old master and die with the luggage, thus providing the most damning condemnation of Falstaff? And was Act V, which is rather bare, to have included Falstaff? The inconsistencies of the Folio give a shadowy outline of another *Henry V* which would have been in the same heroi-comical mode as *1–2 Henry IV*.

If this highly conjectural re-creation holds some truth (and it is not necessary for my point that it be right in every detail), the question is why did Shakespeare alter the course of *Henry V*. It may be that the Oldcastle family objected, and Shakespeare was forced to cut the knight (though he was later to appear in *The Merry Wives of Windsor*, possibly at the Queen's desire). Walter thinks it 'most unlikely that the removal was made for artistic or moral reasons'. But the play we have suffers from a markedly discontinuous sub-plot, and does so in a serious play written by a dramatist who habitually makes his sub-plots comment on and mirror the main action. Whether Shakespeare was subject to external pressure or whether Falstaff's continued presence could not be accommodated to the theme of Henry as ideal king, is perhaps immaterial. The fact is that Fluellen and the 'humorists' throw little light on Henry's role. Well might the First Quarto have been called, 'The Chronicle History of Henry the fift, With his battell fought at Agin Court in France. Togither with Auntient Pistoll. . . .' Pistol could not take the place of Falstaff. He could only be separate from the main plot.

David Jones's intuition is right. The mock soldiers were meant as a humanizing centre. Shakespeare's murder of Falstaff came about, I would guess, because the fat knight could not fit into a national epic without destroying the whole enterprise. To have included Falstaff would have raised too overtly the difficulties already present in the conclusion of *2 Henry IV*. Henry is intended as the ideal Renaissance prototype of a king whose politics are directed by divine grace and human perfection, not by *Realpolitik*. Henry V is an anti-type to the Machiavel. Yet in portraying a king, whose virtues are derived from theory (one ultimately going back to medieval and chivalric concepts), Shakespeare, however true he may have been to the humanists, runs counter to a central discovery of his age—secular politics. The pressure of the times informs Bolingbroke, and for that matter, Edmund, Iago, and Macbeth, as it cannot Henry V. *1–2 Henry IV* owes its power to the exploration of that discovery, which asks whether the good man and the good politician can ever be compatible. In *Henry V*, Shakespeare for the first time turns away from the facts of history, changing them to suit the demands made by his exemplary Christian king. As Charles Barber has observed, 'Throughout *Henry V*, the whole question of the Lancastrian succession is hushed up'[9] as it is not in the earlier plays. The usurpation question is raised in Henry's soliloquy in Act IV only to be ignored. *Henry V* has to avoid the human complexities of the rest of the tetralogy.

Probably *Henry V*, with or without Falstaff, was a noble idea 'impossible of fulfilment' (Tillyard). But enough remains of the alternative half of the play for us to recognize the kind of truth to which David Jones pays tribute and which sustains his own

---

[9] 'Prince Hal, Henry V, and the Tudor Monarchy', *The Morality of Art: Essays Presented to G. Wilson Knight by his Colleagues and Friends*, ed. D. W. Jefferson (1969), p. 74. Further, see the whole of Barber's incisive essay.

writing. Eliot has said that the past is altered by the present as the present is directed by the past: *In Parenthesis* draws strength from *Henry V*, and in doing so reveals the unachieved greatness of its predecessor.

Dean Donne's Monument in St. Paul's

Helen Gardner

IT SEEMS almost sacrilege to question the most famous of all the stories about Donne: Walton's account of how he posed when dying for a picture from which the monument in St. Paul's was carved. It seems also rash, since the late R. C. Bald, in his definitive examination of all the records and traditions concerning Donne in the biography edited with such self-effacing skill and learning by Professor Milgate,[1] accepted the story. But I cannot believe it is true, nor can I accept many of the statements made about the significance of the monument.

It is noticeable that whenever Bald is able to check Walton's statements against other evidence they are usually shown to be inaccurate; and the comment Bald makes on the story of Donne's vision of his wife with a dead child in her arms, added in the final version of the *Life of Donne* in 1675, sums up very well his generally cautious approach to the problem of Walton's reliability. Having demonstrated that Walton's account is 'riddled with inaccuracies', he concludes:

Even so, it is not inconceivable that some such hallucination occurred, and that it was related to Donne's ill-health while he was in Paris. . . . In the course of telling and retelling, the story, no doubt, became more and more circumstantial and therefore less accurate, but the substratum of truth may well be there.[2]

Yet, when he came to tell the story of Donne's last days, Bald threw caution to the winds, declaring 'It would be impossible to improve on Walton's account of Donne's last days, and of its authenticity there can be no question.'[3] Owning that it is unlikely that Walton heard Donne's last sermon, *Deaths Duell*, which was preached at Court, he argues that he must have been able to speak to some who did, and that

for other details, where his own first-hand knowledge could not be

---

[1] R. C. Bald, *John Donne: A Life* (1970).   [2] Bald, 253.   [3] Bald, 525.

drawn upon, he would have had the word of men like Henry King and Thomas Mountfort, who probably saw Donne almost daily during the last weeks of his life. More than thirty years later King wrote to Walton recalling that Donne 'but three days before his death delivered into my hands those excellent Sermons of his now made publick; professing before Dr. *Winniff*, Dr. *Monford*, and, I think, your self then present at his bed side, that it was by my restless importunity, that he had prepared them for the Press'. Here then, is King's testimony to Walton's presence at an episode of some importance that took place in Donne's bedroom during his last illness.

Without denying that Walton was a friend of King and Mountfort, Donne's executors, and that his presence on the occasion that King refers to points to his closeness to Donne and Donne's circle, we may yet doubt whether this necessitates our giving uncritical credence to a story that does not occur in the first version of the *Life* in 1640, but was added in the enlarged and revised version that appeared in 1658, more than a quarter of a century after Donne's death.

In some minor points of fact that occur in the first version of the *Life* (1640) Walton is certainly in error. He declares that after preaching his last sermon, of which a moving account is given, Donne 'hastned to his house, out of which he never moved, untill like S. *Stephen, He was carried by devout men to his grave*'.[4] But Professor Milgate, who was able to examine the records of the Charterhouse, discovered that the day after he had preached *Deaths Duell* Donne was present at an Assembly of the Governors.[5] Donne was remarkably conscientious in attending meetings. Even so, he can hardly when he preached have been in so debilitated a state as Walton describes if on the next day he was able to attend what was only a routine meeting at the Charterhouse. Walton also states that Donne's mother 'died in his house but three moneths before him'.[6] But, in fact, it was just over two months before Donne's own death that his mother died, and she died in her son-in-law's house, being buried at Barking on 28 January 1631.[7] Finally, Walton says that Donne lay fifteen days in his bed-chamber awaiting his end, having completed 'any worldly business undone'; but, as Bald notes, it was only ten days before his death on 31 March 1631 that we find the last entries in the register of

---

[4] *LXXX Sermons* (1640), B6.
[6] *LXXX Sermons*, B5.
[5] Bald, 528.
[7] Bald, 524 n. 4.

St. Paul's which bears his name.[8] These are trivial points; but they confirm that when Walton appears most exact he is least trustworthy. As he emulated the liberty of ancient historians in composing suitable speeches for his hero, so he gave verisimilitude to his narrative by corroborative and circumstantial detail. But in 1658, in telling the story of Donne's posing for his monument, he went much further. Here we are not, I believe, dealing with an inexact memory but with embroidery on a basis of truth.

The facts about the monument are these: that although in his will, signed on 13 December 1630, Donne expresses his desire to be buried in St. Paul's 'in the moste private manner that maye be' in the place 'wch the nowe Residentiaries of that Church have been pleased at my request to assigne for that purpose',[9] he makes no mention of any monument or of any provision for one; that on 18 July 1631 (over three months after his death) his executors arranged with Nicholas Stone for him to make a monument; that Stone's account book records payments to various other carvers for assistance—eight pounds to Humphrey Mayer on 27 February 1632 for 'the fineshen of Doctor doons pictor' (i.e. the effigy), six pounds to Robert Flower 'for the nech of Doctor done and the under stone and the tabell' (i.e. tablet) on 14 May, and, finally, ten shillings to Mr. Babbe 'for Doctor Dones tabell of inscription and blaking the wall' on 30 November,[10] that after the Great Fire the monument was stored with other relics in the crypt of the new St. Paul's and that it was retrieved from there and re-erected some time around 1818.

The monument as it now appears in Wren's St. Paul's shows Donne in his shroud standing on an urn within a shallow, rounded, black niche, with his epitaph on a tablet above. The shroud is drawn back to expose the face and the eyes are closed. The hands, which are joined in front of the body, and the feet are enclosed in the shroud, which is knotted in a ruff above the head and is also knotted in a ruff below the feet.[11] The back of the effigy is flat. As

---

[8] Bald, 530.   [9] Bald, 563.

[10] Bald, 533, quoting *The Note Book and Account Book of Nicholas Stone*, ed. A. J. Fineberg, Walpole Society Publications, vii (1919), 85. The last payment suggests that the monument can hardly have been erected before the very end of 1632 or the beginning of 1633.

[11] This last very curious feature does not appear in the engraving of the monument as it was before the fire in Dugdale's *History of St. Paul's Cathedral* (1658).

the sculptor Hamo Thornycroft pointed out to Gosse, the folds of the shroud fall as they would if the figure were recumbent and not standing. The knees are not straight but slightly bent.

In the original version of the *Life of Donne*, prefixed to *LXXX Sermons* in 1640, Walton concludes his narrative, before his final summary characterization, by telling us of the great concourse at Donne's funeral and that many friends came daily to strew his grave with 'curious and costly flowers' until the stones that had been taken up to make the grave were 'againe by the Masons art levelled and firmed, as they had been formerly, and his place of buriall undistinguishable to common view'. He goes on:

Nor was this (though not usuall) all the honour done to his reverend ashes; for by some good body, (who, tis like thought his memory ought to be perpetuated) there was 100. marks sent to his two faithfull friends and Executors, (the person that sent it, not yet known, they look not for a reward on earth) towards the making of a Monument for him, which I think is as lively a representation, as in dead marble can be made of him.

With some revision of wording this passage was retained in the revised and expanded version of the *Life of Donne* in 1658, with the important addition that the unknown donor was Dr. Simeon Fox, Donne's physician, whose generous act only became known after his death.[12]

Fox died in 1642. Anything that Walton heard from him had plenty of time to undergo some sea-changes in Walton's memory and imagination before he settled to revise and enlarge his *Life of Donne* in 1658 for separate publication. He left at the close of his story his original statement about the monument, which implies that the donor of the 100 marks was inspired to his act of generosity by distress at the fact that Donne's grave was 'undistinguishable

---

[12] The version of this paragraph in 1658, virtually unaltered in the subsequent versions runs: 'Nor was this all the Honour done to his reverend Ashes; for as there be some persons that will not receive a reward for that for which God accounts himself a debter; persons that dare trust God with their Charity, and without a witness; so there was by some gratefull unknowne friend, that thought Dr. *Donne*'s memory ought to be perpetuated, an hundred Marks sent to his two faithfull Friends and Executors towards the making of his Monument. It was not for many years known by whom, but after the death of Dr. *Fox* it was known that he sent it; and he lived to see as lively a representation of his dead friend as Marble can express; a Statue indeed so like Dr. *Donne*, that (as his friend Sir *Henry Wotton* hath expressed himself) it seems to breath faintly, and Posterity shall look upon it as a kind of artificiall Miracle.'

to common view'. He inserted, after an expanded version of a speech he had put into Donne's mouth on the day after he had preached his last sermon, three paragraphs that would appear to derive from information given to him by Fox. The first tells that, on Donne's return from Essex to preach his last sermon, Fox came to him 'to consult his health' and recommended him to drink milk for twenty days. Donne at first refused; but in the end he gave way so far as to drink the hated liquid for ten days. After this he gave up, declaring he preferred death, which he was 'so far from fearing' that he 'longed for the day of his dissolution'. This has the ring of truth, for there seems no reason why Walton should invent such a story, although he turns it to edification. The second paragraph, after a rather uneasy defence of men's desire for glory and for 'having our memory to out-live our lives', tells us that 'Dr. *Donne*, by the perswasion of Dr. *Fox*, yielded at this very time to have a Monument made for him; but Dr. *Fox* undertook not to perswade him how or what it should be; that was left to Dr. *Donne* himself.' The third paragraph then tells the famous story:

This being resolved upon, Dr. *Donne* sent for a Carver to make for him in wood the figure of an *Urn*, giving him directions for the compasse and height of it, and to bring with it a board of the height of his body. These being got, and without delay a choice Painter was in readiness to draw his picture, which was taken as followeth.—Severall Charcole-fires being first made in his large study, he brought with him into that place his winding-sheet in his hand, and having put off all his clothes, had this sheet put on him, and so tied with knots at his head and feet, and his hands so placed as dead bodies are usually fitted for the grave. Upon this Urn he thus stood with his eyes shut, and so much of the sheet turned aside as might shew his lean, pale, and death-like face, which was purposely turned toward the East, from whence he expected the second coming of our Saviour. Thus he was drawn at his just height; and when the picture was fully finished, he caused it to be set by his bed-side, where it continued, and became his hourly object till his death, and was then given to his dearest friend and Executor Dr. *King*, who caused him to be thus carved in one entire piece of white Marble, as it now stands in the Cathedrall Church of S. *Pauls*; and by Dr. *Donn*'s own appointment these words were to be affixed to it as his Epitaph: [the text of the epitaph above the monument follows].

Two things in this story we can accept as unquestionable. There can be no doubt that Donne composed the epitaph that stands above the monument. Not merely the final conceit—'Hic licet in occiduo cinere aspicit eum cujus nomen est Oriens'—but the statement that he took orders 'instinctu et impulsu Sp. Sancti, monitu et hortatu Regis Jacobi', which recalls the 'agente Spiritu S^to, suadente Rege,' in the inscription in the Bible at Lincoln's Inn, and the idiosyncratic method of dating his ordination, 'anno sui Jesu MDCXIV. et suae aetatis XLII', are unmistakable signs of Donne's authorship. We can also accept that Donne, either during his last illness, or after his death, was painted in his shroud.[13] The engraving by Droeshout, prefixed to *Deaths Duell*, is a genuine likeness. The hollow cheeks and sunken eyes do not disguise Donne's features as we know them from other portraits. The engraving shows only the shrouded head and shoulders, set in an oval frame. Beneath there is a Latin motto: 'Corporis haec Animae sit Syndon, Syndon Jesu'. Nobody but Donne could have written this motto. It can only have been written with one purpose: to stand below this picture. So we may accept that it was by Donne's orders that he was painted shrouded for burial. I suggested some years ago that Donne's last sermon, with this striking frontispiece, was published according to his own instructions, and that we should add to his activities in his last illness its preparation for the press and the composition of this epitaph written to stand beneath the portrait of him in his shroud.[14] We can therefore accept Walton's

[13] It is possible, and indeed without Walton's story I think it would have been assumed from the engraving, that the painting was made after death and is not the portrait of a living man but of a dead man shrouded for burial, the equivalent of a death-mask. But whether Donne was so painted before or after death does not affect the argument from the epigraph that the painting was made on his instructions.

[14] *The Divine Poems*, ed. Helen Gardner (1952), 113. I regret that by a carelessly worded sentence I appeared to suggest that Donne was responsible for the title. As Keynes pointed out (*TLS*, 24 Sept. 1938), Walter Colman, in his sole work *La Danse Machabre or Deaths Duel* [1633], complained that his title was 'inuriously conferred by Roger Muchill [i.e. Mitchell, a bookseller from 1627 to 1631], upon a Sermon of Doctor Donnes'. Colman's book was entered under the title 'a booke called *Deaths Duell*' in the Stationers' Register on 13 June 1631. Donne's sermon was entered without a title on 30 September following. Donne had not given titles to any of his separately printed sermons, but had been content to give the place where they were preached, or the occasion, or the text preached from, on the title-page. The fact that we owe the title *Deaths Duell* to the bookseller and not to Donne does not affect the argument from the frontispiece and its epigraph. In editing the sermon Mrs. Simpson, accepting my arguments, preferred the text of the Quarto of 1632 to the text in *LXXX Sermons*.

statement that a painter was summoned, and even agree that he was a 'choice Painter'.[15]

No deep research is needed to challenge the rest of Walton's story: the summoning of the carver, the making of an urn and of a board the height of Donne's body, the lighting of the charcoal fires, the tying of knots at the head and at the feet, the disposition of the hands, and the standing on the urn with the face turned towards the east.[16] We have only to appeal to experience and common sense. I would ask those who accept the story, and who have passed the meridian of this life, to attempt to emulate this extraordinary feat by a dying man. It is tiring enough to stand perfectly still with feet together on the floor for any length of time, as every woman knows who has had to do so while having the hem of a full skirt pinned up. To stand balanced on a small urn, with the feet together, the hands folded and the eyes closed, even for a few minutes, would tax a professional model in good health. Although the charcoal fires would have prevented the invalid from catching a chill, they would also have contributed to the inevitable dizziness. And what, one may well ask, was the point of demanding such an effort from a dying man? Even if a full-length, life-size portrait had been required to serve as model for a sculptor, would an even moderately competent painter have required his subject to stand for him in order to paint a body clothed in so simple a garment as a shroud? If the painter were really so incompetent as to be incapable of painting a shrouded body without a model, anyone of roughly Donne's size could have posed for the figure. Lastly, if the sculptor had this life-size image of the shrouded Donne standing perched on an urn before him, why did he not make the folds of the shroud fall as they would have fallen on a standing figure?

Walton's story may, all the same, have a basis of truth. It remains possible that when Fox told him of Donne's refusal to drink milk, and revealed to him that he was the person who gave the 100 marks

[15] Dr. Roy Strong, whom I consulted, was unable to suggest who might have painted the portrait from which Droeshout made his engraving. It must have been a striking and movingly realistic portrait of Donne either *in extremis* or dead. The engraving contrasts strongly with the beautiful, idealized head which Nicholas Stone carved from its original.

[16] The charcoal fires are a delicious touch, giving vraisemblance, but Donne's standing facing east suggests the same kind of excess of zeal in a model as the actor showed who painted himself black all over to play Othello.

for the monument, he also told him that Donne was persuaded by him that a monument should be erected and that Donne himself gave the directions for it. The portrait may well have been painted for a double purpose: to be engraved as the frontispiece for the sermon and to provide all a sculptor would need in addition to directions: an image of the dead man's face.[17] But if Donne did himself give directions for the design of his monument, in addition to writing his epitaph, can we believe that the monument as erected was made to those directions?

The portrait of Donne in his shroud and the shrouded effigy in St. Paul's have often been spoken of as final examples of Donne's 'terrible morbidity'. I find it strange that the shrouded effigies that are so common in the mid-seventeenth century should be regarded as morbid or macabre. Unlike the horrifying cadavers in various stages of gruesome decay that lie beneath robed effigies in the late fifteenth century, and the less revolting but equally grim reminders of mortality, the skeletons, such as we see beneath the slab on which Robert Cecil in his robes of state reposes at Hat-field,[18] shrouded figures do not proclaim the dominion of death and the empire of the worm, but the Christian hope by which Death is no longer 'an uncouth hideous thing, Nothing but bones'.[19] They express two typical and fundamental Christian conceptions: that the dead are 'asleep in Jesus', and that they will rise again in their flesh at the Last Day. They also provide an implicit rebuke to the worldliness of so many tombs from the Elizabethan age onwards, which seem mainly designed to assert the importance of

[17] The development of the desire for 'true likenesses' in monuments after 1600 is discussed by Eric Mercer, *English Art 1553–1625* (1962), 238–40. Mrs. Esdaile (*English Church Monuments, 1510–1840*, 1946, p. 48) reports, 'There are notes of family portraits being sent in the charge of servants to a sculptor in town in several seventeenth-century sets of household accounts.'

[18] According to Mrs. Esdaile, the cadaver appears 'virtually confined to important ecclesiastics' and fell into disuse by the mid-sixteenth century. The 'skeleton, the skull, or skull and crossbones, the charnel-house itself, all play their part on monuments, both civil and ecclesiastical, although they had ceased to be the central idea and were degraded to the condition of accessories' (K. A. Esdaile, *English Monumental Sculpture since the Renaissance*, 1927, p. 26).

[19] George Herbert, 'Death'. The whole poem seems to breathe the spirit of the recumbent shrouded monuments, particularly at its close:

> Therefore we can go die as sleep, and trust
> Half that we have
> Unto an honest faithfull grave;
> Making our pillows either down, or dust.

worldly success. In contrast to the kneeling or recumbent figures in robes of office or sumptuous clothing, they remind us of the third versicle at the beginning of the service for the Burial of the Dead: 'We brought nothing into this world, and it is certain we can carry nothing out. The Lord gave and the Lord hath taken away; blessed be the Name of the Lord.' Many of the epitaphs on tombs or monuments with shrouded effigies express a sure and certain hope with the sobriety characteristic of Caroline piety. They also frequently express personal as well as religious emotion, and seem the expression of affection and grief rather than of pride in pedigree, connections, or great place. Thus, at Great Maplestead, Essex, Lady Deane (d. 1633), 'who lived the faithful wife and died the constant widow of Sir John Deane' and 'to whose beloved memory' her eldest son 'here prostrate at her feete erects this monument', stands in her shroud with her grieved son lying before her. At Churchill, Somerset, Sara Latch (d. 1644) lies in her shroud with her living husband reclining behind her, his right hand drawing back the shroud so that he may look his last upon her face. At Bassingbourne, Cambridge, a touching memorial of 'her dear & vertuous Brother', Henry Butler (d. 1647), was provided by 'Lady Dingley his most affectionate sister who prayeth

> This stone may lye untill he rise
> To see his Saviour with his eies.'

The two famous Joshua Marshall monuments at East Carlton, Northants, and Chipping Campden, Gloucester, which show a married pair hand in hand issuing from an opened tomb, were both erected by the surviving partners to express their fond hope of a reunion.

There are two quite distinct types of tombs or wall monuments which have shrouded effigies. The first is a development from a common type of late medieval brass: the effigy is recumbent, either on an altar tomb, or on a ledge within a niche, or on a slab upon the floor, with the shroud drawn back to expose the face and the eyes closed as in sleep. The shroud is knotted at the head and, sometimes also, at the feet; at other times the feet are merely enclosed in the shroud, which is not knotted.[20] The second type is the

---

[20] A variant, of which I have only seen two examples, shows the dead man lying on his shroud on his side with the shroud drawn over the body. Nicholas

Resurrection monument. This takes various forms. A common
early form shows a shrouded figure in profile sitting up in a coffin.
Temperance Browne (d. 1634), daughter to Sir Thomas Crewe,
Speaker of the House of Commons, is commemorated in this way
in a wall monument, carved by John and Matthew Christmas, at
Steane, Northants. Her head is lifted, eyes open, and her right
hand is raised. Above her an angel sounds the trump.[21] George
Rodney (d. 1651), buried at Rodney Stoke, Somerset, also sits up
in profile in his coffin with head lifted and both hands raised in
prayer; for him too an angel on billowy clouds sounds the trump.[22]
A more sensational example of this form can be seen at Egham,
Surrey, where Sir John Denham (d. 1639), the father of the poet,
has started up at the summons with his grave-clothes falling from
him and his left hand raised up on high. Below him is a frieze of
skeletons and corpses, among them the head of a recently dead
man, who are starting up to be reclothed in flesh.[23] Less dramatic
than these figures sitting up in their coffins are the frontal shrouded
busts on wall monuments. In St. Giles Cripplegate Constance
Whitney, granddaughter of Donne's friend Sir Thomas Lucy of
Charlecote, who died aged seventeen in 1628, appears under a
shallow arch with cherubs either side. Her shroud is knotted above
her head and drawn back to expose not only her face but also her
unbound virgin locks on either side of her face. Her hands are
lifted in the *orans* pose. In Chelsea Old Church Sara Colville, who
died 17 April 1631, in her fortieth year, the 'happy mother of 8
sons and 4 daughters', similarly appears, but, being a wife and
mother, with no hair exposed.[24] Both ladies have a simple under-

---

Stone thus carved Sir William Curle (d. 1617) on a flat slab at Hatfield. The
head and one arm are bare here and the shroud is transparent, showing the
limbs through; see Mercer, Plate 90b. At Bassingbourne, Henry Butler (d.
1647), a charming young man, hardly more than a boy, lies on his side on a
black slab, with his shroud merely drawn across his body, the arms and legs as
well as the head uncovered. Both these are supremely natural portrayals of a
sleeping figure.

[21] The Brothers Christmas executed a similar monument at East Barsham,
Norfolk, for Mary Calthorpe (d. 1640).

[22] Plate 107 in Esdaile, *English Church Monuments*. Mrs. Esdaile, misled by
George Rodney's youthful lovelocks, wrongly identified him as Ann Rodney.

[23] Thomas Marsham (d. 1638) at Stratton, Norfolk, similarly rises from a
sarcophagus above a grated charnel-house inscribed 'Trophaeum Mortis'.
These two monuments may well be stigmatized as macabre.

[24] Mercer, Plate 90a.

garment beneath the shroud, which shows at the neck and covers the raised arms.

More relevant to this inquiry are the full-length standing figures. An early example is the monument already referred to of Lady Deane, erected in 1634 and ascribed to William Wright of Charing Cross.[25] She is standing on the flat top of a large, round, shallow bowl. Her shroud falls to the ground around her feet, but it is not knotted and one foot is slightly advanced with the knee bent. Her right hand is raised; her left holds the shroud in place. Within the arch above her, two small angels play trumpets, and above her raised head, in a gap in the arch, two angels hold a crown. At Amersham, Bucks., Henry Curwen, who died aged fourteen in 1636, is commemorated in a monument by Edward Marshall.[26] He stands in a pose more classical than Christian, with two angels holding open the doors of his tomb. His right foot rests on an orb and he leans towards the right with both hands resting on another orb standing on an ornamental table. His shroud, knotted at the head, is thrown back to show his long curls and he looks towards the left with an almost coy expression. This rather epicene figure seems at a far remove from other Resurrection figures, his shroud a mere decorative garment. More interesting is Thomas Burman's signed and dated monument to John Dutton (d. 1656) at Sherburne, Gloucestershire. His wife Ann, 'unto whose care the erecting of this Monument was by will entrusted', was the daughter of John King, Bishop of London and sister of Henry King, Donne's executor. The figure, free-standing, in marble stands within a black niche in his shroud. He stands, like Lady Deane, on a large, round, shallow bowl, flat at the top. His feet are free, the left protrudes from the shroud and the right knee is slightly bent, that is, he is advancing on his left foot. The shroud is knotted above the head but falls back to show his hair on either side of the face and a gown tied at the neck with a tassel. His right hand, across the breast, holds the shroud in place, his left hangs down beneath a fold. His head is slightly raised and turned to the right. Sir Geoffrey and Lady Palmer at East Carlton, Northants, and Viscount Campden and his wife at Chipping Campden, Gloucestershire, stand on two shallow, round bowls with one foot advanced

[25] Esdaile, *English Church Monuments*, Plate 110.
[26] Margaret Whinney and Oliver Millar, *English Art 1625–1714* (1957), Plate 29a.

onto the rim of the bowl and the knee bent. They are hand in hand, the other hand holding the shroud in place.[27]

While I cannot claim to have seen by any means all the shrouded effigies in English churches, I have seen enough to say with some confidence that the Donne monument is a very strange one. And, although it is often said to have set a fashion for depicting the dead in their shrouds,[28] I have not seen any that has imitated its curious features. The erect position, standing on an urn, relates it to the full-length Resurrection figures; but the closed eyes and the total enclosure of the hands, and even more of the feet, within the shroud belong to the sleeping recumbent figures on altar tombs or tomb chests. Accepting Walton's story of Donne's posing for his monument, Professor Bald tried to find 'the meaning of the role he was trying to enact':

> It seems to have been Donne's intention to represent the resurrection of the body; the shrouded figure is rising from the funeral urn, and what seems at first glance to be a crouching attitude suggests rather that he is still emerging, and has not yet drawn himself erect. That the resurrection was in Donne's mind is clear from Walton's statement that he faced east while the drawing was being made. . . . But why then the closed eyes? One can only suggest that he is but half aroused, and that he dare not yet open his eyes to the glory of the Lord.[29]

This is ingenious, not to say imaginative. Looking at the monument, as we see it today, we see that Donne, far from 'still emerging', has his feet very firmly set on the ruffed end of the shroud, which is set above the flat top of the urn. Again, the figure can hardly be described as 'crouching'. The torso is erect; it is only the knees that sag. Finally, the extraordinary expression of peace on the face does not suggest he is even 'half aroused'. It is the face of someone sleeping, whose sleep has not been in any way disturbed by the sound of the Last Trump. In fact, the earliest

---

[27] Lady Palmer died in 1655; her husband (d. 1670) erected the monument in his lifetime. Viscount Campden died in 1642; his wife erected the monument in 1664. I suspect the monument at East Carlton, the finer to my taste, is the original and the one at Chipping Campden the replica. Dr. Whinney suggested that the East Carlton monument was by Edward Marshall, a better artist than his son who carved the one at Campden.

[28] The dates show that Donne was rather in tune with the feeling of his age than setting it a model.

[29] Bald, 535–6.

comment we have on Donne's monument, the verses 'Hexastichon Bibliopolae' signed 'Jo. Mar.', prefixed to the *Poems* in 1633, assumes that both the portrait prefixed to *Deaths Duell* and the statue show Donne as dead:

> I see in his last preach'd, and printed booke,
> His Picture in a sheete; in *Pauls* I looke,
> And see his Statue in a sheete of stone,
> And sure his body in the grave hath one:
> Those sheetes present him dead, these if you buy,
> You have him living to Eternity.

The simplest and most obvious explanation of the oddity of the monument would be that the effigy was not originally designed to stand erect upon an urn but was to lie upon a tomb: that Donne was to be shown not as rising at the general Resurrection but as asleep in sure and certain hope. There are some difficulties in accepting this explanation which were pointed out to me by Mr. J. F. Physick,[30] who very kindly examined the monument for me. He reported that the effigy is 'perfectly flat behind, from the top of the urn up to about neck level' and that the ruffed shroud at the feet has also been cut flat, adding that all this 'seems to have been done quite deliberately, as the marble is smooth, and is not simply unworked'. He also noted that the urn (which is not flat at the back) seems to have been carved from a separate piece of marble.[31] Mr. Physick thought that, although the flat back of the effigy would be consistent with its having been carved to lie recumbent, the head, which is not flat but carved behind, did not curve forward sufficiently for it to have been designed to lie on a pillow or cushion. He thought the curve, which is shallow but quite definite, was designed to take into account the profile of the head of the niche itself and suggested that the flattening of the effigy at the

---

[30] Assistant Keeper in the Department of Conservation, Victoria and Albert Museum. Mr. Physick made two visits on my behalf. On the second he writes that 'the Dean's Verger and I, lugging an immense and heavy ladder had to force our way from one end of the Cathedral to the other through hundreds of visitors —something I should not care to do often.'

[31] That the urn was separately carved is confirmed by Dr. Richard Gough, who visited the crypt where the remains of the monuments from the old Cathedral were stored on 19 May 1783. He found the effigy in St. Faith's Chapel and the urn 'flat at top and never open in a separate vault'. (*Sepulchral Monuments of Great Britain,* Part II (1796), p. cccxxiv. Gough's notes are in the Bodleian copy of Dugdale.)

back might have taken place when the monument was reconstructed in order to make the effigy fit into a shallower and narrower
niche than it occupied in old St. Paul's.

This last suggestion seems very probable. Comparison of the
monument as it is at present with the engraving by Hollar in
Dugdale's *History of St. Paul's Cathedral* (1658) shows that the
present niche appears to be considerably shallower and narrower
than the original one. Mr. Physick writes that the effigy at its
widest is a very tight fit and added, 'I do not think I could get my
fingers behind the shoulders.' In the engraving there is plenty of
room round the figure, which gives the impression of being free-
standing, that is carved in the round. The suggestion that the
forward curve of the head was designed to take into account the
profile of the head of the niche seems less likely if we can trust the
engraving which shows the head of the niche with a shallower and
wider curve than the present one. The present niche is also considerably longer than the original one. A pedestal has had to be
provided for the urn to stand upon, and also, possibly, the ruffed
shroud at the feet. Although it and the effigy seem to be carved
from the same piece of marble, it does not appear in the engraving
where Donne's feet, enclosed in the shroud, stand on the urn; nor
is there any sign of it in the engraving of the material stored in the
crypt in J. P. Malcolm's *Londinium Redivivum* (1803). Here
Donne's effigy stands entire, among various more or less mutilated
figures, with his shroud knotted above his head and his feet
enclosed in the shroud but flat on the ground.[32]

Finally I come to the slack knees within folds that fall not towards the feet but sideways away from the knees. Even as late as
the seventeenth century the great majority of recumbent effigies,
clothed or shrouded, lie in the old medieval position, rigid, with
their hands joined above their breasts in prayer. But a new natural-
istic tendency appears in the early seventeenth century, the finest
and most celebrated example being Nicholas Stone's masterpiece:
the effigy of Lady Carey at Stowe Nine Churches, Northants.

---

[32] Hollar's engraving and the engraving of the crypt with its fragments in
J. P. Malcolm's book are reproduced in Sir Geoffrey Keynes's edition of *Deaths
Duell* (Boston, 1973). I am greatly indebted to Sir Geoffrey's admirable 'post-
script' to this elegant reprinting of Donne's last sermon.

The ruffed end, on which Donne so oddly stands without flattening it at all,
makes the effigy correspond with Walton's statement that the shroud in which
Donne posed was 'tied with knots at his head and feet'.

Stone's Note Book records that he was commissioned by Lady Carey in 1617 and set up the tomb in 1619.[33] She is shown asleep, half-turned on to her left side, in her habit as she lived. She wears a finely embroidered bodice over a full skirt under a fur-lined cloak with a riding-hood over her head. Her right hand is on her breast, her left lies by her side. Her knees are flexed, the right leg lying above the left with the sole of the foot showing beneath the hem of her cloak. Ten or so years later a sculptor who has not been identified carved an altar tomb for Anne, Lady Kinloss, who died in 1627 at the age of twenty-two. She was the first wife of Lord Bruce of Kinloss, later first Lord Elgin, and was a great heiress, granddaughter and sole surviving heir of the first Lord Harington, niece of Donne's friend Lucy Bedford and of her brother the second Lord Harington, for whom Donne wrote a long funeral elegy. At Exton, Rutland, among glorious and splendid monuments commemorating the Haringtons and the Noels, she lies asleep in her shroud. The effigy is of remarkable beauty,[34] and, in its setting, is the most moving example I know of the implicit rebuke to worldly vanity that the shrouded effigies present. She lies on her back with her eyes closed. One arm and hand lie outside the shroud which is drawn back to show her face. The shroud is knotted at the head, which lies on a low tasselled pillow with two cherubs carved in a low relief on either side of her head. Her feet are enclosed in the shroud, but it is not knotted at the feet; their soles rest against a heraldic image of an eagle swallowing a snake. Her knees are flexed and not rigid. Comparing the effigy with a photograph of Donne's monument which I took with me, I should say that the knees of the recumbent Lady Kinloss and the knees of the standing Dr. Donne were at about the same angle.[35]

To sum up: it would seem that the effigy, though at present, except for the head, flat at the back, was originally fully carved in the round. And it should now be added that it is only around the

[33] The tomb was set up in Lady Carey's lifetime. She died at the age of eighty-four in 1630. The naturalism of this monument is seen in an even more striking form in Stone's effigy of Sir William Curle at Hatfield made at about the same time.

[34] I find it difficult to believe that anyone but Stone was capable of such work in 1627.

[35] The same relaxed knees can be seen in the shrouded effigy of Lady Frances Knyveton (d. 1643), on the tomb erected by her mother, Alice, Duchess Dudley in St. Giles in the Fields, a rather undistinguished work by Edward or Joshua Marshall.

knees that the folds of the shroud do not fall as for a standing
figure. At the head and shoulders they do not fall back. This
difference between the lines of the folds in the upper half of the
figure and in the lower is one of the features that make the monument so unsatisfactory. (Another is the absurdly small urn, only
just wide enough at the top to take the feet.) The head and face are
very beautifully carved, but the same cannot be said of the figure
as a whole.[36] As has been said, Stone paid an outside carver 'for
the fineshen of Doctor doons pictor'. His account book shows that
he rarely employed outside carvers, and very rarely—on only two
other occasions—for help with the effigy. I cannot help feeling that
something went badly wrong with the commission: that Stone was
directed to make a recumbent figure, but it was then discovered
that the authorities at St. Paul's could not find space for a full-
length figure on an altar tomb, and the effigy had to be adapted to
stand in a niche. This would explain the oddity of the monument;
but whether this explanation is accepted or not, I cannot believe
that it was Donne's own directions that produced the monument
as it was erected.

Although I believe that Walton's anecdote of Donne's posing for
the monument must be rejected on grounds of its inherent
improbability, I think the story has a core of truth. I think we
should accept that Donne was persuaded by Fox that he should
have a monument and that he wished to be shown in his shroud,
asleep in the Lord and, as his epitaph says, 'looking towards Him
whose Name is the Rising'. In order that the sculptor should have
a likeness to carve from, he was painted in his shroud either before
or just after his death. He wished, I believe, his monument to
proclaim what in his poems and so often in his sermons he had
humbly asserted: that in death the Christian's trust can only be
in the mercy of his Creator and the merits of his Saviour.

[36] This is why, for the frontispiece for my edition of the *Divine Poems*, I had
a photograph made of the head alone.

The Poetics of the Critical Act: Dryden's Dealings with Rivals and Predecessors

EARL MINER

ARNOLD'S DREAM that poetry would replace religion had its premiss in religious disbelief. Not surprisingly, the dream has gone unfulfilled. Today some theorists doubt poetry sufficiently to suppose that criticism must replace literature: Arnold's dream now beckons as a critical nightmare. But if this is the modern critical condition, it is not the modern poetic condition. Nor has it always been so for critics. Even today, most of us know in our hearts that all creation is the most fundamental if also usually implicit criticism. This is where Dryden enters. He constantly engaged with other writers, wrote in an astonishing range of translations, of sorts of non-dramatic poetry, of drama, and of prose styles. He was the first English writer aware that he was prosecuting a critical career in which poetic practice and critical precept were counterparts.

To Dryden we owe the realization for English literature that what we can know involves defining self in relation to world, world to self; and that the process of definition involves remembered versions of both, presently understood versions of both, and hitherto unknown versions. The last is the creative part in which poets excel. But it is infeasible without the other two. We see this congeries of definitions in Dryden's prefaces. His explicitness, like Shakespeare's silence, is a personal trait. He constantly joins features of our understanding of the world that usually are thought discrete: literature, other arts, politics, history, religion, science. One of the most public of poets, he is also one of the most personal of critics. In both roles, he is extraordinarily innovative. But he made no pretence to have invented everything, and his translations, allusions, and adaptations show him involved in 'influence' or 'reception', what in the end is best understood as concomitant creation, criticism, and self-definition.[1]

The demonstration of these matters requires an intimate knowledge of the writings of any poet treated, and the simplest writing with which to begin, at least for Dryden, is his prose criticism. In a late essay, *A Parallel Betwixt Poetry and Painting*, he insists that art is founded on imitation of nature and must please (including 'what ought to please' as a norm).[2] This typical Renaissance neo-Aristotelianism and neo-Horatianism is remarkable because he seeks to harmonize two premisses whose relation came about quite accidentally. His discussion makes something else clear. Mimesis pervades Western literature because it assumes not just that nature is imitable, but that it is real, knowable, and shareable. The assumption induces great confidence. Disagreeing with Aristotle over why imitation pleases (*Poetics*, ch. 5), he argues that it involves cognitive and ethical matters: truth through our reasoning and good by exercise of our will. On that basis, 'The imitation of nature is therefore justly constituted as the general, and indeed, the only, rule of pleasing, both in poetry and painting' (Watson, ii. 193).

Dryden posits a freedom in imitation. In portraying character,

---

[1] The fashions of words sometimes make us look silly when the fashion passes. My Ph.D. dissertation was accurately entitled 'The Japanese Influence on British and American Literature' (1955). But 'influence' was then such a disreputable term that for a book the title became pretentious: *The Japanese Tradition in British and American Literature* (1958). Thirteen years later Claudio Guillén, or common sense, had made the word tolerable, as in 'The Aesthetics of Literary Influence', chs. 1 and 2 of *Literature as System* (Princeton: Princeton University Press, 1971). The idea that there is a problem in the transactions between modern and older writers derives from the Romantics, as I have shown in 'The Double Truth of Modern Poetic Criticism' in *Sense and Sensibility in Twentieth-Century Writing*, ed. Brom Weber (Carbondale and Edwardsville: Southern Illinois University Press, 1970), pp. 16–25. After such blame of past writers was translated into the notion of 'dissociation of sensibility' by T. S. Eliot and others, it became, in the fine phrase of Walter Jackson Bate's title, *The Burden of the Past* (Cambridge, Mass.: Belknap Press, 1970). The idea has been greatly extended to a general theory of literary genesis by Harold Bloom in *The Anxiety of Influence* (New York: Oxford University Press, 1973) and later studies. My preferences run more to Dionýz Ďurišin, *Sources and Systematics of Comparative Literature* (Bratislava: Univerzita Komenského, 1974), wooden as its English is; and *Rezeptionsästhetik*, ed. Rainer Warning (Munich: Fink Verlag, 1976); and Wolfgang Iser, *Der Akt des Lesens* (ibid. 1977).

[2] Dryden, *Of Dramatic Poesy and Other Essays*, ed. George Watson, 2 vols. (London: Dent, 1962), ii. 181–208, especially 193–200. Hereafter cited as 'Watson'.

'there is a better or worse likeness to be taken: the better is panegyric, if it be not false, and the worse is a [satire].' He recalls a passage
in the *Poetics* where three writers are said to have depicted people
better, worse, and like (Watson, ii. 202). The artist's imitation
allows for latitude in truth or goodness within a range of moral
cognition while yet preserving the poet's purposes and the reader's
consent.

These important issues seem never to have been aired adequately.
Their centrality to Dryden can be shown in the earlier 'Account'
prefixed to *Annus Mirabilis*. Discussing 'descriptions or images',
he declares that 'historic and panegyric' poetry are 'branches' of
'epic poesy' (Watson, i. 101). Panegyric clearly also implies its
obverse, worse likeness, satire. All this relates very clearly to
Dryden's non-dramatic practice, in which varieties of narrative
predominate. Wonder and grandeur, the high mimesis, involve a
world of time and history, of large numbers of people, and of
strong personalities defined by shared values. In this public world,
Dryden and Milton found what they believed truly real. By serving
supernal ends beyond the contingent, the true narrative, the real
heroic of these poets offered a species of theodicy and asserted
divine providence. Such narrative allowed for subsidiary branches
of praise and blame for better or worse likenesses, as Milton's
Satan shows to perfection. The historical filled the distant heroic
with the matter of time and place.

Two of Dryden's historical concepts have redirected our
thought. One deserves a name, Crites's Question. In *An Essay of
Dramatic Poesy*, Crites asks: 'Is it not evident in these last hundred
years (when the study of philosophy [i.e. science] has been the
business of all the virtuosi in Christendom), that almost a new
nature has been revealed to us?' (Watson, i. 26.) This echoes, and
alters, Sidney's remark on the poet's disdaining to be bound to
reality and growing 'in effect another nature'.[3] Sidney has in mind
centaurs and the like. Dryden has in mind a concept far more
radical: a changing nature. Crites's 'almost' (like Sidney's 'in
effect') betrays some hesitation. And well it might, since such
historicism would ultimately jeopardize Dryden's beliefs in the
uniformity of human nature, the comparability of historical episodes (cyclicity), and mimesis itself.

[3] G. Gregory Smith, ed., *Elizabethan Critical Essays*, 2 vols. (Oxford:
Clarendon Press, 1904), i. 156.

The other, closely related, historical concept is so familiar as to seem always to have existed. But we owe to Dryden our idea of a literary period or age.

> Well then; the promis'd hour is come at last;
> The present Age of Wit obscures the past:
> Strong were our Syres; and as they Fought they Writ,
> Conqu'ring with force of Arms, and dint of Wit;
> Theirs was the Gyant Race, before the Flood;
> And thus, when *Charles* Return'd, our Empire stood.

So Dryden to Congreve (ll. 1–6). This is akin to talk of the dramatists of 'the former age' in *An Essay of Dramatic Poesy* and elsewhere. This conception of a period made possible a genuine historical view of literature and other human enterprises, something Dryden deals with in terms of progress pieces on an art such as painting (*To Sir Godfrey Kneller*) or a technology such as navigation and shipping (*Annus Mirabilis*). With these ideas Dryden laid the basis for historical understanding of literature. They also made him a genuine comparatist. He considered for drama the ancients and, among the moderns, the Spanish, French, and English. He compared Chaucer with Ovid and Boccaccio. In comparing Horace and Juvenal, he declared: ''Tis generally said that those enormous vices which were practised under the reign of Domitian were unknown in the time of Augustus Caesar; that therefore Juvenal had a larger field [as satirist] than Horace' (Watson, ii. 132). From this we see that the historical element helps to distinguish difference and the theoretical helps to identify common elements, as they have tended to do ever since Dryden.

The distinction between differentiating historicism and homogenizing theory is sufficiently clear to allow for some joining of the two for greater effect. In his poetry, the one implies the other in his constant preoccupation with likening, combining. The standard example of congruence between prose and poetry must be *Religio Laici*, whose prose preface covers the very topics of the poem in their order, ending with just the same concern over the poem's style. Yet we read the poem in preference to the prose, for the reasons we return to *Mac Flecknoe*. Poetry matters more than prose, at least when prose attempts the same thing as poetry. When poems give better or worse likeness, each version of the truth holds interest.

It seems agreed that *Mac Flecknoe* uses a theatrical coronation progress for its situation, and that it weaves three major strands: monarchy or politics involving a slight plot; art and especially drama, clearly committing the poem to a critical act; and religion, validating politics and art. The combination is presided over by an implicit heroic standard, with history, panegyric, and satire made immediate. The princes are Richard Flecknoe and Thomas Shadwell, historical characters who inhabit a real world, alive with art; or rather they rule over 'all the Realms of Non-sense' (l. 6), a barbarous Ireland or, more idyllically, 'Some peaceful Province in Acrostick Land' (l. 206). The old topos of the epic poet as king has a new day, especially since the ruler is also a divine, 'As King by Office, and as Priest by Trade' (l. 119). So art becomes politics becomes religion becomes art once more in ceaseless combinatory play.

The additional crucial element in *Mac Flecknoe*, human relationship of father and son, has counterparts in 'To the Memory of Mr. Oldham'. The analogies for the Dryden–Oldham relation begin with heroic *amicitia* as the older and younger poets are compared with Nisus and Euryalus in the *Aeneid*. But the poem ends by assimilating Virgil's Augustus–Marcellus relation to Dryden and Oldham, thereby making Dryden the monarch and Oldham the lost successor. In few words, this poem takes a better likeness to the worse of *Mac Flecknoe* even while sharing many concerns and analogies. Examination would show that various of these elements recur in the Killigrew and Purcell odes, *A Song for St. Cecilia's Day*, *Alexander's Feast*, as well as the addresses to Kneller and Southerne. Of course there are also real distinctions, since Dryden honours the historical integrity in each instance. But the poem to Congreve astonishingly resembles *Mac Flecknoe* in subject and analogy. Again a father–king–artist is unseasonably deposed. Again he addresses his most promising son, a dramatist, with charges. Again different ages are involved. But a far better likeness is taken in the assessment by heroic metaphor of 'Dryden's poetic kingdoms'.

Connections such as those between father and son, ruler and inheritor, artist and king gave him ways to define his relations with his fellow poets. He differs from the Elizabethans in feeling no need to *defend* poesy.[4] But since poesy required doing, he had to

---

[4] See Smith's introduction to *Elizabethan Critical Essays*, i, pp. xxi–xxxi, on 'The Defence' essential to Elizabethan criticism.

consider other doers. As Shakespeare fussed a little over the rival poet, and as Jonson and others fulminated in theatrical wars, he had to consider contemporaries who sometimes had to be thought enemies. For him, this was the arena where self-definition became most heated, problematical.

In recent years much has been made of the anxiety or repression a poet undergoes in trying to overgo a strong predecessor. As Ďurišin says, quoting the Russian Formalist, Tynyanov: 'literary continuity represents . . . a struggle, a tension, often between contradictory developmental trends. "Every literary continuity is, above all, a contest, a disruption of an old compactness and a new alignment of old elements."'[5] As Ďurišin himself puts it better still, 'in every process of reception of literary values, the dominant feature is the act of completion, of finishing, of overcoming, a differentiating act' (p. 54). As we have seen, for Dryden differentiation was to a large extent historical, a matter involving the character of writers in one age as against those in another. This is another way of saying that the writers that create a poet's alarms and arouse the liveliest limbic activity are those in one's own age rather than one's dead predecessors or as yet unborn successors.

We know that he got on unusually well with most of his contemporaries. Was there ever another poet who dealt so warmly with younger contemporaries? Although he owed to truth certain important qualifications in taking a better likeness, what generosity is there in his poems on the dead John Oldham and the dead Anne Killigrew! He could expect no gain from such tributes. But as with Milton in *Lycidas* or Shelley in *Adonais*, he did pay tribute to poets of his time who were lost before they could achieve what they might have. If there were contemporaries who were enemies, there was also that last reviewer, Death, whom any ambitious writer had most to fear.

Of all these poems on artists who were his contemporaries, the most handsome must be the one to his young friend Congreve. Dryden hailed him as a 'promis'd' superior in comedy. He said that Congreve's first play was the best maiden effort he had ever seen. In the poem to Congreve he asserted that *The Double Dealer* proved that at last their age had someone on whom Nature had bestowed a genius equal to Shakespeare's. Before we dismiss this assertion as hyperbolic nonsense, we may ponder a couple of

[5] Ďurišin, op. cit., p. 53.

things. For one, a comparison of Congreve's first two plays with Shakespeare's initial pair would more readily suggest what Dryden claims than the opposite. For another, and especially considering that in *All for Love* Dryden had essayed the Shakespearian topic, such praise of a fellow poet over oneself is as rare as the Phoenix. After all, he is talking about an individual's promise in a new era taking on its character as he enters old age. He is addressing a contemporary of genius, one whose promise might have put him in the class of Shakespeare, Purcell, or Dryden himself. The event shows that Will. Congreve was happier with a sinecure than as a writer. If that is a kind of satire or worse likeness, Congreve rather than Dryden suffers.

In considering his relations with his contemporaries, a double distinction must be held in mind. He mentioned, or is mentioned by, many contemporaries, although he actually addressed or commemorated relatively few. On the other hand, his address to few is relatively many by comparison with most other poets. Together the distinctions imply several things of importance. In general, he proves in the liveliest fashion that any poet understands himself most clearly by taking a relation to contemporaries. In addition, for good or ill, for better or worse likeness, certain writers matter more than others. Such basic matters pertain to all writers. What beyond them distinguishes him is his explicit understanding of his contemporaries, which is to say his explicit self-definition by relation to them. Only a poet who is also an explicit critic and is comfortable in himself and his world could have such composure as his. It is also a feature of his poetic self-portraits that they involve the same kind of comparative exercise, albeit implicit, that we remember from his prose criticism, in which Juvenal is compared with Horace in diffcrent ages or Jonson with Shakespeare in the same. He was generous, and in treating his contemporaries was handsomely willing to take a better likeness, to praise.

From Dr. Johnson on, Dryden's praise of his contemporaries in his prose, especially his dedications, has usually seemed beyond comprehension when it has not seemed fulsome and self-serving. Let us say that there is excess, and then let us ask how often poets err in generosity to their contemporaries. But let us also examine his fine print. Amid the excess, and especially in the poetry, there will also be found a closer likeness of the truth than is supposed. Congreve provided us with a positive instance. Anyone attending

to the poems on such writers as Oldham and Killigrew will see
that they are quite carefully placed by the end of Dryden's tribute.
A less well known example, the poem to Thomas Southerne, con-
soles him for the failure of one of the finest comedies of the time,
The Wives Excuse. The consolation is genuine. And so is the advice:
imitate, he says, Etherege in style and Wycherley in wit.

> Learn after both, to draw some just Design,
> And the next Age will learn to Copy thine.
>
> (ll. 30–1)

Advice direct mingles with comfort, setting Southerne in a context of earlier poets, so that the present may yield to a happy future,
so that the present may be better understood in terms of past and
future, so that indeed there may be some historical continuity in
genuine literary quality.

The poetic evidence of his relation with his contemporaries
includes a number of matters involving Milton. Here was a great
poet with whom he might have felt uneasy, but in fact did not.
Within a decade or so of the publication of *Paradise Lost* and
Paradise Regained, he treated them as classics, as fonts for borrowing and allusion. He essayed what Milton had planned, a dramatic
version of *Paradise Lost*. Like Milton, he found it a mistake and
only published *The State of Innocence* when a corrupt text appeared.
In 1688 Jacob Tonson the bookseller wished to make something
special of *Paradise Lost*, so that besides the illustrations he introduced he asked Dryden for commendatory verses. The contribution is at once stiff and uninteresting. Like their subject, Dryden
required more room for manœuvre. But he knew what he was
doing. He put into English a distich written by the Italian Selvaggi,
honouring Milton's visit to Rome. Milton was so proud of his
being compared favourably to Homer and Virgil (and by an
Italian no less) that he included the verses in his 1645 *Poems*.
Dryden connects his version with *Paradise Lost*, a poem the Italian
never knew. Mediterranean flattery has been translated into just if
not very remarkable criticism.

The poem to Kneller offers a somewhat different definition of
art and life by consideration of a contemporary. Although it has
resemblances with various poems, its chief interest lies in the quite
unusual, dyspeptic tone. The progress of painting turns out to be

as dispiriting as his other progress pieces are optimistic. Painting improved through Grecian times. The Romans kept it alive, but in lesser state. Then came the '*Goths* and *Vandals*, a rude Northern Race' (l. 47). Thereafter the art slept with the ruins of poetry until Raphael and Titian. This leads to Kneller's gift to the poet, a painted version of the Chandos portrait of Shakespeare. Defining himself by Shakespeare (rather pointedly choosing him rather than Kneller as a positive model), he is 'Proud to be less; but of his Godlike Race' (l. 76). That race excels the other one of painters.

> Our Arts are Sisters; though not Twins in Birth;
> For Hymns were sung in *Edens* happy Earth,
> By the first Pair; while *Eve* was yet a Saint;
> Before she fell with Pride, and learn'd to paint.
> Forgive th' allusion; 'twas not meant to bite;
> But Satire will have room, where e're I write.
>
> (ll. 89–94)

The last line is very true, if we allow also for the presence of panegyric as the obverse, for history as part of the public world, and hopes for heroic endeavour. He is also playing a role, Mr. Satirist. The year before he had had fresh access of fame from his translation of Persius and much of Juvenal. As Juvenalis Britannicus he 'bites'. Yet more is involved. He is worried about both arts, about monarchy (the topos for both kinds of artists), and his usual complex of values in 'this Age', 'these Inferiour Times' (ll. 117, 118). Historical insight breeds pessimism in the artist caught like ravished Rome in another 'stupid Military State' (l. 51), the time of King William and his wars, rebellion in Ireland and protest at home, taxes, and harassment of Catholics. His grumpiness over 1688 and All That quite strikingly resembles Milton's in 1660, with the fuming over England's choosing 'a captain back to Egypt'.

The times are not, however, deterministic. If Kneller depresses Dryden, in the same year Congreve buoys him. Many of the same motifs are used: historical development in a progress piece, a monarchy of politics and a kingdom of art in disarray. The people addressed differ. When the vain Kneller had his poem republished after the poet's death, certain questioning passages were omitted. When Congreve published Dryden's plays in 1717, he said very simply, 'I loved Mr. *Dryden*.' Dryden is engaged with his

contemporaries all right, and his use of any one of them in a poem
both reflects and defines his concerns.

The likeness taken need not be simply positive or negative, as
many poems show, although none better than *Mac Flecknoe*. In
this satire presented as panegyric, Dryden unhistorically bestows
upon Flecknoe and Shadwell a love like that between him and
Congreve. Actually, the son of Flecknoe was originally probably
Elkanah Settle.[6] Whether to Settle or Shadwell, the love given is
that Dryden felt for his own real and artistic sons. The king and
Prince of Dulness absolute possess their ranks, because monarchy
and art define each other positively to Dryden. The filial and
paternal relation, the royalty and succession, the art and praise
comically supposed join with prophecy to aid in defining the
nature of the poet. In this ebullient and positive, if therefore more
deadly praise in a worse likeness, Dryden composedly defines
himself as an artist with an assured laughter derived from comic
versions of his own ideals.

Certain other contemporaries were such that he would not fit
them into that scheme of art–politics–religion. One can only
assume of these people, especially as we find them in *Absalom and
Achitophel*, that they seemed important enough to offer genuine
danger of some kind. One such was Buckingham, whom he refuses
to allow a son, as by contrast are Ormonde (Barzillai) and even
Shaftesbury (Achitophel) after a sort, as also notoriously the king.
It is not a little interesting that Dryden's quarrels with the
profligate nobleman (Rochester serves as another example) do not
lead him to accusation of grievous sins and crimes. It would be
impossible to infer from his character of Zimri that the Duke of
Buckingham had deserted his wife for a double adultery and the
killing of his partner's husband. Since Dryden left out these
things, we must assume that he did not choose to define his own
character against such corruption. He chooses rather to consider
Buckingham and Rochester as rival *poets*, challengers to his art.
The Rehearsal is not the worst parody of what is not the best
dramatic kind, the heroic play. But Buckingham and Rochester
must have seemed to be getting up a party against him to deny
him an audience. As we can see, in defining himself against his
contemporaries, he responded differently within a range of a

---

[6] See George McFadden, 'Elkanah Settle and the Genesis of *Mac Flecknoe*',
Philological Quarterly, xliii (1964), 55–72.

number of motifs and situations. As it happens, he responded well to good people and, with the exception of Shadwell and possibly Rochester, duly acknowledged the talents of those whom he opposed. He managed the writer's most difficult critical passage, relation with contemporaries.

As all writers, or anyone acquainted with them, know, their basic concern in taking relation is with their contemporaries. No writer of the past can exert the emotional pressure, good or bad, on a writer that living friends or enemies do. That said, there is of course a proper subject of concern in the less important relation taken by a writer with other writers of some distance in time or space. When Pound extolled the haiku, or Yeats the nō, both arts were being practised in Japan. It is striking that our 'classical' writers have been definitively dead since the sack of Rome, whereas the 'classical past' of the Japanese involved a literary culture across the sea that continued to evolve. No wonder that the Japanese felt the Chinese 'classics' to be almost contemporaneous as well as classical, and no wonder that from time to time they would reject what might seem a contemporary rival.

Dryden is typical of English poets in his dealings with earlier writers. In the Renaissance way, he draws on some with indifference to what we would term plagiarism. He uses some as positive models, others as cautionary examples. But like all artists, he was most interested in qualities that might live for his own purposes. Here is a process of assimilation, an effort to contemporize the past through adaptation, rejection, and all that goes on in a revisionary use of what one wants to one's own ends. A small but telling example occurs in *Mac Flecknoe*, where he dismisses Thomas Dekker (l. 87) along with Thomas Heywood, James Shirley, and one contemporary, John Ogilby (l. 102). No one has bothered to ask why that is the order, but the death years of the four authors are successively 1632, 1641, 1666, and 1676. The past stretching back to a Dekker is brought, as negative example, into temporal line with a present Ogilby.

Translation illustrates the contemporizing best. Dryden was involved in this art from his rendering of Persius and other authors as a schoolboy to his *Fables* in 1700. In nothing else must a poet submit to a predecessor as much as in translation, and it is very significant indeed which poets find translation uncongenial, which give up their own work to translate, and which are at home in both.

As we have seen, Dryden poses as the English Satirist after rendering Persius and much of Juvenal. But he is always finding the poet he is engrossed in possessed of a soul most like his own. Homer, the first book of whose *Iliad* appears in *Fables*, is merely the last example: 'My thoughts are at present fixed on Homer; and by my translation of the first Iliad I find him a poet more according to my genius than Virgil' (Watson, ii. 266). What we call translation represents only the most obvious use of writers in another language or, like Dryden's Chaucer, in an earlier version of one's own tongue. He even speaks of transfusion, which perhaps we can relate to other appropriations ranging from translation and plagiarism to allusion or echo. He was aware of these varieties, and spoke of distinctions between metaphrase, paraphrase, and imitation as progressively 'looser' kinds of translation. The point is important, but for some reason he has been over-credited for it, even as his most profound remark of this kind has gone unappreciated: 'I have endeavoured to make Virgil speak such English as he would himself have spoken, if he had been born in England, and in this present age.' (Watson, ii. 247.) The difficulties of that enterprise are daunting. But any attempt to understand the past without acknowledging one's own presence as understander is less daunting than doomed. He was well aware of the difficulties, adding to the old saying that Virgil was the torture of the grammarian that he was the plague of the translator. Yet he assumes translation to be necessary and that it involves bringing an author into one's own present language.

The obvious purpose of translation, as for any kind of writing, is that it is meant to be read, to have readers. England at that present age consists not solely of John Dryden but also of numerous readers ranging from excellent judges to 'mob readers' who prefer the flashy to 'solid sense and elegant expression' (Watson, ii. 243). The universal stylistic premiss is decorum, engaging the writer with the subject (for translation, another writer's creation) and the audience. To consider only the former is to ignore half the matter of a writer's self-definition. In fact, the audience often matters more than the author translated, just as rival contemporary poets certainly account for more of a writer's concern than does a predecessor.

Dryden's concern with his audience involves so much of his writing in prose and verse as to require a book. Congreve is both subject and part of the audience of the poem addressed to him. Shadwell is part of the audience of real readers and also, as Mac Flecknoe, an audience in the poem. This complicated, rich subject can be reduced to compass only by some such means as considering Dryden's advocacy of Horatian affectivism, teaching and delight. By comparison with critical predecessors and contemporaries, he is generally more liberal in assigning greater importance to pleasure. The liberality implies an easy faith in his relation to his audience. In 1666, he allowed that delight is 'one intention of a play' (Watson, i. 38: the earliest critical use of 'intention'?). Two years later, he argues that 'delight is the chief if not the only end of poesy . . . for poesy only instructs as it delights' (Watson, i. 113–14), distinguishing such pleasure from what may take with audiences of mob readers. In 1670, he allows delight a larger role still (Watson, i. 152), and in 1677 he argues against the redoubtable Rymer that although 'The great end of the poem is to instruct . . . by making pleasure the vehicle of that instruction', 'The chief end of the poet is to please' if the poet is to have an audience (Watson, i. 219). Here we see a writer confident in his art and his age growing yet more certain that he can carry his audience with him in new ventures.

The stresses of the 1680s altered such assurance. The epistle to the reader prefixed to *Absalom and Achitophel* (1681) envisioned an audience harsh or friendly as they are Whig or Tory. In the next year he set before *The Medal* a defiant 'Epistle to the Whigs'. In 1682 he also published his first religious confession, *Religio Laici*, stressing the personal nature of his beliefs: 'For *MY* Salvation must its Doom receive/Not from what *OTHERS*, but what *I* believe' (ll. 303–4). Such self-assertion increases in the poems until 1688, but often as expressions of confidence in himself as man and poet rather than in his audience. By the time he wrote *The Hind and the Panther*, he deliberately wrote above the heads of an audience he expected to be largely hostile to a Catholic poem: 'Much malice mingl'd with a little wit/Perhaps may censure this mysterious writ' (Pt. III, ll. 1–2). Here is a change that has not been discussed but that reveals a great deal about how an author must define self by audience. For Dryden the change can be characterized as a shift from a Protestant insistence on faith (the 'what *I* believe' of *Religio Laici*) to a Catholic stress on good works ('Good life be now my task' in *The Hind and the Panther*, i. 78).

The shift in self-definition by relation to his audience led him to numerous adjustments. These became crucial with the 1688 Revolution, after which he shows a new interest in instructing his audience. In the preface to *Don Sebastian* (1690), he tells us that, in addition to the general moral, there are others 'couched under every one of the principal parts and characters' (Watson, ii. 50). Here is the general moral in the last four lines of the play.

> And let *Sebastian* and *Almeyda*'s Fate,
> This dreadfull Sentence to the World relate.
> That unrepented Crimes of Parents dead,
> Are justly punish'd on their Childrens head.

Let it be declared that such morals seem unbearably reductive of a great play like *Don Sebastian*. Let it be asked if, or how, Dryden meant them.

Fables Ancient and Modern is to some of us his finest achievement, and certainly it is his last work of great scale. In it he is busy supplying morals. This is done by shading, by adding to the offences of the guilty in versions of Ovid to make their punishment more appropriate. He adds emphatic morals where Boccaccio had none. And in translating *The Nun's Priest's Tale*, he extends Chaucer by separating the concluding lines into a labelled 'Moral'.

> The Cock and Fox, the Fool and Knave imply;
> The Truth is moral, though the Tale a Lie.
> Who spoke in Parables, I dare not say;
> But sure, he knew it was a pleasing way,
> Sound Sense, by plain Example, to convey.
> And in a Heathen Author we may find,
> That Pleasure with Instruction should be join'd:
> So take the Corn, and leave the Chaff behind.
>
> (ll. 814–21)

In a shift of emphasis that has not been studied, Dryden alters his early emphasis on religious typology to a dominant religious tropology, moving from what is to be believed to what is to be done, from faith to works, as we have seen in contrasting *Religio Laici* with *The Hind and the Panther*. But for Dryden, if not for Bunyan, tropology signals an alteration of his definition of his relation to his audience. After years of sufficient faith in that relation, he gradually found it necessary to instruct his readers. He does add Horatian affectivism to Chaucer's passage, but teaching has grown more important than delight.

That is too simple. It seems to be accepted that the *Fables* is an integrated collection in which the poems are linked one to the next and, more importantly, are integrated by variations on a number of topics related to the search for the good life: valour, love, parents and children, husbands and wives, politics, history, philosophy, and religion. These are not new in his writing, but they have now been fitted to an easy narrative, rather than absorbed by metaphorical forces that may exchange with each other, as in *Mac Flecknoe*. The art is at once simpler in the foreground and more complex in the larger background. For example, the work opens with *To the Dutchess of Ormond*, which gives a very positive version of love, wife and husband, parents and children, valour, history, and religion. The set becomes highly problematical in the next poem, *Palamon and Arcite*, where in Chaucerian or Robertsonian fashion he emphasizes the results of concupiscence and wrath, especially in a pagan setting. He also places his poems not based on works by other poets toward the beginning and end of the collection, so that their ideal, Christian versions set off the imperfect or heathen in a kind of personal testimony, an ethical proof of his own.

If Dryden feels it necessary to underscore the moral import of his writing, it seems fair to assume two things. He must now think that ethical-religious-philosophical matters are of greater importance than the aesthetic-political-religious complex he had dealt with before. The balance of his interests has altered. It must also be true that he doubts the capacity of all his audience to understand as he wishes them to do without such guidance. Without sifting a great deal of evidence, it is impossible to do more than suggest what is happening. One thing is the enlargement of his audience, and the addition to it of a larger component of women readers, for whom his respect seems to have been less than it was for men educated at the schools and the universities. In the last poem in *Fables, Cymon and Iphigenia*, he begins with a *poëta loquitur* to the Duchess of Ormonde, telling her that this is written for her and 'all the Fair' so that they may discover, 'When Beauty fires the Blood, how Love exalts the Mind' (ll. 38, 40). Here is the old topos of love as education. The hero, Cymon (whose name means 'brute'), awakens to reason as he sees and then loves

Iphigenia. The tale goes on to very different things, however, ending with his seizing her from her promised husband at the marriage altar and subsequently running off with her amid violent homicide.

The moral of love as education proves to be drastically insufficient, and the *Fables* ends bleakly for our possibility of finding the good life in other than religious terms. The discrepancy between the simple moral foreground and the more complex moral background suggests that in the last ten or fifteen years of his life Dryden sought to instruct what he thought the larger portion of his audience, giving them both simpler morals and more explicit guidance. For the choicer few, a far more complicated view of human life is provided by indirection or implication, whether in *Don Sebastian* or in *Fables*. The two audiences are not absolutely distinguished after the earlier Renaissance method of supposed veiled truths for the initiate. Dryden seems careful to make the morals and the simplicities sufficiently inadequate to beckon an attentive reader toward what is more profoundly meaningful.

It must have been important to him, however, that he could assume a saving remnant of a knowing audience. His faith lies in them, in himself, and in the great authors he was, after all, drawing on in *Fables*. Late in life he found security in the sense that he belonged with them, and they with him, even if after 1688 he necessarily felt cut off from the easy relation with his audience that he had enjoyed as playwright, poet, and critic in his earlier years.

This example of a single poet cannot apply in detail to all other writers. It does show, however, that matters of 'reception' or 'influence' belong to a larger class of understanding by definition of self with world. And the relation taken between self and world, involves not merely earlier writers but also contemporary writers and one's audience. Of these three, the last two are immeasurably more important than the first. A writer relates to earlier writers only as they are manifested in their works. Allusion, imitation, appropriation, and translation are the typical symptoms of the relation. Relation to contemporary writers involves something far more emotional—rivalry or at least what can only be termed personality. One may not actually know as a person some contemporary writer, although of course Dryden knew all of importance to some degree. But one feels that they live, and that their writings are not a canon but an evolving career like one's own.

Relation to one's audience is less personal, except of course in special instances, particularly including contemporary writers or people for or about whom one writes. Audiences also change in identity and taste, just as accidents such as sudden political changes can alter one's own position. These matters seem so obvious as to make one wonder if their evident truth has led the ingenious to search out more fanciful explanations.[7]

There is, of course, the historical possibility that what was true for writers of Dryden's time and before was not true for writers of Blake's time and after. It could be argued that the ambition of a Dryden to excel is fundamentally different from the ambition of a Blake to be original. Let us pursue this. We may say that the Romantics sought to free themselves from the tyranny of the past, only to find themselves aboriginal in the strict sense. To begin all over is to have to re-create the past without its faults. To such writers the past becomes a burden only because the present is so terrifyingly free and the future so unpromising.

Yet this interpretation, which may have something to it, does not have enough. In his 'Memorial Verses', Arnold spoke in a definitive phrase of 'Wordsworth's healing power', and we have the testimony of Mill to prove that that was no idle expression. If that was true of Wordsworth with his sorrows over our gradual separation from nature, it was certainly true of the other great Romantic poets. They were all well aware of problems and failure, because they had looked at life. But they got on well with the great poets except those immediately preceding them, as is shown for example by Keats's sudden efflorescence after his discovery of Dryden's odes. The problems they had to deal with and that concerned them most were their fellow poets (even when Wordsworth was Coleridge's friend) and their audiences, which involved the exile of Shelley and Byron. Does one need to dwell on what inhibitions of subject matter Victorian audiences imposed on a Dickens?

The idea that the crucial relation is one between a poet and a predecessor seems to be no more than an allegory for the strains felt by contemporary critics. For no good reason, the idea has got

[7] Hazlitt has, however, put it succinctly on contemporary poets: 'I cannot say that I ever learnt much about Shakespeare or Milton, Spenser or Chaucer, from these professed guides; for I never heard them say much about them. They were always talking of themselves and one another' ('On the Living Poets', third paragraph).

abroad that critics understand literature better than do poets. That
also has a limited truth, since critics have as their business making
explicit for other readers. But that truth has placed unnecessary
burdens on the critic and imperilled two truths of greater
importance. Every critic must bow to the fact that the poet is the
radical, if only implicit, critic, who best understands what is of import in what has gone before and what can be made of what exists at
present. It is preposterous to assume that any critic has ideas
remotely as original as Milton's about the epic, Swift's about satire,
or Joyce's about the novel. It is much healthier to think of the
critic as a reader in Sunday Best than as a Mad Scientist seeking
to re-do creation. It is exciting to enter on to theoretical heights,
but the blood of literary life has difficulty there in keeping pace,
and rather than enable us to see farther, that vantage-point too
often puts us among clouds of obscurity or induces in the critic
pains of high-altitude sickness. When we can all participate as
readers in the great literatures of the world, there is no indignity
in doing so. In writing about what we discover, about the nature
of what is discovered, or even about the nature of discovery, we
play as critics in a no-loss enterprise. To confuse that play with
the enterprise of poets is to enter a game in which the chance of
winning is only illusory, and in which the most intelligent people
are sure to suffer from knowledge of self-inflicted loss. To compare
small things to great, we may say of the finest criticism what
Dryden said of his *Aeneis* in relation to the original.

Lay by Virgil, I beseech your Lordship and all my better sort of judges,
when you take up my version; and it will appear a passable beauty
when the original Muse is absent. But, like Spenser's false Florimel
made of snow, it melts and vanishes when the true one comes in sight.
(Watson, ii. 252)

There is the poet in relation to an older poet and to contemporaries.
And there is the right tone of criticism.

The Discovery of the Date of
Mac Flecknoe[1]

DAVID M. VIETH

I

DURING THE summer of 1953, Jim Osborn and I began research for
what we hoped would be a collaborative book-length study of the
relationship between John Dryden and Thomas Shadwell. Necessarily the project involved the much-discussed problem of the date
at which Dryden composed *Mac Flecknoe*, as well as the event or
events that occasioned this famous lampoon on Shadwell. Earlier
investigators had shown that Dryden wrote *Mac Flecknoe* several
years before it was first printed in an unauthorized quarto pamphlet dated 4 October 1682; the authorized version was not published until 1684. The composition of the poem was assigned to
1678, the date which is given in a notation in John Oldham's
manuscript copy.[2]

It suddenly occurred to me that *Mac Flecknoe* refers to many
events up to and including the publication of Shadwell's comedy
The Virtuoso in the first week of July 1676, but not to any later
events; also, the poem fails to refer to subsequent events in
Shadwell's career that Dryden would surely have exploited if *Mac
Flecknoe* were not already in existence; and, finally, the multiple
attacks on Dryden in the published version of *The Virtuoso* offered
an obvious occasion for his poetical retort.[3]

[1] A summary of this paper formed part of a public lecture, 'Shadwell in
Wonderland, or The Fruits of UCLA: Three Problems Posed by John Dryden's
Mac Flecknoe', delivered at Southern Illinois University in Carbondale on 2
May 1974. The first of the three problems, the early texts of the poem, is covered
in my article 'Dryden's *Mac Flecknoe*: The Case Against Editorial Confusion',
Harvard Library Bulletin, xxiv (1976), 204–45; hereafter called 'The Case
Against Editorial Confusion'. The date and occasion of *Mac Flecknoe* were the
second problem.

[2] For the date of the pamphlet and the date in John Oldham's transcription,
see 'The Case Against Editorial Confusion', pp. 229–30.

[3] Without fully grasping the implications of his words, Mark Van Doren in

I worked up my evidence, arguments, and conclusions about the date and occasion of *Mac Flecknoe* into a rough draft of nearly forty typewritten pages. This typescript, together with a rudimentary set of explanatory notes for the poem (both, twenty-three years later, lying beside me unpublished, with Jim's pencilled comments on them), would constitute a memorandum to myself when we returned to our project, which our discoveries that summer promised to make a substantial, valuable volume on Dryden and Shadwell.

Other obligations intervened. During 1959–60, when my first book on Rochester, *Attribution in Restoration Poetry*, was in preparation, the format of the volume could well have accommodated a chapter on the date and occasion of *Mac Flecknoe*.[4] It was decided, however, to reserve my findings for the joint volume that Jim Osborn and I would complete as soon as I could obtain foundation aid for my part of the undertaking.

The aid was not forthcoming. When George Lord decided to print *Mac Flecknoe* in his initial volume of the Yale edition of *Poems on Affairs of State*, a copy of my typescript of 1953 was made available to the project. Commenting that 'evidence that the poem was circulating in manuscript in 1678 has led Dryden's editors to assign it to that year', Lord continued: 'In a forthcoming study J. M. Osborn and David Vieth argue persuasively that the poem was written even earlier, in response to Shadwell's slighting remarks on Dryden in the dedication to *The Virtuoso* (published in July 1676), and before the production of Shadwell's *Timon* in January 1678.'[5] Lord added that *Mac Flecknoe* seems to be mentioned in 'Advice to Apollo', a verse lampoon probably written in October 1677. Not foreseen was the confusion that might arise from the acknowledgement to Jim and me jointly, although the form was proper enough when Lord's volume was published in 1963.

1920 observed of *Mac Flecknoe*, 'As a satire on Shadwell it would have been as timely in 1676 as it was in 1682. It alludes to no play published by Shadwell later than 1676.' (*The Poetry of John Dryden*, New York: Harcourt, Brace and Howe, 1920, p. 340.)

[4] *Attribution in Restoration Poetry: A Study of Rochester's 'Poems' of 1680* (New Haven and London: Yale University Press, 1963); hereafter called *ARP*.

[5] *Poems on Affairs of State: Augustan Satirical Verse, 1660–1714*, Vol. I: *1660–1678*, ed. George deF. Lord (New Haven and London: Yale University Press, 1963), p. 376. The dating of 'Advice to Apollo' derives partly from prior research by John Harold Wilson, as Lord acknowledges (p. 392).

Confusion was introduced in *Dryden's Poetry*, published in 1967 by Earl Miner, an editor of the California *Works* of Dryden. Miner remarked, referring to an article on *Mac Flecknoe* by George McFadden, 'His evidence strongly supports the belief that the poem was written in 1678. Basing his discussion upon as yet unpublished material of David Vieth, George deForest Lord suggests that "Dryden probably wrote *MacFlecknoe* . . . between July 1676 and December 1677". . . . The argument is complex, plausible, and unconvincing.'[6] As an observation on Lord's single sentence, at that time the sole citation in print of my case for a new dating of *Mac Flecknoe*, such a statement must have seemed bewildering. Not only does it attribute the argument to me alone (correctly, as it happens) rather than to Jim Osborn and me jointly, but by what stretch of the term could Lord's brief summary be called 'complex'?

Meanwhile, with progress stalled on the Dryden–Shadwell volume, it seemed desirable to present my case for the date and occasion of *Mac Flecknoe* in skeletal form as a note in *The Gyldenstolpe Manuscript Miscellany*, edited in collaboration with Bror Danielsson and published in 1967.[7] This procedure, it was hoped, might render a detailed presentation unnecessary. Again the hope was disappointed. Although more than one reviewer noticed my discussion of the date of *Mac Flecknoe*,[8] it escaped listing under Dryden in the annual bibliographies and thus failed to reach some readers. To complicate matters, my case for the new dating of *Mac Flecknoe* could now be credited three different ways: to Osborn and Vieth, to Vieth alone, or to Danielsson and Vieth.[9]

When Volume II of the California *Works* of Dryden, containing

---

[6] Earl Miner, *Dryden's Poetry* (Bloomington and London: Indiana University Press, 1967), pp. 77–8 n.

[7] *The Gyldenstolpe Manuscript Miscellany of Poems by John Wilmot, Earl of Rochester, and other Restoration Authors*, ed. Bror Danielsson and David M. Vieth (Stockholm: Almqvist & Wiksell, 1967), pp. 343–7; hereafter called *Gyldenstolpe*.

[8] James Kinsley commented, 'The note on *Mac Flecknoe* is a persuasive argument for 1676, rather than 1678, as the date of composition. We have all been mesmerized by Oldham's "A⁰ 1678" ' (*The Library*, 5th ser., xxiii (1968), 363). The reference by Frank Brady in 'Recent Studies in The Restoration and Eighteenth Century', *Studies in English Literature*, viii (1968), 553, would have been seen by all serious students of English literature of 1660–1800.

[9] This last form is adopted in B. J. Frye's very useful casebook, *John Dryden: Mac Flecknoe* (Columbus, Ohio: Merrill, 1970).

Mac Flecknoe, came out in 1972, it did not mention the *Gylden-stolpe* volume, which had been published five years before. Responsibility for the new dating of the poem was given to George Lord, who 'develops this ingenious theory, following an unpublished study by James M. Osborn and David Vieth'.[10] Hence the theory could now be acknowledged four different ways: Osborn and Vieth, Vieth alone, Danielsson and Vieth, or Lord assisted by Osborn and Vieth. The California discussion, whatever its sources, moves closer to my views than one would guess from its disclaimer that 'the theory rests on supposition rather than on fact' (ii. 301).

Such tactics damage the study of Dryden. Countless recent publications continue to give 1678 as the date of *Mac Flecknoe*. To cite just one example, a monograph on Shadwell's plays, using *Mac Flecknoe* as a point of reference throughout, assumes that Dryden wrote the poem in 1678.[11] A bibliography of Dryden studies published in 1975 fails to list the *Gyldenstolpe* discussion.[12]

Since 1963, when my case for the date and occasion of *Mac Flecknoe* was first briefly presented in print, no valid evidence or argument has been advanced against it. Therefore my task in this essay is not to offer a new argument, but to clarify views that are already accepted by scholars in a position to judge them. As for the volume on Dryden and Shadwell in which this essay was to have appeared, Jim Osborn and I regretfully recognized early in the 1970s that we would never have the opportunity to complete it as a collaborative effort.[13]

II

The search for the date of *Mac Flecknoe* began in earnest

[10] *The Works of John Dryden*, Vol. II: *Poems 1681–1684*, ed. H. T. Swedenberg, Jr., and Vinton A. Dearing (Berkeley, Los Angeles, London: University of California Press, 1972), p. 301 n. 10. Another footnote credits Lord alone (iii. 306 n. 28). Footnote 10 misrepresents my *terminus a quo* for the composition of *Mac Flecknoe* as 26 June 1676, which is the date appended to the dedication of *The Virtuoso*, not that of the advertisement in the *London Gazette*.
[11] Don R. Kunz, *The Drama of Thomas Shadwell* (Salzburg: Institut für Englische Sprache und Literatur, Universität Salzburg, 1972).
[12] John A. Zamonski, *An Annotated Bibliography of John Dryden: Texts and Studies, 1949–1973* (Folkestone: Dawson, 1975), pp. 121–5.
[13] Material from the proposed volume has nevertheless appeared elsewhere. Besides the present essay, the most substantial items are my article 'The Case Against Editorial Confusion' and Jim Osborn's paper on 'Upon a late fall'n Poet', cited in n. 52 below.

between the two world wars. Controversy exploded in 1918 with Percy L. Babington's ill-judged contention that *Mac Flecknoe* was written, not by Dryden, but by John Oldham. As Babington was answered by H. M. Belden and George Thorn-Drury, attention turned to the question of the date at which Dryden composed his poem, with additional evidence and arguments contributed by Harold F. Brooks and R. Jack Smith.[14] These contributions established beyond doubt that *Mac Flecknoe* was in existence several years before 4 October 1682, the date which Narcissus Luttrell inscribed on his copy of the quarto. The following items carry varying degrees of weight:

(*a*) If, as was formerly believed, Dryden wrote *Mac Flecknoe* shortly before 4 October 1682 in answer to Shadwell's *The Medal of John Bayes*, dated 15 May 1682 by Luttrell, then it is strange that he attacked Shadwell again only five weeks later in the character of Og in *Absalom and Achitophel*, Part II, which Luttrell dates 10 November 1682.[15]

(*b*) Unlike Dryden's satire on Og for 'Writing Treason' as well as for 'Writing dull', *Mac Flecknoe* significantly fails to mention Shadwell's political or religious leanings. These had become highly relevant by 1682, when Dryden and Shadwell were actively supporting opposite factions. The description of *Mac Flecknoe* in the 1682 quarto as 'a Satyr upon the True-Blew-Protestant Poet, T.S.' is transparently an insertion by the publisher, 'D. Green', to give an appearance of topicality.

(*c*) *Mac Flecknoe* is mentioned, almost eight months before its first publication, in *The Loyal Protestant and True Domestick Intelligence* for 9 February 1681/2: '. . . he would send him [Shadwell] his Recantation next morning, with a *Mac-Flecknoe*, and a brace of Lobsters for his Breakfast; All which he knew he

---

[14] Percy L. Babington, 'Dryden not the Author of "MacFlecknoe"', *Modern Language Review*, xiii (1918), 25–34. H. M. Belden, 'The Authorship of *Mac-Flecknoe*', *Modern Language Notes*, xxxiii (1918), 449–56. G. Thorn-Drury, 'Dryden's "Mac Flecknoe." A Vindication', *Modern Language Review*, xiii (1918), 276–81, and 'Some Notes on Dryden', *Review of English Studies*, i (1925), 187–90. Harold Brooks, 'When Did Dryden Write *MacFlecknoe*?—Some Additional Notes', *Review of English Studies*, xi (1935), 74–8. R. Jack Smith, 'The Date of *Mac Flecknoe*', *Review of English Studies*, xviii (1942), 322–3. The question is summarized in Mark Van Doren, *John Dryden: A Study of His Poetry* (New York: Henry Holt and Co., 3rd edn., 1946), pp. 267–78, and Hugh Macdonald, *John Dryden: A Bibliography* (Oxford: Clarendon Press, 1939), pp. 28–9.

[15] Luttrell's dates here and later are taken from Macdonald's bibliography.

had a singular aversion for.' Presumably the reference is to manuscripts of the poem in circulation.

(*d*) There may be an allusion to *Mac Flecknoe* in a song in Thomas D'Urfey's comedy *Sir Barnaby Whigg*, probably acted in early summer 1681.[16] In the second of two stanzas, Sir Barnaby, who is almost certainly a caricature of Shadwell, says of himself:

> I got Fame by filching from Poems and Plays,
> But my Fidling and Drinking has lost me the Bays;
> Like a Fury I rail'd, like a Satyr I writ,
> *Thersites* my Humour, and *Fleckno* my Wit.
> But to make some amends for my snarling and lashing,
> I divert all the Town with my Thrumming and Thrashing.

The last line may allude to the water pageant in lines 35–52 of *Mac Flecknoe*, especially to Shadwell's 'threshing hand'.[17]

(*e*) In the lampoon *The Tory-Poets*, dated by Luttrell 4 September 1682, 'Dryden' speaks:

> Alas! says *Bays*, what are your Wits to me?
> *Chapman's* a sad dul Rogue at *Comedy*;
> *Shirley's* an Ass to write at such a rate . . .[18]

Dryden had written harshly of Chapman's *Bussy D'Ambois* in his dedication of *The Spanish Friar*, 1681. *Mac Flecknoe* refers twice

---

[16] Judith Milhous and Robert D. Hume, 'Dating Play Premières from Publication Data, 1660–1700', *Harvard Library Bulletin*, xxii (1974), 392. Unless corrected from this source, all dates of play performances are taken from *The London Stage*, Part I: 1660–1700, ed. William Van Lennep *et al.* (Carbondale: Southern Illinois University Press, 1965). Titles of plays are normalized to the form used in *The London Stage*. Students of Restoration literature have not always distinguished carefully between features of a play's performance (e.g. the prologue and epilogue) and features that belong only to its publication (e.g. a preface or dedication). In what follows I am aware that theatrical records for 1660–1700 are distressingly meagre, but conclusions must be based upon the evidence available.

[17] D'Urfey's first stanza reads (III.ii):

> Farewell my Lov'd Science, my former delight,
> *Moliere* is quite rifled, then how should I write?
> My fancy's grown sleepy, my quibling is done;
> And design or invention, alas! I have none.
> But still let the Town never doubt my condition;
> Though I fall a damn'd Poet, I'le mount a Musician.

This song parodies Dryden's popular lyric beginning 'Farewel, fair *Armeda*, my Joy and my Grief'.

[18] *The Complete Works of Thomas Shadwell*, ed. Montague Summers, 5 vols. (London: Fortune Press, 1927), v. 281.

to the Jacobean playwright James Shirley (ll. 29, 102), whom Dryden, according to R. Jack Smith, had not mentioned previously in print. Be that as it may, the line in *The Tory-Poets* seems to reflect an acquaintance with *Mac Flecknoe*, which was not published until a month afterward.

(*f*) Evidently *Mac Flecknoe* is echoed in the lampoon *Rochester's Farewell*, written in July 1680,[19] and in poems composed by John Oldham from 1679 to 1682. For example, a couplet in *Rochester's Farewell*,

> Lewd Messaline was but a type of thee,
> Thou highest, last degree of lechery,

appears to echo Dryden's

> *Heywood* and *Shirley* were but Types of thee,
> Thou last great Prophet of Tautology.[20]

It is more likely that these other poems borrowed from *Mac Flecknoe* than that the reverse occurred.

(*g*) John Oldham's manuscript copy of *Mac Flecknoe* includes the notation 'A⁰ 1678' to the left of the title. Whatever its precise signification, this note points to a date of composition well before the poem was first published in the quarto of 1682.

Thus far, conclusions seem inescapable. Too many scholars, however, have considered Oldham's note a reliable indication of the date of composition and have proceeded to seek the occasion of *Mac Flecknoe* in events of 1678. Among the events suggested are Flecknoe's alleged death in that year; a supposed quarrel with Henry Herringman, who ceased to be Dryden's publisher after the appearance of *All for Love* in March 1678; and an indirect insult to Dryden in Shadwell's dedication to the Duke of Buckingham of his tragedy *The History of Timon of Athens*, published about February 1677/8. But it is not certain that Dryden's poem refers to Flecknoe's death, or even that Flecknoe died in 1678.[21] Nor is the reference to Herringman particularly hostile ('Bilk't *Stationers*

---

[19] The date is established in *Gyldenstolpe*, pp. 361–2.

[20] *Rochester's Farewell* is quoted from *Poems on Affairs of State: Augustan Satirical Verse, 1660–1714*, Vol. II: *1678–1681*, ed. Elias F. Mengel, Jr. (New Haven and London: Yale University Press, 1965), p. 224.

[21] E. S. de Beer, 'Dryden: "The Kind Keeper." The "Poet of Scandalous Memory"', *Notes and Queries*, clxxix (1940), 128–9; Thorn-Drury, 'Dryden's "Mac Flecknoe." A Vindication', p. 278.

for Yeomen stood prepar'd,/And *H[erringman]* was Captain of the Guard' (ll. 104–5).

The fact is that Oldham's date has been accorded too much reverence. Meticulous though he was in dating his own works, in this instance Oldham merely acted as scribe for another man's poem, and there is no way of knowing how many careless copyings intervened between his transcription and Dryden's original draft. Dates of this kind, giving only the year, are common in poetical texts of the Restoration period. Experience shows that 'frequently they vary from the true date of composition by a year in either direction, and sometimes by as much as two years, though rarely by a longer interval'.[22] In terms of this rule, Oldham's date indicates that *Mac Flecknoe* was probably written in 1677, 1678, or 1679, but quite possibly as early as 1676 or as late as 1680.

In 1932, Daniel Morley McKeithan maintained that the occasion of *Mac Flecknoe* was probably Shadwell's dedication of *Timon*, with its praise of *The Rehearsal*, Buckingham's farce in which Dryden was ridiculed as Mr. Bayes. McKeithan's reasoning is circular, however. He argues that (1) if *Mac Flecknoe* was written in 1678, it was probably occasioned by the publication of this dedication in February, but also (2) since this dedication would have offended Dryden, he probably wrote *Mac Flecknoe* in 1678.[23] No doubt Dryden would have found the dedication of *Timon* annoying, but it is only one of Shadwell's repeated attacks on him, and by no means the most severe—less severe, for example, than the dedication of *The Virtuoso*. Also, if *Timon* occasioned *Mac Flecknoe*, it is strange that Dryden's poem makes no clear reference to this play, concentrating instead upon earlier plays by Shadwell.

---

[22] *ARP*, p. 28. Objecting that my date for *Mac Flecknoe* 'rests on supposition rather than on fact', the California editors appeal to 'Oldham's dating as an anchor of fact' (ii. 301). It is a fact that 'A⁰ 1678' appears in Oldham's notebook, but what does the fact signify?

The California edition speaks of 'the two passages Oldham transcribed' and 'the 103 lines he did not transcribe' (ii. 299–300), an account that would scarcely be given by anyone who had examined the text he claims to be editing. The missing 102 lines—not 103—would have just filled the two leaves that are now lacking from Oldham's notebook, as is implied elsewhere in the California volume (ii. 428).

[23] Daniel Morley McKeithan, 'The Occasion of *MacFlecknoe*', *PMLA*, xlvii (1932), 766–71.

III

Mac Flecknoe refers to numerous events up to and including the publication of *The Virtuoso*, which was advertised in the *London Gazette* for 3–6 July 1676, but it does not refer to any later event. It provides a well-informed review of Shadwell's activities as a dramatist until the first week of July, a cut-off point implying that *Mac Flecknoe* was composed shortly thereafter. The distribution of references is illustrated for the years 1660–80 in the chart on page 72.

References to events of the 1660s are scattered, with the density increasing towards the end of the decade. Flecknoe's *Love's Kingdom* receives two references by title, at least one of these to a printed edition (ll. 122–5, 143); the play was acted 'probably not later than fall 1663' and published in 1664.[24] There is one clear reference to Etherege's first play, *The Comical Revenge* (l. 153), acted about March 1663/4, and another to his second play, *She Would if She Could* (l. 153), produced on 6 February 1667/8. Although *Mac Flecknoe* does not mention Shadwell's first play, *The Sullen Lovers* (acted 2 May 1668), or his second, *The Royal Shepherdess* (produced on 25 February 1668/9), it gives the title of his lost play, *The Hypocrite* (l. 92), which was acted about 14 June 1669. Dryden's own heroic drama, *Tyrannic Love*, probably acted 24 June 1669, gets a single reference (l. 78).

There are certainly three allusions and probably a fourth to the acting version of Shadwell's comedy *The Humorists* (10 December 1670), as well as a probable allusion to Shadwell's preface (published early in 1671).[25] Specifically named are the play's title (l. 92) and one of its characters, Raymond (l. 93). Four lines of *Mac Flecknoe* (ll. 189–92) parody four lines of the epilogue to *The Humorists*, to which Shadwell calls special attention by quoting them boastfully in the preface to the play. Moreover, Flecknoe's exhortation that Shadwell's fools should be 'Not Copies drawn, but Issue of thy own' (l. 160) probably echoes this epilogue.[26]

[24] Milhous and Hume, 'Dating Play Premières', p. 380.

[25] Dated 1671 on its title-page, *The Humorists* was in print by 20 April, as is shown by letters from Shadwell to the Duke and Duchess of Newcastle (*Works of Shadwell*, ed. Summers, i. lxxxiii).

[26]   Expect not then, since that most flourishing Age,
       Of *BEN*, to see true Humor on the Stage.
       All that have since been writ, if they be scan'd,
       Are but faint Copies from that Master's Hand.

(*Works*, ed. Summers, i. 254).

1660 1661 1662 1663 1664 1665 1666 1667 1668 1669 1670 1671 1672 1673 1674 1675 1676 1677 1678 1679 1680

Love's Kingdom (acted) .. .. 1663 X

The Comical Revenge (acted *c.* Mar.) .. .. .. 1664 X
Love's Kingdom (pub.) X

She Would if She Could (acted 6 Feb.) .. .. 1668 X
The Sullen Lovers (acted 2 May) .. ..

The Royal Shepherdess (acted 25 Feb.)
The Hypocrite (acted *c.* 14 June) .. .. .. 1669 X
Tyrannic Love (acted *c.* 24 June) X

The Humorists (acted 10 Dec.) .. .. 1670 XXXx

The Humorists (pub.) .. .. 1671 x
The Rehearsal (acted *c.* 7 Dec.) x

The Miser (acted Jan.) .. .. 1672 X
Epsom Wells (acted 2 Dec.) Xx
1673

The Tempest (acted *c.* 30 Apr.) .. .. .. 1674 x

Calisto (acted 15 Feb.) .. .. 1675 x
Psyche (acted 27 Feb.) XXXXx
The Libertine (acted 12 June) .. ..

The Man of Mode (acted 11 Mar.) XX
The Virtuoso (acted 25 May) .. .. .. 1676 XXXXXXxxx
Epsom affair (17 or 18 June) x
The Virtuoso (pub. early July) xxxxx
John Ogilby dies (4 Sept.) .. ..
Ibrahim (pub. summer or autumn) .. .. ..
Duke of Newcastle dies (25 Dec.) .. .. ..
1677

Timon (acted *c.* Jan.) 1678
Timon (pub. *c.* Feb.) .. ..
A True Widow (acted) .. ..

A True Widow (pub.) 1679
The Woman Captain (acted *c.* Sept.)

The Woman Captain (pub.) 1680

X—definite reference or allusion.   x—probable reference or allusion.

Although lines 57–9 of *Mac Flecknoe* refer generally to Davenant's *The Siege of Rhodes*, the phrase 'Lute and Sword' in this passage implies that Dryden's primary allusion is to the burlesque of Davenant's opera in Act V of *The Rehearsal*, acted about 7 December 1671.

Shadwell's fifth play, *The Miser*, acted in January 1671/2, is mentioned once by title in *Mac Flecknoe* (l. 91). His popular comedy *Epsom Wells*, acted 2 December 1672, is represented by the charge that he was assisted in its composition by Sir Charles Sedley (ll. 163–4) and possibly by the charge of borrowing from Etherege (l. 184).[27]

The 'subterranean wind' at the end of *Mac Flecknoe* (l. 215) probably echoes the song 'Arise, arise! ye subterranean winds', which Shadwell wrote for his operatic version of the Dryden–Davenant *Tempest*, produced about 30 April 1674. Similarly, Dryden's line 'The fair *Augusta* much to fears inclin'd' (l. 65) probably echoes the passage beginning 'Augusta is inclin'd to fears' in the prologue to John Crowne's *Calisto*, produced at Court on 15 February 1674/5.

Shadwell's opera *Psyche*, produced on 27 February 1674/5, receives four separate references in *Mac Flecknoe* (ll. 53–6, 90, 125, 179–80). The title alone occurs four times. Mention is made of St. André, the choreographer of the work, and Prince Nicander, one of its chief characters. There may be an echo of the prologue to *Psyche* in 'Like mine thy gentle numbers feebly creep' (l. 197).[28]

---

[27] But the latter accusation could apply to *The Virtuoso*; see n. 32 below. In its note to lines 163–4 (ii. 324), the California Dryden neglects to mention the reference to 'Shadwell's unassisted former scenes' in Rochester's satire *Timon*, composed during the spring of 1674. See my edition, *The Complete Poems of John Wilmot, Earl of Rochester* (New Haven and London: Yale University Press, 1968), p. 65; hereafter called *Complete Poems*. Line 42 of *Mac Flecknoe*, 'The like was ne'er in *Epsom* Blankets tost', evidently does not refer to *Epsom Wells*; see n. 33 below.

[28] 'His Subject's humble, and his Verse is so; / . . . He would not soar too high, nor creep too low' (*Works of Shadwell*, ed. Summers, ii. 281). Elsewhere in *Mac Flecknoe* are a reference to *Psyche*'s humble 'numbers' (l. 55) and the line 'Or swept the dust in *Psyche*'s humble strain' (180). Elkanah Settle, in his preface to *Ibrahim* (published summer or autumn 1676), noted the 'humble style' of *Psyche*, 'written so feebly' (*The Preface to Ibrahim by Elkanah Settle*, ed. Hugh Macdonald, Oxford: Published for the Luttrell Society by Basil Blackwell, 1947, pp. 2, 4). *Psyche* was Shadwell's only play in rhymed verse.

I have not counted among the allusions to *Psyche* Dryden's use of the words 'Dominion' (l. 141) and 'Province' (ll. 187, 206), which occur prominently in

Oddly, *Mac Flecknoe* does not mention Shadwell's successful tragedy *The Libertine*, acted in early June 1675, unless 'Thy Tragick Muse gives smiles' is a glancing allusion (l. 198). It may be significant that no performance of *The Libertine* is recorded for the theatrical season of 1675–6, whereas *Psyche* was performed at least three times. This season witnessed the première of Etherege's finest play, *The Man of Mode*, acted 11 March 1675/6, which receives two adjacent references in *Mac Flecknoe* (ll. 151–2, 153).

Two months later occurred the première of Shadwell's best play,[29] *The Virtuoso* (acted 25 May 1676), which gets more attention in *Mac Flecknoe* than any other work by Shadwell. There are references to the five years allegedly required to write *The Virtuoso* (l. 149); to Bruce, one of two 'Gentlemen of wit and sense' in the play (l. 93; also 212); to the oratory of Sir Formal Trifle (ll. 165, 168–9); to the blanket-tossing inflicted upon Sir Samuel Hearty (l. 42) and his practice of 'selling bargains' (l. 181); and to the episode of the trap door in which Bruce and Longvil participate (ll. 212–13). There are probable echoes of Shadwell's prologue (ll. 155–6)[30] and epilogue (l. 148).[31] The accusation that 'thou whole *Eth'ridg* dost transfuse to thine' (l. 184) appears to refer primarily to *The Virtuoso*.[32]

Shadwell's preface (*Works*, ed. Summers, ii. 279). Settle makes fun of the same words (*The Preface to Ibrahim*, ed. Macdonald, pp. 4–5).

[29] In my opinion, and apparently in that of Michael W. Alssid, who calls it Shadwell's 'most vigorous "humors" satire' (*Thomas Shadwell*, New York: Twayne, 1967, p. 8). *The Virtuoso* was chosen to represent Shadwell in the Regents Restoration Drama Series (ed. Marjorie Hope Nicolson and David Stuart Rodes, Lincoln: University of Nebraska Press, 1966).

[30] *Mac Flecknoe:*

> Yet still thy fools shall stand in thy defence,
> And justifie their Author's want of sense.

Shadwell's prologue (*Works*, ed. Summers, iii. 103):

> He's sure in Wit he cann't excel the rest,
> He'd but be thought to write a Fool the best.

[31] With *Mac Flecknoe*'s 'Pangs without birth, and fruitless Industry', compare the conclusion of Shadwell's epilogue (*Works*, ed. Summers, iii. 182):

> You know the pangs and many labouring throws,
> By which your Brains their perfect births disclose. . . .
> And if this Birth should want its perfect shape,
> And cannot by your care its death escape,
> Th' abortive Issue came before its day,
> And th' Poet has miscarry'd of a Play.

[32] George R. Noyes argued that Dryden's line refers to Shadwell's borrowings

Although line 42, 'The like was ne'er in *Epsom* Blankets tost', applies to the blanket-tossing of Sir Samuel Hearty, the traditional claim that it also refers to *Epsom Wells* is unconvincing.[33] Instead, '*Epsom*' probably alludes to the scandalous brawl at that town on the night of 17 June 1676, or very early the following morning. This widely publicized affair, which involved Etherege, Rochester, and other gentlemen-rioters, resulted in the death of a certain Captain Downs. It began with the revellers tossing in a blanket some fiddlers who refused to play for them. Similarly, the line in

---

in *Epsom Wells* from Etherege's *She Would if She Could*, which Shadwell in his preface to *The Humorists* had called 'the best Comedy that has been written since the Restauration' (*The Poetical Works of John Dryden*, Boston: Houghton Mifflin, 1909, p. 962; rev. edn., 1950, p. 970). Without diminishing the validity of Noyes's conclusion, one may feel that the resemblances between *The Virtuoso* and *She Would if She Could* are even closer. Besides the two witty young couples (Courtall and Freeman, Gatty and Ariana / Bruce and Longvil, Miranda and Clarinda), there is the lecherous older married woman (Lady Cockwood / Lady Gimcrack) and her dupe of a husband (Sir Oliver Cockwood / Sir Nicholas Gimcrack), although Sir Nicholas as virtuoso owes as much to Shadwell's own Sir Positive At-All as to Etherege's Sir Oliver. The older married woman attempts to seduce both witty young men—unsuccessfully in Etherege, successfully in *The Virtuoso*. In both plays, she causes confusion with forged letters to the young men from the young ladies. The roles of Lady Cockwood and Lady Gimcrack were both created by Mrs. Shadwell (and those of Courtall and Bruce by William Smith).

Since *Mac Flecknoe* already describes *Epsom Wells* as 'larded with wit' by Sedley (ll. 163–4), Dryden would scarcely imply, twenty lines later, that it also borrowed 'whole *Eth'ridg*'. There was a revival of *She Would if She Could* during the theatrical season of 1675–6, probably in February. Thus it was fresh in the minds of the audience that saw *The Virtuoso*.

Dryden's words 'transfuse' and 'transfus'd' (ll. 184, 185) may have been chosen to recall Sir Nicholas Gimcrack's ridiculous transfusions of blood between a mangy spaniel and a sound bulldog and from a sheep to a madman (*Works*, ed. Summers, iii. 128–30).

[33] As I observed in print in 1963, '*Epsom-Wells* contains no reference to tossing in a blanket, nor is there any reason why the implements of Sir Samuel's humiliation should be called "Epsom" blankets.' Dryden must have been specially conscious of Rochester's activities about this time, for he had recently been attacked in Rochester's 'An Allusion to Horace' (*ARP*, pp. 142–4).

The California edition repeats the traditional explanation of '*Epsom* Blankets' (ii. 317) and that of lines 177–8—'Where did his wit on learning fix a brand, / And rail at Arts he did not understand?'—which it calls 'apparently an allusion to the satire on experimental science in *The Virtuoso*' (ii. 325). But *The Virtuoso* does not satirize, and certainly does not 'rail at', the true experimental science of the Royal Society; see Joseph M. Gilde, 'Shadwell and the Royal Society: Satire in *The Virtuoso*', *Studies in English Literature*, x (1970), 469–90. Rather, Shadwell railed constantly at the 'Arts' of heroic drama, as in the epilogue to *The Virtuoso*, quoted below, p. 79.

Mac Flecknoe is part of a mock-celebration of Shadwell's prowess as a musician (ll. 35–59).

The conclusion that *Mac Flecknoe* refers not only to the acting but also to the published version of *The Virtuoso* (advertised 3–6 July 1676) rests upon a combination of probable allusions to Shadwell's dedication, together with the circumstance that this was Shadwell's harshest attack on Dryden thus far.[34] Of Shadwell's five '*Northern Dedications*' to the Duke or Duchess of Newcastle (l. 170), only this one attacks Dryden. Shadwell indeed 'Promis'd a Play' in the dedication,[35] although in the play itself he had repeatedly 'dwindled to a Farce' (l. 182). He boasts more conspicuously of his 'New Humours' (l. 188) than he ever had before.[36] Shadwell's dedication mentions the four lines in the epilogue to *The Humorists* that Dryden parodies in *Mac Flecknoe* (ll. 189–92), and his reference to 'the Preface to the *Humorists*, written five Years since' may have been distorted into Dryden's insinuation that *The Virtuoso* took five years to write (l. 149).

Concerning later events *Mac Flecknoe* is silent, as the chart on page 72 shows.[37]

IV

Not only does *Mac Flecknoe* mention no event after the publication of *The Virtuoso* in early July 1676; it fails to mention

[34] Elkanah Settle scolds Shadwell because 'instead of addressing himself with that Duty and Respect he owed to so illustrious a Patron, he fills up almost a whole Dedication with condemning other Mens parts' (*The Preface to Ibrahim*, ed. Macdonald, p. 9).

[35] 'I have endeavoured, in this Play, at Humour, Wit, and Satyr, which are the three things . . . which your Grace has often told me are the life of a Comedy' (*Works of Shadwell*, ed. Summers, iii. 101).

[36] 'Four of the Humors are entirely new; and (without vanity) I may say, I ne'er produc'd a Comedy that had not some natural Humour in it not represented before, nor I hope ever shall' (*Works*, ed. Summers, iii. 101). Settle's preface to *Ibrahim* ridicules Shadwell for 'those *four intirely new* Humours he speaks of' in the dedication of *The Virtuoso* (ed. Macdonald, p. 8).

[37] Apparent allusions to later events do not stand up under examination. The suggestion that 'flayle of Sense' (l. 89) alludes to Stephen College's 'Protestant flail' lacks corroboration (Samuel H. Monk, 'Shadwell, "Flail of Sense": "MacFlecknoe" Line 89', *Notes and Queries*, ccv (1960), 67–8). A metaphor of parturition in the prologue to Shadwell's *Timon of Athens*, similar to those in *Mac Flecknoe*, is a commonplace that occurs more prominently in the epilogue to *The Virtuoso* (*Poetical Works of Dryden*, ed. Noyes, 1950, p. 1060). 'The fair *Augusta* much to fears inclin'd' (l. 65) need not allude to the Popish Plot hysteria, especially since it echoes the prologue to Crowne's *Calisto*, 1675 (see above, p. 73).

events that Dryden surely would have utilized if *Mac Flecknoe* were not already in existence.

The crux is Shadwell's tragedy *The History of Timon of Athens*, published probably in February 1677/8,[38] whose dedication to Buckingham McKeithan believed to be 'the insult that moved Dryden to action' (p. 770). We can at least concede that if Dryden had not already written *Mac Flecknoe, Timon* would have goaded him into writing it. As an adaptation of Shakespeare, Shadwell's play would have interested Dryden because his own *All for Love* was produced at nearly the same time. In his dedication, Shadwell remarks smugly of his reworking of Shakespeare, 'Yet I can truly say, I have made it into a Play.'[39] Buckingham, who had ridiculed Dryden as Mr. Bayes, is lauded for having 'so clearly shown the excellency of Wit and Judgment in your Self, and so justly the defect of 'em in others, that they at once serve for the greatest example, and the sharpest reproof. And no man who has perfectly understood the *Rehearsal*, and some other of your Writings, if he has any *Genius* at all, can write ill after it.'

Doubtless irritating to Dryden were two elements in the play itself, which was probably acted in January 1677/8. The character of the Poet, like Drybob in *The Humorists* and Crambo in Shadwell's adaptation of Newcastle's *The Triumphant Widow*,[40] represents Shadwell's usual ridicule of the kinds of plays Dryden preferred. In the Poet's inflated 'Heroick style', a lion becomes 'the fierce *Numidian* Monarch of the Beasts', a bull 'the mighty Warriour of the horned Race' (iii, 200).[41] Also, Alcibiades's

---

[38] Licensed 18 February 1677/8 and entered in the Stationers' Register on 23 February.

[39] *Works of Shadwell*, ed. Summers, iii. 194.

[40] And Bayes in *The Rehearsal. The Triumphant Widow* was acted 26 November 1674, licensed 27 November 1676, advertised in the *Term Catalogues* on 12 February 1676/7, and dated 1677 on its title-page. Crambo hates Ben Jonson for having 'no Wit' (p. 61), a distorted reflection of the attitude Shadwell had attributed to Dryden. Elkanah Settle, however, complained of Shadwell that 'Having a Play, call'd the *Triumphant Widow*, given him to bring into the Duke's Playhouse, he spitefully foists in a Scene of his own into the Play, and makes a silly Heroick Poet in it, speak the very words he had heard me say' (*The Preface to Ibrahim*, ed. Macdonald, p. 5). Newcastle's holograph of the play was printed as *A Pleasante & Merrye Humor off A Roge By William Cavendish Duke of Newcastle*, ed. Francis Needham, Welbeck Miscellany No. 1, 1933.

[41] Several remarks given to the Poet seem to be satirical hits at Dryden's 'Apology for Heroic Poetry and Poetic Licence', published less than a year

penultimate speech concludes with a dose of the democratic political theory being advocated by Buckingham and Shaftesbury:

> . . . when the Government
> Is in the Body of the People, they
> Will do themselves no harm; therefore henceforth
> I do pronounce the Government shall devolve upon the
> People, and may Heav'n prosper 'em.[42]

Dryden was currently rebutting such ideas in his dedication of *All for Love*.[43] Given these features of *Timon*, the fact that it is not once mentioned in *Mac Flecknoe* virtually assures that Dryden's poem must have been written earlier.

Further evidence, if any is needed, is the absence from *Mac Flecknoe* of any reference to Shadwell's next play, *A True Widow* (possibly first acted 21 March 1677/8; published 1679).[44] In Shadwell's dedication to Sir Charles Sedley, dated 16 February 1678/9, the force of the insult to Dryden depends upon an implicit comparison of *All for Love* and Sedley's *Antony and Cleopatra* (acted 12 February 1676/7). Sedley, Shadwell tells us, showed

in *Antony* and *Cleopatra*, the true Spirit of a Tragedy, the only one (except two of *Johnson's*, and one of *Shakespear's*) wherein *Romans* are made to speak and do like *Romans*: there are to be found the true Characters of *Antony* and *Cleopatra*, as they were; whereas a *French* Author would have made the *Ægyptian* and the *Roman* both become *French* under his Pen. And even our *English* Authors are too much given to make true History (in their Plays) Romantick and impossible; but in this Play, the *Romans* are true *Romans*, and their Style is such:

---

earlier. See George McFadden, 'Elkanah Settle and the Genesis of *Mac Flecknoe*', *Philological Quarterly*, xliii (1964), 70–1.

[42] *Works of Shadwell*, ed. Summers, iii. 272. The social and political aspects of *Timon* are examined by P. F. Vernon, 'Social Satire in Shadwell's *Timon*', *Studia Neophilologica*, xxxv (1963), 221–6; Gunnar Sorelius, 'Shadwell Deviating into Sense: *Timon of Athens* and the Duke of Buckingham', *Studia Neophilologica*, xxxvi (1964), 232–44; and Alan S. Fisher, 'The Significance of Thomas Shadwell', *Studies in Philology*, lxxi (1974), 225–46.

[43] Published in March 1677/8. See especially the passage on pp. 6–7 of my Regents Series edition of *All for Love* (Lincoln: University of Nebraska Press, 1972).

[44] Milhous and Hume, 'Dating Play Premières', p. 387. In contributing the prologue to *A True Widow*, Dryden merely fulfilled a normal playhouse duty carrying no implications concerning his personal relationship with Shadwell. His prologue does not refer specifically to Shadwell's play and was later printed with Aphra Behn's *The Widow Ranter* (1690).

and I dare affirm, that there is not in any Play of this Age so much of the Spirit of the Classick Authors, as in your *Antony* and *Cleopatra*.[45]

Likewise not mentioned in *Mac Flecknoe* are Shadwell's *The Woman Captain* (1679) and *The Lancashire Witches* (1681).

V

The Virtuoso, especially its dedication to the Duke of Newcastle, comprises the most extensive, corrosive attack that Shadwell directed at Dryden prior to *The Medal of John Bayes* in 1682. Thus its publication early in July 1676 is a likely occasion for the composition of *Mac Flecknoe*.

Compared with the dedication, the attacks on Dryden in the play itself (acted 25 May 1676) seem mild, consisting mostly of Shadwell's customary sneers at heroic drama. There are references to 'plaguy Rhiming Plays, with scurvy Hero's worse than the Knight of the Sun, or *Amadis de Gaul*' and 'a dull Rhiming Play, with nothing in't but lewd Heroe's huffing against the Gods'[46]— probably alluding to Maximin in Dryden's *Tyrannic Love*, which was revived at the other playhouse a week before *The Virtuoso* was acted (18 May 1676). In Shadwell's epilogue (iii. 181):

> But of those Ladies he despairs to day,
> Who love a dull Romantick whining Play;
> Where poor frail Woman's made a Deity,
> With senseless amorous Idolatry;
> And sniveling Heroes sigh, and pine, and cry.
> Though singly they beat Armies, and huff Kings,
> Rant at the Gods, and do impossible things;
> Though they can laugh at danger, blood, and wounds;
> Yet if the Dame once chides, the milk-sop Hero swoons.
> These doughty things, nor Manners have nor Wit;
> We ne'r saw Hero fit to drink with yet.

In the play, the foolish Sir Samuel Hearty cultivates the 'repartee' that Dryden, in his earlier critical controversy with Shadwell, had considered more important in comedy than Jonsonian humours (iii. 108, 121, 131, 171).

Shadwell's dedication assails Dryden for preferring repartee in comedy, for not appreciating humour, for allegedly condemning

---

[45] *Works of Shadwell*, ed. Summers, iii. 283–4.

[46] *Works of Shadwell*, ed. Summers, iii. 116, 134; also 154 and 103 (prologue, ll. 5–6).

all Ben Jonson's plays, for writing inferior plays himself, and for
his pension as Poet Laureate:

Nor do I hear of any profest Enemies to the Play, but some Women,
and some Men of Feminine understandings, who like slight Plays
onely, that represent a little tattle sort of Conversation, like their own;
but true Humour is not liked or understood by them, and therefore even
my attempt towards it is condemned by them. But the same people, to
my great comfort, damn all Mr. *Johnson's* Plays, who was incomparably
the best Dramatick Poet that ever was, or, I believe, ever will be; and I
had rather be Authour of one Scene in his best Comedies, than of any
Play this Age has produced. That there are a great many faults in the
conduct of this Play, I am not ignorant. But I (having no Pension but
from the Theatre, which is either unwilling or unable to reward a Man
sufficiently for so much pains as correct Comedies require) cannot allot
my whole time to the writing of Plays, but am forced to mind some
other business of Advantage. (Had I as much Money, and as much
time for it) I might, perhaps, write as Correct a Comedy as any of my
Contemporaries.

Preceding this barrage are shots at Dryden for 'the affectation of
some *French* words' in the character of Melantha in *Marriage a la
Mode* and for considering 'downright silly folly a Humour'.[47]

Compounding these insults in *The Virtuoso* was Rochester's
attack on Dryden, coupled with praise of Shadwell, in 'An Allusion
to Horace', written during the winter of 1675–6. Rochester recalls
the issues in the earlier controversy between Dryden and Shadwell:

> But does not Dryden find ev'n Jonson dull;
> Fletcher and Beaumont uncorrect, and full
> Of lewd lines, as he calls 'em; Shakespeare's style
> Stiff and affected; to his own the while
> Allowing all the justness that his pride
> So arrogantly had to these denied?
> And may not I have leave impartially
> To search and censure Dryden's works, and try
> If those gross faults his choice pen does commit

---

[47] iii. 101–2. In his 'Defence of the Epilogue' appended to *The Conquest of
Granada*, Dryden, in a conciliatory gesture to Shadwell, had allowed that 'for
Ben Jonson, the most judicious of poets, he always writ properly, and as the
character required; and I will not contest farther with my friends who call that
wit: it being very certain that even folly itself, well represented, is wit in a larger
signification' (*Of Dramatic Poesy and Other Critical Essays*, ed. George Watson,
2 vols., London: Dent, 1962, i. 178).

> Proceed from want of judgment, or of wit;
> Or if his lumpish fancy does refuse
> Spirit and grace to his loose, slattern muse?

Shadwell, on the other hand, is praised in terms that anticipate the dedication of *The Virtuoso* (and even *Mac Flecknoe*):

> Of all our modern wits, none seems to me
> Once to have touched upon true comedy
> But hasty Shadwell and slow Wycherley.
> Shadwell's unfinished works do yet impart
> Great proofs of force of nature, none of art:
> With just, bold strokes he dashes here and there,
> Showing great mastery, with little care,
> And scorns to varnish his good touches o'er
> To make the fools and women praise 'em more.[48]

About April 1676, Rochester learned that Dryden was displeased with 'An allusion to Horace': 'You write me word, That I'm out of favour with a certain Poet. . . .'[49] Evidently Dryden decided to take separate revenges on his two adversaries, postponing his retort to the Earl until the preface to *All for Love* early in 1678.[50]

VI

Mac Flecknoe, then, was written after the publication of *The Virtuoso* early in July 1676 and almost certainly before the production of Shadwell's *Timon* in January 1677/8. Additional evidence

[48] *Complete Poems*, pp. 122–5. With the fourth and fifth lines of Rochester's passage on Shadwell, compare *Mac Flecknoe*'s 'Trust Nature, do not labour to be dull' (l. 166) and 'What share have we in Nature or in Art?' (l. 176). The echo is noted in *Poems on Affairs of State*, ed. Lord, i. 378. The third line of the same passage is mentioned in Dryden's preface to *All for Love*, where he criticizes Rochester for having 'called a slow man hasty, or a hasty writer a slow drudge' (ed. Vieth, p. 24).

[49] *The Rochester Savile Letters*, ed. John Harold Wilson (Columbus: Ohio State University Press, 1941), p. 41.

[50] If *Mac Flecknoe* was triggered by the publication of *The Virtuoso*, it seems futile to seek an occasion in some obscure action by Richard Flecknoe that might have angered Dryden. For investigations taking that line, however, see John Harrington Smith, 'Dryden and Flecknoe: A Conjecture', *Philological Quarterly*, xxxiii (1954), 338–41; McFadden, 'Elkanah Settle and the Genesis of *Mac Flecknoe*', p. 60 n. 12; Maximillian E. Novak, 'Dryden's "Ape of the French Eloquence" and Richard Flecknoe', *Bulletin of the New York Public Library*, lxxii (1968), 499–506; Helmut Castrop, 'Dryden and Flecknoe: A Link', *Review of English Studies*, N.S., xxiii (1972), 455–8. As I suggested (*ARP*, p.250), Flecknoe was probably chosen as a typical poetaster in place of the more notorious Edward Howard, who was Dryden's brother-in-law.

points to a date of composition closer to the earlier limit than to the later. Quite possibly *Mac Flecknoe* was struck off during the summer of 1676 just after *The Virtuoso* was published.[51]

A straw in the wind is an otherwise unknown lampoon on Dryden, headed 'Upon a late fall'n Poet. Suppos'd to be Written by Mʳ Shadwell', which appears immediately following *Mac Flecknoe* in the 'Yale MS.' that figured so prominently in my *Attribution in Restoration Poetry*.[52] This lampoon can be assigned on internal grounds to late March 1678. Although it is probably not by Shadwell or an answer to *Mac Flecknoe*, its placement implies that to the scribe who assembled this manuscript miscellany about spring 1680, *Mac Flecknoe* was the earlier of the two poems.

More substantial is the apparent reference to *Mac Flecknoe* in the lampoon 'Advice to Apollo', which 'was probably produced by Rochester and his fellow wits who assembled at Woodstock in mid-October 1677'. Dryden is described as one

> Who but begins to aim at the renown
> Bestow'd on satirists, and quits the stage
> To lash the witty follies of our age.
> Strike him but gently that he may return,
> Write plays again, and his past follies mourn.[53]

Mac Flecknoe is the only satire Dryden wrote anywhere near this date which was likely to be known to the authors of 'Advice to Apollo' and their intended audience. Moreover, apart from the

---

[51] The opinion of Maximillian E. Novak—'The witty lines [of Dryden's *Mac Flecknoe*] are of the kind a writer savors over a period of years. That he worked on it between 1674 and 1678 is not at all unlikely'—is no more credible than Dryden's claim that Shadwell took five years to complete *The Virtuoso*. A poet who could translate the entire works of Virgil in *three* years did not need *five* years to compose an original poem only 217 lines long ('Dryden's "Ape of the French Eloquence"', p. 499). In a class with Novak's is George McFadden's opinion that 'a lapse of four or five years seems natural between the completion of his first satire and its original begetting' ('Elkanah Settle and the Genesis of *Mac Flecknoe*', p. 55). My investigation of the early manuscripts of *Mac Flecknoe* in 'The Case Against Editorial Confusion' does not support the theory that Dryden's poem passed through several authorial versions over a period of years.
[52] *ARP*, pp. 73, 486. The manuscript is now catalogued as Yale University Library MS. Osborn Shelves b. 105. 'Upon a late fall'n Poet' was discussed by Jim Osborn in a paper delivered in 1974 at the Clark Library and published in *John Dryden II* (Los Angeles: William Andrews Clark Memorial Library, 1978), pp. 27–52.
[53] *Poems on Affairs of State*, ed. Lord, i. 392–4.

question of the precise date of 'Advice to Apollo', the quoted passage locates *Mac Flecknoe* during Dryden's 'retirement' from the stage, between the production of *Aureng-Zebe* (17 November 1675) and that of his next play, *All for Love* (12 December 1677). *Mac Flecknoe*, we can conclude, already existed in the autumn of 1677.

In his essay 'The Author's Apology for Heroic Poetry and Poetic Licence', published with *The State of Innocence* in early February 1676/7 and written during the preceding summer or autumn,[54] Dryden rounded off his discussion of 'imaging' in poetry by remarking,

Mr. Cowley lies as open too in many places:

Where their vast courts the mother waters keep, etc.

For if the mass of waters be the mothers, then their daughters, the little streams, are bound, in all good manners, to make courtesy to them, and ask them blessing. How easy 'tis to turn into ridicule the best descriptions, when once a man is in the humour of laughing, till he wheezes at his own dull jest![55]

This takes us into the milieu of *Mac Flecknoe*, which burlesques the line quoted from Cowley's *Davideis* as 'Where their vast Courts the Mother-Strumpets keep' (l. 72). It has not been noticed how surprisingly feeble, under the circumstances, is Dryden's illustration in the 'Apology' of how to turn Cowley's line 'into ridicule'. The whole passage has the look of an 'inside joke', intelligible to the few who recognized how this line had already been parodied in *Mac Flecknoe*,[56] but superficially plausible to those not 'in the know'. Dryden's reticence about *Mac Flecknoe* is apparent in his reluctance to publish the poem until 1684.

William Cavendish, 1st Duke of Newcastle, to whom Shadwell had addressed four of his five '*Northern Dedications*', including the dedication of *The Virtuoso*, died on 25 September 1676. *Mac Flecknoe*, however, mentions these '*Northern Dedications*' as if they

[54] Charles E. Ward, *The Life of John Dryden* (Chapel Hill: University of North Carolina Press, 1961), p. 116. *The State of Innocence* was advertised in the *Term Catalogues* on 12 February 1676/7 and in the *London Gazette* for 8–12 February.

[55] *Of Dramatic Poesy and Other Critical Essays*, ed. Watson, i. 205.

[56] The alertness of contemporary readers in such matters is shown by the copyist of *Mac Flecknoe* who returned Dryden's parody of this line to Cowley's original version. See 'The Case Against Editorial Confusion', pp. 225–6 n. 49.

would continue indefinitely (l. 170). One may doubt that Dryden's sense of discretion would have allowed him even this mildly disparaging allusion during the months following the Duke's death.[57] Similarly, *Mac Flecknoe* refers to 'Uncle *Ogleby*' as if he were still alive—or at least as much alive as 'Father *Fleckno*' (ll. 173–4).[58] John Ogilby died on 4 September 1676.

A long-standing puzzle is the relationship between *Mac Flecknoe* and the attack on Shadwell in the preface that survives in a few copies of Elkanah Settle's tragedy *Ibrahim*, published in summer or autumn 1676.[59] The two attacks display such 'striking similarities', as George McFadden had demonstrated, that one must probably have influenced the other. 'There is indeed a possibility that Settle helped Dryden to the principal donnée of *Mac Flecknoe*', observes McFadden, whose evidence and arguments, he concludes, 'indicate that Dryden supplemented his recollection of the Shadwell plays . . . by consulting Settle's attack'.[60] What does not seem to cross McFadden's mind, perhaps because he assumes without question that *Mac Flecknoe* was written in 1678, is the obvious explanation: Settle's preface borrows from Dryden's poem. As Earl Miner has shown in a set of parallels between poems by these two authors, the borrowing, as one might expect, is invariably by Settle from

[57] By 1863, however, Dryden could call Shadwell 'the *Northern Dedicator*' in *The Vindication of the Duke of Guise*.

[58] Thereby contrasting ironically with the lines Dryden parodies in *Aeneid*, iii. 342–3 and xii. 439–40, where 'pater Aeneas' (Flecknoe) is alive, whereas 'avunculus Hector' (Ogilby) is dead. In line 102 of *Mac Flecknoe*, however, Ogilby, who was a very old man when he died, is listed with Heywood and Shirley. Among Ogilby's protean accomplishments was the preparation by him and William Morgan of an elaborate map of London that was published in 1677, very close to the date of *Mac Flecknoe* (facsimile, ed. Charles Welch, London and Middlesex Archaeological Society, 1895).

[59] Acted *c.* March 1676, licensed 4 May 1676, entered in the Stationers' Register on 7 July 1676, advertised in the *Term Catalogues* on 22 November 1676, and dated 1677 on the title-page.

[60] 'Elkanah Settle and the Genesis of *Mac Flecknoe*', pp. 67–9. Besides accepting the conclusions in McKeithan's 'The Occasion of *MacFlecknoe*', McFadden contends that Dryden's poem satirizes an 'anti-poet' modelled upon Settle rather than upon Shadwell. Thus he is in the odd position of maintaining that *Mac Flecknoe* attacks a person (Settle) and was occasioned by a work (*Timon*) which it never mentions! Earl Miner finds McFadden's reasoning 'excellent', adding, 'His evidence strongly supports the belief that the poem was written in 1678' (*Dryden's Poetry*, p. 77 n.). Paul J. Korshin agrees that McFadden's article 'corroborates the traditional date' (*From Concord to Dissent: Major Themes in English Poetic Theory 1640–1700*, Menston: Scolar Press, 1973, p. 132 n. 40).

Dryden, by the poetaster from the great poet.[61] A *terminus ad quem*
for the date of Settle's work is the reference to 'an *Ibrahim*, with
the Preface torn out' in the lampoon 'A Session of the Poets'
written about November 1676 (*ARP*, pp. 309–10). Since time
would have been required for Settle's preface (influenced by *Mac
Flecknoe*) to be written, published, and noticed by the anonymous
author of 'A Session', the date of *Mac Flecknoe* is effectively
pushed back to the summer of 1676.

From the vantage-point of summer 1676, *Mac Flecknoe* emerges,
not only as a specific response to *The Virtuoso* and a general review
of Shadwell's dramatic career, but as a selective review of the
theatrical season of 1675–6. A pertinent question is why the
dramatist that Dryden chose to set over against Shadwell should
have been George Etherege—rather than, for example, William
Wycherley. Wycherley and Etherege were both on equally good
terms with the Rochester–Shadwell and Dryden–Mulgrave factions. If Wycherley had been praised more extensively than
Etherege in Rochester's 'An Allusion to Horace' (probably written
before the première of *The Man of Mode*), Etherege was Rochester's
companion in the Epsom brawl in June.

The answer seems to be that the two new 'smash-hit' comedies
of the season were *The Man of Mode* and *The Virtuoso*, produced
at the Duke's Theatre in March and May respectively.[62] Besides a
prologue and probably a song by Sir Carr Scroope, *The Man of
Mode* had an epilogue by Dryden himself. Also, *She Would if She
Could*, Etherege's last previous play, originally produced eight
years before, was revived earlier in the season (*c.* February 1675/6).
Wycherley, on the other hand, produced no new play during the
season of 1675–6. *The Country Wife*, although revived late in this
season (16 May 1676), had its première the preceding winter (12
January 1674/5), while *The Plain Dealer* was not produced until

[61] Earl Roy Miner, 'Dryden's "MacFlecknoe"', *Notes and Queries*, cci
(1956), 335–7.

[62] In the prologue to *The Virtuoso*, Shadwell's opening gambit appears to be
a comparison between his play and *The Man of Mode* (*Works*, ed. Summers,
iii. 103):

> You came with such an eager appetite
> To a late Play, which gave so great delight;
> Our Poet fears, that by so rich a Treat,
> Your Palates are become too delicate. . . .
> In the last Comedy some Wits were shown;
> In this are Fools that much infest the Town.

the following winter (11 December 1676). *The Man of Mode* and
The Virtuoso, as was normal for two successful plays, were both
published (by Henry Herringman) after the end of the season in
June and were advertised together in the *London Gazette* (3–6
July) and the *Term Catalogues* (22 November).

Shadwell's *Psyche*, to which *Mac Flecknoe* gives so much attention, was performed at least three times during the season of
1675–6 (25 September and 8 October 1675, c. January 1675/6).
There was a revival of *Tyrannic Love* (18 May 1676), the only one
of Dryden's heroic plays to be mentioned in *Mac Flecknoe* ('And
little *Maximins* the Gods defy', l. 78). Appropriately, in bringing
to a close the season of 1675–6, *Mac Flecknoe* itself comes to a
close by re-enacting the memorable trap-door episode from *The
Virtuoso*.[63]

Why is the date of *Mac Flecknoe* important? The layman may
well wonder. Biographically, since this was Dryden's first great
poem, it is important to know that *Mac Flecknoe* was probably
written five full years before his next great poem, *Absalom and
Achitophel*. Also, in the whole of world literature, no other author
of comparable stature has had his reputation demolished as completely as *Mac Flecknoe* demolished Shadwell's. Hence the poem
should at least be placed chronologically within the web of relation-
ships among Restoration writers.

Mac Flecknoe has long awaited recognition as the crowning
literary achievement of 1676, the year I have elsewhere termed
'the apex of the "high Restoration"'.[64] This year included the last
plays of Etherege and Wycherley, the finest writers (before Congreve) of the finest branch of Restoration drama, its comedy. The
last heroic play by the undisputed master of the genre, Dryden's
Aureng-Zebe, was produced just before the year began (17 November 1675). By 1676, the year of his 'apotheosis as the half-angelic,
half-diabolical Dorimant', Rochester had written almost all of
his best poems (*ARP*, p. 177).

The overwhelming challenge that confronted Dryden, as well as

---

[63] As well as alluding to the story of Elijah and Elisha, to the use of this story
in Cowley's verses 'On the Death of Mr. Crashaw', to Shadwell's lyric 'Arise,
arise! ye subterranean winds', and to the 'subterranean wind' of *Paradise Lost*,
i. 231.

[64] In my essay 'Divided Consciousness: The Trauma and Triumph of
Restoration Culture', *Tennessee Studies in Literature*, xxii (1977), 52, which
develops more fully the views adumbrated in my two concluding paragraphs.

Rochester, Etherege, Wycherley, and their contemporaries, was how to register the traumatically fragmented 'modern' consciousness of the 1660s and 1670s while still maintaining continuity with earlier seventeenth-century traditions—how, in Dryden's words, to 'transfuse' one into the other, but not 'so transfus'd as Oyl on Waters flow'. *Mac Flecknoe*, in 1676, not only describes this artistic dilemma but enacts and resolves it.

Admiration in the Comedies of Thomas Southerne

Eugene M. Waith

One of the best-publicized developments in the history of English drama is the sad change of heart (and I use all these words advisedly) that came over the writers of comedy as the eighteenth century neared and then arrived. The publicity is, of course, due in large measure to the efforts of one of those who helped to bring the change about—the divine whose view of the English stage was so very dim. Naturally, then, the virtuous and weepy comedy that began to appear at this time has often been seen as the consequence of Jeremy Collier's attack on immorality and profaneness. Libertines must no longer prosper nor the clergy be mocked. It has also been explained that the success of Collier and the contemporary societies for the reformation of manners was related to the increasing influence of the ladies in the audience and to the rise of the middle classes, that historical phenomenon to which our attention is always being called, whether we are reading about Elizabethan or Georgian England, France in the time of Richelieu or Louis XVI, or all of western Europe in the industrial revolution. Middle-class or, as we now say, bourgeois morality was on the march as the seventeenth century ended, we are told, and the old aristocratic *savoir vivre* ended too.

It was the change in the moral climate that struck both Joseph Wood Krutch and John Harrington Smith. One charted the gradual triumph of conscience over comedy; the other described the rise, decline, and last-ditch fight of the 'gay couple', who are unfortunately apt to be confused today with an 'odd couple', but, in Smith's terminology, were the witty fair one and her sparring partner, the free-thinking beau, whose wit-combats proclaim their independence of standard morality.[1]

---

[1] *Comedy and Conscience after the Restoration* (New York, 1924); *The Gay Couple in Restoration Comedy* (New York, 1971; orig. 1948).

Ernest Bernbaum emphasized a shift in underlying assumptions about human nature from the traditional belief in depravity to faith in basic goodness,[2] or from what I have called the hard view to the soft view. Concomitant with this shift or, as some would say, responsible for it, was the increasing importance of emotional appeal in what is after all known as *sentimental* drama, both comic and tragic. Arthur Sherbo wrote about the nature of this appeal and the techniques of the playwrights who made it.[3] He considered that the sentimental dramatist was 'concerned primarily to arouse pity for distressed virtue and admiration for innate human goodness' (p. 100). Since he wished, so far as it was possible, to distinguish between essentially sentimental plays and those with only certain sentimental characteristics, he was very selective, and resolutely put aside even *Love's Last Shift*, often called the first sentimental comedy. This bold decision has been disputed by B. R. S. Fone, who argues that the morality, the benevolence, and the pity expected in sentimental comedy are present there from first to last.[4]

I mention these accounts of the transformation of comedy not to disagree with them, for I accept the considerable number of shared assumptions they contain, and do not wish at this time to choose sides where they disagree. But the mention of these assumptions will serve as a reminder that most discussions of the history of comedy present a picture of rather abrupt change in the moral and emotional landscape, sometimes said to have occurred precisely in 1696. Anticipations of the change are, of course, recognized—tremors, so to speak, preceding the great quake— and after it some rickety remains of older structures are perceived. Without denying the change, I want to call attention to certain strands of continuity which may help to make the transitional period in comedy more understandable. Thomas Southerne, whose career spanned the time from Dryden to Gray, and whose comedies have long been recognized as portents of things to come,[5] seems to be a useful playwright to examine in this connection. The significance of his comedies can, however, be seen more clearly in

[2] *The Drama of Sensibility* (Gloucester, Mass., 1958; orig. 1915).
[3] *English Sentimental Comedy* (East Lansing, Mich., 1957).
[4] 'Love's Last Shift and Sentimental Comedy', *Restoration and 18th Century Theatre Research*, ix (1970), 11–23.
[5] See esp. John Wendell Dodds, *Thomas Southerne, Dramatist* (New Haven, 1933), pp. 50–5.

relation to accepted ideas about the nature of comedy and the audience to which it was addressed.

According to a tradition extending back to Aristotle, comedy was supposed to expose the follies of ordinary people to ridicule. The emblem for this function of comedy was the mirror: in the often-quoted words attributed to Cicero by Donatus, 'comedy is an imitation of life, a mirror of custom, an image of truth'.[6] Thus considered, comedy closely resembles satire, which was also sometimes represented as a mirror in which fools might see their reflections. In both cases the implication is that the image of folly will be ridiculous and hence laughable. But, as William K. Wimsatt pointed out in a memorable introduction to some essays on comedy, 'laughter has always been one of the chief embarrassments of the comic theorist.'[7] We need look at only three major English critics to be sure that this is so. Sidney, in *An Apology for Poetry*, says:

But our Comedians thinke there is no delight without laughter; which is very wrong, for though laughter may come with delight, yet commeth it not of delight, as though delight should be the cause of laughter; but well may one thing breed both together: nay, rather in themselues they haue, as it were, a kind of contrarietie: for delight we scarcely doe but in things that haue a conueniencie to our selues or to the generall nature: laughter almost euer commeth of things most disproportioned to our selues and nature. Delight hath a ioy in it, either permanent or present. Laughter hath onely a scornful tickling. For example, we are rauished with delight to see a faire woman, and yet are far from being moued to laughter.

As a subject for comedy he commends Hercules with Omphale, 'For the representing of so strange a power in loue procureth delight: and the scornefulnes of the action stirreth laughter.'[8] In the *Discoveries* Jonson has the strikingly similar observation: 'Nor, is the moving of laughter alwaies the end of *Comedy*, that is rather a fowling for the peoples delight, or their fooling.'[9] Closer to the

[6] *Theories of Comedy*, ed. Paul Lauter (New York, 1964), p. 27.

[7] *English Stage Comedy*, ed. W. K. Wimsatt, Jr. (New York, 1955), p. 4. See also his informative editorial comments in another collection, *The Idea of Comedy* (Englewood Cliffs, N.J., 1969), to which I am indebted.

[8] *Elizabethan Critical Essays*, ed. G. Gregory Smith, 2 vols. (Oxford, 1904), i. 199–200.

[9] *Ben Jonson*, ed. C. H. Herford and Percy and Evelyn Simpson, 11 vols. (Oxford, 1925–52), viii. 643, ll. 2629–31.

time with which we are concerned is Dryden's comment in his preface to *An Evening's Love*: '. . . the business of the poet is to make you laugh: when he writes humour, he makes folly ridiculous; when wit, he moves you, if not always to laughter, yet to a pleasure that is more noble.'[10]

The embarrassment is clear. Some laughter is rather low or ill-natured or both, and these critics would prefer to see comedy appeal to a more cultivated audience for a finer response. Sidney's mention of a fair woman and the power of love in this connection points to a kind of comedy which did just that—to romantic comedy, though of course he would not have recognized the term. And Dryden's distinction reminds us of the wit so often found in the romantic comedies of Shakespeare, Fletcher, and others. If the 'mirror of custom' is the emblem for that sort of comedy which depicts satirically the follies of the everyday world, a corresponding emblem for romantic comedy might be, as I have suggested elsewhere, that magic mirror made for Britomart by Merlin, the 'world of glass' in which she sees the object of her quest, Sir Artegall (*Faerie Queene*, iii. 2). Here is a mirror that reflects ideals and gives delight. Neither mirror, it must be said, gives an exact likeness. One makes slightly grotesque; the other reflects not a surface but inner desire. To be just, one would have to say that both sorts of mirror are operative in romantic comedy, but the presence of this 'world of glass' tends to elevate the tone considerably and to provide that 'pleasure which is more noble'. While comic theorists continued to write in the terms of an Aristotelian or Ciceronian definition, romance began to affect both theory and practice.[11]

The elevation which Sidney, Jonson, and Dryden thought desirable might be manifested both in idealized images and in witty conversation, which is also, in a way, an idealized image. Both were the stock-in-trade of the writer of romance, and particularly of the seventeenth-century French romance, which catered to a society bent on self-improvement. The reform of manners and letters was, after all, the avowed goal of those formidable ladies who presided over the *salons*. So nuances of feeling and of expression were cultivated in the works of Madeleine

---

[10] *Essays of John Dryden*, ed. W. P. Ker, 2 vols. (Oxford, 1926), i. 143.

[11] A conflict between lowness of subject matter and refinement of dialogue is to be found even in Aristotle's comments on comedy, as Wimsatt points out (*Idea of Comedy*, p. 10). See especially the *Nicomachean Ethics*, iv. 8.3–7.

de Scudéry, for instance, and the crowd of fashionable folk in
Madame de Rambouillet's 'blue room' were delighted to recognize
the flattering reflections of themselves in the mirror of *Le Grand
Cyrus*.

When English playwrights in the latter part of the century rifled
these romances for the plots of both their heroic plays and their
witty comedies, they assumed a similar relationship between
fictional characters and audience. In a familiar passage from the
epilogue to the second part of *The Conquest of Granada* Dryden
would have his spectators believe that imitation of them is solely
responsible for the superiority of Restoration drama to its predecessors:

> If Love and Honour now are higher rais'd,
> 'Tis not the Poet, but the Age is prais'd.
> Our native Language more refin'd and free.
> Our Ladies and our men now speak more wit
> In conversation than those Poets writ.[12]

Dryden's implication that the witty and the virtuous will see themselves in *The Conquest of Granada* is in itself a piece of flattery.
More truly one might say that they could see themselves there as
they might like to be.

In the most witty comedies of that time the heightening and
refinement were not a matter of moral superiority but of elegance.
The manners of the clever rakes could make them feel at home
with heroes. Consequently, it is a little less surprising to find that
the libertine Florimell and Celadon in *Secret Love* were inspired,
like the heroic lovers in that play, by some of the characters of
Mlle de Scudéry. Even Etherege's unromantic lovers are not so
far removed from the tradition of romance as they are sometimes
thought to be. If there is little moral uplift in such plays, there is
notable elevation of a sort, and while there is certainly satirical
laughter at the expense of those who have not learned how to
behave, there is also delight in the performance of those who have.

I suggest, then, that dissatisfaction with the laughter of low
comedy and liberal use of the materials of romance to achieve a
more refined product opened the way for the portrayal of a 'joy
too exquisite for laughter' in *The Conscious Lovers*,[13] though what

---

[12] Wimsatt, *Idea of Comedy*, pp. 55–6.
[13] Preface, l. 29, in the edition of Shirley Strum Kenny (Lincoln, Neb., 1968)

Steele meant by these words was something quite different from
what Dryden meant by a pleasure 'more noble' than laughter.
Closely related to the concern on the part of writers in the romance
tradition for elevation and refinement was the aim of arousing
admiration. Admirable characters appeared in most romantic
comedies and were given prominence in Shakespeare's last
romances, Fletcher's tragicomedies, and Corneille's *comédies
héroïques*, but above all, as this term of Corneille's reminds us,
they were found in heroic drama, where wonder at some greatness
of spirit was the characteristic effect. In Dryden's *Secret Love*, to
which I have already referred, heroic characters intended to arouse
precisely this response appeared in one plot while witty, libertine
characters appeared in the genuinely comic plot. The two varieties
of heightened characters, while in a sense sharing the same world,
were assigned to different actions. In some of Southerne's plays
'wonderful' characters and situations are introduced into comic
plots, but in a way that hardly recalls Shakespeare or Corneille, for
the admirable is now stamped with the hallmarks of the late
seventeenth century. To focus on this aspect of Southerne's
technique is to see comedy in the process of transforming itself by
borrowing directly from the contemporary version of heroic drama
a special kind of heightening.

For his first play, the tragedy of *The Loyal Brother*, performed
in 1682, Southerne chose a Persian setting. In the romances and
plays of the seventeenth century the great potentates of this region,
splendidly attired, were likely to commit crimes with extraordinary
ruthlessness or else rise to acts of generosity exceeding those of
most Christian princes. They were naturals for heroic drama. Since
Southerne's 'loyal brother', a prince of unflinching virtue, was
intended as a flattering portrait of the Duke of York, the play was,
among other things, a political allegory. But I am not concerned
with this aspect or even, to any great extent, with the character of
the hero. He is named Tachmas, is in love with and beloved by
Semanthe, and is the brother of Seliman, the sophy, who is also in
love with Semanthe. Two underlings who have been eclipsed by
the prince's military glory plot his destruction by fanning the
flames of Seliman's jealousy. Brought to Semanthe's apartment,
where he has been told, ambiguously, that 'she in private enter-
tains a Lover' (II. 3; i. 29),[14] Seliman overhears a platonic love-

[14] Unless otherwise noted, quotations are taken from *The Works of Mr.*

scene, loses control of his passions, and banishes Tachmas. By the
end of Act III he has become so infuriated by Semanthe's continued
coldness to him that he orders his brother's death. Here occurs the
first major scene. Tachmas is on a scaffold, awaiting execution.
Seliman is on hand to see it carried out. To intervene for the prince
their mother arrives first, and drenches Seliman with a flow of
rhetoric reminiscent of Seneca's Jocasta in *The Phoenician Women*
or Shakespeare's Volumnia. She is followed by Semanthe, who
makes an equally passionate plea as both women, on their knees,
hold the sophy. Then, like Antony, beleaguered by Octavia and his
little daughters, he begins to melt, as Semanthe sees:

> A Blush confus'dly wanders in his Cheeks
> And now he turns away. O blessed Change!   (III. 4; i. 46)

At last he makes Semanthe and his mother rise:

> Yes you have conquer'd, and I blush to think,
> I could so long resist such wondrous Virtue.   (ibid.)

Though he is not quite ready to give Semanthe to Tachmas, he
feels virtue winning 'apace' upon his soul, and expects to make
this final gesture when his 'rebel Passions' have subsided. The
villains have not given up, however. They make one more, almost
successful, attempt to discredit Tachmas by means of a forged
letter, and are thwarted only by a loyal officer. In the second major
scene, where the evil characters all get their just deserts, Seliman
does not play a large part, but the last speech of the play is his.
Released from the domination of his passions, he speaks of how
'Virtue shines out again in its full Blaze' (v. 3; i. 70), and keeps his
promise of giving Semanthe to his loyal brother.

   These two scenes are typically heroic, but heroic in a particular
way. They solicit admiration not only for the virtuous characters
who have endured unjust treatment but for the capacity to recognize virtue, to forgive, to be compassionate and generous. This is
a sort of heroism that one associates with the later Dryden and
with some of Racine and Otway.

   Southerne's next dramatic work, two years later, was *The
Disappointment, or The Mother in Fashion*, which he called simply

Thomas Southerne, 2 vols. (London, 1721). Scene-numbers are mine, however,
based on indications of a change of scene. Volume and page in this edition are
given after act and scene.

'a play'. Though it is more comedy than anything else, John W. Dodds is right in saying that it 'points forward to his main achievement in the theatre—the development of a sentimental problem drama'.[15] One part of the action is closely analogous to the situation of Seliman and Semanthe. Here we have a married couple, the jealous Alphonso and the virtuous Erminia. The villain of the piece is Alberto, a rake, whose plans to seduce both Erminia and Angelline, an unmarried girl, are frustrated by his cast-off mistress. The devices are characteristically comic—a waiting-woman suborned, a *meretrix* posing as a mother (the 'mother in fashion'), and the bed-trick played twice by the same woman on the same man, thanks to two disguises. In the midst of these jolly goings-on are the scenes with Alphonso and Erminia which have so different a tone. Alphonso, finding a love-letter to his wife on which Alberto has forged the duke's signature, confesses to his friend Lorenzo that he is insanely jealous. Lorenzo, defending her, stirs the husband's pity and persuades him to visit his wife. When he does so, however, he behaves like Othello, questioning and accusing her. Unlike Othello, he relents when she faints, and the scene ends with an emotional reconciliation. He is still unhappy about the letter, however. To test Erminia he pretends to go away, so that he and Lorenzo can see what happens (this part of the plot is borrowed from a famous episode in *Don Quixote*, already dramatized several times). Lorenzo, having become suspicious of Alberto but then convinced again of Erminia's innocence, arranges another interview between husband and wife which makes the climactic scene of the fourth act. Erminia is all submissive love, begging on her knees for a kind word as Semanthe begged for the life of Tachmas. Alphonso is overcome by her virtue, and makes his friend lift her to her feet, as he stands transfixed by knowledge of his unworthiness. 'Then I will rush upon you with my Charms', she says, with a Restoration heroine's full awareness of her power. 'Thou art too good for Man,' says Alphonso (IV. 1; i. 139).

Unfortunately, since certain suspicious circumstances have not yet been explained, Alphonso's jealous fit comes on again in the fifth act. This time he is only just prevented from killing both Alberto and Erminia, but is once more brought to believe in her innocence and repent for his suspicions. Thus Alphonso's fever-chart is very similar to Seliman's, and once again, a major com-

---

[15] *Thomas Southerne*, p. 49.

ponent of the effect of the two big scenes is the recognition of virtue. If we say that virtue is made admirable here, we must include in our meaning of the term not merely moral approval but wonder at conduct 'too good for Man'. The characters on-stage experience this admiration, and the audience may admire both the admiring and the admired. Hence it is not enough to say that *The Disappointment* is a didactic play or a play of moral reformation. It is also a play about man's marvellous capacity for goodness—a play for those sufficiently cultivated to appreciate such refinement of human nature.

Southerne was nothing if not an experimenter. When he next returned to the stage after a six-year absence, he scored his first resounding success with *Sir Antony Love, or The Rambling Lady*, a lively and rather libertine comedy with a breeches part for Mrs. Montfort. He proved that he could write comedy in a familiar Restoration mode. There is little admiration for virtue here, but a lot of amusement at folly and misunderstanding. In the play which followed, *The Wives Excuse, or Cuckolds Make Themselves*, he again depicted lechery rampant, but also, as in *The Disappointment*, some admirable virtue. Though the play now seems much more interesting than *Sir Antony Love*, it was a failure in its time. Southerne blamed the fashionable sparks, 'who were affronted at Mrs. *Friendall*', his virtuous heroine, speaking against her in public, he implied, largely in order to seem more wicked than they were able to be in private (Epistle Dedicatory (i. 262)).

Mrs. Friendall is, in any case, a character worthy of attention. She is not in love with her husband like Erminia. She considers him, in fact, her cross, but is determined to bear it as well as she can (v. 3; i. 338), knowing Friendall to be foolish, unfaithful, and something of a coward. Lovemore, who appears to be sincerely in love with her, seeks to give her a 'wives excuse' for infidelity by showing up her husband's cowardice, but she covers up for Friendall and even goes to ingenious lengths to protect his reputation, not out of pure generosity, but to protect her own reputation. She explains to Lovemore that what she did was 'not for the Commendation of your Wit, nor as a Debt to him, but to my self, foreseeing a long Life of Infamy, which in his Follies I was marry'd to; and therefore sav'd myself by saving him' (IV. 1; i. 322). In other words, she has her honour to think of, like Chimène or Sophonisba. Lovemore is impressed. 'Your Conduct every way is excellent, but there it was a Master-piece indeed, and worthy Admiration' (ibid.). Yet at this point, as previously, Mrs. Friendall offers Lovemore no encouragement.

What gives this exchange its special interest is its relation to the rest of the play. There is not, as in *The Disappointment*, a sharp contrast between scenes of licentious intrigue and scenes of virtuous sentiment. Lovemore is an intriguer, more truly devoted to the object of his pursuit than the rake Wilding, for instance, but equally set on an adulterous affair. Mrs. Friendall, though virtuous, is worldly-wise and indulges in the same sort of cynical banter as the other ladies, some of whom are playing a fast game. The surface of the comedy is uniformly that of a polite society in which adherence to forms only barely conceals a great deal of moral laxity. Perfectly aware of what is going on, Mrs. Friendall determines to live according to standards which most of her friends have put aside. She is not quite alone, however. Mrs. Sightly, though less heroic than Mrs. Friendall, apparently rewards none of the men who pursue her, among whom is Mr. Friendall. Eventually she tells his wife about his attentions. One of her admirers, Wellvile, is also among the more honourable members of this group. He is a critic of society, who pretends to be writing a play called *The Wives Excuse*, and who aids in the exposure of the most despicable of the characters, Mr. Friendall and Mrs. Witwoud. Between the best and the worst characters are several who are neither very good nor very bad, but comply with the way of the world.

For the denouement of the piece Southerne assembles almost all his large cast at the Friendalls'. The occasion is a masquerade, but the action is an unmasking of the sexual intrigues of this licentious society. Just before the principal revelation, there occurs a confrontation between Mrs. Teazall, a plain-speaking old woman, who blasts 'the wicked ways of Living in this Town' (v. 3; i. 342), and Wilding, who brazenly defends his libertinism. He then goes on to make public one of the more scandalous intrigues and to engineer the discovery of Mr. Friendall and Mrs. Witwoud on a couch in the next room.

Although such an ending to the action might seem to throw the emphasis of the play on a satirical exposure, encouraging a sudden glory of Hobbesian laughter at the worst characters, and only a bit of delighted sympathy with the best, Southerne's treatment of the situation in fact prompts a more complicated response. Friendall is thoroughly discredited, to be sure, and has to grant his wife separate maintenance. We may suppose that she will eventually give herself to Lovemore, for whom she has confessed her fondness earlier in the act (v. 3; i. 338), but her last words are to her husband: 'I must be still your Wife, and still unhappy' (p. 346). Whether or not she decides to console herself with a lover, she has suffered precisely the sort of public humiliation she has sought to avoid. Nor does Mrs. Sightly make any promises to Wellvile. Though he has saved her from serious embarrassment at the least by revealing a plot to procure her for Wilding, she suspects him of using the favour to oblige her to him. Happiness for these two basically good characters is also uncertain. How different it all is from the ending of *The Way of the World*, for instance, where not only are the villainous schemers shown up, but Jack has Jill and a lot of money!

John Harrington Smith saw *The Wives Excuse* as a revival of Wycherley's manner, but as going even beyond Wycherley in the condemnation of free gallantry. Southerne, he believed, 'saw the world as infected with a blight which could attack even honest love' (p. 148). The combination of satirical attack with the portrayal of sterling worth may indeed be reminiscent of *The Plain Dealer*, but in *The Wives Excuse* the scourging is considerably less brutal and the ending less romantic. What distinguishes Southerne's comedy from most of those with which it can be compared is its simultaneous appeal for admiration and for an awareness that the admired virtues may never bring happiness, never be properly rewarded. Faith in an ideal and cynical acceptance of the world as it is seem to exist side by side as complementary views, neither of which triumphs over the other. This 'complementarity', if I may borrow from Norman Rabkin the term he borrowed from atomic science,[16] even differentiates *The Wives Excuse* from *The Relapse*, where the admirable Amanda converts Worthy to virtue as Loveless relapses into the arms of Berinthia. There, with a fine impartiality, Vanbrugh allows both the wicked and the good to prosper. Southerne moves us to admiration and compassion for a heroine whose virtue, as the world sees it, may not last, but, if it does last, will deny her the chief happiness she might expect. If Vanbrugh's comedy permits the responses expected in both the old libertine comedy and the new proto-sentimental comedy, one response each

[16] *Shakespeare and the Common Understanding* (New York, 1967), p. 22.

to two situations, Southerne, by his treatment of single situations, in a sense arouses both responses only to frustrate them. Perhaps bewilderment or the desire to have it one way or the other was responsible for the audience's lack of enthusiasm.

In Southerne's next comedy, *The Maid's Last Prayer, or Any Rather than Fail*, of 1693, the maid of the title is a virgin of forty-five who makes one final and successful effort to marry herself off, though she does not get the man she wants. The ending is similar to that of *The Wives Excuse* in that most of the characters, with the possible exception of one very clever rake, have to settle for something less than their desires, but virtue is in short supply. Laughter of a satirical kind seems to be the one response envisaged. In the two following plays there is plenty to admire, but they are tragedies, the great successes of Southerne's career, *The Fatal Marriage* of 1694 and *Oroonoko* of 1695. The various sorts of admiration evoked by the main plots of these plays belong to another story. I may note in passing, however, that both plays have comic underplots, and that in *The Fatal Marriage* there is a momentary suggestion in a comic scene of the kind of situation Southerne incorporates in *The Wives Excuse*. Julia, the free-speaking but loyal wife of a jealous husband, says to a would-be seducer, 'But for the future, Sir, you may believe there are Women, who won't be provok'd to injure their Husbands' (IV. 1; ii. 145).

After *Oroonoko* came two more tragedies, *The Fate of Capua* in 1700 and, nineteen years later, *The Spartan Dame*, most of which Southerne had written in the late eighties but had been unable to have performed on account of political censorship. His last play, performed in 1726, when he was sixty-six, was a comedy called *Money the Mistress*, in which, once more, noble gestures are made in the midst of prevalent chicanery. The setting is the English garrison at Tangier. Mariana is in love with Mourville, a French lieutenant-colonel who has been captured by the Moors. Davila, her father, who wants her to marry the English Colonel Warcourt, is quite content to leave Mourville unransomed and thus safely out of the way, but Mariana, aided by her high-spirited cousin Harriet, works out a scheme for rescuing him. The girls disguise themselves and pay Davila to lead them into the enemy camp. An initial clue to Harriet's character is furnished by her taking along, over Mariana's protest, a gift of jewels generously sent by Warcourt despite his knowledge that Mariana is not interested in him;

Harriet is not only high-spirited but shrewd. The Moorish guard allows Mariana to take Mourville's place, since no one seems interested in ransoming him and it appears that someone is likely to pay well for Mariana's release. Mourville's initial response to Mariana's unexpected appearance is suitably romantic: 'My *Mariana*! O Astonishment!' he says, and in a moment, 'Thou art all Wonder' (II. 3; p. 19).[17] When Harriet tells him about War-court's gift he worries about the seductiveness of money, but at this point one is free to suppose that he is thinking only of the danger that Mariana might be won away from him. Soon it becomes clear that he is much more vulnerable than she. He agrees, after some hesitation, to leave Mariana with the Moors and go with Harriet to seek ransom. It is Warcourt who ransoms her, however, because her father has reason to think his fortune has been lost at sea. Harriet, who turns out to be not only shrewd but utterly unprincipled, pawns Mariana's jewels and persuades Mour-ville to marry her.

The ending of the play is much less bleak than this sequence of events might suggest. When the pawning of the jewels comes to light Mariana, ignorant of the marriage, tries to protect Mourville by saying she is his wife and gave him the jewels. She swoons when Harriet reveals the truth, but this does not prevent Harriet from justifying what she and Mourville have done on the basis of love—and financial prudence. Somewhat softening the effect of her selfishness and materialism, two other characters make gestures almost as noble as Mariana's. Warcourt, always magnanimous, again offers himself to Mariana, and her father forgives her for running away. Though the play concludes with a somewhat jarring assertion of the sin of disobedience to a father, the net effect of the denouement is obviously more than an emotional reinforcement of this moral. Mariana's brutal disillusionment, followed by the comfort of her father's decency and Warcourt's marvellous generosity, is somewhat analogous to the rapid succession of responses expected of the spectator. Harriet's perfidy is already known to us, but her callous justification of it is still shocking. Then, since Southerne punishes the two betrayers by a final turn of the plot which impoverishes Harriet and restores Davila's wealth, we are allowed some harsh pleasure at the discomfiture of

[17] All quotations from *Money the Mistress*, too late to be included in the 1721 *Works*, are taken from the 1726 edition.

the wicked. But alongside this sentiment, I would suggest, must be a delight that includes admiration for Mariana, Warcourt, and Davila. As Mariana is too overcome by conflicting feelings to make any immediate answer to Warcourt, asking for time to forget her misdeeds, so we may be aware of several different responses to the situation, no one of which absolutely prevails.

I hope it is quite clear that I do not claim for Southerne any monopoly on admiration in comedy during this transitional period. I have already mentioned Vanbrugh, and both Cibber and Steele immediately come to mind also. A glance at two of their plays will suffice for illustration and for certain distinctions. The last act of Steele's *The Lying Lover* of 1703 is full of admirable behaviour. One character attempts to take the blame for a supposed murder in order to save his friend, who naturally finds this conduct admirable, while the victim, not dead after all, is lost in admiration of such noble friends. The epilogue asserts that the author soared above the mere effort to excite mirth,

> And chose with pity to chastise delight.
> For laughter's a distorted passion, born
> Of sudden self-esteem and sudden scorn;
> Which, when 'tis o'er, the men in pleasure wise,
> Both him that moved it and themselves despise;
> While generous pity of a painted woe
> Makes us ourselves both more approve and know.[18]

Here admiration is firmly linked to the appeal to pity and tears. My second instance is from Cibber's *The Careless Husband* of 1704, where admiration is enlisted to serve the comedy's moral intentions. The famous 'steinkirk scene' leads to a meeting between Sir Charles Easy and Lady Easy, in which Sir Charles, who has been altogether too easy, recognizes his wife's 'generously tender' treatment of him and confesses that her 'wondrous conduct' has touched his conscience. His reformation is greeted by her ecstatic plea: 'Oh my dear! Distract me not with this excess of goodness' (v. vi. 109–10).[19] Thinking of Dryden's Dorax, saying to Don Sebastian, 'O stop this headlong Torrent of your goodness', one might be tempted to say that heroic drama, good old soldier that it was, never died; it just faded away into sentimental comedy. Of

---

[18] *Richard Steele*, ed. G. A. Aitken, Mermaid Series (London, 1894), p. 187.
[19] *The Careless Husband*, ed. Wm. W. Appleton (Lincoln, Neb., 1966), p. 103.

course this would be a gross simplification, but also a partial truth. What Southerne's plays show is that admiration very similar to that called for in heroic drama came to be invoked even in comedy which was not notably sentimental—neither extraordinarily tearful nor mainly didactic. My suggestion is that it was natural for a kind of comedy that had its roots in romantic sensibility, and had been progressively elevated in order to appeal to cultivated spectators, to borrow certain effects from heroic drama, which had a common origin and had appealed to the same sort of people. Moral reformation, however important, was not solely, and perhaps not mainly, responsible for this particular effect. Nor do I think the continual rising of the middle classes had much to do with it. Although the audiences may have been more middle-class, the important fact was that they had cultivated sensibilities which were once thought to be aristocratic. They could admire admirably.

Pope's Copy of Chaucer

Maynard Mack

I

LIKE HIS creed, Pope's taste in English poetry was catholic. From his early twenties, and perhaps earlier, he had the portraits of 'Dryden, Milton, Shakespear, &c.' in his chamber—'round about me, that the constant remembrance of 'em may keep me always humble.'[1] We have no way of knowing whether '&c.' included at this time a Chaucer; but eventually, in the Twickenham villa, there would be 'a Chausor in a black frame', perhaps one and the same with the 'grave old Chaucer . . . from Occleve' that Spence was shown among drawings dating from Pope's study-days with Jervas in 1713.[2] There can be no doubt, at any rate, that from his earliest years he thought of Chaucer as one of the exemplars to whom an aspiring English poet must put himself to school. His *January and May*, a free translation of *The Merchant's Tale*, was published in 1709 in company with his earliest work, *The Pastorals*; his version of *The Wife of Bath's Prologue*, apparently written at about the same period, appeared only five years later in 1714; his *Temple of Fame*, adapted from the third book of *The Hous of Fame*, followed speedily in 1715; and there is a surviving brief verse anecdote in Chaucer's manner that, though not published till 1727, clearly dates from his youthful efforts to learn to write by imitating various poetic styles.[3] 'I read Chaucer still', he told Spence in 1730, at the start of his own most creative decade, 'with as much pleasure as almost any of our poets. He is a master of

---

[1] *Correspondence of Alexander Pope*, ed. George Sherburn, 5 vols. (Oxford, 1956), i. 120. Referred to hereafter as *Correspondence*.

[2] *Observations, Anecdotes, and Characters of Books and Men*, ed. J. M. Osborn, 2 vols. (Oxford, 1966), No. 108. Hereafter designated 'Spence'. For the 'Chausor' at Twickenham, see the inventory taken of Pope's goods at his death, reprinted in *The Garden and the City: Retirement and Politics in the Later Poetry of Pope, 1731–1743* (Toronto, 1969), p. 255.

[3] See *The Twickenham Edition of the Poems of Alexander Pope* (hereafter, *TE*), vi. 41–2.

manners and of description, and the first tale-teller in the true enlivened natural way.'[4]

Pope's admiration for Chaucer being what it was, it may be counted a piece of good fortune that his copy of Chaucer's works survives. This is the black-letter folio edited by Speght and printed in London by Adam Islip in 1598. It was presented to Pope in 1701, when he was thirteen, by a Gabriel Young of whom we know nothing further. On the title is written, presumably in Young's hand, 'Gab. Young his booke', and on the flyleaf, in Pope's printing hand: 'Ex Libris/ALEXANDRI POPEI;/Ac è Dono/GABRIELIS YOUNG 1701'.[5] The date of gift accords well with what we know from other sources about Pope's early reading. When he had done with his more or less formal education at the hands of family priests and in two or three small Roman Catholic schools (all which seems to have been behind him by the time he was 12 or 13), he applied himself to reading and 'in a few years . . . had dipped into a great number of the English, French, Italian, Latin, and Greek poets'; 'I followed everywhere as my fancy led me, and was like a boy gathering flowers in the woods and fields just as they fall in his way. I still look upon these five or six years as the happiest part of my life.'[6] It must have been during this time, just beginning when Young made his gift, that Pope first read Chaucer.

II

Pope does not mark his books either extensively or consistently. Many that we know he read bear no scriptural signs of it. When he does make a marginalium, it is likeliest to be an inverted single comma, less frequently inverted double commas, occasionally a cross. Scarce indeed is the verbal marginalium, and when one occurs it is almost invariably editorial rather than critical or appreciative in intent. The only verbal marginalium in his Chaucer, for instance, that serves other than an indexing function relates ll. 1975–80 of *The Knight's Tale*, describing the bleak situation of Mars' temple, to the similar passage in Statius'

---

[4] Spence, No. 411.

[5] For an account of the books still surviving from Pope's library, with their inscriptions and present locations, see 'Pope's Books: A Biographical Survey, with a Finding List', in *English Literature in the Age of Disguise*, ed. M. E. Novak (Los Angeles, 1977), pp. 209–305. Pope's Chaucer is at Hartlebury.

[6] Spence, Nos. 14–15, 21, 24.

Thebais (7.34 ff.)—'Vide desert. Do-/mus Martis in/Statio. Th. 7.'
—that modern editors of Chaucer also cite.[7]

Verbal marginalia of the indexing kind appear most often in the translation of the *Romaunt of the Rose*. Here, in the neat carefully formed script of his early years, he catalogues in the margins for easy reference the season, places, and persons of the poem. 'Description/of May', he writes at ll. 52 ff., beside an encomium of springtime that he will recall in beginning his own *Temple of Fame*, as he will also recall the spring-dream convention; and with the next entry begins his marginal catalogue in earnest: 'The Garden /inclos'd wth/a Wall, ad-/ornd with/Figures on/the outside.'

Successively from this point on, he identifies in the margin: 'The Picture/of/I. Hate' (ll. 147 ff.), 'Villany' (ll. 166 ff.)—for some reason, he passes over Chaucer's Felonye at 162 ff.—'II./Covet-uosness' (*sic*) (ll. 181 ff.), 'III./Envy' (ll. 247 ff.), 'IV./Sorrow' (ll. 301 ff.), 'V./Old Age' (ll. 349 ff.), 'VI./Hypocrisy' (ll. 413 ff.), and 'VII./Poverty' (ll. 449 ff.). In the second line of the portrait of Poverty, he has underscored, with a sensitivity to the condition of the poor that he will retain all his life, Chaucer's poignant last two words:[8]

> And alderlast of everichone
> Was painted Povert al alone. (449–50)

Commas also signal the portrait's later lines:

> And she was put, that I of talke,
> Ferre fro these other, up in an halke[.]
> There lurked and there coured she[,]
> For poore thing where so it be
> Is shamefast, and dispised aie[.] (463–7)

Having inspected the portraits on the outward walls, the Lover

[7] Pope was probably unaware of the more direct source in Boccaccio's *Teseide*. He mentions Boccaccio only once (in the defense of allegory prefixed to his *Temple of Fame*) and then in a way that suggests no familiarity.

[8] Quotations in this essay are from Pope's 1598 text with its spelling preserved. Line-numbers, lacking in 1598, are supplied from *The Poems of Chaucer*, ed. F. N. Robinson (Cambridge: Houghton, Mifflin, 1933), except in the case of *The Plowman's Tale*, where they have been supplied from the text in Skeat's *Supplement: Chaucerian and Other Pieces* (Oxford, 1897). Punctuation (in square brackets) is also supplied from these texts, 1598 having very little. When a 1598 reading differs conspicuously from a modern one, the modern reading is supplied (in square brackets) immediately following the 1598 reading. Sentences or verses required to make passages singled out by Pope's marginal commas intelligible are similarly supplied (in square brackets), as are occasional glosses of difficult words, the latter being distinguished by 'i.e.' Except when otherwise noted, the marginal commas in Pope's Chaucer are single commas.

next approaches the gate and its guardian in a passage that Pope characterizes with the words: 'The Entrance/of the Garden,/& the Portress/Idleness describ'd.' The description of Idleness evidently captured his imagination, for he has bordered it with commas:

> Her heere was as yelow of hew
> As any basen scoured new[;]
> Her flesh tender as is a chike[,]
> With bent browes, smoth and slike[;]
> And by measure large were
> The opening of her iyen clere[,]
> Her nose of good proporcion[,]
> Her iyen gray, as is a faucon[,]
> With swete breath, and well favoured [savoured] [,]
> Her face white, and well coloured[,]
> With little mouth and round to se[;]
> A clove chinne eke had she[.]
> Her necke was of good fassion
> In length and greatnesse[,] by reason[,]
> Without bleine, scabbe, or roine[;]
> Fro Hierusalem unto Burgoine
> There nis a fairer necke, iwis[,]
> To fele how smoth and soft it is[;]
> Her throte also white of hew
> As snow on braunch snowed new[.]
> Of body full well wrought was she. . . .   (539–59)

Similarly arresting seems to have been the account of Idleness's life-style, also set apart with commas—though whether from the viewpoint of a ripening moralist or with such a touch of envy as a boy growing up in a devout household in rural Berkshire might feel, we shall never know:

> She had a lusty life in May[:]
> She had no thought, by night ne day[,]
> Of nothing, but if it were onely
> To graieth her well and uncouthly.   (581–4)

III

The Lover now enters the garden, and the sights met with are marginally catalogued in the same manner as the murals. First, 'The Garden/itself' (ll. 645 ff.), then 'Mirth, and/His Retinue' (ll. 729 ff.), then 'Gladness' (ll. 743 ff.), then 'Curtesie' (ll. 795 ff.), and finally, now seen closer up, 'Mirth describ'd' (ll. 817 ff.). Gladness, dancing with Mirth, is in fact described so irresistibly that she too attracts Pope's commas:

> She semed like a rose newe
> Of colours [colour], and her flesh so tender
> That with a brere small and tender [slendre]
> Men might it cleve. . . .   (856-9)

At this point, several new figures appear. One is 'The God/of Love' (ll. 877 ff.), accompanied by Swete-Loking who holds two bows and ten arrows. Pope ignores Swete-Loking altogether, but takes full account of his weaponry: 'The Bows/of Love' (ll. 923 ff.), 'The 5 gol-/den Arrows' (ll. 949 ff.), 'The 5 other/Arrows' (ll. 971 ff.). Other figures that he identifies marginally include 'Beauty' (ll. 1003 ff.), 'Richesse' (ll. 1033 ff.), and 'Bounty' (ll. 1149 ff.)—Chaucer's Largesse. Fraunchise (ll. 1211 ff.), for no clear reason, he passes over, like Felonye and Swete-Loking earlier, but is so taken in the immediately ensuing lines with the conduct of Youthe and her partner that only a border of commas can do it justice:

> Her lemman was beside alway
> In such a gise that he her kiste
> At all times that him liste[,]
> That all the daunce might it see[.]
> They make no force of previtie[;]
> For who so spake of hem ivel or wele[,]
> They were ashamed never a dele[,]
> But men might sene hem kisse there
> As it two yong doves were.   (1290-8)

Delicious lines! from which in the dear dead days before the Pill young men and maidens wove their dreams.

IV

Through the next several pages—taking us from the de Lorris to the de Meun fragment—Pope pursues his marginal cataloguing with such thoroughness that it amounts to a synopsis: 'The Garden/describ'd' (ll. 1349 ff.), 'The Well/of/Narcissus' (ll. 1455 ff.), 'The Roser' (ll. 1649 ff.), 'The Au-/thor shot/with the/5 Arrows' (ll. 1715 ff.), 'The Precepts/of Love' (ll. 2175 ff.), 'Here begins/the descrip-/tion of a/Man in/Love, &/continues/to page/

128' (ll. 2361 ff.), 'The Pains/of Love' (ll. 2537 ff.), 'Comforts/of/ Love' (ll. 2691 ff.), 'Reason/describd' (ll. 3193 ff.), 'The Speech/of Reason/persuad-/ing ag^{st}/Love' (ll. 3217 ff.), 'He rejects/her advice,/and consults/a Friend' (ll. 3305 ff.), 'Endeavours/to prevail on/Danger in/vain' (ll. 3395 ff.), 'Pity and/Bounty/overcome/ Danger' (ll. 3499 ff.), 'Fair Welcome/introduces/him to the/ Roser' (ll. 3609 ff.), 'Venus pro-/cures him/a Kisse' (ll. 3573 ff.), 'Scandal pro-/vokes Jea-/lousy ag^{st}/him' (ll. 3799 ff.), 'Shame/ would/quiet/Jealousy' (ll. 3861 ff.).

Here, quite abruptly, the marginal indexing stops, though we are still nearly 4,000 lines from the end of the translation. Fortunately, some comma-ed passages before this point and several after, the last within 250 lines of the close, assure us that Pope is still paying attention to the poem and not simply to its plot. The passages that elicit his commas before this point have to do, in the first instance, with the contrary symptoms undergone by the Lover when he is wounded by the God of Love's arrows:

> Both great anoie, and eke swetnesse
> And ioye meint with bitternesse[.]
> Now were they easie, now were they wood[;]
> In hem I felt both harme and good[;]
> Now sore without allegement[,]
> Now softing with oyntment[;]
> It softened here, and pricked there[:]
> Thus ease and anger togither were.   (1919–26)

In the second instance, it is the notion that false lovers grow fat— like clerics—that attracts his marginal notations:

> It is no wonder though they be fat[;]
> With false othes her loves they gat[.]
> For oft I se such losengeours
> Fatter than Abbots or Priours.   (2691–4)

In the third case, the centre of his interest appears to be in the attributes of Reason as allegorically represented:

> But she was neither young ne hore[,]
> Ne high ne low, ne fatte ne lene[,]
> But best, as it were in a meane[.]   (3196–8)

The rest of the comma-ed lines—those that come after the marginal catalogue ends—are all touched in some degree by de Meun's satiric view of ecclesiastics, a view to which the young

Pope already seems responsive. The first passage concerns lechery:

> Shame, shame (said Jelousy)
> To be bitrashed great drede have I[.]
> Lechery hath clombe so hie
> That almost blered is mine eie[;]
> No wonder is, if that drede have I[.]
> Over all reigneth Lechery[,]
> Whose might groweth night and dey[.]
> Both in Cloistre and in Abbey
> Chastite is werried over all[.]   (3909–17)

The remaining three passages deal with hypocrisy. Dame Abstinence-Streyned and Fals-Semblant decide to visit Wicked-Tonge in disguise:

> As it were in a pilgrimage
> Like good and holie folke unfeined.

Abstinence-Streyned conspicuously displays her psalter and beads, which, as the poet lets us know, as much reveal what she is as hide it:

> For they were given her, I wote weale[,]
> God wote[,] of a full holie Frere
> That saied he was her father dere. . . .
> And with so great devocion
> They made her confession
> That they had oft for the nones
> Two heddes in one hode at ones. (7362–3, 7373–6, 7383–6)

Fals-Semblant also disguises himself, and off they go:

> And forthe she walked soberlie[;]
> And false Semblant saint [i.e. cinctured][,] ie vous die,
> And [Had][,] as it were for such mustere[,]
> Doen on the cope of a Frere
> With chere simple, and full pitous[:]
> His loking was not disdeinous
> Ne proude, but meke and full pesible[.]
>   About his necke he bare a Bible. . . .   (7405–12)

So apparelled, they deceive even Wicked-Tongue. And they would deceive you too, the poet suddenly exclaims, addressing his readers and using the transformation of Fals-Semblant (from a

'Jolie Robin' into 'a Jacobin') to launch an ironic challenge to the
religious orders as a whole:

> But sothly what so men him call[,]
> Frere Preachours been good men all[;]
> Her order wickedly they bearen[,]
> Such Minstrelles, if they wearen.
> So been Augustines, and Cordilers
> And Carmes, and eke sacked Freres[,]
> And all Freres shode and bare[,]
> Though some of hem been great and square. . . .

As Antony was to say on a somewhat more emergent occasion, So
are they all, all honourable men! And is there not some residue of
this vision of multiplicity and masquerade, and more especially of
the last line but one, in the panorama pointed out by Settle to
Theobald in the *Dunciad*?

> Men bearded, bald, cowl'd, uncowl'd, shod, unshod,
> Peel'd, patch'd, and pyebald, linsey-woolsey brothers,
> Grave mummers![9]

V

Chaucer's translation of Boethius draws Pope's commas more
selectively. That he knew the original early seems evident from
his youthful translation of Metrum 9 of the third book, which is
obviously related more closely to the Latin than to Chaucer.[10] In
the *Essay on Man* too, and occasionally in other contexts like the
treatment of riches in Bathurst, there are passages that unquestionably have their long roots in the *Consolation*, whatever their
immediate inspirations may be. The only part of the work that
attracts Pope's commas in Chaucer's version, however, is the last
third of Book III. There Philosophy sets out to show Boethius
that temporal goods are only fragments of a One that sustains all
things and is their goal. The stages in the argument that bring
forth Pope's commas[11] are these:

I have shewed thee (qd she) that the things that ben required of [i.e.
are sought by] many folke, ne been not very goods ne perfite. For they
ben divers, that one from that other. And so as eche of hem is lacking
to other, they ne have no power to bring a good, that is full and absolute.

---

[9] *Dunciad* (1729), iii. 106–8.   [10] *TE* vi. 73–4.
[11] In the Boethius translation, always double commas.

But then at erst been they very good, when they been gathered togider all into one forme, and into one werking: so that thilk thing that is suffisant, thilke same is power, and reverence, noblesse, and mirth. (Prosa 11, ll. 18–30)

The thynges then (qd. she) that ne been no goods, when they been divers, and whan they beginnen to be all one thyng, then been they goods, ne commeth it not then, by the getting of unity, that they bee maked goods? (Ibid., ll. 37–43)

Then must thou graunten (qd. she) by semblable reason, that one and good be one same thyng. (Ibid., ll. 50–1)

And who so would renne in the same manner by all thyngs, he should seen that without doubt, every thyng is in his substaunce, as long as it is one. And when it forleteth to be one, it dieth and perisheth. (Ibid., ll. 79–83)

Nowe looke upon the Herbes and Trees [Boethius has asked whether, being soulless, they can be credited with the same 'appetite to dwellen, and to duren' as animals and human beings] for they weren firste in such places, as ben convenable to hem: in whiche places they mowe not dien ne drien, as longe as her nature may defende hem. For some of hem wexen in fieldes, and some wexen in Mountaignes, and other wexe in Mareis. . . . For nature yeveth to every thinge, that is convenient to him, and travaileth that they ne dye, as long as they have power, to dwellen and to liven. (Ibid., ll. 109–16, 120–4)

[This concern may be seen in seed too, providing 'a fondement, and edifice'] for to duren not onely for a tyme, but right as for to dure perdurably by generacion. [And the thinges eke, that men wenen ne have no soules, ne desire they not[,] by semblable reason, to kepen that is his, that is to sain, that is according to her nature, in conservacion of her being and enduring?] For wherefore els beareth lightnes the flambes up, and the weight presseth the earth adoune, but for as much as thilke places, & thilke movings be convenable to everich of hem. [Ne I treat not now here, of wilful movings of the soule that is knowing, but of naturell entencion of things, as thus:] right as we swallowen the meate that we receiven, and ne thinke not on it, and as we draw our breath in sleping, that we wete not while we slepen. (Ibid., ll. 143–4, 150–5, 173–7)

Phil. But (qd she) thilke thing that desireth to be & dwell perdurably, hee desireth to ben one. . . . All things then (qd she) requiren good, and thilke maist thou discriven thus: good is thilke thing, that every wight desireth. (Ibid., ll. 213–15, 227–30)

And for as much as we have gathered and comprehended, that good is thilke thing, that is desired of al, then mote we nedes confesse, that good is the fine of all things. (Ibid., ll. 252-6)

And if so it be that the Muse and the doctrine of Plato singeth sothe, all that every wight learneth, he ne doeth nothing else then, but recordeth, as menne recorden thinges that ben foryeten. (Metrum 11, ll. 46-51)

[Then saied I thus. I accord me greatly to Plato, for thou recordest and remembrest me these things, yet the second time,] that is to say, first when I lost my memorie, by the contrarious coniunccion of the bodie with the soule [and eftsones . . . by the burden of my sorowe. . . .] (Prosa, 12, ll. 4-6)

Thou ne wendest not (qd she) a little here before, that men should doubt, that this worlde is governed by God. (Ibid., ll. 23-5)

Have I not nombred and saied (qd she) that suffisaunce is in blisfulnesse. And we have accorded, that God is thilke same blisfulnesse. (Ibid., ll. 58-61)

[Philosophie. Wenest thou (qd she) that God ne be almightie? Boecius. No man is in doubt of it certes (qd I). Philosophie. No wight ne doubteth it, if he be in his minde (qd she.)] But he that is almightie, there nis nothing that he ne may? Boecius. That is sooth (qd I). Philosophie. May God do evil (qd she)? Boe. Nay forsoth (qd I). Phi. Than is evill nothing (qd she) sith that he may done none evil that may done al things. (Ibid., ll. 159-67)

[Boethius then sums up what Philosophy has taught him and in the summary speaks a sentiment to which Pope gives commas] . . . when thou began at blisfulnesse [in Book II], thou saiedst that it is a soveraine good, and that God is the blisfulnesse. . . . (Ibid., ll. 179-81)

VI

Pope's assignment of commas among the original poems seems exceptionally random and, considering that he imitated and translated some of them, rather disappointing. One passage is singled out in *The Parliament* (in Pope's text, *Assemblie*) *of Fowls*. This is the familiar quatrain:

> For out of the olde feldes, as men saieth[,]
> Cometh all this new corne, fro yere to yere[,]
> And out of old bookes, in good faieth[,]
> Cometh all this newe science, that men lere[.]   (ll. 21-5)

In the third book of *The Hous of Fame*, on which his own *Temple* is based, the magnifying powers of the wall of beryl draw double commas:

> That shone lighter then a glas[,]
> And made wel more then it was
> As kinde thing of fame is;[12]   (ll. 1289–92)

and the wry third line in the description of the fourth company of suppliants—those who have lived virtuously but seek no credit for it—draws a single comma: 'But certaine they were wonder fewe'. That is the sum total of his markings.[13]

More interesting, though also limited in number, are the passages signalled by commas in the *Canterbury Tales*. *The Merchant's Tale* lacks markings of any kind, despite the care with which Pope must have read it for his *January and May*, and *The Wife of Bath's Prologue* has only an indexing 'Jenkin' inserted at l. 509 to identify the Wife's fifth husband. The Miller's retort to the Reeve, on the other hand, during the interchange following *The Knight's Tale*, receives commas for its first two lines:

> And saied, leve brother Oswolde[,]
> Who hath no wife is no cockolde[.]   (ll. 3151–2)

and for its practical-minded conclusion:

> An husband should not been inquisitife
> Of Goddes privete; ne of his wife[,]
> For so he find Goddes foison there,
> Of the remnaunt nedeth not to enquere.   (ll. 3163–6)

Of the two passages in *The Reeve's Tale* similarly distinguished, one satirizes the parson's intent to marry his granddaughter (daughter to Miller Simken, the tale's hero and butt) with a dowry got from church gains:

> For holy churches good mote ben dispended
> On holy churches blode[,] that is discended[;]   (ll. 3982–3)

the other shows Simken taking advantage of the manciple's illness to steal meal and corn more boldy than before:

> For that before, he stale but curteisly[,]
> But now he was a theef outrageously.   (ll. 3997–8)

[12] Pope's text lacks line 1291, which considerably clarifies the meaning: 'To semen every thing, ywis'.

[13] With the exception of the numeral 100 prefixed to line 1340 and the numeral 300 prefixed to line 1762, for reasons not clear to me.

In *The Squire's Tale*, Pope's commas again appear twice. In both cases, they seem intended to signal observations of psychological interest, the kind of thing that Pope must have had in mind in stressing Chaucer's mastery of 'manners'. The first notes the response of ignorance to whatever is unfamiliar or complex:

> As leude people demen comenly
> Of things that ben made more subtelly
> Than they can in her leudnesse comprehende[,]
> They demen gladly to the badder ende[.]   (ll. 221–4)

The second, in lines often quoted, dwells on human nature's love of freedom and change:

> Men loven of kinde newfanglenesse[,]
> As briddes don, that man in cages fede[.]
> For thogh thou night & day take of hem hede[,]
> And strawe her cage faire and soft as silke[,]
> And give hem sugre, hony, breed and milke[,]
> Yet right anon as his dore is up[,]
> He with his fete wold sporne adoun his cup[,]
> And to the wood he wold, and wormes eate.   (ll. 610–18)

The only other genuine tale to elicit Pope's commas is the Franklin's. The beautiful lines on Winter—

> Phebus waxed old, and hewed ylike Laton[,]
> That afore in his hote declinacion
> Shone as yᵉ brenning gold, with stremes bright[;]
> But now in Capricorne adoun he light[,]
> Where as he shone full pale, I dare well sain[.]
> The bitter frost, with the slidder rain[,]
> Destroyed hath the grene in every yerde[.]
> Janus sit by the fire with double berde
> And drinketh of his bugle horne the wine[;]
> Beforn him stont braune of the tusked swine[,]
> And nowell crieth every lustie man.   (ll. 1245–55)

receive both an indexing marginal 'Winter' and a border of commas. The other passages in the tale that receive Pope's attention are both from the Franklin's dimissal of 'maistrie' in relations of friendship and love:

> For one thing[,] sirs, safely dare I seine[,]
> That frends, everich other must obeine
> If thei wol long holden company[.]

Love will not be constrained by maistrie[.]
When maistrie cometh, the God of Love anon
Beateth his wings, and farewell[,] he is gon[!]
Love is a thing, as any spirit free[.]
Women of kind desiren liberte. . . .   (ll. 761–8)

[Pacience is an high vertue[,] certaine[,]
For it venquisheth, as these clerkes saine[,]]
Things that rigor shall never attaine:
For every word, men may not chide or plaine[.]
Lerneth to suffer, or els, so mote I gone[,]
Ye shall it lerne whether ye wol or none[;]
For in this world[,] certaine, no wight there is
That he ne doth or saith sometime a mis[.]
Ire, sicknes, or constellacion[,]
Wine, wo, or changing of complexion
Causeth full oft, to don a misse or speken. . . .   (ll. 773–83)

Three of these lines (764–6) are quoted (in a note attributed to Pope) in the 1751 edition of his works[14] as a gloss or source for Eloisa's exclamation (ll. 75–6):

Love, free as air, at sight of human ties
Spreads his light wings, and in a moment flies,

and the idea contained in them, enlarged to a political principle, reappears in the *Essay on Man*'s account of the growth of human communities in the Golden Age:

Converse and Love mankind might strongly draw,
When Love was Liberty, and Nature Law.[15]

As for the second passage, with its record of the trivial influences often affecting human conduct, this may have stood out for Pope even in his younger days, afflicted as he often was with headaches, fevers, chills, nausea, and other ailments. It seems also a fair anticipation, though doubtless not at all a source, of some of the caprices

[14] As quoted in 1751, the lines do not accord with either the Speght text (1598, 1687) or the Urry text (1721) and are probably therefore quoted from memory or adapted to make them more intelligible.

[15] Pope's meaning is considerably more pointed (and perhaps touched with a pragmatic wisdom akin to the Miller's) in a manuscript version of this couplet:

And half the Cause of Contest was remov'd,
When Beauty could be kind to all who lov'd.

and inconsistencies to be celebrated eventually in his *Epistle to Cobham*.

VII

The poem in the Chaucer volume that most of all calls out Pope's comma-form annotations is *The Plowman's Tale*. This is a poem of 1,380 lines in eight-line stanzas rhyming ababbcbc, attributed nowadays not to Chaucer but to the anonymous author of *Pierce the Plowman's Crede*, a book which was also in Pope's library and carried his annotations.[16] Both works have Wycliffite leanings, *The Plowman's Tale* taking the form of a quasi-debate between a 'Pellican', representing Wycliffite 'true Christianity', and a 'Griffon', representing the church hierarchy and religious orders. Pope's commas begin to appear toward the end of Part II, with these lines:

> Christ badde Peter kepe his shepe
> And with his sword forbade hem smite[;]
> Swerd is no tole with shepe to kepe
> But to shepherdes that shepe woll bite[.]
> Mcthinketh such sheperdes ben to wite
> Ayen her shepe with swerd that contend[;]
> They drive her shepe with great dispite.
> But all this God may well amend.

Pope also commas these lines in the immediately following stanza:

> A swerd no sheperd usen ought
> But he would slee, as a bochour.
> For who so were Peters successour
> Should bere his shepe till his backe bend[,]
> And shadow hem from every shoure[;]
> And all this God may well amend[.]   (ll. 573–80)

The only respect, says the poet, in which the officers of the church are truly the heirs of Peter is in following him where he *diverges* from the example of Christ—a sentiment that Pope again marks:

> They folow Peter forsoth in this[,]
> In all that Christ would Peter reprehend.   (ll. 609–10)

[16] I have not been able to see this book, though it was offered for sale a few years ago. Its eighteenth-century owner, Thomas Warton the younger, had it from Warburton, coheir to Pope's library, and noted on the flyleaf that it contained marginalia by Pope, including a brief prose summary of its argument, which is again a satire on the religious orders. For details, see the account of Pope's books cited above, no. 103.

At the end of the section, following a reminder that if the secular powers let the powers spiritual become powers temporal, they may be dispossessed by them, the last stanza closes: 'The king and lords now this amend' (l. 700). To this line, Pope allots double commas.

Much of the tale's third section is given to the unholy lives that the church's holy men lead. They are to be found

> At the wrestling, and at the wake[,]
> And chiefe chauntours at the nale[,] [i.e. in the alehouse]
> Market-beaters, and medling make[,]
> Hoppen and houten with heve and hale[;]
> At faire fresh, and at wine stale[;]
> Dine and drinke, and make debate:
> The seven Sacraments set a saile [at sale][,]
> How kepe such the kaies of heavcn gate? (ll. 869–76)

They are keen for 'tything' and 'offring' and fees, but pay small attention to duties:

> And twise on the daie he woll sing[;]
> Goddes priestes nere none such[!]
> He mote on hunting with dogge and biche[,]
> And blowen his horne, and crien hcy[!]
> And sorcerie usen as a Witche[;]
> Such kepen evill Peters key.   (ll. 887–92)

They encourage idolatry:

> Yet they mote have some stocke or stone
> Gailie painted, and proudly dight[,]
> To maken men leeven upon
> And saie that it is full of might[;]
> About such, men set up great light[;]
> Uther such stockes shull stand therby
> As darke as it were midnight,
> For it make no mastrie.   (ll. 893–900)

They pretend one thing but do another; for though one of them may tell his fellow that

> He goth to Masse anon right[,]
> And saieth he singeth out of sinne[!]
> His birde abideth him at his inne
> And dighteth his diner the meane while.   (ll. 975–8)

When the Griffin challenges the Pelican to censure monks and convents, the latter replies:

> Sainct Benet, that her order brought[,]
> Ne made hem never on soch manere[;]
> I trow it came never in his thought
> That they should use so great power.

> That a man should a Monke lord call[,]
> Ne serve on knees, as a king[.]
> He is as proud as Prince in pall[,]
> In meat, and drinke, and all thing[;]
> Some wearen miter and ring[,]
> With double Worsted well idight,
> With roiall meat and rich drinke[,]
> And rideth on a courser as a knight. (ll. 993–1004)

What makes it all worse, says the Pelican, is that they have rejected the poor, from whom most of them derive:

> And commenly such ben comon [comen]
> Of poore people, and of hem begete[,]
> That this perfection han inomen[;]
> Her fathers riden nat but on her fete
> And travailen sore for that they eat[,]
> In povert liveth[,] young and old[;]
> Her fathers suffreth drought and weat[,]
> Many hungry meales, thurst, and cold.

> And all this the Monkes han forsake
> For Christes love and sainct Benete[;]
> To pride and ease have hem take[;]
> This religion is evill beseat[.]
> Had they been out of religioun
> They must have hanged at the plow,
> Threshing and diking fro toune to toune
> With sory meat, and not halfe inow. (ll. 1029–44)

The single-line reprise which opens the following stanza—'Therefore they han this all forsake' (l. 1045)—draws double commas and concludes Pope's markings.

VIII

As I have sought to stress above, Pope's markings afford no very reliable guide to the extent of his reading of Chaucer. It is always possible, to be sure, that he made some of his Chaucerian translations from a copy now lost that, if recovered, would show additional signs of his interest. Much more probably, it seems to me, the annotations we find in his Speght were elicited from him during first or early readings, after which (for whatever reasons) he simply happened to make no more in that volume. Though the evidence from the extant books is spotty, one may fairly say that he seems more often impelled to annotate during his youth than later.

But all this is guesswork. So far as the surviving marginalia are concerned, it is not in what they tell us about the degree of the poet's acquaintance with his great predecessor that their value lies, but in their record of particular passages that at one moment or another struck him as notable. Without them one would not necessarily have guessed, I think, his patient interest in the apocryphal *Plowman's Tale*, in the *Consolation*, and in the entire translation of the *Romaunt*—this last possibly a further signal that the marginalia date from his younger days. Nor would one necessarily have anticipated, especially if the date is correctly presumed to be early, so warm and pervasive a response to censure of the religious orders, a circumstance that makes one doubly regret the absence of markings from the margins of the General Prologue.

As for the annotations as a whole, perhaps they serve us best if they help us remember how like our own—miscellaneous, many-faceted, almost mysterious—the attention of other readers is, including that of poets. The well-turned phrase, the striking image, the sentiment 'whose Truth convinc'd at Sight we find', the reminiscence of some scene or character met with before, the triggering of a prejudice, the figure of January sipping his wine by the fire (one wonders at which of his two faces), the ingratiating vision of a boy and girl kissing—'As it two yong doves were', the delectable incongruities of feeling to be savoured in

> For so he find Goddes foison there,
> Of the remnaunt nedeth not to enquere,

together with that window suddenly opened on more sobering considerations: 'Than is evill nothing (qd she) sith that he may done none evil that may done all things'—al these elements and many more enter into Pope's marginal record and by their very variousness and arbitrariness help us qualify our all too frequent conception of the man as a one-dimensional *arbiter elegantiarum* and manufacturer of smart couplets.

A Supplement to *The Portraits of Alexander Pope*

JOHN RIELY AND W. K. WIMSATT

INTRODUCTION

WILLIAM KURTZ WIMSATT'S *The Portraits of Alexander Pope* was published by the Yale University Press in 1965. Over the course of fifteen years spent intermittently gathering the material for the book, Professor Wimsatt brought to light more than two hundred portraits, which he arranged under 81 primary numbers, for as many distinct types. Inevitably, some authentic likenesses of Pope failed to appear for the occasion. But the book, once published, had the ultimately salutary effect of bringing a number of 'lost' or unrecorded portraits out of hiding. The purposes of this Supplement are those of the book: to serve as guide to the iconography of Pope and as biography of Pope, in so far as his portraiture can enlarge our understanding of the man and his work.

Although fresh information about some of the previously known portraits is presented here, the Supplement consists primarily of new entries describing portraits that were 'not in Wimsatt' or that were mentioned only in Appendix 2 as 'Unexplained Allusions to Pope Portraits'. A 'new' portrait, whether an original or a replica, is indicated by an asterisk in the heading of the entry. The present whereabouts of portraits that have changed hands since 1965 is given if known, but no attempt has been made to bring up to date the ownership of every item. The use of the book in conjunction with the Supplement is assumed throughout. The original format has been followed as closely as possible; the same short-titles for frequently cited sources are used, with the sole addition of '*Portraits*' to refer to the book itself.

The Supplement to the *Portraits* was begun as a collaboration about two years before the death of W. K. Wimsatt in December 1975. The files which he had accumulated up to that time were turned over to me for further investigation, and I agreed to undertake the actual writing of the Supplement. We later decided to offer it as a joint contribution to the Festschrift honouring James M. Osborn, 'the Lord Oxford among Pope collectors of the present age'. Before Professor Wimsatt's death, we were able to have several sessions together in which we discussed the material in hand. But he did not live to read any of the entries I have written, and he should not be held responsible for any errors of fact or judgement which they may contain. In completing the Supplement on my own, I have liked to imagine the pleasure he might have had in the discoveries and discriminations that came after his death.

J.C.R.

ACKNOWLEDGEMENTS

Our thanks must go first to the private owners and institutional custodians of the portraits we discuss and reproduce below. We deeply appreciate their kindness and friendly co-operation. We are also indebted to the many others who volunteered information or patiently answered our inquiries and requests for help. Whenever possible, their particular contributions are acknowledged under the relevant entry in the Supplement.

We offer further thanks to those who assisted us in other ways too various to detail: Marcia Allentuck, Mary Bennett, Beverly Carter, Malcolm Cormack, James Dickie, James David Draper, Ellen S. Dunlap, Joan M. Friedman, Theodore Hofmann, Richard Jeffree, Herman W. Liebert, Michael McCarthy, Hamish Miles, Richard Ormond, Jules David Prown, Alvaro Ribeiro, Basil Skinner, and Robert R. Wark. The London offices of Sotheby's and Christie's cheerfully dealt with our queries concerning auction sales conducted by them. Dealers and their associates in 'the trade' have similarly facilitated our research.

Sir Ellis Waterhouse and David Piper provided expert counsel and information from their unrivalled knowledge of English painters and portraiture. In addition to reading the manuscript, John Kerslake, Maynard Mack, and Margaret Wimsatt have supported our undertaking with their learning and encouragement.

A generous grant from the Paul Mellon Centre for Studies in British Art (London) Limited has made it possible for us to include the illustrations.

CHARLES JERVAS (*c.* 1675–1739)

3.2a. CRAYON (CHALK) DRAWING ON BUFF PAPER, POSSIBLY BY CHARLES JERVAS. HENRY E. HUNTINGTON LIBRARY AND ART GALLERY, SAN MARINO, CALIFORNIA.*

In 1967 the Huntington Library acquired an anonymous drawing, 8½×6½ inches, inscribed in pencil on an old mount (probably in an eighteenth-century hand) 'Alex. Pope Poet.' The drawing is executed in black chalk heightened with white, with touches of pen and wash on the head. It previously belonged to Bruce Bradford and, before him, to Dr. Max A. Goldstein. Pope's likeness, particularly as recorded in various drawings by Jonathan Richardson, is sufficiently evident in this rather freely sketched portrait to warrant the inscription. The pose of the figure, as well as the dress, most closely resembles that of Jervas's full-length (no. 3.2) among the finished portraits of Pope, although there are notable differences. It seems possible that this is a preliminary sketch by Jervas for the painting, but authenticated drawings by Jervas are not available for comparison. There are also similarities to the three-quarter-length portrait by Richardson at Hagley Hall (no. 9.1). A good discussion of the evidence is contained in Robert R. Wark, *Early British Drawings in the Huntington Collection 1600–1750* (San Marino, 1969), page 25; the drawing is reproduced (for the first time) on page [100].

3.3. LINE ENGRAVING, BY J. H. ROBINSON, AFTER CHARLES JERVAS, 1819.

The original copperplate for the engraving having the Portuguese letters was acquired in May 1972 from Suckling & Co., London, by Professor Rosemary E. Cowler, of Lake Forest College, Lake Forest, Illinois. The over-all size of the plate is 12×9 inches; the frame around the picture of Pope measures 6$\frac{13}{16}$×4$\frac{15}{16}$ inches. On the back of the plate is engraved 'G. Harris/31 Shoe Lane/ London.'

3.3a. AQUATINT ENGRAVING, BY ROBERT HAVELL, JUNIOR,
AFTER CHARLES JERVAS, c. 1825.*

Robert Havell, Junior (1793–1878), known chiefly as the engraver of Audubon's *The Birds of America* published between 1827 and 1838, was responsible for *The Naturorama; or, Nature's Endless Transposition of Views on the Thames . . . London: Published by Havell and Co. 79, Newman Street, Oxford Street; L. Lorant, 24, Hart Street, Bloomsbury; and sold by all Booksellers. Price £1. 4s.* It consists of eighteen coloured aquatints of views on the Thames from Richmond to Oxford ('The Drawings taken from nature, By R. Havell, Jun.'), with 'a moveable Scene of Pope in his grotto, By which is added a rich fore-ground of mechanical perspective'. The 'moveable Scene' is a cut-out aquatint, $7\frac{13}{16} \times 5\frac{1}{2}$ inches, depicting Pope seated in an armchair at the riverside entrance to his grotto at Twickenham; it is intended to fit over any of the eighteen views, in the manner of a frame, so that Pope is always in the foreground. (View no. 11 is identified as Pope's villa, but actually represents Lady Howe's house, which replaced the villa pulled down by her in 1807.) This is *BMEP* 7. The portrait of Pope is loosely derived from Jervas's seated full-length painting (nos. 3.1 and 3.2).

Robert Havell, Jr., was in business with his father at 79 Newman Street, Oxford Street, for several years after 1823.[1] The *Naturorama* was probably published before 1827, when the younger Havell began to be employed by Audubon on *The Birds of America*.

A copy of the *Naturorama* in the Paul Mellon Collection, Yale Center for British Art, has the eighteen views, along with the framing device, contained in a solander box of contemporary design ('NATURORAMA' on the spine); a coloured aquatint having a unique view of the Thames framed by Pope in his grotto is mounted on the front of the box. This aquatint is reproduced in George Paston [Emily Morse Symonds], *Mr. Pope, His Life and Times* (London, 1909), 2, facing page 544.[2]

---

[1] William B. Todd, *A Directory of Printers and Others in Allied Trades, London and Vicinity, 1800–1840* (London, 1972), p. 93. See also George Alfred Williams, 'Robert Havell, Junior, Engraver of Audubon's "The Birds of America" ', *Print-Collector's Quarterly*, 6 (1916), 227, 230–6, 242.

[2] We are indebted to Dr. James Dickie, who saw another copy of the *Naturorama* exhibited at the Fitzwilliam Museum, Cambridge, in February 1969, and kindly brought it to our attention.

SIR GODFREY KNELLER (1646–1723)

5.1a. OIL PAINTING, BY OR AFTER SIR GODFREY KNELLER.
SIR GILBERT INGLEFIELD, LONDON.*

Sir Gilbert Inglefield has in his possession a portrait of the 1716 Kneller type which closely resembles the signed and dated version owned by Lord Barnard, no. 5.1. On the back is a printed extract from a sale catalogue: '196 SIR G. KNELLER—a three-quarter life-size Portrait of Alexander Pope 35 ins. × 27 ins., in old carved frame.' A note in the hand of Sir Gilbert's mother reads, 'Bought at Allestree sale', and there is also an old label (perhaps late nineteenth-century), 'P & D Colnaghi & Comp^y/Print Warehouse/ 13 & 14 Pall Mall East.'[1] Sir Gilbert has kindly informed us that the sale at Allestree Hall, Derbyshire, the seat of the Johnson family, took place c. 1928–32; the portrait of Pope was presumably lot 196 in the sale.[2] He thinks that his mother acquired the painting because of a possible earlier connection with the Englefield (Inglefield) family.

Anthony Englefield (c. 1637–1712) was Pope's elderly Catholic neighbour at Whiteknights in Berkshire, about nine miles away from Binfield and near the village of Englefield. He was 'a lover of poetry and poets' who may have introduced the young Pope to literary men. Pope occasionally saw his friend John Caryll, who was related to the Englefields, at Whiteknights, and it was there that he became acquainted with Martha and Teresa Blount, the granddaughters of Anthony Englefield. His friend Henry Englefield (d. 1720) was their uncle.[3] It is reasonable to suppose that the Englefields might have had a Pope portrait of the 1716 type (either by Kneller himself or a good contemporary replica), but such a provenance for this painting remains uncertain.

[1] Mr. Patrick Matthiesen of Colnaghi's tells us that the firm was located in Pall Mall East between 1824 and 1911, but that their records of this period are presently inaccessible.
[2] Efforts to locate a copy of the sale catalogue have been unsuccessful. The sale was apparently held at Allestree.
[3] George Sherburn, *The Early Career of Alexander Pope* (Oxford, 1934), pp. 37, 48.

5.8. OIL PAINTING, BY OR AFTER SIR GODFREY KNELLER.

This portrait, which was previously traced to Bernard Halliday of
Leicester, and offered for sale in his catalogue no. 63, new series,
issued in July 1923, came to light in September 1965 at Sylvia
Tearston Antiques, then located at 1019 Third Avenue, New York
City. In 1969 the painting was sold to a private collector in New
York whose identity has not been disclosed.[1]

[1] This much information was gleaned from a conversation with Sylvia Tearston in September 1976.

6.2. OIL PAINTING, BY SIR GODFREY KNELLER, 1721. THE BARON
HOME, THE HIRSEL, COLDSTREAM, BERWICKSHIRE.

The portrait painter and copyist George Perfect Harding (d. 1853)
compiled a manuscript *List of Portraits, Pictures. In Various
Mansions, of the United Kingdom* over a period of years after 1804.
This painting is recorded in the *List* (vol. 2, page 29) as 'Alexander
Pope profile in a circle' among the pictures then in the Earl of
Home's possession at The Hirsel.[1]

The portrait was exhibited in the Kneller exhibition at the
National Portrait Gallery, November 1971–January 1972, and is
discussed and illustrated in the catalogue by J. Douglas Stewart,
Sir Godfrey Kneller (London, 1971), pages 9, 65 (no. 82). In his
discussion Professor Stewart suggests that the shape of the profile,
with its slightly parted lips and upturned head and eyes, may
derive from portraits of Alexander the Great, specifically the well-
known ancient 'medal' (i.e. coin) of the deified Alexander, in which
he is shown in profile to right, with the horns of Ammon.[2]

In *The Temple of Fame*, written perhaps two or three years
before the epistle *To Mr. Addison, Occasioned by his Dialogue on
Medals*, Pope offers this glimpse of Alexander:

> High on a Throne with Trophies charg'd, I view'd
> The *Youth* that all things but himself subdu'd;
> His Feet on Sceptres and *Tiara's* trod,
> And his horn'd Head bely'd the *Lybian* God.[3]

He glossed the passage in a note: 'Alexander *the Great: The* Tiara
was the Crown peculiar to the Asian *Princes: His Desire to be thought
the Son of* Jupiter Ammon *caus'd him to wear the Horns of that God,
and to represent the same upon his Coins, which was continu'd by*

several of his Successors.' Just about this time Pope received a letter from his friend John Caryll, in which Caryll, in a witty and flattering way, compared Pope to Alexander the Great. ''Tis certain', Pope wrote in his reply,

the greatest magnifying glasses in the world are a mans own eyes, when they look upon his own person; yet even in those, I appear not the great Alexander Mr Caryll is so civil to, but that little Alexander the women laugh at. But if I must be like Alexander, 'tis in being complimented into too good an opinion of my self: they made him think he was the son of Jupiter, and you persuade me I am a man of parts.[4]

Pope's consciousness of a connection between himself and Alexander the Great is not expressed openly until many years later in the *Epistle to Dr. Arbuthnot* (published in 1735)—

> I cough like *Horace*, and tho' lean, am short,
> *Ammon*'s great Son one shoulder had too high,[5]

—although his early awareness of a pun on the name Alexander may be taken for granted. It seems not unlikely that Pope may have asked Kneller to portray him in the manner of 'Alexander Ammon', a provocative imitation of the medal.[6]

[1] Harding's *List* is in the National Portrait Gallery. Mr. John Kerslake kindly brought this reference to our attention.

[2] The coin is a tetradrachma issued during the reign of Lysimachos (323–281 B.C.), King of Thrace. Two examples differing slightly from each other are documented and illustrated in Peter R. Franke and Max Hirmer, *Die Griechische Münze* (Munich: Hirmer Verlag, 1964), pp. 118–19 and pl. 176.

[3] *Twickenham* 2. 265–6 (ll. 151–4).

[4] Pope to Caryll, 25 January 1710/11 (*Correspondence 1.* 114; cf. ibid. 9).

[5] *Twickenham* 4. 104 (ll. 116–17).

[6] Professor Stewart has further suggested to us that the position of the profile—to the right in the medal of Alexander, to the left in Kneller's portrait of Pope—may be significant. The sequence follows the normal one for British sovereigns from one generation to the next. An example of the medal in the collection of Pope's friend Lord Winchilsea is mentioned in Nicola Francesco Haym, *The British Treasury; Being Cabinet the First of our Greek and Roman Antiquities of all Sorts* [*Del Tesoro Britannico*] (London, 1719–20), *1.* 81–2, *2.* 4–5. Pope might have seen Lord Winchilsea's medal or read the description of it in Haym's book.

6.4.   OIL PAINTING, ATTRIBUTED TO JONATHAN RICHARDSON, AFTER SIR GODFREY KNELLER. WALKER ART GALLERY, LIVERPOOL.

This portrait, which had been at Croxteth Hall, Liverpool, the seat of the Earls of Sefton, since at least 1863, remained there until the death *sine prole* of the seventh Earl in 1972. At the Croxteth Hall Sale, 17–20 September 1973, it was sold by Christie's, lot 1020, to the Walker Art Gallery.[1]

Pope, writing to John Caryll on 25 June 1711, says: 'I keep the pictures of Dryden, Milton, Shakespear, &c., in my chamber, round about me. . . . I wish I had Mr Caryll's there, that I might have something to make me proud, when I reflected on his friendship. The extreme goodness with which you accept the offer I too impudently made you of mine, can never be enough acknowledged.'[2] Pope here seems to refer to a finished portrait ready for presentation to Caryll, although his statement need not be so interpreted: he may simply have offered to have himself painted for Caryll. No portrait of Pope at this date is known. In any event, the letter shows that Pope and Caryll were likely to have exchanged portraits with each other.

Caryll's eldest son, John Caryll, Jr., died during his father's lifetime in 1718, aged 30, leaving a son, John Baptist Caryll (1713–88), the last of his family. This last John Caryll married the Hon. Dorothy Molyneux, daughter of the fifth Viscount Molyneux, of Croxteth Hall, and died without issue in 1788.[3] The Molyneux were an old Catholic family whose descendant, Charles William Molyneux, conformed to the Church of England and was created Earl of Sefton, in the Irish peerage, in 1771. The fact that John Baptist Caryll directly inherited his grandfather's property, was related to the Molyneux by marriage, but had no heir to receive his own property, suggests a situation in which a portrait of Pope originally belonging to John Caryll, Sr., might have passed into the possession of the Molyneux family (after 1771, Earls of Sefton). This would have probably occurred, if at all, during the third quarter of the eighteenth century; an inventory of Croxteth Hall made in 1745 contains no mention of a Pope portrait.[4]

The painting has been attributed on stylistic grounds to Jonathan Richardson the elder.[5]

[1] The painting is no. 8564 in the forthcoming Foreign Schools catalogue compiled by Edward Morris of the Walker Art Gallery (listed as 'Studio of Sir Godfrey Kneller').

[2] *Correspondence I.* 120. This is 'Unexplained Allusions' no. 1 in *Portraits*, p. 349.

[3] Joseph Gillow, *A Literary and Biographical History, or Bibliographical Dictionary of the English Catholics* (London, 1885–1902), *I.* 421; Howard Erskine-Hill, *The Social Milieu of Alexander Pope* (New Haven, 1975), pp. 83, 101–2.

⁴ MS. inventory in the Lancashire Record Office, Preston (information from Mr. Edward Morris). Dorothy (Molyneux) Caryll died in 1760. By 1768 Caryll had disposed of all his estates; he then went to Italy to join the Young Pretender. He remained on the Continent until his death twenty years later. See Erskine-Hill, loc. cit.

⁵ John Kerslake, *Early Georgian Portraits* [*in the National Portrait Gallery 1714–1760*] (London, 1977), *I.* 219, n. 8.

6.4a. OIL PAINTING, PROBABLY FROM THE STUDIO OF KNELLER. MRS. W. K. WIMSATT, NEW HAVEN, CONNECTICUT.*

This portrait was offered for sale by Appleby Bros. Ltd., 10 Ryder Street, London, in April 1967, having been purchased 'some time ago by the late Mr. Arthur Appleby'; it was acquired from them by W. K. Wimsatt. It appears to be either a work from Kneller's studio or a very good early replica. The original size of the canvas has apparently been slightly reduced, probably in the process of relining.

6.5a. OIL PAINTING, AFTER SIR GODFREY KNELLER. ICONOGRAPHY COLLECTION, HUMANITIES RESEARCH CENTER, UNIVERSITY OF TEXAS, AUSTIN.*

This painting was lot 49, 'The Property of a Nobleman', in Christie's sale on 20 November 1964; it was purchased by 'York'. A year later, the portrait was owned by the House of El Dieff, Inc. (Lew David Feldman), New York City, and was offered for sale in their illustrated catalogue *Sixty Five* (1965), item no. 42. It was acquired from them by the University of Texas in November 1965.¹

The anonymous 'Nobleman' (the vendor of the portrait in 1964) has been identified as Henry Vernon St. John (1896–1974), sixth Viscount Bolingbroke.² Lord Bolingbroke, who succeeded his father, the fifth Viscount, in 1899 (when he was only three years old), lived at Lydiard Tregoze, the Wiltshire seat of the Viscounts Bolingbroke, until 1943, when he sold the property to the Corporation of Swindon and retired to a house in Hampshire.³ He had inherited the Pope portrait from his father, who was born in 1820 and succeeded to the title in 1851.⁴ From what is known about the interests of the fifth Viscount—and, indeed, the third and fourth Viscounts as well—it appears highly unlikely that he would have bought a portrait of Pope. It is much more probable that this painting came to Lydiard Tregoze during the lifetime of the second Viscount, Frederick St. John (1734–87).

Frederick was the nephew and heir of the first Viscount, the celebrated Henry St. John, Pope's intimate friend. He succeeded his uncle to the title in 1751 and lived at Lydiard Tregoze. His uncle had never resided there; having surrendered all interest in the place to his half-brother, the second Viscount St. John (Frederick's father), in 1739, he lived during his retirement at the family manor house at Battersea. If he was the original owner of this portrait—a possibility for which concrete evidence is lacking[5] —the portrait would probably have been at Battersea at the time of his death, and possibly as late as 1763. In that year, when Frederick sold the Battersea estate to Viscount Spencer, the portrait might have been removed to Lydiard Tregoze. The painting itself, however, has rather the appearance of being a posthumous copy, though perhaps done quite early after Pope's death.[6]

[1] Miss Ellen S. Dunlap, Research Librarian at the Humanities Research Center, has kindly furnished information for this entry.

[2] Thos. Agnew & Sons, on behalf of Lord Bolingbroke, consigned the portrait to Christie's in July 1964 for sale at auction (information from Mr. Robert Frey of the House of El Dieff, Inc.).

[3] The history and ownership of Lydiard Tregoze are outlined in two articles by Christopher Hussey in *Country Life*, *103* (19, 26 March 1948), 578–81, 626–9.

[4] According to Miss Catherine McLean, the companion and housekeeper of the late 6th Viscount Bolingbroke, the portrait was included in a list compiled after the 5th Viscount's death. We owe this information to Mr. Frank T. Smallwood, of London, who has generously shared with us his research on the history of the St. John family.

[5] Bolingbroke must have owned more than one portrait of Pope, but the references in Pope's correspondence are indefinite; see *Portraits*, pp. 144–5.

[6] On the back of the canvas is written in pencil 'Jarvis Pinxit'. Charles Jervas, whose half-length painting of Pope *c.* 1714 (no. 2.1) is the earliest portrait by a named artist, predeceased Pope by five years.

7.2a. OIL PAINTING, AFTER SIR GODFREY KNELLER.

MR. AND MRS. JOHN C. RIELY, NEW HAVEN, CONNECTICUT.*

This portrait came to light in a miscellaneous sale conducted by Phillips, Son & Neale, London, on 24 October 1966; it was lot P6, described in the catalogue, page 21, as 'Hogarth (after): Portrait of a Man leaning on "Homer."'[1] The painting reappeared as lot 108, 'The Property of a Gentleman', in Christie's sale of

Fine English Pictures on 17 March 1967, and was purchased by Chas. J. Sawyer, the well-known London booksellers. The following year, Sawyer sold it to Lew David Feldman of the House of El Dieff, Inc., New York City, who offered it in his catalogue *Seventy* (1969), item no. 68. It was acquired from him by John C. Riely in October 1973.

The portrait is briefly described and illustrated in *The Scriblerian*, 6 (Spring 1974), 62–3. Sir Ellis Waterhouse has recently suggested to us that it may have been painted by Thomas Gaugain (1748–1805), an engraver and copyist who is known to have been employed by the second Earl Harcourt.[2] Kneller's original (no. 7.1), painted for the first Earl Harcourt, was presumably the portrait of Pope from which a copy was made for Lord Onslow in 1792.[3] It is possible that this replica is the one done for Lord Onslow, though it may well have been executed earlier.

[1] Mr. Richard Jeffree recognized the portrait as Pope and kindly informed us of the sale.

[2] Cf. the copy of Allan Ramsay's portrait of Horace Walpole, painted by Gaugain ('Gogain') for Lord Harcourt; see C. Kingsley Adams and W. S. Lewis, 'The Portraits of Horace Walpole', *The Walpole Society 1968–70, 42* (1970), 18–19, no. A. 14. 2.

[3] See *Portraits*, pp. 62, 201 n. 3.

7.5a. OIL PAINTING, AFTER SIR GODFREY KNELLER.
MISS ELEANOR POYNTON, CHRISTCHURCH, NEW ZEALAND, 1968.*

In a letter of February 1966, Mr. Gordon Cooper, of Ulverston, Lancashire, described a Pope portrait of the 1722 Kneller type then in his possession. Mr. Cooper's father had become the owner of the painting a half-century earlier, when it was part of the estate of his cousin, a Dr. Poynton. It was later decided that the portrait should go to a relative of Dr. Poynton, Miss Eleanor Poynton, who was then living in Christchurch, New Zealand; it was sent to her in 1968. Nothing is known about the provenance of the painting before c. 1920.

7.6a. CRAYON DRAWING (PASTEL), AFTER SIR GODFREY KNELLER.
K. T. WHITTY, ESQ., MALVERN, WORCESTERSHIRE, 1967.*

This crayon drawing was acquired by Mr. Kenneth Whitty at an antiques fair held at Malvern, Worcestershire, in June 1966. It had apparently passed through several hands during the previous two decades, but its earlier history remains obscure.

The drawing is mounted on a wood board, on the back of which is written in ink 'S^r. G. Kneller'. The writing does not resemble authentic examples of Kneller's signature, and may safely be considered merely an inscription.[1] If the drawing were by Kneller himself, it would be unique; attribution by comparison with similar works is impossible, as no crayon drawing by Kneller as finished as this one is known. Moreover, the fact that it is so finished argues strongly for its being a copy after the 1722 Kneller type of portrait and against its being a study for the original painting (no. 7.1).

[1] If a signature, it would doubtless have been on the drawing itself rather than on the back; 'S^r·' would not have been used. But the hand may well be eighteenth-century.

7.6b. CRAYON PAINTING (PASTEL), AFTER SIR GODFREY KNELLER. THE ESTATE OF THE LATE THEODORE BESTERMAN, BANBURY, OXFORDSHIRE.*

No. 7.2 in *Portraits*, pages 62–3, is a replica, oil on canvas, of the 1722 Kneller type, now at the Humanities Research Center, University of Texas at Austin. When this painting was sold at Christie's on 27 June 1924, it was attributed to George Knapton; the sale catalogue further stated that 'This picture was purchased at Ashby Lodge, Ashby St. Legers, Northamptonshire.' The portrait seems to have been first recorded during the early nineteenth century in G. P. Harding's *List of Portraits, Pictures. In Various Mansions, of the United Kingdom*, where it is listed (vol. 1, page 149) as 'Alexander Pope—[Knapton]' among the pictures then at Ashby Lodge, the seat of George Henry Arnold.[1] In his account of Ashby Lodge in *The History and Antiquities of the County of Northampton* (London, 1822–41), *1.* 247–8, George Baker notes that in the hall is 'Pope, the poet, *Knapton*'.

Pictures, prints, and books, the property of Lumley Arnold, were sold by Phillips at Ashby Lodge on 20–2 April 1854, in 721 lots (Lugt 21852).[2] Lot 144 in the sale was a 'Portrait of Pope; *the engraved picture*', by 'Knapton'; it was sold to 'Waters' for £3. 5s. 0d.[3] This was almost certainly the painting now at Texas. Also in the Ashby Lodge Sale was another portrait of Pope, by 'Rosalba', sold as lot 13 to 'Rudd' for £8. 15s. 0d.[4] The fact that

PLATE 1

5.1a. Oil on canvas. 36 × 28 in. Colours similar to those of no. 5.1. Inscribed in lower left: 'Alexander Pope'. Sir Gilbert Inglefield, London.

PLATE 2

6.4a. Oil on canvas. 28¼ × 23 in. Colours similar to those of no. 6.2. Mrs. W. K. Wimsatt, New Haven, Connecticut.

PLATE 3

6.5a. Oil on canvas. 29½ × 24½ in. Colours similar to those of no. 6.2. Inscribed within panel below: 'ALEX^R POPE', OB', 1744', ÆTAT', 56,'. Iconography Collection, Humanities Research Center, University of Texas, Austin.

PLATE 4

7.2a. Oil on canvas. 29 × 24 in. Colours similar to those of no. 7.1. Mr. and Mrs. John C. Riely, New Haven, Connecticut.

PLATE 5

7.5a. Oil on canvas. 30 × 24¾ in. Colours similar to those of no. 7.1. Miss Eleanor Poynton, Christchurch, New Zealand, 1968.

PLATE 6

7.6a. Crayons on buff paper, mounted on wood board. 18 × 14 in. (approx.).
Colours less brilliant than those of no. 7.1; coat faded blue instead of green. In-
scribed in ink on backing board: 'Sr· G. Kneller'. K. T. Whitty, Esq., Malvern,
Worcestershire, 1967.

PLATE 7

7.6b. Crayons on paper. $23\frac{1}{4} \times 17\frac{1}{2}$ in. Background dark grey; cap and lining of coat pinkish mauve; coat greenish blue, tending to turquoise; shirt white; eyes brown; flesh tints pink and delicate; lips red. The Estate of the late Theodore Besterman, Banbury, Oxfordshire.

PLATE 8

19x. White marble. Height (without pedestal) 21½ in. Width below shoulders 20 in. Chin to crown 9¼ in. Width at ears 6¾ in. Inscribed on front of pedestal: 'POPE'. Yale Center for British Art, Paul Mellon Collection.

PLATE 9

31a. Lead pencil on vellum. $7\frac{5}{8} \times 5\frac{1}{8}$ in. Richardson the younger's stamp 'R' on front, in right magin; inscribed in pencil on back bottom centre: 'Mr Pope' with Richardson the elder's monogram stamp 'JR' in lower right; in lower left: 'by Richardson' in a later hand. Yale Center for British Art, Paul Mellon Collection.

PLATE 10

56x. Oil on canvas. 39 × 33 in. Background, dark brown tree trunks with olive-green foliage, in the distance grey obelisk and patches of dark blue sky; ledge greyish red; loose gown brown with yellowish highlights, representing satin; waistcoat cobalt blue; shirt white; hair dark brown with grey at hairline; eyebrows black; eyes brown; flesh tints deep pink, with reddish lips. On letter held in right hand: 'For Mr Richardson.' Yale Center for British Art, Paul Mellon Collection.

PLATE 11

61.1a. Polished white marble. Height (without pedestal) 19½ in. Width at shoulders 17¼ in. Chin to crown 9¼ in. Width above ears 7¼ in. Inscribed on front of pedestal: 'Promissum ille sibi voluit prænoscere Cælum/Nec novus ignotas hospes adire domos.' Mrs. Gerrit P. Van de Bovenkamp, New York City.

PLATE 12

57–61.6. White marble. Height (without pedestal) 15½ in. Width at shoulders 12 in. Chin to crown 9¼ in. Width above ears 7¼ in. Inscribed on back above pedestal: 'Nollekens f^t.' Benjamin Sonnenberg, New York City.

PLATE 13

57–61.7a. White marble, on a pedestal of veined marble. Height (including pedestal) 20½ in. Eyes not incised. Reg. & Muriel Andrade Ltd., Plympton, Devon, 1967.

PLATE 14

57–61.28. Sèvres *biscuit* porcelain, with gilt letters and border. Diameter 5½ in. 'ALEXANDRE POPE NE' A' LONDRE.' Miss M. Mellanay Delhom, Charlotte, North Carolina.

PLATE 15

63.1a. Oil on canvas. 29¾ × 24¾ in. In a painted oval. Background greyish brown; cap dark grey-green (like evergreen), with highlights representing velour; outer garment deep reddish brown; waistcoat dark brown, almost black; shirt white; flesh tints sallow; lips deep pink. W. G. Skillicorn, Esq., Ellesmere, Shropshire.

PLATE 18

66.21. *Elysium and Tartarus, or the State of Final Retribution*, detail of centre panel. Oil on canvas. Coat brownish purple; neckcloth white. Royal Society of Arts, London.

the portrait was attributed to Rosalba Carriera is good evidence that it was a crayon painting (pastel).

In February 1972, a pastel portrait of the 1722 Kneller type, belonging to Mr. C. B. J. Gledhill, was brought to the National Portrait Gallery for examination. Two labels on the backing board of the picture were noted at that time. The first label was inscribed as follows: 'Pope   I bought at Mr Lumley Arnolds sale, Ashby Lodge, Northamptonshire in 1854. Baker in his history of the County mentions this portrait by Knapton and which several persons connected with Ashby say was painted from life. . . . T. Christy'. The other label appeared below: 'Pope/Baker's Northamptonshire gives it by Knapton in his account of portraits at Ashby/ Cat Ashby Sale 13'.[5] It seems clear enough that the portrait owned by Mr. Gledhill in 1972 was the same one sold at Ashby Lodge, lot 13, in 1854. Since Baker's *Northampton* mentions only one Pope portrait at Ashby Lodge and gives it to Knapton, it is not difficult to see how the other (pastel) portrait could have been confused with it—particularly as Knapton worked in both crayons and oils. Indeed, the pastel portrait, in addition to the oil painting (no. 7.2), may be the work of Knapton.

Mr. Gledhill's portrait was sold at Christie's on 14 November 1972, lot 65 ('Various Properties'), to Thos. Agnew & Sons. It was acquired from Agnew's by Dr. Theodore Besterman, the director of the Voltaire Foundation, who died in November 1976. Christie's sale catalogue notes that the portrait was formerly owned by S. R. Christie-Miller. Sydney Richardson Christie-Miller (1874–1931), of Clarendon Park, Salisbury, Wiltshire, was a grandson of Thomas Christy (d. 1877), of Brooklands, Essex; the latter was doubtless the 'T. Christy' who acquired the portrait at the Ashby Lodge Sale.

The Christie catalogue offers an attribution to William Hoare, the originator of another well-known Pope portrait type (see below, nos. 63.1a and 63.3x). Like Knapton, Hoare painted portraits in crayons as well as oils. But the colours in his crayon paintings are generally more brilliant than those of Knapton, who preferred pale, low-keyed tones which can often appear rather drab.[6] The colouring of this portrait is bright enough to suggest Hoare, although Knapton's responsibility cannot be ruled out.

[1] See above, no. 6.2.
[2] Auctioneer's annotated copy of the sale catalogue in the records of Phillips, Son & Neale, deposited in the British Library.

[3] Knapton's replica was never engraved; the catalogue description mistakenly implies that it was the original of this type, whereas George White's well-known mezzotint engraving (no. 7.8) was taken from Kneller's signed and dated painting of 1722.

[4] The printed catalogue entry for lot 13 reads 'A Portrait of Matthew Prior', but the name has been crossed out by the auctioneer and 'Pope' substituted (see n. 2 above).

[5] 'Rudd', whom the annotated sale catalogue names as the purchaser of lot 13 at Ashby Lodge, was probably a dealer bidding for 'T. Christy'. Mr. John Kerslake kindly communicated the information on the labels.

[6] Waterhouse, *Painting in Britain*, p. 233; Edward Mead Johnson, *Francis Cotes* (London, 1976), p. 4.

7.12. PEN-AND-INK DRAWING ON PAPER, AFTER KNELLER.
MICHAEL PAPANTONIO, NEW YORK CITY.*

Mr. Michael Papantonio, of the Seven Gables Bookshop, New York City, has in his personal collection an elaborately designed example of calligraphy which includes a portrait of Pope on a large sheet of paper, 17½×10 inches. A bust-length image of Pope, probably copied from George White's mezzotint engraving (no. 7.8) of Kneller's painting (but without the hand and arm supporting the head), appears in an oval frame, wreathed by ivy, bay leaves, and flowers, at the top of the sheet. 'ALEXAND. POPE.' is written below the portrait in large letters. To the left, a book is open to the title-page of 'The Works of Alexander Pope, Esq. . . . 1753' (Warburton's edition, 9 vols., 1753), with a trumpet leaning on end; to the right, there is a leaf of paper headed 'The Rape of the Lock,' with a lyre standing upright. The middle portion of the sheet contains, in parallel columns, two 'Odes' by Pope, the 'Ode on Solitude' ('Happy the man . . .') and 'The Dying Christian to his Soul, Ode' (the second of his adaptations from Hadrian), each with elegant title-pieces. At the bottom of the sheet, below the odes, is a rural landscape perhaps intended to suggest Pope's *Pastorals* or *Windsor-Forest*; to the right, at what looks vaguely like the entrance to his grotto, transposed into the landscape, is a coffin on which rests a death's head. The whole—portrait, odes, and landscape—is composed within an ornamental border.

This unusual specimen of calligraphy, though skilful in its treatment of word and image, is probably the work of an amateur during the third quarter of the eighteenth century, after 1753.

PETER SCHEEMAKERS (1691–1781)

19X. MARBLE BUST, PROBABLY BY PETER SCHEEMAKERS.
YALE CENTER FOR BRITISH ART, PAUL MELLON COLLECTION.*

The appearance of a life-size white marble bust of Pope, attributed to Peter Scheemakers the younger, in an exhibition held by the London fine arts dealer Cyril Humphris 11–22 September 1972, invited speculation that a bust of this description owned by Pope's friend and physician Dr. Richard Mead had at last been recovered. The bust was acquired from Humphris by Mr. Paul Mellon in October 1972.[1] Dr. Mead died in 1754. In the sale of sculpture from his collection, conducted by Langford on 11 March 1755 (Lugt 871), lot 63 was a white marble bust of Pope 'by Mr. Scheemaker', sold, according to John Nichols, to 'Gen. Campbell' for £18. 7s. 6d.[2] This is 'Unexplained Allusions' no. 12 in *Portraits*, page 350. 'Gen. Campbell' was doubtless John Campbell (1694–1770), a regular army officer who was promoted to lieutenant-general in 1747 and who succeeded his cousin as fourth Duke of Argyll in 1761. The bust was probably taken to Combe Bank, his seat near Sundridge, Kent.

A portion of the collection of John, Duke of Argyll, 'Lately Deceased', sold by Langford and Son on 19–23 March 1771 (Lugt 1905), included only pictures. The bust of Pope disappears from public notice, and was apparently not included in any of the various sales of fine art belonging to the Dukes of Argyll, beginning in 1798 and continuing at intervals into the present century.[3] At a sale held by Dowell's of Edinburgh at Roseneath Castle, Dunbartonshire, a seat of the Duke of Argyll, on 7–11 October 1940, lot 588 was a 'Sculptured white marble bust of a gentleman, on marble pedestal, under glass shade'.[4] It is possible that this anonymous bust may be eventually identified as the bust now in the Mellon collection, even though the latter has a pedestal (probably not the original one) inscribed 'POPE'.

The close resemblance of the Mellon marble to the stone bust of Pope in the Temple of British Worthies at Stowe (no. 19 in *Portraits*, pages 129–36), constitutes new evidence concerning Scheemakers's probable role in the creation of the Worthies. Recent research has helped to illuminate his connection with the annals of Stowe. We now know that in 1737 he was commissioned by Lord Cobham to carve the four Ancient Worthies for the Temple of Ancient Virtue.[5] He may also have executed the sculptured relief of Britannia for the Temple of Concord and Victory. As for the sixteen busts in the Temple of British Worthies, it is evident that they were produced in two series. The eight busts of the first series were originally placed around a small domed temple designed by James Gibbs; George Vertue, who saw them there in July 1732, noted the names of seven (omitting, probably inadvertently, Hampden) and added: 'these busts by Mr. Rysbrake'. They were subsequently transferred to the present semicircular shrine designed by William Kent c. 1735. The Revd. Jeremiah Milles, who visited Stowe in July 1735, recorded that the first series of busts, plus Inigo Jones, was in place in the new temple, apparently before the remaining seven busts were ready.[6] These seven busts, including that of Pope, are slightly larger and coarser in detail than those of the first series. Scheemakers, who was replacing Rysbrack at Stowe about this time, was very likely commissioned to complete the second series.

The marble bust of Pope may be compared stylistically with the signed bust of Lord Cobham by Scheemakers, originally in the Temple of Friendship at Stowe and now in the Victoria and Albert Museum,[7] and with four unsigned but authenticated busts of Spenser, Shakespeare, Milton, and Dryden at Hagley Hall, given to Pope by Frederick, Prince of Wales, and bequeathed by him to Lord Lyttelton.[8] The neat, regular pattern of the hair and the somewhat flat, schematic folds of the drapery are characteristic of Scheemakers rather than of Rysbrack. It seems possible that the Stowe bust and the marble bust in the Mellon collection were both made from a model which is today unknown. At Scheemakers's sale 6–7 June 1771, on his retirement from business, lot 44 included a cast of a 'head' (i.e. bust) of Pope—an indication that Scheemakers was accustomed to producing repetitions of his original portrait.

---

[1] The bust is described and illustrated in Humphris's catalogue, *British Portrait Sculpture during the Neo-classic Period*. Mr. Humphris informs us in a recent letter: 'Our record of its acquisition no longer exists and I can only say, from memory, that it was acquired privately . . . from someone who could not, or would not, give an earlier history.'

[2] John Nichols, *Literary Anecdotes of the Eighteenth Century* (London, 1812–15), 6. 220 n. An annotated copy of the sale catalogue in the Yale University

Library confirms the price stated by Nichols, but does not name the purchaser. The bust is described as life-size in the catalogue (in Latin) of Mead's collections also issued by Langford in 1755, *Museum Meadianum*, p. 251.

[3] None of the sale catalogues consulted at the Frick Art Reference Library lists a bust of Pope, though our search cannot claim to be exhaustive.

[4] Copy of the sale catalogue at the Scottish National Portrait Galley; the entry was kindly communicated by Dr. Duncan Thomson, who also supplied helpful information about the Argyll estates. Sir Ellis Waterhouse brought the Roseneath Sale to our attention.

[5] Payment is recorded in Lord Cobham's account book, 1736/41, among the Stowe MSS. in the Henry E. Huntington Library. The Ancient Worthies are no longer at Stowe, but have been located recently in Northamptonshire; one of them, Homer, is signed by Scheemakers. We owe this information to Mr. George Clarke of Stowe School, and to Michael Gibbon's article 'The History of Stowe—XV: Garden Ornaments' in *The Stoic*, 25 (March 1972), 62–8.

[6] Milles's description of Stowe is in British Library Add. MS. 15776, ff. 1–10: 'An Account of the Journey yt Mr Hardness & I took in July 1735'. See Gibbon, op. cit., p. 63, and George Clarke, 'Grecian Taste and Gothic Virtue: Lord Cobham's Gardening Programme and its Iconography', *Apollo*, 97 (June 1973), 566–71.

[7] See Margaret Whinney, *English Sculpture 1720–1830* (Victoria and Albert Museum, London, 1971), no. 15.

[8] The busts are illustrated in G. W. Beard, 'Alexander Pope', *Apollo*, 57 (January 1953), 4–6.

JONATHAN RICHARDSON (1665–1745)

31a. PENCIL-ON-VELLUM DRAWING, BY JONATHAN RICHARDSON, *c.* 1736. YALE CENTER FOR BRITISH ART, PAUL MELLON COLLECTION.*

This drawing was presumably included in the posthumous sale of prints and drawings from the collection of Jonathan Richardson the younger on 5 February 1772.[1] Its subsequent history is unknown until it was sold in a small mixed lot at Bonham's in October 1963 to L. G. Duke, of London. Duke died in 1971. The drawing was lot 121 in the sale of English drawings and watercolours from the Duke collection, Part VII, at Sotheby's on 29 April 1971; it was purchased by John Baskett for Mr. Paul Mellon. In 1975 the drawing was given to the Yale Center for British Art as part of the Paul Mellon Collection.

The portrait may be compared with two other pencil-on-vellum drawings by Richardson, no. 31 (dated '30 Aug: 1736') and no. 33 ('15 Feb. 1736'), in *Portraits*, pages 176–7. The appearance of the face and the style of the drawing both suggest a similar date for this work.

¹ See *Portraits*, pp. 148–9.

42a.   ETCHING, BY JONATHAN RICHARDSON, PROOF BEFORE
       INSCRIPTION OF NO. 43.1. DAVID BAXTER, BOURN,
       CAMBRIDGESHIRE.

The etching recorded as no. 42 in *Portraits*, page 187, is apparently a counterproof of an early state of the etching which, when completed, was the medallion 'Amicitiæ Causa' (no. 43.1).

In a letter of July 1972, Mr. David Baxter, of Bourn, near Cambridge, kindly reported that he has in his possession an etching identical to no. 43.1 except for the absence of the lettering 'Amicitiæ Causa. J. Richardson f.' This impression, apparently a proof before inscription, is illustrated in I. R. F. Gordon, *A Preface to Pope* (London and New York, 1976), page 22.

55.2a.   OIL PAINTING, AFTER JONATHAN RICHARDSON.
         PROFESSOR MAYNARD MACK, NEW HAVEN, CONNECTICUT.*

At Sotheby's on 15 July 1952, lot 280 ('The Property of a Gentleman') was a 'Portrait of Alexander Pope, half-length, his head half turned to the left, in oils, canvas, unframed (28 in. by 24 in.).' The purchaser was Mr. J. A. Pearson, an Eton dealer and art collector. The painting remained in Mr. Pearson's hands until his death in early 1966. In August of that year, it was acquired from John A. Pearson Ltd. by Professor Maynard Mack. This is 'Unexplained Allusions' no. 41 in *Portraits*, page 354.

When the portrait arrived in New Haven, it was found to have on the back two small paper labels: one, pasted on the stretcher, was inscribed '8920/H'; the other, on the frame, 'Roscoe Pope'. The fact that the picture was sold 'unframed' at Sotheby's in 1952 adds to the uncertainty of how the frame (apparently supplied by Mr. Pearson) came to be so labelled.

It has recently come to light that William Roscoe, the editor of Pope's *Works* (10 vols., 1824), was given a portrait of the poet by his friend the Revd. W. Parr Greswell, probably in 1825. Greswell wrote to Roscoe from Denton, near Manchester, on 23 January 1826:

Concerning the Picture which to my great gratification proved an agreeable present to you . . . being formerly in the frequent habit of intercourse with Thomas Falconer Esq[r] of Chester who in the days of my juvenility bore a high reputat[n] as a literary character and an encourager of studious young Men I had frequently noticed particularly a Portrait of Pope in his possession. After my removal to Manch[r] I saw little of M[r] Falconer but know that at his decease his establishm[t] was broken up & presume that by order of his Ex[rs] the picture in quest[n] with many other articles must have been sold by auction. In one of my late rambles about the streets of Manch[r] entering an old book shop—I observed the Picture now in your possession. . . . The recognition was that of an old & familiar acquaintance, though nearly 40 years must have elapsed since our last meeting so natural & spontaneous as to forestal every kind of doubt or question whether it were or not the identical Picture which M[r] Falconer formerly possessed. I found it indeed battered & worse for time & ill usage. . . . I immediately secured it with the pleasing intent[n] of sending it to you. . . .[1]

Thomas Falconer (1738–92), classical scholar and antiquary, was sufficiently well known as a patron of literature to be called the 'Mæcenas of Chester' by Anna Seward.[2] His younger brother, Dr. William Falconer of Bath, owned a profile portrait of Pope painted by Edward Wright, after Richardson, now in the Guild Hall at Bath (no 52.9 in *Portraits*, pages 212–13). The 'Roscoe Pope' thus emerges from a deep context of West Country littérateurs, Pope and Richardson a generation or two back. The present portrait, whether or not it is the one given to Roscoe by Greswell, apparently derives from the painting in the Fitzwilliam Museum (no. 55.2) signed by Richardson and dated 1742. Although Richardson's work varies considerably in quality, the handling here seems too insensitive and amateurish to be his.

[1] Roscoe Paper 1877, Liverpool Public Library. Professor D. H. Weinglass, whose extensive research on William Roscoe has yielded new information about several Pope portraits, kindly brought this letter to our attention.

[2] Anna Seward to Lady Gresley, 10 August 1792 (*Letters of Anna Seward* [Edinburgh, 1811], 3. 167).

56x. OIL PAINTING, BY JONATHAN RICHARDSON, 1738.
     YALE CENTER FOR BRITISH ART, PAUL MELLON COLLECTION.*

In a letter of 28 November 1738 to his patron Lord Burlington, William Kent tells of accompanying Pope on a rainy Sunday morning to visit the elder Richardson:

I got drest & went with him to Richarsons & had great diversion he shew'd three picturs of Lord Baulingbrok one for himself for Pope, another Pope in a mourning gown with a strange view of the garden to shew the obelisk as in memory to his mothers Death, the alligory seem'd odde to me. . . . the son of Richardson & Pope agree'd that popes head was Titziannesco, the old long Glow worm sayd whe have done our best.[1]

This is 'Unexplained Allusions' no. 4 in *Portraits*, page 349—'a picture,' Professor Mack has written, 'one would give a good deal to recover.'[2]

The portrait seems to have gone unrecorded until 1793, when it was engraved in stipple by R. Clamp for publication in Sylvester and Edward Harding's *Shakespeare Illustrated*. The engraving (no. 56.1 in *Portraits*, page 222) presents a severely cropped view of the painting, completely omitting Pope's right hand, which holds a letter addressed 'For Mr Richardson', as well as the garden background with the obelisk in the distance. The printed inscription identifies the subject as 'A POPE ESQ^r,/From an Original Picture by Richardson/in the Possession of Antony Storer Esqr'.

Anthony Morris Storer (1746–99), of Purley Park, near Pangbourne, Berkshire, was a man of fashion who had a brief career in Whig politics. About 1781 he underwent a 'conversion' to antiquarianism and print-collecting—'the last patina,' writes Horace Walpole, 'I should have thought a Macaroni would have taken.' He paid visits to Walpole at Strawberry Hill and was shown 'hosts of portraits of the dead'.[3] Storer died unmarried, leaving his valuable collection of books and prints to Eton; the rest of his property, including his pictures, miniatures, and china, was willed to his nephew, Anthony Gilbert Storer (1782–1818), who succeeded him at Purley Park. At his death the pictures presumably passed to his only son, Major A. M. Storer (1813–1902), of Purley Park. In 1924 many of the pictures were in the possession of Major Storer's granddaughter, Mrs. Evans, of Chalcombe House, Banbury, Oxfordshire.[4] It is not certain that the portrait of Pope descended to Mrs. Evans, but quite possibly it did. Three portraits originally in the collection of Anthony Morris Storer were sold at Sotheby's on 9 December 1964, lots 172–4, 'The Property of the Storer Trust (Sold by Order of Mrs. I. Evans and the Trustees)'. Pope by Richardson was not one of them,[5] but a few years later, on 24 November 1972, the painting appeared at auction as lot 62

('Various Properties') in Christie's sale of *Fine English Pictures*. The portrait was purchased by John Baskett for Mr. Paul Mellon, who gave it to the Yale Center for British Art for the Paul Mellon Collection the following year.

Kent's letter of 1738 supplies a reliable date for the portrait. Richardson's 'alligory' (as Kent calls it) represents his most ambitious effort as painter-in-ordinary to Pope during the prolific decade of 1732–42. It is also the initial version of the final Richardson portrait-type, in which Pope is portrayed three-quarter face to left.[6]

Pope's mother died in 1733. Two years later he was 'building' the stone obelisk to her memory in his garden at Twickenham. He placed it on higher ground at the end of a narrowing avenue of cypress trees, so that it became 'the point of visual and emotional climax for the observer in the garden'.[7] Walpole speaks of 'the solemnity of the termination at the cypresses that lead up to his mother's tomb'.[8] The obelisk in the background thus establishes the theme of the poet in mourning for his mother. Pope wears a loose gown of a sombre brown (but not black) for 'second' or 'half' mourning.[9] His head is said to be 'Titziannesco'—probably a reference to the 'warmth, and mellowness, and delicacy of colouring' that Richardson greatly admired in the paintings of Titian,[10] and to the rather free handling of the paint itself.

[1] *Correspondence 4.* 150.

[2] Maynard Mack, *The Garden and the City: Retirement and Politics in the Later Poetry of Pope 1731–1743* (Toronto, 1969), p. 29.

[3] Walpole to Lord Strafford, 13 June 1781; to Lady Ossory, 13 June 1781 (*The Yale Edition of Horace Walpole's Correspondence*, ed. W. S. Lewis *et al.* [New Haven, 1937–], 35. 359, 33. 273).

[4] See Granville Proby's Preface to Tancred Borenius and J. V. Hodgson, *A Catalogue of the Pictures at Elton Hall* (London: The Medici Society, 1924), p. xii, and the 'Pedigree of Proby and Allen Families', facing p. ix.

[5] Messrs. Ellis Peirs and Young Jackson, of London, solicitors for the Major A. M. Storer Will Trust, have kindly informed us that the portrait is not listed in inventories of the Storer estate carried out in 1918 and 1946. The Trust was wound up in 1970. The portrait may therefore have passed to one of the other grandchildren of Major Storer rather than to Mrs. Evans.

[6] Cf. no. 55.2a above. The presentation of the figure is reminiscent of the bust-length Milton—dressed in a flowing robe, with right arm resting on a ledge in front of him—in Richardson's group portrait of *c.* 1734 at Capesthorne. See *Portraits*, p. 141.

[7] Mack, op. cit., p. 28. See also pp. 50 (plate 19), 285–6.

[8] 'Essay on Modern Gardening' (1771), in Isabel W. U. Chase, *Horace Walpole: Gardenist* (Princeton, 1943), p. 29.

[9] Second mourning followed the period of deep or full mourning, when black

clothing was generally worn. The favoured colours for suits of second mourning at this time were grey or brown. In a letter of 1738 to her London agent, Elizabeth Purefoy requests 'patterns of Cloath of a fashionable colour for second mourning for my son' (*The Purefoy Letters 1735–1753*, ed. G. Eland [London, 1931], 2. 217).

[10] Richardson, 'The Theory of Painting', in *The Works of Jonathan Richardson* (London, 1792), p. 68.

LOUIS-FRANÇOIS ROUBILIAC (1705?–1762)

57.1. TERRA COTTA BUST, BY L.-F. ROUBILIAC, *c.* 1738.
THE BARBER INSTITUTE OF FINE ARTS, UNIVERSITY OF BIRMINGHAM.

This bust, presumably the model for the four signed and dated marbles by Roubiliac that are known today, had belonged to Mrs. E. C. L. Copner (the former Mrs. Michael R. H. Murray) and on her death passed to Mr. Christopher Murray. It was sold at Sotheby's on 19 June 1970, lot 47 ('The Property of Christopher Murray, Esq.'), to Mrs. S. Barrow for John Baskett, for £20,000, the highest price ever to have been paid at auction for a piece of pre-twentieth-century English sculpture. The bust was acquired from Baskett by Mr. Paul Mellon, who, after being denied permission to export the bust, sold it to the Barber Institute of Fine Arts at Birmingham in late 1970.

The bust was at one time painted white; caustic used to remove the paint caused discoloration in the terracotta. Since its acquisition by the Barber Institute, the bust has undergone successful treatment in deionized water in order to remove the discoloration.

58x. PLASTER 'MASK', POSSIBLY FROM NO. 58a. ICONOGRAPHY
COLLECTION, HUMANITIES RESEARCH CENTER, UNIVERSITY OF TEXAS, AUSTIN.

This 'mask' of Pope, which belonged to the late Mrs. Arundell Esdaile and is referred to in her book *Roubiliac* (London, 1928), page 48, as a 'bronzed life-mask', was acquired from the House of El Dieff, Inc., New York City, by the University of Texas in 1960. Close examination of the object reveals a seam in the plaster running vertically down the middle—clear evidence that it was cast in a mould made from a bust, and that it is not, therefore, a life-mask in the proper sense of the term.

60.2a. PLASTER BUST, REPLICA OF NO. 60.1. K. D. DUVAL (BOOKS AND
     MANUSCRIPTS), FRENICH, FOSS, PITLOCHRY, PERTHSHIRE.

This bust, which Mr. Kulgin D. Duval acquired in 1964 and which is recorded in *Portraits*, page 244, was offered for sale in Mr. Duval's Winter 1974 catalogue, item no. 89. It is there described as 17 inches high (the same height as no. 60.2), rather than 16½ inches, as previously stated, and 'is thought to have come from Yorkshire'. The bust is still in Mr. Duval's possession.

61.1a. MARBLE BUST, BY OR FROM THE WORKSHOP OF L.-F. ROUBILIAC.
     MRS. GERRIT P. VAN DE BOVENKAMP, NEW YORK CITY.*

This bust, along with an oil painting of the Van Loo type (no. 66.7a below), descended among the heirlooms of the Earls Poulett at Hinton St. George, their seat in Somerset. At Sotheby's on 1 November 1968, lot 14 ('The Property of the Right Hon. the Earl Poulett, Removed from Hinton House, Somerset') was 'A fine pair of English white marble busts from the workshops of Louis François Roubiliac, one of Isaac Newton . . . the other bust of Alexander Pope'; the busts were acquired by Cyril Humphris, 23 Old Bond Street, London. In 1969 Humphris sold the bust of Pope to Mr. Armand G. Erpf, of New York City. On Mr. Erpf's death in 1971, the bust passed to his widow, who is now Mrs. Gerrit P. Van de Bovenkamp.[1]

    The general appearance and style of the bust relate it to the signed marble of 1741 owned by Lord Rosebery, no. 61.1, although the head is slightly larger and the drapery is in certain details even more like that of the terracotta, no. 57.1. An attribution to Roubiliac, or at least to his workshop, seems warranted by the over-all quality of the portrait; the absence of a signature perhaps indicates that the bust is posthumous, though probably made not long after Pope's death. The inscription on the pedestal, *Promissum ille sibi voluit prænoscere Cælum/Nec novus ignotas hospes adire domos*, is closely adapted from Ovid's *Fasti 3*. 159–60, a passage concerning preparedness for the afterlife.[2]

[1] The companion bust of Newton is now in the collection of Mr. Benjamin

Sonnenberg, who also owns a marble bust of Pope by Nollekens (no. 57–61.6 below).

[2] The inscription seems generally related to ideas expressed in the *Essay on Man*, especially ll. 281–94 of the First Epistle concerning '*the* absolute Submission *due to Providence, both as to our* present *and* future *State*' (*Twickenham 3.* i. 49–51).

57–61.1. BRONZE HIGH RELIEF, BY L.-F. ROUBILIAC. YALE CENTER FOR BRITISH ART, PAUL MELLON COLLECTION.

In July 1966 Mr. Paul Mellon acquired from Cyril Humphris, London, a bronze medallion of Pope, identical in size and type to no. 57–61.1 in *Portraits*, pages 248–50. This example is set in an oval wood frame, painted black, with a wood backing that bears an illegible inscription written in ink. The two bronze medallions of Pope now known were clearly taken from the same mould.

57–61.2. MINIATURE MARBLE BUST, ROUBILIAC TYPE. YALE UNIVERSITY ART GALLERY.

Miss Gladys Singers-Bigger, the owner of this bust in 1965, presented it to the Yale University Art Gallery the following year. It was exhibited at the Art Gallery in February 1967. See 'Recent Gifts and Purchases', *Yale University Art Gallery Bulletin, 31,* no. 3 (Winter 1967–8), 19, where the bust is illustrated.

57–61.6. MARBLE BUST, BY JOSEPH NOLLEKENS, AFTER ROUBILIAC. BENJAMIN SONNENBERG, NEW YORK CITY.

The provenance of this bust before 1965, so far as it is known, is given in *Portraits*, page 252. It was sold at Sotheby's on 18 June 1965, lot 81, to Ronald A. Lee. Mr. Lee, a dealer in works of art, soon afterwards sold the bust to Cyril Humphris, from whom it was acquired by Mr. Benjamin Sonnenberg.[1] The bust is mentioned in Desmond Fitz-Gerald's article 'A New Yorker's Unusual Collection', *Apollo, 85* (March 1967), 168, where the companion bust of Sterne by Nollekens is illustrated, figure 11, with a caption mistakenly identifying it as Pope. The bust of Pope is illustrated here for the first time.

[1] Mr. Howard Ricketts, who negotiated the sale between Mr. Lee and Mr. Humphris, was helpful in tracing the recent migrations of the bust. Mr. Sonnen-

berg is also the owner of a companion marble bust of Laurence Sterne by Nollekens, sold at Sotheby's 18 June 1965, lot 82, to R. A. Lee; the pair of busts was formerly in the collection of Lord Hore-Belisha.

57–61.7a. MARBLE BUST, ROUBILIAC TYPE. REG. & MURIEL ANDRADE
LTD., PLYMPTON, DEVON, 1967.*

This bust, though similar in format to the Garrick marble now at the Shipley Art Gallery (no. 60.1), may be described simply as a freely executed version of the Roubiliac type. It was advertised for sale by Reg. & Muriel Andrade Ltd., 8 Boringdon Villas, Plympton, Devon, in the *Connoisseur, 164* (January 1967), xxxix. Mr. Philip Andrade, of the successor firm Philip Andrade Ltd., informs us that he is unable to trace the person to whom the bust was sold, but he kindly supplied the photograph that we reproduce here.

57–61.8. PLASTER BUST, ROUBILIAC TYPE.
NATIONAL PORTRAIT GALLERY NO. 2483.

This bust, which is described in *Portraits*, pages 254–5, as being a terracotta, is in fact made of plaster and painted terracotta colour. It is discussed in John Kerslake, *Early Georgian Portraits [in the National Portrait Gallery 1714–1760]* (London, 1977), *I*. 217–18.

57–61.9. PLASTER BUST, ROUBILIAC TYPE, PROBABLY BY JOHN
CHEERE. STOURHEAD, WILTSHIRE.

The first exhibition devoted to the work of the sculptor John Cheere was held successively at Temple Newsam House, Leeds, and at Marble Hill House, Twickenham, May–September 1974. The plaster bust from Stourhead was included in the exhibition, and is no. 64 (illustrated, plate 12) in the catalogue compiled by Terry Friedman and Timothy Clifford, *The Man at Hyde Park Corner: Sculpture by John Cheere 1709–1787* [1974]. The catalogue entry states in part: 'Although there appears to be no documentation to identify this plaster as John Cheere's work, the modelling, the bronzing technique and the use of a curved-panelled socle are characteristic of his productions. The presence of other Cheere plasters at Stourhead . . . makes him an almost certain candidate for this piece, of which no other example has been traced.'

The plaster statuette of Pope signed 'Cheere Ft 1749' at the Castle Museum, York (no. 57–61.15), was also exhibited in *The Man at Hyde Park Corner*, catalogue no. 63 (illustrated, plate 10).

57–61.12. PLASTER BUST, ROUBILIAC TYPE, POSSIBLY BY CHARLES
HARRIS. ASTON HALL, BIRMINGHAM, AND TRINITY
COLLEGE, CAMBRIDGE.

In the field of mass-produced plaster sculpture, the work of Charles Harris (d. 1795) may be easily confused with that of John Cheere (see above, no. 57–61.9). None of Harris's plasters has been positively identified, but he published *A Catalogue of the Statues, Bass Reliefs, Bustos, &c. of Charles Harris, Statuary, Opposite to the New Church in the Strand, London*, n.d., which lists a large number of white and bronzed plaster statues, statuettes, and busts, including nearly every subject also available from Cheere.[1] Terry Friedman and Timothy Clifford have pointed out that the plaster bust of Pope originally at Shardaloes, Buckinghamshire, and now at Aston Hall, Birmingham (one of a set including Shakespeare, Milton, Newton, Locke, and others), might someday be identified as Harris's work.[2]

[1] Friedman and Clifford, *The Man at Hyde Park Corner* [1974], p. 11.
[2] Ibid.

57–61.13. PLASTER BUST, DERIVED FROM THE ROUBILIAC TYPE.

The bust of Pope that is mentioned in *The Ambulator*, 8th edition, 1796, page 267, as being situated in an aperture in the rock of Pope's grotto at Twickenham, was placed there at least as early as 1775. In the journal of the American loyalist Samuel Curwen, who lived in England during the period of the Revolution, the following entry for 25 August 1775 appears:

[At] Welbore Ellis's seat late Mr. Popes we alighted, and . . . entered the gardens and grotto; the latter being arches under the middle of the House, about man's heigth, admitting a prospect into the largest shady contemplative walk in the garden from the River. It is almost 5 feet in width, faced with small flint stones, cristal and some other kinds stuck into mortar, with the angles out . . . 2 or 3 niches filled with the busts of Pope and I forget who else. . . .[1]

The politician Welbore Ellis (created Baron Mendip in 1794)

inherited Pope's house in 1772 from his father-in-law, Sir William Stanhope, who had carried out extensive alterations to the house and garden by 1760.[2] A second bust of Pope, in white marble, described in *The Ambulator* as being 'over an arched way, leading to the new gardens' (i.e. the gardens added by Stanhope), is also mentioned in Curwen's journal.[3]

[1] *The Journal of Samuel Curwen, Loyalist*, ed. Andrew Oliver (Cambridge, Mass.: Harvard University Press for the Essex Institute, Salem [owner of the MS. journal], 1972), *1.* 57. We are indebted to Mr. Oliver for bringing the journal entry to our attention before it was printed in full for the first time in his edition.

[2] R. S. Cobbett, *Memorials of Twickenham: Parochial and Topographical* (London, 1872), pp. 284–7.

[3] Oliver, loc. cit. See *Portraits*, p. 257 n. 1.

57–61.21. WEDGWOOD CAMEO MEDALLION, ROUBILIAC TYPE.

The earliest example of this portrait medallion known to us, dated *c.* 1790, is owned by Mr. Eugene D. Buchanan, of Highland Park, Illinois. The white image of Pope, $2\frac{5}{8}$ inches high, is mounted on a blue jasper oval plaque, $3\frac{1}{4} \times 2\frac{1}{2}$ inches; the name 'Pope' is impressed below the image. This medallion was formerly in the possession of Frederick Rathbone, the well-known Wedgwood dealer, and later in the collection of David Davis.[1] It was exhibited (no. 162) at the Twelfth Wedgwood International Seminar held at the Smithsonian Institution, Washington, D.C., on 3–6 May 1967, and is described and illustrated in Robin Reilly and George Savage, *Wedgwood: The Portrait Medallions* (London, 1973), pages 281–2.

A white-on-black jasper medallion of Pope, image 3 inches high, in the collection of Mrs. Robert D. Chellis, of Wellesley, Massachusetts, was made at the Etruria Wedgwood factory *c.* 1910.[2] Another such medallion, in white-on-green jasper, was made for Professor Maynard Mack in 1965 from mould no. 271–8 at Barlaston; the height of the image is $2\frac{1}{2}$ inches.

The images of Pope in these three examples differ not only in height but in fine sculptural detail. Moreover, these images appear to be related very closely to one another, as well as to the Roubiliac type. The three dates—1790, 1910, and 1965—suggest successive remakings and progressive simplifications of an original mould probably designed by William Hackwood or John Flaxman the younger.[3] Small variations in detail may be due to finishing touches applied to the moulded image before firing.

[1] Information kindly communicated by Mr. Buchanan.
[2] Mrs. Chellis has generously shared with us her expert knowledge of Wedgwood medallions.
[3] All three examples are discussed and illustrated in W. K. Wimsatt, 'Portraits of Alexander Pope', *The Twelfth Wedgwood International Seminar* [New York, 1976], pp. 108–10.

57–61.24. LINE ENGRAVING, AFTER ROUBILIAC, BY H. GRAVELOT.

The variant impression described in *Portraits*, page 264, as having 'a heavier hatched shading under the lower right quarter of the medal and in general a heavier shading of hair, face, neck, and garment, than the British Museum impression' reproduced, is now in the possession of Mrs. Allen T. Hazen, New York City, the gift of Margaret Wimsatt in August 1976.

57–61.27. OIL PAINTING, 'THE JOHN BACON FAMILY', *c.* 1742–43, WITH GRISAILLE WALL MEDALLION OF POPE, AFTER ROUBILIAC, IN THE BACKGROUND. YALE CENTER FOR BRITISH ART, PAUL MELLON COLLECTION.*

In 1968 Mr. Paul Mellon acquired from Spink and Son, Ltd., London, an anonymous oil painting, $30\frac{1}{8} \times 51\frac{5}{8}$ inches, of an English family in an interior; it was at that time attributed to Arthur Devis (1711–87). The subject of this conversation piece has recently been identified by Ellen D'Oench as John Bacon (1709–52), F.R.S., F.S.A., his wife Catherine, and their four children; the setting is probably their house in London. The picture was apparently painted in 1742 or 1743.[1] John Bacon, a member of the landed gentry of Northumberland, was a governor of Bethlehem and Bridewell Hospitals. Various scientific instruments shown in the painting attest to his serious interest in astronomy and other branches of science.[2]

The significant feature for us in this instance is an oval portrait of Pope, one of four grisaille medallion portraits of British worthies adorning the far wall of the drawing-room. The other three subjects are Francis Bacon (no relation), Milton, and Newton. All of them are bust-length portraits of approximately life size, each set within a painted square or rectangle, in grey monochrome. The profile of Pope, facing left, is an adaptation of Roubiliac's image similar to that of the Wedgwood cameo medallion, no. 57–61.21.

Medallion portraits of modern worthies, painted to give the appearance of stucco relief, are an unusual feature of interior decoration at this period; for a later grisaille ceiling medallion of Pope (after Dassier), see *Portraits*, pages 273–4, no. 62.6. Mr. Edward Croft-Murray has called our attention to an interesting analogue, part of a scheme of decoration at Knole (Kent) carried out by an architectural and ornamental painter about 1728. On canvas panels (now detached, but perhaps originally belonging to the staircase) is painted, in grey monochrome, a series of 'busts' of English poets. This decoration was undertaken for Lionel Sackville, first Duke of Dorset; the artist may have been a member of the Hauduroy family.[3]

---

[1] We are greatly indebted to Mrs. D'Oench for information about the painting. A copy of her unpublished study, which discusses in detail many aspects of the painting and contains extensive documentation of the evidence, is deposited in the Yale Center for British Art. Although Mrs. D'Oench argues against a new attribution to William Verelst (*fl.* 1729–56), his authorship remains a possibility.

[2] The painting was included in the exhibition *The Pursuit of Happiness: A View of Life in Georgian England* at the Yale Center for British Art, 19 April–18 September 1977, and is described and illustrated in the catalogue, no. 42.

[3] See Edward Croft-Murray, *Decorative Painting in England 1537–1837* (London, 1962–70), 2. 302. Mr. Croft-Murray informs us that among the papers of the Sackville family (Kent Archives Office, Maidstone) is a record of payments made at this time to an artist named Hauduroy. Mark Antony Hauduroy (or Hoduroy) (*fl. c.* 1735–7) is known to have been employed as a decorative painter at Dyrham Park and at Chandos House, London; see Croft-Murray, 2. 218.

57–61.28. SÈVRES WHITE PORCELAIN MEDALLION, ROUBILIAC TYPE. MISS M. MELLANAY DELHOM, CHARLOTTE, NORTH CAROLINA.*

Miss M. Mellanay Delhom, Curator of the Delhom Gallery and Institute for Study and Research in Ceramics at the Mint Museum of Art, Charlotte, North Carolina, has in her personal collection a circular cameo medallion of Pope produced at the Sèvres factory in France. It is made of white unglazed porcelain of the type known as *biscuit*, used extensively in Sèvres manufacture of figures, groups, and ornamental objects during the second half of the eighteenth century. The profile image of Pope, facing right, is a free rendering of the Roubiliac type which may be compared (though in a different medium) with Gravelot's engraving, no. 57–61.24. Miss

Delhom owns two other medallions of the same kind, representing
Voltaire and Rousseau, both marked with the Sèvres royal cipher.[1]

Production of *biscuit* portrait medallions began at Sèvres about
1766 and continued well into the nineteenth century. They were
relatively inexpensive, popular items; a wide variety of subjects
(royalty, famous men, classical and mythological figures) was
available, some in more than one size. Many of the original models
and moulds are preserved at the Sèvres Museum.[2]

[1] Two Sèvres medallions (one dated 1778) of Benjamin Franklin are described
in Charles Coleman Sellers, *Benjamin Franklin in Portraiture* (New Haven,
1962), pp. 365, 372–3 (nos. 1, 10); illustrated, pls. 12, 14.

[2] A list of 'Bustes en ronde bosse' is given in Comte Xavier de Chavagnac and
Marquis de Grollier, *Histoire des manufactures françaises de porcelaine* (Paris,
1906), pp. 278–80. Neither the model nor the mould for the medallion of Pope
has apparently survived. See also Pierre Verlet, Serge Grandjean, and Marcelle
Brunet, *Sèvres* (Paris, [1953]), *1*. 36.

JACQUES-ANTOINE DASSIER (1715–1759)

62.3. LINE ENGRAVING, BY HUBERT-FRANÇOIS GRAVELOT,
      AFTER DASSIER.

Only one example of this engraving is known; it is now in the
possession of Mrs. Allen T. Hazen, New York City, the gift of
Margaret Wimsatt in August 1976.

62.8. REPRODUCTIONS OF GEMS, BY JAMES TASSIE, MOSTLY AFTER
      DASSIER. SCOTTISH NATIONAL PORTRAIT GALLERY.

The original gem for no. 14368 in the 1791 *Catalogue* of Tassie's
reproductions, described as a cornelian belonging to William
Warburton, is probably *not* the same as a cornelian portrait seal of
Pope on a ring which Warburton had given to Dr. John Brown
(1715–66). See *Portraits*, page 276 and note 5, where the later
provenance of the ring is misquoted from *The Poetical Works of
Alexander Pope*, ed. Robert Carruthers (London, 1853–4), *2*. iv.
The quotation should read: 'Dr. Brown left the ring to Dr.
William Stephens, who left it by will to James Edwards, Esq.; and
Mr. Edwards left it, also by will, to his wife, now Mrs. Butt, of
Trentham, Staffordshire.'

A wax impression made from the seal ring when it was owned by James Edwards (1757–1816), the well-known bookseller in Pall Mall, is affixed to a letter written by Edwards to William Roscoe, 27 December 1810, now among the Roscoe MSS. at Liverpool.[1] Edwards concludes his letter with a postscript: 'The Seal of the Letter is the Head of Pope done for Warburton & presented by Pope to him mention^d in the late Vol. of his Correspond^ce with Hurd.'[2] The seal impression on the letter is the same size as Tassie's no. 14368, but differences in the nose, the curl at the nape of the neck, and the collar are further evidence supporting the hypothesis that Warburton owned more than one portrait seal of Pope.

[1] Roscoe Paper 1424, Liverpool Public Library. The misquotation from Carruthers's edition was noticed by Professor D. H. Weinglass, who also brought the Edwards letter to our attention and provided us with an excellent photograph of the seal impression for study.

[2] See *Portraits*, p. 276, n. 5.

62.8a. BLACK BASALT INTAGLIO SEAL, BY JEAN VOYEZ, AFTER DASSIER. VICTORIA AND ALBERT MUSEUM.*

No. 14366 in the Tassie *Catalogue* of 1791 is a reproduction, cameo as well as intaglio, of a portrait gem of Pope in cornelian (owner not named). The image is identical to that of a mould preserved at the Barlaston Wedgwood Museum, no. 816,[1] and to a basalt seal (oval, height $\frac{13}{16}$ inch) owned in 1965 by Mr. Alfred Fairbank. See *Portraits*, page 275.

In 1967 the Victoria and Albert Museum acquired five unmounted intaglio seals and one cipher seal mounted with 'self shank', black basalt ware, made by Jean Voyez. The recent discovery of these seals was announced by Patrick Synge-Hutchinson in his article 'The Only Known Examples of Jean Voyez's Seals', *Connoisseur*, *161* (April 1966), 212–15. One of the five unmounted intaglios is a portrait of Pope, height $\frac{11}{16}$ inch, the image of which is very similar to Tassie's no. 14366.[2] On the back of the Pope intaglio is impressed the number '74', which corresponds to an entry in *A Catalogue of Intaglios and Cameos, after the Most Esteemed of the Antiques. Made by J. Voyez, Sculptor, Member of the Royal Society of Artists of Great Britain. And to be Sold at his House at Cowbridge, near Newcastle, Staffordshire; and at M.*

Swinney's, in Birmingham, published by Voyez in 1773. The numbered entry reads: '74. Alexander Pope, Cornelian.' This may be interpreted as meaning (as with the Tassie *Catalogue*) that the original portrait gem from which Voyez had taken a cast was carved in cornelian. The owner of the cornelian is not specified. A modern plaster cast made from the Voyez intaglio of Pope is illustrated in Mr. Synge-Hutchinson's article, page 215, figure 5.

Jean Voyez (*fl.* 1767–91) was briefly employed by Wedgwood as a modeller in 1768–9. Following a dispute with Wedgwood, who accused him of stealing clay models and plaster moulds, he worked for various other pottery firms. From 1773 to 1776 he was engaged in his own manufacture and sale of basalt seals in competition with Wedgwood.[3] The close similarity of Voyez's seal of Pope to Tassie's no. 14366 (and to mould no. 816 at Barlaston) suggests that they derive from a common source.

[1] An impression taken from the Wedgwood mould is illustrated in W. K. Wimsatt, 'Portraits of Alexander Pope', *The Twelfth Wedgwood International Seminar* [New York, 1976], p. 107, fig. 14.

[2] Mr. J. V. G. Mallet, Keeper of the Department of Ceramics at the Victoria and Albert Museum, kindly supplied details concerning the intaglio seal of Pope. Additional help was given by Mr. Synge-Hutchinson.

[3] The known facts of Voyez's career are presented in R. J. Charleston's well-documented article 'Jean Voyez', *Transactions of the English Ceramic Circle, 5,* part 1 (London, 1960), 8–33; a transcription of Voyez's *Catalogue* of 1773 is printed in an Appendix, pp. 34–41, with illustrations.

WILLIAM HOARE (1707?–1792)

63.1a. OIL PAINTING, BY OR AFTER WILLIAM HOARE.
W. G. SKILLICORN, ESQ., ELLESMERE, SHROPSHIRE.*

Nos. 63.1 and 63.2 in *Portraits,* pages 283–7, are engravings of an oil painting of Pope, by William Hoare of Bath, that was formerly in the Buckingham collection at Stowe and afterwards in the possession of Sir Robert Peel. This picture, probably painted for Pope's friend Robert Nugent (later Earl Nugent), was the prototype for later versions executed by Hoare in oils and in crayons (see no. 63.3x below). It was last traced in the sale of *Peel Heirlooms* in 1917.

Mr. W. G. Skillicorn, of Ellesmere, Shropshire, reported to the

National Portrait Gallery in 1969 that he had recently acquired the oil painting which is the subject of the present entry. The painting was in poor condition when examined at the Portrait Gallery in 1970, but has since been carefully cleaned by a conservator at the Walker Art Gallery. Both the face and the dress closely conform to the engravings (which vary slightly from each other) of the Stowe–Peel portrait; the size of the canvas is the same. An important clue as to the possible provenance of Mr. Skillicorn's picture exists in the form of a name faintly impressed on the top of the stretcher: 'PeeL'. This barely visible inscription (possibly the remains of a paper label which has been removed) would appear to identify it as being the 'lost' Stowe–Peel portrait, although the evidence cannot be said to prove the case.[1] The somewhat mechanical quality of the painting seems difficult to reconcile with a version having the prestige of the Stowe–Peel portrait, but this aspect in itself does not disqualify it.

[1] A wooden label on the frame when Mr. Skillicorn acquired the painting stated that the subject is 'POPE, BY RICHARDSON'. Picart's engraving of 1807 (no. 63.1) names Richardson as the painter of the Stowe picture, but this portrait type was clearly the property of Hoare rather than Richardson.

63.3X. CRAYON PAINTING (PASTEL), BY WILLIAM HOARE, *c.* 1743.
PROFESSOR MAYNARD MACK, NEW HAVEN, CONNECTICUT.*

Pope's last visit to his friend Ralph Allen at Bath took place in July 1743. The small house party at Prior Park which included Martha Blount, Allen's protégé William Warburton, and (briefly) George Arbuthnot, went off disastrously and led to an estrangement between Pope and Allen.[1] It may have been at this time, or possibly during an earlier visit, that Pope sat to Hoare for the portrait which presumably came into Martha Blount's possession a few months later.

An inscription, apparently in the artist's hand, in faded red crayon on the back of the picture, reads: 'For Mrs Blount to be left at the Lady Gerard's in Welbeck Street by Oxford Chappel'. Elizabeth, Lady Gerard, the widow of Sir William Gerard, 6th Bt., was a close friend of Martha Blount. We learn from Pope's letter of 23 November 1743 to Slingsby Bethel that 'She [Miss Blount] is now at Lady Gerard's house (within three doors of that in which she formerly lived) in Welbeck Street, Oxford Chappel.'[2]

In his will, dated 12 December 1743, Pope refers to '*Mrs*. Martha Blount, *younger Daughter of Mrs*. Martha Blount, *late of* Welbeck-Street, Cavendish-Square.'[3] The inscription, viewed in the light of these statements, is a reasonable ground for assigning a probable date of 1743.

The portrait closely resembles the oil painting of Pope by Hoare (no. 63.4, now in the Osborn Collection at Yale) which was formerly in the collection of Richard Hurd, Bishop of Worcester, at Hartlebury Castle, and which is described in a list compiled by Hurd's nephew in 1813 as 'Mr. Pope—painted by Mr Hoare of Bath from an original in Crayons by himself.'[4] The likelihood of the present portrait being the 'original in Crayons' is supported by the fact that the outline of an earlier rendering of the cap is discernible—a feature which suggests that the artist was working from life.

The picture was reproduced for the first time in *Country Life, 140* (15 September 1966), 618, alongside the National Portrait Gallery's pastel by Hoare (no. 63.3a). At that time it belonged to Mr. J. F. Hickman, of Roughton House, Bridgnorth, Shropshire. Mr. Hickman bought it some years earlier from a Worcester antique dealer, who told him that it had been in the possession of another dealer for a considerable time. In February 1967 Mr. Hickman sold the portrait to Professor Maynard Mack. It appears as the frontispiece to his book *The Garden and the City: Retirement and Politics in the Later Poetry of Pope 1731–1743* (Toronto, 1969), and is discussed in detail on page 279.

[1] *Correspondence 4.* 462–4; Benjamin Boyce, *The Benevolent Man: A Life of Ralph Allen of Bath* (Cambridge, Mass., 1967), pp. 145–9.
[2] *Correspondence 4.* 485.
[3] *The Life of Alexander Pope, Esq; With a True Copy of His Last Will and Testament* (London: Charles Corbett, 1744), p. 62.
[4] *Portraits*, p. 291.

63.20. OIL PAINTING, AFTER WILLIAM HOARE.
DAWSONS OF PALL MALL.

This portrait, acquired about 1935–6 by Dr. A. N. L. Munby, Fellow and Librarian of King's College, Cambridge, remained in his possession until his death in December 1974. It was lot 606 in the sale of the Munby collection (second part) at Sotheby's on 5 April 1976, and was purchased by the bookseller Charles W.

Traylen, of Guildford, Surrey. The painting was subsequently acquired from Traylen by Messrs. Dawsons of Pall Mall (Rare Books and Manuscripts), and was offered for sale by them in July 1976.

64.2a. STIPPLE ENGRAVING, AFTER WILLIAM HOARE. FRONTISPIECE TO VOL. 2 OF POPE'S *Miscellaneous Poems*, BALTIMORE, 1814.*

Two small stipple engravings of this type (*Grolier* 96 and 98) are mentioned in *Portraits*, page 301, with an example of each located in the collection of W. S. Lewis, Farmington, Connecticut. A very similar, but not identical, stipple engraving, in a double-line frame, $3\frac{5}{8} \times 2\frac{1}{8}$ inches, appears as the frontispiece to *The Miscellaneous Poems of Alexander Pope, Esq. with the Life of the Author. In Two Volumes. Vol. 2. Baltimore: Published by Neal, Wills & Cole. Benja. Edes, Printer. 1814*. The inscription under the engraving reads: 'Alexander Pope Esqr/from an original drawing.'—but it is doubtless copied from Pierre Condé's stipple engraving of 1797 (no. 64.2).

64.14. PEN-AND-WASH DRAWING, AFTER WILLIAM HOARE. ULSTER MUSEUM, BELFAST.*

In 1973 Mr. Hugh Crawford, of Sheet, Petersfield, Hampshire, donated to the Ulster Museum, Belfast, a full-length drawing of Pope, almost certainly copied from Condé's stipple engraving of 1797 (no. 64.2). The drawing is executed in pen and ink and pale sepia wash over pencil, on thin white wove paper, $7 \times 4\frac{1}{2}$ inches, pasted on a card. The inscription 'Alexander Pope Esqr.' is written in ink on the card, below the drawing. On the back of the card is transcribed in ink, in the same hand as that of the inscription, the explanatory note printed by Warton in 1797 ('Warton's edition of Pope's works'). The name 'C. Victoria Williamson' (in a later hand) appears below it, along with the notation '2097/3'. The drawing was probably made in the early nineteenth century.[1]

---

[1] Mr. John Kerslake brought this drawing to our attention, and Mr. Martyn Anglesea, of the Ulster Museum, kindly furnished information about it.

JEAN-BAPTISTE VAN LOO (1684–1745)

66.7a. OIL PAINTING, AFTER J.-B. VAN LOO. ROBERT H. TAYLOR, PRINCETON, NEW JERSEY.*

This portrait seems to be first mentioned ('Alexander Pope. Kneller.') in an account of the pictures at Hinton St. George, Somerset, the seat of the Earls Poulett, communicated by 'P. Q.' to the *Gentleman's Magazine, 82*, part 2 (September 1812), 213. It is also recorded in the 'List of the principle Pictures at Hinton' in John Preston Neale, *Views of the Seats of Noblemen and Gentlemen in England, Wales, Scotland, and Ireland*, Second Series, *4* (London, 1828), after plate [29]: 'Alexander Pope—Sir G. Kneller.' This is 'Unexplained Allusions' no. 20 in *Portraits*, page 351.

The painting remained at Hinton St. George until its sale at Sotheby's on 5 February 1969, lot 23 ('The Property of the Rt. Hon. the Earl Poulett'), to 'Spiller'. Shortly thereafter, it was purchased by Cyril Humphris, 23 Old Bond Street, London. The picture was in their hands until it was resold at Sotheby's on 12 May 1971, lot 41, to Chas. J. Sawyer, the London booksellers, who offered it in their illustrated catalogue no. 286 (1971), item no. 518 ('by Charles Jervas'). It was acquired from Sawyer's by Mr. Robert H. Taylor in June 1973.[1]

As Kneller and Jervas both died before 1742, the *terminus a quo* for the Van Loo type of Pope portrait, this repetition could not have been painted by either of them. It has the appearance of being a late eighteenth-century copy.

[1] Information kindly supplied by Cyril Humphris and by Nancy N. Coffin, Curator of the Robert H. Taylor Collection.

66.11. CRAYON 'PAINTING' (PASTEL), AFTER J.-B. VAN LOO.

This portrait was acquired at auction by William H. Robinson Ltd., of 16 Pall Mall, London, in 1952, and was still in their possession in August 1961. The picture reappeared in a sale at Sotheby's on 6 July 1977, lot 367 ('The Property of a Gentleman'), but did not meet the reserve price and was therefore bought in. Its present ownership remains anonymous.

66.15. MEZZOTINT ENGRAVING, BY J. FABER, AFTER J.-B. VAN LOO, *c.* 1744.

The first of three states of this engraving, described by J. Ch. Smith *1.* 413 (Faber no. 294) and corrected by Charles E. Russell, *English Mezzotint Portraits* (London, 1926), *2.* 96, lacks any inscription ('Three examples known'—but not located). Professor Maynard Mack of Yale University owns an impression of the first state, acquired some years ago from Frederick B. Daniell & Son, 32 Cranbourn Street, Leicester Square, London.

66.15a. BLACK CRAYON AND PENCIL DRAWING ON WHITE PAPER, AFTER J.-B. VAN LOO. H. P. KRAUS, NEW YORK CITY.*

H. P. Kraus (Old and Rare Books, Manuscripts, Maps), 16 East 46th Street, New York City, is the present owner of an anonymous drawing, $7\frac{5}{8} \times 5\frac{11}{16}$ inches, inscribed 'Alexander Pope, Poet anglois. m. 1744/son age 57 ans.' The similarity of the inscription to that of Faber's mezzotint ('ALEXANDER POPE/Poeta Anglus./OB: A? 1744 ÆTAT: 57/. . .') supports the conclusion that the drawing was done from the mezzotint.

66.16a. WATERCOLOUR DRAWING, BY E. F. BURNEY, AFTER J.-B. VAN LOO. F. J. DU ROVERAY, 1806.*

In a letter of 22 January 1806 to George Baker, F. J. Du Roveray (the publisher of illustrated editions of Milton, Gray, and Pope) mentions eight 'portraits done for him by Burney', including 'One of Pope . . . in water-colours, and in perfect preservation'.[1] This drawing was doubtless the design for a rectangular line engraving, $4\frac{13}{16} \times 3\frac{1}{2}$ inches, that appears as the frontispiece to volume 1 of *The Poetical Works of Alexander Pope. A New Edition. Adorned with Plates . . . London: Printed for F. J. Du Roveray, By T. Bensley, Bolt Court,* 6 vols., 1804. The portrait of Pope, contained within an oval, is derived from the Houbraken engraving, no. 66.16. The portrait is surrounded by drapery; below it is an allegorical scene (possibly intended to represent the Three Graces with the infant Pope) on an oblong panel, with a ewer and a lyre in the foreground. The inscription reads: 'Drawn by E. F. Burney.//Engraved by Ls Schiavonetti./A. POPE./Published 1st

October 1804, by F. J. Du Roveray, London.' The engraving is *BMEP* 51, *Grolier* 71.

Edward Francesco Burney (1760–1848), Fanny Burney's first cousin, is chiefly known today for his popular book illustrations, although he also painted portraits in oils and a number of large watercolour scenes (often satirical) from contemporary life.[2] The present whereabouts of the frontispiece design commissioned by Du Roveray is not known.

[1] British Library Egerton MS. 2679, f. 13. Professor D. H. Weinglass kindly brought this letter to our attention.

[2] The fullest published account of Burney's work is in Hanns Hammelmann and T. S. R. Boase, *Book Illustrators in Eighteenth-Century England* (New Haven, 1975), pp. 21–3. Patricia Crown, who has recently completed a doctoral dissertation on Burney, was helpful in identifying the portrait of Pope mentioned in Du Roveray's letter.

66.16b. OIL PAINTING, BY G. W. NOVICE, AFTER J.-B. VAN LOO.
STEPHEN PARKS, NEW HAVEN, CONNECTICUT.*

Dr. Stephen Parks, Curator of the Osborn Collection, Yale University Library, is the owner of a small oil painting of Pope of the Van Loo type, but in the reversed pose of the Houbraken engraving (no. 66.16), purchased at a sale by Dowell's of Edinburgh, 26 March 1965, lot 65. The painting, which is on a wood panel 6⅝×5½ inches, is inscribed in ink on a paper label pasted on the back: 'Alexander Pope, Esquire, in 173[5]/Poet, Ætati 47./ Novice after Jervas.' The initials 'G. W. N.' are painted below the label. The portrait was doubtless copied from the Houbraken engraving or from one of the numerous derivative engravings of the Van Loo type.

George W. Novice was a painter of genre scenes who exhibited three works at the Royal Academy between 1828 and 1833, and four works at the British Institution between 1824 and 1832.[1]

[1] Algernon Graves, *The Royal Academy of Arts* (London, 1905–6), 5. 392; Graves, *The British Institution* (London, 1908), p. 404.

66.20. OIL AND TEMPERA PAINTING, BY WILLIAM BLAKE, AFTER VAN LOO, *c.* 1800. CITY ART GALLERY, MANCHESTER.

In a letter of November 1965, Dr. F. G. Grossman, then the Deputy Director of the City Art Gallery, Manchester, suggested plausibly that Blake's head of Pope is derived from Faber's mezzotint engraving (no. 66.15), which preserves the direction of the pose in Van Loo's painting, rather than from the Houbraken engraving (no. 66.16), in which the image is reversed.

The eighteen frieze-panels executed by Blake for the library of Turret House, Felpham, Sussex (the seat of his friend and patron William Hayley), have been recently discussed in Edward Croft-Murray, *Decorative Painting in England 1537–1837* (London, 1962–70), *2*. 71–2, 171–2; six of the panels, including that of Pope, are illustrated, pages 152–4, plates 143–8.

66.21. MURAL PAINTING, 'ELYSIUM AND TARTARUS', BY JAMES BARRY, WITH VIGNETTE PORTRAIT OF POPE, AFTER VAN LOO. ROYAL SOCIETY OF ARTS, LONDON.*

Between 1779 and 1783 the Irish 'history painter' James Barry (1741–1806) was engaged on the last of his six monumental canvases for the Great Room of the Royal Society of Arts in the Adelphi. The theme of this great allegorical series is 'the progress of human culture and knowledge'. The sixth picture, entitled *Elysium and Tartarus, or the State of Final Retribution*, was executed in three panels (12 feet high, 42 feet long overall). In April 1783, when all six pictures were exhibited for the first time, the *Elysium* represented 117 ancient and modern worthies, arranged according to their interests and achievements.[1]

A vignette portrait of Pope, after Van Loo, appears among a group of literary figures in the centre panel of the *Elysium*, above the outstretched arm of an angel strewing flowers. Barry probably copied the portrait from one of the many derivative engravings of the Van Loo type.[2] A newspaper report of the 1783 exhibition pointed out that the artist had taken several of his portraits 'from the frontispieces of books [placing them] in Heaven in the very attitude given them by the booksellers', and mentioned Newton, Locke, and Pope as examples of this 'plagiarism'.[3] Pope is immediately surrounded by familiar likenesses of Dryden, Gray, William Mason, and Sterne.

The *Elysium* was etched by Barry with the publication date of 1 May 1791 (four states known). A preparatory study for the etching, in brown ink and wash, is in the British Museum.

[1] For a detailed account of the genesis and composition of the *Elysium*, see

David Allan, 'The Progress of Human Culture and Knowledge: James Barry's Paintings for the Royal Society of Arts at the Adelphi in London, 1777–1801—Part Two: The Fifth and Sixth Pictures', *Connoisseur, 188* (February 1975), 98–106. We wish to thank Mr. Allan, Curator-Librarian of the Royal Society of Arts, and Dr. Christopher White, Director of Studies at the Paul Mellon Centre for Studies in British Art, for generously undertaking to have the Pope vignette specially photographed for the Supplement. Professor William L. Pressly has provided helpful counsel and information for this entry.

² See *Portraits*, p. 329.

³ *St. James's Chronicle*, 13–15 May 1783. We owe this reference to David Allan.

APPENDIX 2:
UNEXPLAINED ALLUSIONS TO POPE PORTRAITS

42. Dawson Turner to William Roscoe, 20 May 1823: 'The Rev. C. Taylor [Charles Benjamin Tayler (1797–1875)], curate to Dr Hay Drummond at Hadleigh [Suffolk], has an original portrait of Pope by Jervis, of a kitcat size, painted when he was not more than 20 years of age, & when his deformity had not yet come on, & supposed to be the only likeness of him at that early time of life' (Roscoe Paper 4921, Liverpool Public Library).

APPENDIX 3:
PORTRAITS MISTAKENLY CALLED POPE, AND SOME OTHERS

2. This painting, which has been described at one time or another as a self-portrait of Pope or as an allegorical work painted by him, was presented by the late Caroline Newton to Bryn Mawr College and now hangs in the Miriam Coffin Canaday Library. The drawing in red chalk said to be by Pope—one of two extant designs related to the painting—is in the collection of Mr. Philip Hofer, Cambridge, Massachusetts.

27. This unique 'composite' portrait of Pope is now in the possession of J. C. Riely, New Haven, Connecticut, the gift of Margaret Wimsatt in May 1976.

28. Further information about this picture comes from Professor D. H. Weinglass, who kindly informs us that William Ford, the Manchester bookseller, wrote to William Roscoe on 6 October 1823: 'I have also a very curious, early Picture of Pope, which represents him, I shd think, about 16 or 17 & said to be by Sir Godfrey Kneller. If a Drawing of it, or a Lithographed print of it for your Work, for it has now been engraved wd be acceptable, it is at your Service also' (Roscoe Paper 1562, Liverpool Public Library). Ford had possibly acquired the portrait said to be Pope at the William Davies Sale at Christie's in 1821. But Roscoe made no use of it to illustrate his edition of Pope's *Works*. Ford wrote to him again on 11 October 1823: 'The portrait of Pope, I conclude you do not want, as you do not mention it, but if I should Lithograph it, you would probably be desirous of having one, as I consider it a genuine Portrait of him, and from circumstances which I am in possession [of], have no doubts of its originality' (Roscoe Paper 1563).

29. At Christie's 16 July 1965, lot 82 ('The Property of the Rt. Hon. Lord Burton, and formerly part of the Collection of the late Rt. Hon. The Baroness Burton') was a portrait described as follows: 'Richardson. Portrait of Alexander Pope, half length, in brown dress and red cap, holding a book—*inscribed* [at top of canvas: 'ALEXANDER POPE. J. RICHARDSON.']—29 in. by 24 in.' It was purchased by Mr. Earle W. Newton, of St. Augustine, Florida, who had previously acquired a replica of the Van Loo type, no. 66.5. The subject of this portrait, whose dress is similar to that of Pope in Kneller's portrait of 1716, has an aquiline nose and a pointed chin—features which tell against its being Pope.

30. In the catalogue of Colnaghi's *Exhibition of English Drawings, Watercolours, and Paintings*, 14 November–7 December 1973, no. 57 is George White (*c.* 1674–1732), 'Portrait of a Gentleman, possibly Alexander Pope,' in coloured chalks, 358×275 mm, signed in black lead and dated 1732 (illustrated, plate 20). The subject is clearly not Pope.

31. A postcard of recent issue, copyright London Borough of Richmond upon Thames, shows a full-length portrait of a man identified as follows: '5. Alexander Pope by Jonathan Richardson

(1665–1745), *oil on canvas* A191'. Mr. Derek Jones, Chief Librarian and Curator of the Libraries Department, London Borough of Richmond upon Thames, informs us that the painting was so identified when it was sold to the Hon. Mrs. Nellie Ionides. This portrait from the Ionides collection is now at the Orleans House Gallery, Twickenham. The postcard has been withdrawn from sale.

APPENDIX 4:
NOMINAL PORTRAITS OF POPE

6. Commentators who discuss the engraving (first and second states) of Hogarth's painting *The Distressed Poet* have assumed that the print on the wall above the poet's head represents Pope thrashing Edmund Curll. Ronald Paulson, in 'New Light on Hogarth's Graphic Works', *Burlington Magazine*, *109* (May 1967), 283, offers new evidence which suggests that the print is intended to show Curll thrashing Pope. Paulson writes: 'It is likely that most contemporaries who were aware of the unsavoury tussle over the publication of Pope's letters considered that Curll emerged the victor. Moreover, of the two figures, the prone one with cap and narrow face more nearly resembles Pope than the other hefty figure with his three-cornered hat and periwig.' See also Paulson's *Hogarth's Graphic Works*, revised edition (New Haven, 1970), *1*. 174–6 (no. 145), 323.

Down Chancery Lane

James Sutherland

I HOPE that the theme of this volume permits contributors to be mildly anecdotal, for I have reached a time of life when it is difficult to be anything else; but if I may have to ask for the indulgence of some readers, I feel sure that my old friend Jim Osborn would have forgiven, and might even have welcomed, a measure of reminiscence on such an occasion. At all events, when we first met in the early 1930s, and he was working on Edmond Malone at Oxford, I was spending a good deal of my spare time at the Public Record Office in Chancery Lane; and it is mainly my fortunes and misfortunes in that vast repository of documents that I wish to recall here. The tall uniformed doorkeeper with whom I used to exchange friendly platitudes about the weather (an old soldier by the look of him) must long since have been gathered to his fathers, and I have never met any of his replacements, for it is getting on to forty years since I last visited that neo-Gothic building. But for some half-dozen years I was a fairly regular *habitué*. There I would sit, like Hogarth's industrious apprentice at his loom, poring over the documents that were brought to me, untroubled by thought or the need to think, but buoyed up by an unconquerable hope that one day something (I had no idea what, but something quite remarkable) would turn up on my table. Inevitably I made a few discoveries, although most were modest and none was spectacular; but I worked there long enough to realize that for the literary scholar a vast amount of interesting material still lies hidden there waiting to be discovered, and that at the present rate of extraction it will last much longer than North Sea oil.

My involvement with the Public Record Office began when I was a lecturer at University College, London. The head of my department, C. J. Sisson, had already made some notable discoveries among the Elizabethan records there, and was to make many more; and he liked his young men to publish. I did not think that the Record Office was my natural haunt, and for some time I resisted all suggestions that I might work there, but in the end I weakened and went. I had, of course, to be looking for something, and I was soon working my way through a succession of Chancery bills of complaint brought by early eighteenth-century booksellers and printers. I had equipped myself with a sixpenny magnifying glass to help me read illegible words, and in the early stages I was assisted by a paper published by Margaret Dowling (an ex-student of Sissons's, and by now R. B. McKerrow's secretary), entitled 'Public Office Research: The Equity Side of Chancery, 1558–1714'.[1]

Anyone deciding to work in the Record Office has to reconcile himself to a good deal of drudgery, unless he has a research assistant to do the preliminary sifting for him. With an income of £500 I was inevitably my own research assistant; and since I had elected to work among Chancery proceedings, the initial drudgery lay in going slowly through the Six Clerks indexes, and noting down likely names of plaintiffs and defendants. (A Six Clerk was one of the six official clerks formerly connected with the Court of Chancery, whose duty it was to file, under the name of the complainant, bills (and answers) as they came in.) It would perhaps be an exaggeration to say that the Six Clerks indexes are chaotic: names, it is true, were entered under the first letter of the complainant's surname, though not in alphabetical order within any given letter. But since Chancery proceedings were notoriously slow and might often last for some years, the answers of defendants were often separately indexed, and may indeed turn up in any of the Six Clerks divisions. Worse still, documents irretrievably mislaid may not turn up at all, and it is possible to find an answer or answers to a bill without ever finding the original bill of complaint.

On my way through the Six Clerks indexes I kept in mind the names of all the booksellers I could remember, and soon acquired a promising list. Whenever I was able to visit the Record Office I would fill in as many requests for Chancery bills as I thought the staff would accept, and would go on searching in the indexes for further names while waiting for the documents to arrive. But of course, if I was going to all this trouble, it was only sensible to make a note of any more illustrious names that might turn up, such as Pope or Swift, who—if they proved to be the right Pope or Swift—would be a greater catch than any mere bookseller. Un-

---

[1] *Review of English Studies*, viii (1932), 185–200.

fortunately, however, when they did their indexing the Six Clerks entered plaintiff and defendant by their surnames only; and when I had written out my slip and a Chancery bill duly arrived on my table, I would find, as often as not, that '*Pope* v. *Philips*' was concerned with the complaint of Richard Pope of Aston Clinton, Gent. about a messuage or tenement falsely and injuriously claimed by Thomas Philips of the said parish of Aston Clinton, and that '*Swift* v. *Dennis*' dealt with the attempt of Isaac Swift of Clerkenwell, scrivener, to recover a bad debt from Christopher Dennis of Cripplegate, haberdasher. The whole exercise bore some resemblance to an archaeological dig, but would perhaps be more accurately pictured as opening a succession of oyster shells hoping to find a pearl. In the course of the next few years, as my heap of oyster shells grew to be a mound, I duly discovered my little quota of pearls, although none of them was perhaps of top quality. But I never turned in to the Record Office from Chancery Lane without feeling a slight quickening of the pulse, for I was now thoroughly hooked on what was a sort of gambling game. It was the sort of gamble that might be expected to appeal to a young Scot: I had nothing to lose but my time, and of that in those far-off days I had plenty.

So far I have emphasized the irksome, unglamorous, and often frustrating aspects of research among the Chancery records. But one had one's lucky days. For some time I had been noting and examining all the suits in which the plaintiff was 'Gay', only to find when the documents reached me that they had nothing to do with the author of *The Beggar's Opera*. But one morning I unrolled a bill marked '*Gay* v. *Astley*', and the first word that caught my eye was 'Polly'. What I had come upon was an answer to John Gay's bill of complaint against Thomas Astley and others for pirating his handsome six-shilling quarto of *Polly* in 1729. From Astley's answer I learned that he had a collaborator in the piracy, James Watson, and that Astley himself had employed Samuel Ayris as his printer. I was now committed to working my way through the letter G in all the Six Clerks indexes—not in itself a herculean task, since surnames beginning with G are not particularly common. I never, in fact, succeeded in tracing Gay's bill of complaint, in which presumably he was asking for an injunction to prevent further piratical publication of his play; but in due course I located three 'further answers' of James Watson (but not his first answer, which was no doubt attached to Gay's bill), and an answer put in by Samuel Ayris. I had stirred up a hornets' nest, and as I went on examining the various bills in which the plaintiff was 'Gay', I came upon an answer by Francis Jeffery, two answers by Robert Walker, and four by Thomas Read—all dealing with *Polly*. Eventually it became apparent that I had on my hands, not one pirated edition of the play, but five, published only a few days after the appearance of Gay's own edition, and of course selling at a considerably lower price.

I now had enough material to form a fairly clear idea of what had been going on. But anyone working on a Chancery suit has an obligation to search through all the collateral records that may have a bearing on the case, since, if he goes on to publish his findings, it is unlikely that anyone else will think it worth his while to go over the same ground again. I therefore applied myself to the indexes of Decrees and Orders, Depositions and Affidavits, and was able to find a few documents that threw further light, but not much, on the progress of Gay's suit. I was still trying to find the final decision of the Court when war broke out in 1939, and access to the Record Office was suspended *sine die*. Fortunately the outcome of the action was recorded by Sir William Blackstone.[2] When Gay died in December 1732, the Court of Chancery was still proceeding at the snail's pace of 'Jarndyce and Jarndyce' in *Bleak House*; but his two sisters entered a bill of reviver, and at length on 23 December 1733, long after it could have mattered much what happened to *Polly*, they were granted a perpetual injunction.

When I came to put together the scattered evidence I had so painstakingly collected I was faced with several problems of interpretation. At that point I had evidence of four pirated editions: two 'Printed for T. THOMSON', one 'Printed for *Jeffery Walker*', and one 'Sold by T. READ'. From the answers of Astley and Watson I had learned that 'T. Thomson' was, as I had suspected, a fictitious name, intended to conceal the identity of the real publishers, and that they had produced two unauthorized editions of *Polly*, one of 2,000 copies, and a second of 1,000 copies. I had also learned that the printing had been shared equally by Watson and Astley, Watson printing the first half of the play, and Astley employing Samuel Ayris to print the rest. This division of labour could have been due to their desire to shorten the job and

[2] *Commentaries on the Laws of England, Book the Second* (1766), p. 407.

get their pirated edition on the market as early as possible; but from Astley's answer it appeared that in his bill of complaint Gay had charged Astley and Watson with having caused their edition to be printed by several hands, 'the better to carry on their fraud and design'. In his answer Astley expressly denied any such intention, but for anyone familiar with the devious defence often entered by eighteenth-century lawyers his denial is less than convincing: Astley was probably hoping to show that he had not printed a play called *Polly*, only a part of it. It is significant that when Samuel Ayris put in his answer he, or his lawyer, thought it a sufficient defence to deny that he had printed 'all or any' of the editions mentioned in Gay's bill—and again this was literally true. No such defence was available for Thomas Read, but he tried to get round the strict letter of the law by claiming that in his edition there were alterations on every page, that the title-page was different, viz. THE Second Part of THE BEGGAR'S OPERA, and that the music and preface had been omitted—the implication being that whatever he had printed and sold it was not Gay's *Polly*.

When I came to look at the two 'T. Thomson' editions, I soon found myself out of my bibliographical depth, and I had the good sense to enlist the help of Mr. Graham Pollard. His examination of the two Bodleian copies introduced a startling complication. In the first copy he looked at (which I shall call X) he duly found that signatures A–E had been set by one printer, and signatures F–I by another. But on comparing X with the second copy (Y) he found that the whole of Y had been set by the printer responsible for composing signatures A–E in X, i.e. by Watson. This baffled me, but not Mr. Pollard. Watson, he suggested, must have double-crossed his partner, and in addition to printing 2,000 copies of signatures A–E for the first edition, and 1,000 for the second, he must then have over-printed A–E by an unspecified number of copies, and set one of his men to print the same number of copies of F–I. He would then have at his disposal, unknown to Astley, enough additional copies of A–I to constitute a separate edition of *Polly*, of which the Bodleian's Y is a specimen. I cannot reproduce here the whole of Mr. Pollard's reconstruction of what must have happened in Watson's workshop; but in the account I finally gave of those Gay piracies[3] I acknowledged my debt to

---

[3] ' "Polly" among the Pirates', *Modern Language Review*, xxxvii (1942), 291–303.

him, and I repeat that acknowledgement now. I take credit for
some honest spadework, but without his help in interpreting the
evidence I had dug up I should have been

> one whose hand,
> Like the base Indian, threw a pearl away
> Richer than all his tribe.

I had not been working for many months among my Chancery
suits when I had the good fortune to meet Miss Eleanore Boswell
(later Lady Murrie), who was already well versed in the ramifications of the Public Record Office, and had turned her knowledge to
good account in *The Restoration Court Stage* (1932). She kindly
drew my attention to several Chancery suits in which Daniel
Defoe (or Foe) was either plaintiff or defendant, and in the course
of following those up I came upon several more. Eventually I was
able to report on nine different actions relating to his business
activities between 1678 and 1695, which went some way towards
filling a biographical gap in his early career.

About the same time, by examining two other Chancery documents dated 1728 and 1730 I was able to clear up the mystery
surrounding the last years of Defoe's life. The facts, as they had
been narrated by Defoe's biographers, were undoubtedly puzzling.
In the last letter he is known to have written, dated 12 August 1730
'about two Miles from Greenwich, Kent', Defoe tells his son-in-
law, Henry Baker, that his mind is sinking under a weight of
affliction, and that he has received a blow from 'a wicked, perjur'd,
and contemptible enemy'; he would dearly like to see Baker and
his beloved daughter Sophia, but it would not be safe for them to
visit him. On 24 April 1731, he died in a lodging-house in Rope-
makers Alley, and in September 1733 letters of administration on
his goods and chattels were granted to one Mary Brooke. To anyone familiar with Defoe's past history the natural assumption
would be that money troubles had caught up with him again, and
that in his old age he had been driven into hiding to escape the
demands of an unsatisfied creditor.[4] But to his mid-Victorian
biographer William Lee such an assumption was intolerable: the
author of *Robinson Crusoe*, the owner of a fine house in Stoke
Newington, could not possibly have died insolvent. It was true,

---

[4] This was in fact the suggestion of Walter Wilson in his *Memoirs of the Life
and Times of Daniel De Foe*, 3 vols. (1830).

he admitted, that 'under some real or supposed necessity of personal concealment' he appears to have made a temporary transfer of his property to one of his sons and retired to Rope-makers Alley ('perhaps the most agreeable place of residence within the limits of the City'); but his old debts had long since been settled, and Mary Brooke was no doubt merely his landlady seeking to recover a few weeks' rent due to her when Defoe died, all alone, in her house. As for the 'wicked, perjur'd, and contempt-ible enemy', this was almost certainly (if, indeed, Defoe was not simply suffering from mental delusions) his old Tory employer Nathaniel Mist, for whom he had worked on *Mist's Weekly Journal*, and who was now trying to betray him in some unspecified way to the Whig government. All in all, Lee's determination not to allow Defoe to leave the world as an insolvent debtor is a classic case of special pleading. His guess that Mary Brooke was only an unsatisfied landlady was accepted by later biographers, and soon hardened into fact.

The truth should have been made known in 1912. In that year a contributor to *Notes and Queries* drew attention to a Chancery suit, '*Foe* v. *Brooke*' (1728), but unaccountably dismissed it in a few words, explaining that it would be only wasting space to enter into the details of Defoe's bill. Yet when I came to examine this bill I found that it contained a full recapitulation by Defoe of the steps he had taken to reach a settlement with his creditors sub-sequent to his first and second bankruptcies many years before. After his second bankruptcy he had assigned his estate and all his effects to his friend James Stancliffe, who had acted as his trustee to come to a final composition with his creditors, and he had also handed over to Stancliffe all the receipts and releases he had received from creditors already satisfied. He never doubted that Stancliffe would return the receipts and account for any balance that remained after all his creditors had been paid, but before that could happen Stancliffe died. Thereupon Samuel Brooke, weaver, took administration of Stancliffe's estate, and (according to Defoe) agreed to give him his discharge and deliver up to him all his papers and receipts. But unfortunately he too died before he was able to carry out his promise. On Brooke's death his widow —and here at last we come to Mary Brooke—took administration of her husband's estate, and promised to give him his discharge as her husband had intended to do. But now, after all those years, she, together with some other persons, had commenced several actions in the King's Bench and Exchequer courts to recover debts which they alleged to be still outstanding. That, at any rate, was Defoe's story. Unable, however, to produce the documents that would show he had satisfied all his creditors, he made over his estate to his eldest son Daniel, and then went to ground to escape his pursuers.

There is a moral here for scholars. When an earnest young student asked Dr. Martin Joseph Routh, the venerable President of Magdalen College, Oxford, then in his ninety-first year, for some axiom, some precept that he could carry through life, the old gentleman replied: 'I think, sir, since you care for the advice of an old man, sir, you will find it a very good practice *always to verify your references*, sir.' To that I would add that on this and some other occasions I have found it a very good practice to verify other people's references, which is no doubt what the old man had in mind.

I suspect that the Public Record Office is a *terra incognita* to most literary scholars, and is likely to remain so. I also suspect (and I could put this more forcibly) that the scholar who chooses to work there is looked upon by most of his colleagues as at best a harmless drudge, a manual labourer of the intellectual world, one of whom it may be said 'our servants will do those things for us'. It may be so, and I accept my share of dullness. But because I had found it interesting, even fascinating, to dig for some years in that *hortus siccus*, it never occurred to me that others might assume that I was not interested in anything else. I had no right to make such an assumption. When R. B. McKerrow died in 1940 and I was asked to succeed him as editor of the *Review of English Studies*, one of the new friends I made was Elmer Edgar Stoll. The other day I was looking at a letter of his, dated March 24 1947, which must have been in reply to one of mine telling him that I was giving up the editorship of *RES* so that I could have more time for writing. Stoll had been catching up on his reading, and his letter began: 'I have just finished your *Medium of Poetry*, belatedly.' ('Belatedly' was right: it had appeared in 1934.) Stoll went on to say some kind things about this now forgotten book, and I could see that he felt he owed me some sort of apology, though I could not for the life of me think why. But a little further on it all became clear: 'No wonder you are retiring from the unremunerative work of editing, when you can write a book like this.' I can still remember how I suddenly realized, with a mild sense of shock, the image Stoll must have had of me, and of others like me: an editor, a middleman facilitating the communication of ideas between producer and consumer, but not one who was likely to have any ideas of his own. He may even have cast a disenchanted eye over the severely factual account I had given in *RES*, 'Some Early Troubles of Daniel Defoe', when I wrote up the Chancery suits I have already mentioned, and he may well have placed me there and then in my appropriate category. If Stoll did not, Jonathan Cape certainly did. I had written to that excellent publisher asking him if he would be interested in a life of Defoe that I was now thinking of writing, and to show that I knew something about the subject I enclosed the two papers on Defoe that I had published. Mr. Cape, who was a kindly man, invited me to go and see him, but it soon became clear that my two learned articles, bristling with footnotes about Chancery proceedings, had made a fatal impression. He told me in the nicest possible way how such things should be written; and then, as I was leaving, he pressed into my hands a copy of the book he had been holding up to me as a model, Bonamy Dobrée's *Variety of Ways*. But if Mr. Cape, on the evidence available to him, had decided that, biographically speaking, I was fit only to 'settle Hoti's business', I felt he had not got me quite right; and 'if you care for the advice of an old man, sir', I would say we are sometimes too ready to relegate our academic contemporaries to exclusive categories. The twentieth century is hardly likely to be regarded by future generations as an age of tolerance; but I will confess I am often surprised by the animosity that one kind of scholar is prepared to show to another. To my mind, the critic and the scholar are not incompatible, and indeed I have little expectation of profit and delight unless I am reading the work of one who is both. In any case, as the song says in *Oklahoma*, 'The farmer and the cowboy should be friends.'

For the next few years I gave most of my spare time to Defoe. I had abandoned the hunt for him in Chancery, and was now looking for any traces he might have left in State Papers Domestic for the reigns of Queen Anne and George I. Those papers would arrive on my desk in amorphous bundles tied up with white tape, and I found them fascinating. When I was not at the Record Office I was at the British Museum reading my way through the volumes of newspapers in the Burney collection for the same period, and I found them equally absorbing. Anyone who has done what I was now doing will know the difficulty of keeping the end in sight (in my case a life of Defoe), and not getting sidetracked by all the other interesting material that one keeps on turning up. I must have reached some sort of compromise, for the life of Defoe got itself written; but I also filled about twenty notebooks with the literary and historical debris that came my way. What I had been reading in State Papers Domestic was mainly the day-to-day business of the Under-Secretary's office, and much of that consisted of the reports of informers on the authors of pamphlets, newswriters, printers, publishers, and even street hawkers, turning an honest or dishonest penny, who had offended the government, and of the examination of those offenders, and the measures taken to deal with them. Since early eighteenth-century newspapers, like those of the present day, tended to concentrate their attention on people who got into trouble, I would come across the same names again in the *Post Boy*, the *Flying Post*, *Mist's Weekly Journal*, and the rest, until in time Robert Mawson, George Flint, Mrs. Elizabeth Powell, Francis Clifton, Nathaniel Mist, and many more became old friends, and I felt a sort of compulsion to find out what happened to them. I do not seek to defend this, I even recognize that it became something of an obsession; but I think I can explain it. As a Scot I have inherited from my ancestors a strong sense of fact, and an antiquarian interest in the past because it is not the present; and as a scholar I have always wanted, as far as possible, to enter into and re-create for myself the daily life of the period I am studying—though it is now a widely held axiom that this is impossible. I mention all this now because it led to another book which, against his better judgement, I persuaded my publisher to accept. This was *Background for Queen Anne*, containing short biographies of such bygone celebrities and nonentities as the hard-drinking journalist, Burridge the Blasphemer, the young printer John Matthews who was hanged in 1719 for publishing a seditious pamphlet called *Vox Populi*, John Lacy, the self-inspired leader of the Modern Prophets, and poor Charlotte Addison, the only child of Joseph Addison and the Countess of Warwick, who had teenage problems, but who died an old maid at Bilton Manor, the fine country house that Addison had bought for his own old age. *Background for Queen Anne*, however, was doomed from the start: it appeared in 1939 just before the outbreak of war, when readers had more urgent and important things to think about, and it is now a forgotten book about the forgotten. Not quite forgotten, though: one of its few readers was James M. Osborn, and it is cited by him (*non omnis moriar*) in a note to his classic edition of Joseph Spence's *Anecdotes*.

While all this was going on, I was also working on an edition of the *Dunciad* for the 'Twickenham' Pope. This poem had already been heavily annotated by Pope himself, and by his eighteenth- and nineteenth-century editors; but here and there (an experience familiar to anyone who has done much editing) I would come upon a passage that had unaccountably been left alone, although it seemed to call for explanation. One such passage occurs in the speech of the florist (iv. 403–18):

> Soft on the paper ruff its leaves I spread,
> Bright with the gilded button tipt its head,
> Then thron'd in glass, and nam'd it CAROLINE.

Since it was clear from the last line of his speech that the florist was referring to a carnation, I went straight to Philip Miller's *Gardener's Dictionary*, where I soon found (Art. 'Caryophyllus') detailed instructions for the culture of this favourite eighteenth-century flower; and paper ruff, gilded button, and glass all became clear. This was annotation at its most painless: it is one's failures that are most likely to stay (and fester) in the mind. I hate to think how many fruitless hours I spent trying to identify 'Mummius' (iv. 371 ff.), for whom I found at least half a dozen possible candidates; and how many more hours in trying to find Pope's source for 'Blest in one Niger, till he knows of two' (iv. 370), with its implication that a gold coin of the short reign of C. Pescennius Niger was known by only one surviving specimen. I fully realize that if I never solve this last problem life will still go on, and that in annotating the *Dunciad* (which frequently involved writing notes on Pope's notes) I was always in danger of being myself the sort of dunce of whom he said:

> To future ages may thy dulness last,
> As thou preserv'st the dulness of the past.

But that I accepted as an occupational hazard for any conscientious editor of the poem; and the only silly reaction came from Dr. Leavis, who said firmly, 'It is not the edition in which the *Dunciad* should be read. The material is one thing, the poetry another. . . . Notes are not necessary; the poetry doesn't depend upon them in any essential respect.' I have always had a preference for understanding what I read, and it surprised me to find Dr. Leavis making such a sharp distinction between the 'poetry' and the meaning; but perhaps he did not express himself very well.

I tend to think of editing not as an adventure, but as a discipline, and as a relevant application of such knowledge as one possesses or takes the trouble to acquire. But occasionally pure accident plays a part in one's labours. When I was editing Lucy Hutchinson's *Memoirs of the Life of Colonel Hutchinson* a few years ago, I felt fairly sure that I would have to base the text on the first edition published by the Revd. Julius Hutchinson in 1806, since Sir Charles Firth, who had edited the *Memoirs* in 1885 and who wrote the lives of John and Lucy Hutchinson for *DNB*, had stated that the manuscript was lost. Naturally I made a number of inquiries, searched through the manuscript catalogues of various libraries, and even went to Somerset House to look at the will of Canon F. E. Hutchinson, who was a descendant; but all without result. I therefore got to work on the text of 1806, and spent several months on it, before going on to the explanatory annotation. When I had all but completed my notes, it occurred to me that it might be as well to work through the indexes to *Notes and Queries* to make sure there was nothing I had missed. (Any well-organized scholar would probably have thought of this much sooner.) Fortunately I began at the year 1970 and worked backwards, instead of beginning at 1849 and working forwards; and in no time at all I came on an entry for 1923, 'HUTCHINSON, Lucy, manuscripts'. On consulting the relevant volume I found that the manuscript of the *Memoirs* had been purchased in 1922 by the Nottingham Corporation from a London firm of antiquarian booksellers, and that it was now in the Nottingham Castle Museum. So far as the text was concerned, I was now back to square one; but this almost accidental discovery enabled me not only to print the text cleared of the many small errors or improvements made by the editor or his printer in 1806, but to add about 9,000 words which, for one reason or another, the Revd. Julius Hutchinson had felt unable to print. If there is a moral here, it is not on this occasion, 'Always verify your references', but 'Leave no stone unturned.'

I will end with another accidental discovery, of no importance in itself, but worth recording, I hope, for its singularity. Towards the end of the War, when I was living in the Berkshire village of Long Wittenham, an army officer and his wife became our nearest neighbours. My wife and I called on them, and when we grew to know them better I discovered that the lady belonged to the Dering family in Kent, a daughter of the tenth baronet. I remember saying to her that the only thing I knew about her family was that in 1711 one of her ancestors, Sir Cholmely Dering, had been killed in a duel with Colonel Richard Thornhill.[5] Her family home, Surrenden Manor, had been sold, and the contents dispersed; but some months after she came to live at Long Wittenham the family archives arrived in about a dozen wooden boxes, and she kindly gave me permission to look at them. The first few boxes I opened were filled with legal deeds in vellum, with beautiful wax seals attached to them, stretching from medieval times to the seventeenth century. These were of no great interest to me; but then I opened a box filled mainly with correspondence. About the third or fourth time I dipped into this box I came up with a small crumpled piece of paper. Yes; it was Richard Thornhill's challenge to Sir Cholmely Dering: 'May the 8th 1711—Sir, I shall be able to go Abroad Tomorrow Morning,[6] and desire you would give me a Meeting with your Sword and Pistols, which I must insist on. . . .' The following morning the two men fought with pistols at close range in Tothill Fields, and Dering fell, living only long enough to forgive his friend, and to take all the blame for what had happened.

The odds against my making this particular discovery must have been astronomical. That the fatal challenge should have been preserved by the dead man's family was entirely natural. But for me to come upon it was surely the purest accident. From all the English towns and villages in which she might have settled, Sir Cholmely's twentieth-century descendant had to choose Long

[5] I knew this because I had read about it many years before in John Ashton's *Social Life in the Reign of Queen Anne* (1880, ii. 192–4), and because I have one of those fly-paper memories to which facts just stick. And I knew who Richard Thornhill was because I had written my B.Litt. thesis on Nicholas Rowe, and Rowe had addressed a charming poem to him when they were both young men.

[6] The two men had quarrelled on 27 April, and in the ensuing fracas Thornhill had been thrown to the ground, and had some of his teeth knocked out by Dering stamping on him. At Thornhill's trial on 18 May, evidence was given that his injuries were severe and that they had brought on a fever. (John Ashton, op. cit. ii. 192–3.)

Wittenham (population, *c.* 300). There she had to meet with one of the only persons alive who was likely ever to have heard of Sir Cholmely's fatal duel (I do not think the lady herself had), and to allow him to rummage in her family papers, recently recovered from a long storage. . . . As I have said, a matter of no consequence; but as Major Bagstock (old Joey B.) might have said: 'Queer, sir, devilish queer.'

The Chesterfield House Library Portraits

DAVID PIPER

THIS ACCOUNT of the Chesterfield Library portraits was outlined very informally in a talk after lunch at Yale in the early 1960s. Photographs were handed round the table as if in some game of recondite Snap: there was some agreeable clucking. Amongst those present were W. K. Wimsatt, the iconographer of Pope though with other claims to fame, and James M. Osborn. (Sight of the two together has more than once reminded me, in not irreverent affection, of Pooh Bear with Piglet.)

Jim Osborn's interest in British literary portraits was long held, and acquisitive. His most remarkable acquisitions were doubtless the portrait of Whythorne, the only surviving painting of the musician and first of English autobiographers (and incidentally one of the most charming of Elizabethan portraits); and that plump, bright-eyed, little boy of seven years old that surfaced in a London sale-room unwarily when Wimsatt was in England in hot pursuit of Pope: Wimsatt promptly and correctly identified it as the long-lost portrait of Pope as a child that Spence had recorded; Osborn bought it. Desiderata might elude him—the missing pastel by Rosalba of Spence never appeared, though not for want of being searched for—but his collection included reputable and contemporary portraits of Addison, Pope, Dryden, and several others. If in this field, he could be prone to optimism as to identifications, he was in good company, and even if some may have hesitations in admitting that his Dryden is Dryden, it must certainly be agreed at the very least as a most gallant try. Literary portraits were of course a secondary pursuit, but I am sure that he agreed with Carlyle's contention that 'the Portrait was a small lighted *candle* by which the Biographies could for the first time be *read*, and some human interpretation be made of them'.

Before this volume was overtaken by time, to become a memorial volume rather than a Festschrift (though I trust it remains that as well), contributions were asked, if I recall correctly, to offer

variations on the theme of literary discovery. I cannot claim much
virtue of discovery, as the remaining nucleus (which is in fact 16
out of 21) of the Chesterfield Library portraits appeared together *en
bloc* at Christie's in 1951. Had Jim Osborn been aware of them, they
would surely now be in New Haven; however, he was not aware,
while Sir Louis Sterling was, and it was Sterling who bought them
and subsequently gave them, with his own library, to London University, where, in the Sterling Library and the Palaeography Room
of the University Library, they abide. Jim, however, did once express regret to me that he had not known when they came up for sale,
and asked me to signal him if I were ever to identify one of the
missing ones coming on the English market, if London did not want
it. I was never lucky enough to be able to do that, but at least I can
now, though too late, offer him full account of the whole lot.
Although almost all the work on this reconstitution of the Chesterfield Library portrait set was done a decade and more ago, it was
never published, in the hope that cleaning of the paintings would
make a perhaps more definitive account possible. Libraries—
especially British libraries in the national economic crisis omnipresent at the time of writing—have, however, other priorities for
spending money on, than the furbishing of pictures, especially
when the latter are in perfectly sound physical condition, as these
are. Cleaning of the pictures may be further decades off, and the
images they present—even if some of them are somewhat and
indefinably blurred by later overpaint—are near enough to those
originally presented: it seems justifiable to publish them now.

THE PORTRAITS

The Whig statesman, Philip Stanhope (1694–1773), 4th Earl of
Chesterfield, is now famous for his *Letters* to his son, and as the
recipient of one of the most magisterial rebukes in the English
language, from Dr. Johnson. Chesterfield had various London
habitations—St. James's Square, then Grosvenor Square: from a
house in the latter he married in 1733 his next-door neighbour, the
Countess of Walsingham, daughter of the Duchess of Kendal
(better known as 'the Schulenburg', one-time mistress of George
I). Part of the attraction of the marriage (Chesterfield in the same
year took on a new mistress, Lady Frances Shirley) was the bride's
comfortable financial situation (endowed by a royal gift of £50,000
plus £3,000 p.a. from the Civil List). Chesterfield's hankering to

build himself a truly impressive town mansion did not really crystallize, however, till after his mother-in-law's death in 1743, his wife being the heiress. The building of Chesterfield House in Mayfair was under way by 1747, when he wrote to Mme de Monconseil: 'Je me ruine actuellement à bâtir une assez belle maison ici, qui sera finie a la Françoise, avec force sculptures et dorures.' He was into it, if somewhat incompletely, by spring 1749 —then, on 31 March, he wrote that there was 'yet finished nothing but my *boudoir* and my library; the former is the gayest and most cheerful room in England, the latter the best.'

The site was near the south-west extremity of Mayfair, on the corner of what are now South Audley Street and Curzon Street (one says 'on the corner', but the grounds ran a long way east along the north side of Curzon Street: the whole site was about half the size of Berkeley Square). The house fronted west, towards Hyde Park, and at that date it was as much *urbs in rure* as *rus in urbe*, as no houses stood between it and the park: so solitary that Chesterfield could describe it as 'situated among a parcel of thieves and murderers'. But it was always amongst the grandest of Mayfair houses, even after it lost much of its gardens in 1870, and was fashionable until its destruction in 1934, the last inhabitant being the Earl of Harewood and his wife, the Princess Royal. By then the Chesterfield connection had long ceased—all except that of Chesterfield's Library portraits, or most of them. Not all the house's splendours were destroyed though dispersed on demolition: the great staircase and its columns, which Chesterfield's architect had re-used from an earlier demolition, that of the fabulous mansion of the Duke of Chandos, Canons Park, in 1744, went to adorn a cinema in Broadstairs, only to be destroyed by bombing in the War of 1939–45; other elements perhaps fared better, such as the fine fireplace from the house, which can now be found in the Metropolitan Museum, New York.[1] But from the library, claimed by Chesterfield with no false modesty simply as the 'best' room in England, I have come across no survivors from the furnishings and fittings other than the portraits.

Some years before it was demolished, however, H. Avray Tipping published a thorough and well-illustrated survey of the house in two articles in *Country Life*.[2] To these the present account

---

[1] *Met. Mus. Bulletin* (Feb. 1963), pp. 202 et seq.
[2] *Country Life*, li (1922), 235–42, 308–14.

owes a great deal, for they included a photograph of the library as
it then was (Pl. 27). Chesterfield's furniture would have been both
other and otherwise dispersed, but shelving, plaster work, and
structure of the room were as they had been (except the wind dial
over the fireplace, an interpolation of 1790). Chesterfield's architect
was Isaac Ware, a distinguished representative of the second
generation of British Palladian architects—and as such, not an
obvious choice in the light of Chesterfield's pleasure in announcing
his new house to his French correspondent as to be finished 'a la
Françoise, avec force sculptures et dorures'; this suggests a much
stronger rococo accent than most of the house in fact had, apart
perhaps from the 'boudoir'. Perhaps Chesterfield exaggerated the
Frenchness to please his correspondent. The Library certainly was
composed with a classical decorum and symmetry, the most lively
decorative element being the vigorous carving of the wood or
plaster frames for the portraits, but even that does not spill over
its confines. Chesterfield was no longer a young man when he
built this room, but nearer sixty than fifty when it was done,
tending to withdraw a little from the world owing to his increasing
deafness, and perhaps appreciative of a certain calm, a handsome
but not too exciting luxury, in his surroundings. The lapidary
inscription that marched in dignity round the walls under the
cornice is from Horace: NUNC VETERUM LIBRIS, NUNC
SOMNO, ET INERTIBUS HORIS,/ DUCERE SOLLICITÆ
JUCUNDA OBLIVIA VITÆ.[3] This is in key—celebrating the
virtues of books but also of somnolence—with that vein of light
irony that sometimes characterizes Georgian gravities, like the
memorial to the favourite greyhound that the visitor discovers at
the back of the Temple of British Worthies at Stowe.

The adornment of libraries with portraits of authors was no very
novel conceit. It follows Roman precedent, and Lipsius's *De
Bibliothecis Syntagma* (1602) has a whole chapter on the use of
portraits in libraries, tracing the habit via Pliny back to Asinius
Pollio. English readers, if they needed any authoritative support,
would find it easily in Evelyn's translation of Gabriel Naudé's
Instructions Concerning Creating of a Library, where again a
chapter deals with 'Ornamentation and decoration necessarily to
be observed'. However, the more usual kind of portraiture
employed was the sculptured bust; this has implicit classical

[3] Horace, *Sat.* II. vi.

PLATE 19

2. Edmund Spenser (?); copy from a lost painting of *c.* 1580/90. Sterling Library.

PLATE 20

5. William Cartwright; artist unknown. Sterling Library.

PLATE 21

7. Sir John Denham; artist unknown, *c.* 1661. Sterling Library.

PLATE 22

8. Abraham Cowley (*or* ? Sir Henry Vane the Younger); artist unknown. Sterling
Library.

PLATE 23

10. William Wycherley; by Thomas Murray, *c.* 1700. Sterling Library.

PLATE 24

11. Thomas Otway; by John Riley, *c.* 1680/85. Sterling Library.

PLATE 25

Dean Swift

13. Jonathan Swift; by Charles Jervas, 1718 (?). Sterling Library.

echoes, made explicit if a toga is indicated (and the wig omitted), and also presides over, and as it were articulates, bays of bookcases very aptly. The most spectacular surviving example in England of the felicitous use of busts in a library is that at Trinity College, Cambridge, but the habit became quite common through the eighteenth century, and statuaries' workshops like those of the Cheeres seem to have produced casts from moulds in stock in some quantity. More modest libraries might use engraved portraits, framed, and even now one occasionally sights them, yellowing with age, still *in situ* where later generations have not drastically refurbished (as at Chastleton in Oxfordshire). The use of painted portraits was not necessarily less modest than that of busts, and Chesterfield was neither the first nor the last to use them. I suspect Clarendon already had them (anyway Aubrey noted a Samuel Butler over the fireplace in Clarendon's library). At Knole, the literary portraits in the Poets' Parlour (many of them still there) were noted by 1728, and there were other sets, including those on the dispersal of which Chesterfield drew for his own.[4]

It would not have been surprising if he had settled for busts rather than paintings, for the year after the library was finished he sent over a set of four literary busts (Shakespeare, Milton, Dryden, and Pope) to his friend Mme du Boccage in Paris. But he had been collecting painted portraits of poets long before the library even started building. The engraver and antiquary George Vertue noted that Chesterfield was buying at the sale of the Halifax collection in 1739/40, and jotted down the details of some of the purchases.[5] Later, in 1748, when the library was building, Vertue recorded Chesterfield's intention to put in it 'the portraits of many most memorable Poets heads of this nation . . . he bought at several times from Ld. Oxford, Lord Hallifaxes collection . . . many others are coppyed to the size he wants'. The Halifax library and library portraits were probably accumulated by Charles Montagu, 1st Earl of Halifax (1661–1715), rather than by his nephew (the 1st Earl of the second creation), after whose death they were sold, 6–10

---

[4] I have attempted an outline of the history of adorning libraries with portraits elsewhere, in 'The Development of the British Literary Portrait up to Samuel Johnson', *Proceedings of the British Academy*, liv. 51–76, q.v. for detailed references.

[5] G. Vertue, Notebooks IV and V, *Walpole Society*, xxiv (1936), 165, and xxvi (1938), 70.

March 1739/40. The Oxford collection was of course that of
Edward Harley, 2nd Earl of Oxford, accumulated to accompany
his books at Wimpole; his poets' heads were sold after his death,
8–13 March 1741/2. One Captain Boden appears to have bought
for Chesterfield at this sale—at least, most of the portraits bought
by Boden at that sale are reasonably identifiable in Chesterfield's
collection later.[6]

The catalogue that follows this account records possible sources
for each of Chesterfield's library portraits. There is no evidence as
to who did those that were copied for him (except perhaps that
of Rowe), as Vertue states 'many' were. In contrast to some other
libraries, the poets represented were all British and included no
classical authors. The set is especially notable in that it includes
important and unique originals, besides the copies. Thus the
portrait of Denham (Pl. 21) is the only one of that poet known, and
that of Otway (Pl. 24) the only painting of him known; the Wycherley (Pl. 23) is an original, and the Swift (Pl. 25) may be the first of
the several versions that the painter, Jervas, made of this portrait.
Amongst those that were dispersed, that of Sidney is a rare and
authentic contemporary portrait, while the Shakespeare (Pl. 26) is
of considerable interest in the evolution of succeeding generations'
views as to what the Bard ought to have looked like (the Spenser
(Pl. 19) still amongst the set, may be allowed to have more than
merely mythological interest). The set runs from the founding
father, Chaucer, to poets whom Chesterfield must have known, the
latest being Pope. The purpose was obviously not to assemble
heroic, classicizing, ideal portraits, but rather historic likenesses. On
the other hand, it looks as though the fashion for literary portraits,
colliding with a supply of authentic likenesses that was strictly
limited, was producing already, if not outright fakes, then identifications that were at least optimistic. Milton was a prime desider-
atum, but Chesterfield ended up with two apparently that were, on
and off, called Milton although neither is in fact a portrait of him.
One is now called Cartwright (Pl. 20) and may be him; the other,
still inscribed as Milton, is quite certainly Waller. (The date of the
inscriptions is uncertain: there seem at least two styles.) Cowley

---

[6] The Halifax sale is F. Lugt, *Repertoire des Catalogues de Ventes*, Vol. I,
1600–1825 (1938), No. 497: priced copies of the catalogue exist but none with
buyers' names. Of the Oxford sale (Lugt, op. cit., No. 553) priced copies with
buyers' names exist.

may be Cowley (Pl. 22) but is more likely to be Sir Henry Vane the Younger (a confusion neither would have relished).

It is not known exactly when the portraits were actually installed in their florid carved frames in Chesterfield's library, but probably in 1749. There they apparently stayed for two centuries. Lord Brougham commented on them briefly in the *Quarterly Review* in 1845.[7] George Scharf (first Director of the National Portrait Gallery) made detailed notes and sketches of them between 27 September and 8 October 1869, from which the original order can be re-established.[8] That, however, must have been at the time of, or shortly before, the sale of the house by the Chesterfields to Magniac, the famous Victorian collector, and then, in 1869 or soon after, the library portraits were removed to the Chesterfield country house at Bretby. There they stayed—apparently anyway —still in a library setting, until the contents of that house were sold on the premises by Leedam and Harrison, 15–25 July 1918. The library portraits were then bought by Lascelles (later Earl of Harewood) who had already acquired Chesterfield House and no doubt had considerable satisfaction in putting them back in their original setting. By 1922, when Avray Tipping wrote up the house for *Country Life*, they were back—but not all of them, as some had gone astray at the 1918 sale and been missed by Lascelles. So, in the 1922 photograph, one sees over the fireplace, instead of the Shakespeare, now at Stratford-upon-Avon, a version of Titian's 'François I', but the most intriguing intruder is, over the door to the right, a version of Reynolds's 'Blinking Sam' portrait of Dr. Johnson himself. One wonders, was it in this very room that Johnson's stately letter of rebuke to Chesterfield was delivered to him?

In 1934, the house was demolished, and the portraits migrated again, and their present simple wood frames no doubt date from that period. They stayed first in one Lascelles house, Goldsborough Hall, then moved to another, Harewood House, until, after the War, they were brought up to London once again, but this time for sale, at Christie's (29 June 1951). Then they were bought for Sir Louis Sterling. Ten years later, in 1961, they were installed in what should prove their permanent home, the Sterling

---

[7] *Quarterly Review*, lxxvi (1845), 484.

[8] Scharf's sketch-books (S.S.B.) are preserved in the National Portrait Gallery archive.

Library in the University of London library in the Senate House. Of those that 'got away', three are at present unlocated; one (Sidney) had already found its niche in the Hall-i'-th'-Wood Museum, Bolton, and the Shakespeare soon afterwards found its place in the Birthplace at Stratford-upon-Avon.

I am grateful to the Goldsmiths' Librarian of the University of London and his colleagues for help, and for permission to reproduce a selection of the portraits; also to *Country Life* for permission to reproduce a photograph of the Library in 1922, and to the Director of the Shakespeare Birthplace Trust, Stratford-upon-Avon.

CATALOGUE—THE CHESTERFIELD LIBRARY PORTRAITS

A. 1–17: Portraits now in the Sterling Library, University of London

1. CHAUCER

1340?–1400
Artist unknown

Perhaps the head of Chaucer from the Halifax sale 1739/40, 4th day, lot 17 (£6. 6s.), and if so probably a copy made for the 1st Earl of Halifax; noted by Vertue (Notebooks IV, 165) as 'Chaucer a painted head on cloth modern'. There was a Chaucer in the Oxford sale, 5th day, lot 31, bought by Boden, but it was a larger size (Kitcat).

A version of the usual portrait-type of Chaucer, all versions of which derive ultimately from the image recorded by Occleve in his *De Regimine Principum* (British Library: Harleian MS. 4866). This was posthumous but based on memory, and Occleve's verses alongside make clear that it was intended as a likeness, and it is in fact thus one of the earliest portrait likenesses, in the modern sense, in England. See Roy Strong, *Tudor and Jacobean Portraits* (1969), vol. i, pp. 47 and 48; and vol. ii, plates 82–5 for the principal early versions.

2. SPENSER

1552?–1599
After a contemporary portrait   *Plate* 19

Inscribed: Ætatis. Suæ. 32 [?] ANNO DŌI. 186 [*sic*]. Apparently a copy, late seventeenth-century(?) of a genuine late sixteenth-century painting. Likely to be the portrait in the Oxford Sale 1741/2, 'Spenser the Poet', 1st day, lot 34, bought by Boden £2. 6s. od.

I have found no record of any painting of Spenser before 1719, when Vertue (Notebooks I, 58) noted 'a picture of Spencer in Poses of Coll. Guyse'. This is presumably the portrait of which Vertue later (1727) made an engraving dedicated to John Guyse. The engraving is of the same type as the Oxford/Chesterfield portrait, and it has some-times been assumed that it was done directly from our painting. How-ever, Vertue elsewhere (MS. list of his own engravings: colln. W. S. Lewis, Farmington) notes that the original was 'a painting on bord [*sic*]'. The Chesterfield painting is on canvas, and while it does seem to have been enlarged at some stage (from about 24 × 20 inches to nearer the standard 30 × 25 inches), it is unlikely to have been transferred from panel to canvas. The Guyse version is at present untraced: John Guise (1682 or 3–1765) became the great benefactor of Christ Church, but the Spenser is not traced among the 250 or more pictures in his great collection which came to Christ Church on his death. (See J. Byam Shaw, *Paintings by Old Masters at Christ Church, Oxford* (1967), Introduction. A protégé of Guise, J. C. le Blon, produced a colour mezzotint of a Spenser, very likely the same type, but I have not seen an impression.)

Besides the Guise and the Chesterfield ones, other recorded early versions of this type include one from the Harcourt collection, Nuneham Courtenay (conceivably identical with the Guise version, but inscribed, according to Scharf (National Portrait Gallery, S.S.B. 75, fo. 47ᵛ), 1596, AET 36), and one by (?Benjamin) 'Wilson' at Pembroke College, Cambridge (given 1771). The Guise image has become the most widely broadcast image of Spenser (via Vertue's and later engravings), and the Chesterfield version the best-known painted version of it. In the highly hypothetical story of Spenser's iconography it is of considerable import-ance; but its relationship, if any, to Spenser himself remains doubtful— not only because of its late emergence, but because of the clash of interpretations of the varying inscriptions of date and age that the versions bear. But if 1586, age 32, were correct, that could fit Spenser. The Chesterfield image has in any case the oldest tradition of identifi-cation with Spenser, even if not nearly old enough for certainty. A rival type of portrait is first recorded in 1762, known as the 'Kinnoull' type. It clearly represents a different man, and it can have no special claim.

3. BEN JONSON

1573?–1657
Artist unknown, after a portrait of *c.* 1620 by A. van Blijen-berch

A later copy of the most popular type of portrait of Jonson, the original of which was probably a painting by A. van Blijenberch of about 1620:

this original may be the version No. 2752 of the National Portrait Gallery. See Roy Strong, *Tudor and Jacobean Portraits* (1969), vol. i, pp. 183–4 (though he believes No. 2752 also to be a later copy).

The Chesterfield version may have been copied for the Earl of Chesterfield. It was not, however, strictly one of the library portraits. It was hung (in 1869, and doubtless always) elsewhere in the house, whereas in the Library the portrait representing Jonson was one of the larger, threequarter length, ones. See notes on the missing portraits below, and, for the location at Chesterfield House of this version, Scharf's note (National Portrait Gallery, S.S.B. 83, fo. 57).

4. EDMUND WALLER

('John Milton')
1608–87
After the painting by Cornelius Johnson, 1629

Inscribed as Milton, but certainly Waller. The confusion about portraits called Milton in the Chesterfield Library set is mysterious (see also No. 5, Cartwright, below), but this one seems to have been correctly identified as Waller by 1869 (*sic.* Scharf, National Portrait Gallery, S.S.B. 83, fo. 65). It is a copy (perhaps commissioned by Lord Chesterfield) of a painting by Cornelius Johnson of Waller as a young man, which is or was recently still in the Waller family's possession. The head of this portrait-type was engraved (with costume altered) as Waller by P. Vanderbanc, inscribed *Ætatis Suæ 23*.

5. WILLIAM CARTWRIGHT

1611–43
Artist unknown   *Plate 20*

Bought by Lord Chesterfield at the Halifax sale (1739/40, 2nd day, lot 39) as Milton, and noted by Vertue (Notebooks IV, 165) as *Milton leaning on his hand—fictitious*. It was still inscribed with Milton's name in 1869 (Scharf, National Portrait Gallery, S.S.B. 83, fo. 60), and a similar painting (oval) at Ickworth is also known as Milton. The image, however, corresponds to, and probably derives directly from, P. Lombart's portrait engraving of Cartwright for the latter's *Poems and Plays* of 1651. The source of Lombart's engraving, in which the features are shown very summarily, is problematic: it is posthumous, and may represent more generically a poet in his melancholy than Cartwright specifically. The pose follows of course the traditional one of melancholy as in Ripa and elsewhere. No other type of portrait of Cartwright is known for comparison.

6. SAMUEL BUTLER

1612–80
After a painting by Gerard Soest of *c.* 1670 (?)

From the Halifax sale, 1739/40, 2nd day, lot 32; noted by Vertue (Notebooks IV, 165) as *Butler a Coppy*. From a threequarter length by Gerard Soest, of perhaps *c.* 1670. Autograph versions of this are in the National Portrait Gallery and the Bodleian Library. The type had been engraved first by an anonymous mezzotinter; then by J. Faber Senior; and by Vertue. See David Piper, *Catalogue of the Seventeenth Century Portraits in the National Portrait Gallery* (1963), pp. 49–51.

7. SIR JOHN DENHAM

1615–69
Artist unknown, *c.* 1661   *Plate 21*

Shown wearing the red ribbon of a Knight of the Bath, which he became at the coronation of Charles II, 23 April 1661. Probably from the Oxford sale, 1741/2, 4th day, lot 4: *Sir John Denham—an oval*; bought by Boden £4. 10s. od. There is clearly much repaint, but the present image is probably fairly close to that originally shown; the style may be similar to that of Isaac Fuller, and this is apparently basically an original of 1661 or soon after. No other portraits are known for comparison; the ribbon of the Bath supports the traditional identification. The earliest engraving of this type, as Denham, seems to be J. Collyer's, for Johnson's *Poets* of 1779; the earliest engraving inscribed as being specifically from the Chesterfield painting is by Le Goux, 1793.

8. ABRAHAM COWLEY (?)

1618–67
Artist unknown   *Plate 22*

Possibly from the Oxford sale, 1741/2, 3rd day, lot 31: Mr. Cowley, bought by Boden, £3. 15s. od. The identification must, however, be regarded with caution (and the identification of at least one of Oxford's literary portraits—that by Isaac Fuller now in the Tate Gallery—once known as 'Cleveland', was certainly not merely wrong but deliberately faked). The features and hair-style agree very precisely with the best-known portrait-type, by Lely, of Sir Henry Vane the Younger, and far less so with fully authenticated portraits of Cowley. Nevertheless, apparently an original of some power of the period (*c.* 1650–60), close to the style of Isaac Fuller. For authenticated portraits of Cowley, see David Piper, *Catalogue of the Seventeenth Century Portraits in the*

National Portrait Gallery (1963), pp. 85–6, and 393. Several versions of Lely's *Vane* exist (see R. B. Beckett, *Lely* (1951), No. 543; one version is reproduced by J. Willcock's *Life of Sir Henry Vane* (1913), p. 82, and the type was engraved, as Vane, by Faithorne (reversed) in 1662).

9. DRYDEN

1631–1700

After a painting by John Riley of *c.* 1685

From the Halifax sale, 1739/40, 2nd day, lot 38; noted by Vertue (Notebooks IV, 165), as *Dryden a Coppy. a wig on—after Riley*. John Riley's original of *c.* 1685 is in the Maxwell-Stuart collection. After Riley's death, 1691, his partner and successor, Closterman, also produced versions of this portrait: one was in the Ilchester collection. For the original, see David Piper in the *Burlington Magazine*, ciii (1961), 105–6, and fig. 26.

10. WYCHERLEY

1640–1716

By Thomas Murray, *c.* 1700   *Plate 23*

From the Halifax sale, 1739/40, 4th day, lot 18; described by Vertue (Notebooks IV, 164) as *Wycherley a head large wigg. painted from the life by Murray*. As an oldish man, perhaps *c.* 1700; the painter Thomas Murray was a pupil of Riley's. This, rather than the portrait at Knole ascribed to Kneller, may be the one referred to by Spence as having been painted originally wigless, but with the wig added at the sitter's insistence. If so, there were two versions, as according to Spence the one in question belonged to Alexander Pope (see Joseph Spence, *Observations, Anecdotes, and Characters of Books and Men*, ed. James M. Osborn (1966), vol. i, p. 41, with reproduction of the Chesterfield portrait).

11. OTWAY

1652–85

By John Riley, *c.* 1680–5   *Plate 24*

From the Halifax sale, 1739/40, 4th day, lot 15; described by Vertue (Notebooks IV, 165) as *Mr Otway—a well painted picture, by Riley, the original* (see also Vertue, Notebooks v, 70). Probably of *c.* 1680; the only known painting of Otway. Engraved by W. J. Alais (private plate, for Grosart).

12. PRIOR

1664–1721
By or after Jonathan Richardson

Perhaps from the Halifax sale, 1739/40, 6th day, lot 12 (but if so, cut down, as that is described as half-length), but more likely a copy commissioned by Chesterfield and perhaps from the artist of the original, Jonathan Richardson. Richardson's original of 1718 was repeated in many variations and versions, as in the Portland collection at Welbeck (threequarter length, signed, formerly in Lord Oxford's collection); in the Bathurst collection, Cirencester; and elsewhere. See R. W. Goulding and C. K. Adams, *Catalogue of Pictures . . . at Welbeck Abbey* (1936), No. 450.

13. SWIFT

1667–1745
By Charles Jervas, 1718 (?) *Plate 25*

Possibly the portrait in the Oxford sale, 1741/2, 3rd day, lot 37 [as one of a number of half-lengths], *Dean Swift by Mr Jarvis*, bought by Boden £11. 0s. 6d., but if so, cut down. Correspondence between Oxford, Jervas, and Swift, 1723–5, shows that Oxford then owned a half-length of Swift 'the same which Mr Jervas drew in Ireland' (probably in 1718) and, according to Swift, 'more like me by several years than another he drew in London' (in 1710). Whether or not the Chesterfield version is the Oxford one, the quality is lively and on that score it could well be Charles Jervas's original. See the full discussion apropos the National Portrait Gallery version, in David Piper, *Catalogue of the Seventeenth Century Portraits in the National Portrait Gallery* (1963), pp. 337 8.

14. CONGREVE

1670–1729
After a painting of 1709 by Sir Godfrey Kneller

From the Halifax sale, 1739/40, 1st day, lot 14; described by Vertue (Notebooks IV, 165) as *Congreve by Sir G. Kneller the same as is printed*. A copy (or conceivably a studio repetition) of Kneller's Kitcat Club portrait (signed and dated 1709) now in the National Portrait Gallery. See David Piper, *Catalogue of the Seventeenth Century Portraits in the National Portrait Gallery* (1963), pp. 80–1; J. D. Stewart, *Sir Godfrey Kneller*, National Portrait Gallery (1971), p. 41, No. 46 (reproduces further Kneller's drawing for the head, now in the Witt collection, Courtauld Institute).

15. ADDISON

1672–1719
After a painting by Sir Godfrey Kneller of *c.* 1710

Presumably copied for Lord Chesterfield, from Kneller's Kitcat Club portrait of Addison now in the National Portrait Gallery (of *c.* 1710, signed). See David Piper, *Catalogue of the Seventeenth Century Portraits in the National Portrait Gallery* (1963), pp. 1–2.

16. NICHOLAS ROWE

1674–1718
By Jonathan Richardson after a painting of *c.* 1715 by Sir Godfrey Kneller

Perhaps from the Oxford sale, 1741/2, 1st day, lot 25: 'Mr Rowe 3 qrs by Mr Richardson', bought by Boden £1. 12*s*. 6*d*. ('3 qrs', or 'three-quarters', was used to define a head-and-shoulders, 'head', or bust-length portrait). If this is the Oxford portrait though, it must be a copy by Jonathan Richardson after Sir Godfrey Kneller. Kneller's signed original of perhaps about 1715 is recorded in the St. Quentin family collection at Scampston Hall (reproduced in *Country Life*, cxv (1954), 1036). Another copy is at Knole, and the portrait-type was engraved by Vertue. There is nothing improbable in Richardson's copying a Kneller.

17. ALEXANDER POPE

1688–1744
After a painting of 1716 by Sir Godfrey Kneller

Possibly cut down from the Kitcat size portrait, from the Oxford sale 1741/2, 4th day, lot 41; but (as suggested by Wimsatt) that is probably the one now in the Barnard collection, Raby Castle, which is signed and dated by Kneller 1719. The Chesterfield portrait is more likely to be a later copy of this type commissioned by Chesterfield. Sir Godfrey Kneller produced several versions of this portrait; the Barnard version, though signed and dated 1719, is not the first, as John Smith's mezzo-tint engraving of 1717 of this type gives the date of origination as 1716. Good versions are in the Bathurst collection, Cirencester, the Crawford collection, Balcarres, and elsewhere. For full discussion and illustrations of known versions, including the Chesterfield one, see W. K. Wimsatt, *The Portraits of Alexander Pope* (1965), pp. 35–49.

B. 18–22: The Portraits now dispersed from the Library set

Five portraits originally in the Chesterfield House Library had been detached from the set nearly thirty years before the set was finally sold at Christie's in 1948. All five were sold as separate lots (and in two separate places) in Chesterfield sales in 1918, and were missed by the Earl of Harewood when he acquired the main body of the portraits. Only one belonged to the smaller, head-and-shoulders, series: that of Sir Philip Sidney. This was unique in that series in being on wood; originally, it was smaller than the others, and no doubt Chesterfield had it made up to fit the frame, but it was perhaps already reduced back to its original size by the time it was sold in 1918. It was by then anyway already separated from the set, and its place in the Library, when Lord Harewood replaced the set there in or after 1918, was taken by the head and shoulders of Ben Jonson. This, as noted earlier, had come from elsewhere in the house and not from the Library. The 'Jonson' in the Library was one of the four larger pictures that originally hung over the three doorways and the fireplace, and which Lord Harewood had not acquired with the rest of the set. Only two of the five detached from the set have so far been identified.

18. SIR PHILIP SIDNEY

1544–86
By or after John de Critz, *c.* 1585
Hall-i'-th'-Wood Museum, Bolton

Noted by Scharf (National Portrait Gallery, S.S.B. 83, fo. 54) amongst the other smaller portraits in the Library in 1869, with a detailed sketch and comments: 'on panel . . . a genuine picture'. Sold Christie's, 31 May 1918, lot 85; bought for Lord Leverhulme and subsequently presented by him to the Hall-i'-th'-Wood Museum, Bolton, where it abides. It is a contemporary version of a portrait of Sidney originated probably by John de Critz, *c.* 1585, and either by de Critz or from his workshop. It is on panel, $18\frac{5}{8} \times 14\frac{7}{8}$ inches; it was probably made up to match 30×25 inches for Lord Chesterfield, and was the only painting on panel in the smaller set. It was bought for Chesterfield at the Oxford sale in 1741/2, and was engraved by Vertue—the first state indicates that the painting was in the Oxford collection, the second state changes the inscription to indicate that it had become Chesterfield's property.

For this and other versions, see A. C. Judson, *Sidney's Appearance*

(Bloomington, 1958), pp. 37–42 (reproducing the Chesterfield/Hall-i'-th'-Wood version, plate 9); David Piper, 'Some Portraits by Marcus Gheeraedts II and John de Critz Reconsidered', *Huguenot Society*, vol. xx (1960); Roy Strong, *Tudor and Jacobean Portraits* (1969), vol. i, pp. 290–3.

19. SHAKESPEARE

1564–1616
Attributed to Pieter Borseller, *c.* 1660–70
Shakespeare's Birthplace, Stratford-upon-Avon   *Plate* 26

From the Halifax sale, 1739/40, 3rd day, lot 13; £18. 18*s.* o*d.*, as by Zuccaro. In the Chesterfield Library it hung centrally, in the place of honour over the fireplace. When moved to Bretby after 1870 it seems to have slipped from favour, and it is probably to be identified with lot 270 I of the Bretby Hall sale by Leedam and Harrison, Burton-on-Trent, July 1918—as an 'Unknown Man' but catalogued amongst the other literary portraits and with the unusual measurements of 4 foot square, which tallies with the Shakespeare. Its subsequent history was restless, even after its appearance at Christie's, 2 December 1949, lot 163. It was for a time at the Shakespeare Festival Theatre, Stratford, Connecticut, until by the generous gift of Lincoln Kirstein, it found a permanent and apt home at Stratford-upon-Avon.

It is of course posthumous, but represents an important stage in the development of Shakespeare's portraiture. He is shown seated, one arm flung out. The head is a modified and elegant version of the 'Chandos' portrait of Shakespeare, while the composition of the whole modulates the staid Jacobean image of the 'Chandos' into the exclamatory, baroque rhetoric of the tradition of Van Dyck. An attribution to Pieter Borseller, a Dutch artist working in England after the Restoration, *c.* 1660–70, has been suggested (by Sir Oliver Millar). The painting seems to be of that period rather than earlier, though it reminded Scharf of the style of the portrait of Francis Beaumont at Knole, which seems to be of the early seventeenth century. See David Piper, *O Sweet Mr Shakespeare I'll have his Picture* (National Portrait Gallery, 1964).

20. BEN JONSON (called)

Artist unknown
Unlocated

Perhaps the portrait from the Halifax sale, 1739/40, 1st day, lot 11. One of the larger portraits, hanging over a door in the Library. Scharf made a sketch of it (National Portrait Gallery, S.S.B. 83, fo. 57) indicating that it was inscribed 'Johnson' and adding 'something like Ben Jonson'. The sketch shows a standing three-quarter length, panel, with pen and ink-pot. It may have been somewhat doubtfully identified as Jonson; the design does not correspond with any authenticated portrait-type of him. Perhaps Chesterfield sale, Christie's, 31 May 1918, lot 48. Not located (for the portrait of Ben Jonson used by Lord Harewood for the Library set, see above, No. 3).

21. DORSET (Charles Sackville, 6th Earl of Dorset, better known as Lord Buckhurst)
    1638–1706

    Artist unknown
    Unlocated

A threequarter length, hanging over one of the doors. Sketched by Scharf (National Portrait Gallery, S.S.B. 83, fo. 55), but not a version of any portrait of Dorset recorded so far. Chesterfield sale, Christie's, 31 May 1918, lot 35, as by Kneller; bought by 'Glen'.

22. ROCHESTER (John Wilmot, 2nd Earl of Rochester)
    1647–80

    By or after Sir Peter Lely
    Unlocated

A threequarter length standing, hanging originally over one of the Library doors. Scharf's sketch of it (National Portrait Gallery, S.S.B. 83, fo. 56) shows it to be a version of a portrait originated by Lely *c.* 1677 (engraved head and shoulders only by R. White, 1681). Several versions exist: at Hinchingbrooke; at the Victoria and Albert Museum (reproduced by H. B. Butler and C. R. L. Fletcher, *Historical Portraits 1600–1700* (1911), p. 206); and elsewhere. The type is recorded as Lely's by R. B. Beckett, *Lely* (1951), No. 444. Sold in the Bretby Hall sale, Leedam and Harrison, Burton-on-Trent, July 1918, lot 270 H.

Johnson's First Club

JAMES L. CLIFFORD

SAMUEL JOHNSON has often been thought of as the patron saint of clubbability, the inspiration of many informal and formal groups. There are numerous Johnson Clubs and Johnson Societies throughout the world, sometimes made up of scholars or experts, but usually devoted to conversation and friendly discussion among members with widely divergent interests. Johnson himself never praised specialized societies concentrating on a narrow subject; he preferred smaller groups, which stimulated the interchange of intelligent argument between those in different disciplines. The famous Club described by Boswell is a good example.[1] At their dinners a celebrated painter, a politician, a journalist, a musicologist, a doctor, a government official, and a pensioned literary man could talk about a wide variety of topics. The Club, indeed, has become the model of hundreds of similar groups.

Because of Boswell, and because of the preservation of numerous records, much is known about The Club and its history. But we know very little about Johnson's earliest convivial gathering, known as the Ivy Lane Club. Boswell, in the *Life*, devotes only two sentences to describing it.[2] Almost everything known about the Ivy Lane Club comes from Sir John Hawkins, one of the original members. In his authorized life of Johnson (1787), written almost forty years later, Hawkins gives many details about the members and some of the topics they discussed, but he leaves many unanswered questions.[3] Exactly when was the Ivy Lane

---

[1] At the time of his death, James M. Osborn was working on an authoritative book, *The Club: The Founders' Era,* which will be published when completed by his Research Assistant, Mrs. Ardelle C. Short.

[2] *Boswell's Life of Johnson* . . . ed. G. B. Hill, rev. and enl. L. F. Powell (Oxford, 1934–64), i. 190, hereafter referred to as *Life.*

[3] See Hawkins, pp. 219 ff. Hawkins digresses a good deal, and I indicate when something appears away from the main discussion of the Ivy Lane Club. Whenever a quotation is not documented it comes from Hawkins's main account.

Club started? Who chose the members? When and why did it disband? And did the group later change its name or transfer to another club? The subject certainly calls for further investigation.

According to Hawkins, during the winter of 1749 a group of friends began meeting every Tuesday evening at the King's Head, Horseman's well-known beefsteak house in Ivy Lane, between Paternoster Row and Newgate Street. Here near St. Paul's they would begin with supper including wine, and then talk for the rest of the evening, stopping about eleven o'clock, the accepted time to break up. Apparently, the cost of supper and wine was equally divided among those who attended.

Hawkins tells us that there were ten members in all: three physicians, one lawyer, one bookseller, one merchant, one elderly church dignitary and a youthful theologian intended for the Nonconformist ministry, one practising journalist, and one hack writer who aspired to be a dramatist and lexicographer (Johnson himself). The group was certainly heterogeneous—displaying wide interests—for the most part young men of whom scarcely any ever attained renown. Modern readers will recognize no member equal to Reynolds, Burke, or Goldsmith. Indeed, apart from Johnson himself, only Hawkins and Hawkesworth are known to twentieth-century scholars. The rest are merely names, remembered, if at all, because of their connection with Johnson.

Nevertheless, it was an interesting group, and contributed in many ways to the development of its founder. We call Johnson the founder because he apparently took the initiative in forming the group. After long hours struggling in the attic at Gough Square over the preparation of copy for the dictionary, and with his wife, Tetty, frequently ill or recuperating in the country, Johnson desperately needed relaxation and diversity. Dining with a club seemed a suitable answer.

So far as we can learn, Johnson was responsible for the choice of most of the members. The majority were his friends; others represented acquaintances who had impressed him with their willingness to talk, or at least to hear him talk. And so, after some negotiations, some time during the winter of 1749, they agreed to form what we call the Ivy Lane Club. They continued to meet for the next six or seven years, until about 1756 or 1757. It is impossible to tell just when they disbanded, or whether all the original members remained active during this whole span of time. We do know that at least one member (Dr. Edmund Barker), annoyed by some of Johnson's gibes, showed up less and less.[4]

Why was the club limited to ten members? From an anecdote in an unpublished manuscript in the Fitzherbert papers in Derbyshire it is clear that Johnson did have strong feelings about the necessity for confining groups of this kind to small, or at least manageable numbers.[5] A lady whose daughter about this time attended a school run by Mrs. John Hawkesworth at Bromley in Kent met Johnson, who used to visit the Hawkesworths with his wife. Later another daughter heard her mother tell about one occasion when in a numerous company someone brought up the subject of 'the most elegible number to form an agreeable society'. When Johnson kept silent, one of the company asked for his opinion, 'upon which he gravely replied, "between The Muses & the Graces."' That is, between a maximum of nine and a minimum of three. Actually for the Ivy Lane Club Johnson went slightly over his limit of nine. Perhaps he thought it possible to have nine Muses in addition to himself. Amusingly enough, at the beginning of the successor Club in 1764 membership was originally intended to be limited to nine, but it, too, soon went up to ten, and gradually to forty.

Who, then, were the ten founding members of the Ivy Lane Club? In 1749 John Hawkins was an articled clerk, working for an attorney and solicitor, still unmarried and financially insecure. Hawkins had known Johnson for at least eight or nine years, having first met him through Cave and the *Gentleman's Magazine*. Hawkins had published poems and moral essays and was a keen musical enthusiast. Fanny Burney, many years later, recorded a conversation she heard between Johnson and Mrs. Thrale when Hawkins's name was mentioned as one of Johnson's friends whom, like Garrick, he would never allow others to abuse.[6] Only Johnson could provide a fair balance between good and bad traits.

---

[4] Hawkins, p. 234.

[5] In Derbyshire Records Office, Matlock (D239, pp. 14–15), a volume of anecdotes of the life of Sarah Perrin, who married William Fitzherbert. She was the daughter of William and Frances Perrin. Her sister, Mary, who attended Mrs. Hawkesworth's School, died in 1756 at the age of 13. I quote with the permission of Sir John Fitzherbert of Tissington Hall, the present owner of the manuscript.

[6] *Diary and Letters of Madame D'Arblay*, ed. A. Dobson (1904–5), i. 58–9.

Hawkins, Johnson insisted, was basically an honest man, though penurious and sometimes mean and brutal. Then he described how Hawkins and he had

once belonged to the same club, but that as he eat no supper after the first night of his admission, he desired to be excused paying his share.
'And was he excused?'
'Oh yes; for no man is angry at another for being inferior to himself! we all scorned him, and admitted his plea. For my part I was such a fool as to pay my share for wine, though I never tasted any. . . .'

As Johnson had to admit, Hawkins was 'a most *unclubable* man!'

Although we cannot be certain that the club Johnson referred to in this anecdote was that at Ivy Lane, the evidence points that way. During these years Hawkins had been elected to the Madrigal Society, whose records show he never paid his dues.[7] Later, after Hawkins married a well-to-do wife he became more generous. Moreover, during the Ivy Lane years Johnson refused to drink any wine, though by 1764, when the successor Club began, Johnson's attitude towards the grape had somewhat relaxed. Still, with all his unappealing qualities Hawkins probably had much information to offer when the talk touched on music and poetry.

John Hawkesworth, auother associate of Johnson's at the *Gentleman's Magazine*, by this time had become one of his best friends. As pointed out earlr, Jeohnson, with his wife, Tetty, often visited the Hawkesworths in Bromley, Kent. Apparently Hawkesworth had taken over most, if not all, of Johnson's duties at St. John's Gate. In a print used as an introduction to the collected issues of 1747 (perhaps produced late in 1747 or early 1748) Johnson and Hawkesworth are shown as Cave's principal helpers.[8] And although by 1749 Johnson was ostensibly giving all his time to work on the dictionary he probably was frequently consulted by Cave and Hawkesworth on various decisions for the magazine. Born a Londoner, Hawkesworth had worked in his youth as a goldsmith and watchmaker, and later entered a lawyer's office.[9] Not a scholar in the academic sense, Hawkesworth proved to be an excellent journalist, demonstrating a keen mind and wide interests. No one else could better imitate Johnson's style, a fact

[7] Information obtained from Bertram H. Davis.
[8] See bound copy of *Gentleman's Magazine* for 1747, facing general title-page.
[9] A complete account of Hawkesworth is being prepared by John Abbott of the University of Connecticut at Storrs.

which makes the identification of Johnson's later work for the magazine extremely difficult. Doubtless Hawkesworth brought to the Ivy Lane Club meetings news of current books and recent events to be written up for the magazine, as well as problems of all sorts.

John Ryland, who was married to Hawkesworth's sister, had started out as a lawyer, but by this time was an active West Indian merchant and business man. At times he had contributed to the *Gentleman's Magazine*, and once briefly took over Hawkesworth's duties at St. John's Gate.[10] Ryland was a devout dissenter in religion and a firm supporter of the Hanoverians in politics. Indeed, Johnson used to attack him as a 'Republican and a Roundhead'. But at the same time Ryland had an abhorrence of those radicals who kept talking about 'Liberty and Equality'. He was, as John Nichols later called him, a 'Whig of the Old School'. Although disagreeing with many of his positions, Johnson undoubtedly respected Ryland's 'strict integrity' and 'forcible manner'.

Another member whom Johnson probably first met through Cave and the magazine was John Payne, who had started as an accountant in 1746, but about the time of the founding of the Ivy Lane Club had moved into publishing. Later he was the publisher of Johnson's *Rambler* and *Idler* essays and of Hawkesworth's *Adventurer*. Later still he gave up publishing and finally became Chief Accountant of the Bank of England. Once in late 1749 he actually brought proofs of a volume he was publishing to a club meeting to seek advice from those who were there.[11] Undoubtedly he was a very valuable connection for various club members.

Of the younger physicians, none of whom ever became eminent, Johnson's favourite was Richard Bathurst. As Arthur Murphy later expressed it, 'Dr. Bathurst was the person on whom Johnson fixed his affection. He hardly ever spoke of him without tears in his eyes.'[12] And Mrs. Thrale records that he once spoke of him as 'my *dear dear* Bathurst, whom I loved better than ever I loved any human creature'. Another time he said to Mrs. Thrale: 'Dear

[10] John Nichols, *Literary Anecdotes* (1812–15), ix. 500–1.
[11] Hawkins, p. 276. Michael Marcuse of Catholic University believes that this occurred at the gathering on Tuesday 5 December 1749. Lauder's *Essay on Milton's Use and Imitation of the Moderns*, the work referred to, was published on 14 December.
[12] *An Essay on the Life and Genius of Samuel Johnson, LL.D.* (1792), reprinted in *Johnsonian Miscellanies*, ed. G. B. Hill (Oxford, 1897), i. 390.

Bathurst ... was a man to my very heart's content: he hated a fool, and he hated a rogue, and he hated a *whig*; he was a very good *hater*', though to suggest that it was Bathurst's politics which endeared him to Johnson would be an oversimplification.[13] To be sure, his Tory inclinations must have been one part of his attraction, but Johnson evidently had other personal reasons for his admiration for Bathurst.

William McGhie was also one of Johnson's favourites; indeed Hawkins suggests that Johnson 'may almost be said to have loved him'. He was a Scot, 'one of those few of his country whom Johnson could endure'. He had earned a doctor's degree in Scotland, but when he came to London found that London was already 'overstocked with Scotch physicians', though later he became attached to Guy's Hospital.[14] 'A learned, ingenious, and modest man', McGhie was always treated with civility by Johnson, but McGhie could never move ahead in his profession, and died young in poverty, buried by contributions of his friends. According to his good friend Tobias Smollett he was a poet, as well as a physician.

The third physician, Edmund Barker, was a very different sort. As a dissenter, he had studied physic at Leyden, where he had been a fellow student with another member, Samuel Dyer, and had returned to England just about the time of formation of the Ivy Lane Club. Although very intelligent, Barker was, so Hawkins described him, 'a thoughtless young man, and in all his habits of dress and appearance so slovenly as made him the jest of all his companions'. But it was not careless dress which irritated Johnson. He was slovenly enough himself. Although Barker was an excellent classical scholar and metaphysician who had read widely in the Italian poets (skills which probably had led to his election), he had other traits which did not endear him to Johnson. It was Barker's religious and philosophic position which constantly stirred up antagonism. As a professed Unitarian, Barker was an enthusiastic

---

[13] *Anecdotes of the late Samuel Johnson, LL.D.* (1786), reprinted in *Johnsonian Miscellanies*, i. 158, 204.

[14] Lewis M. Knapp, *Tobias Smollett: Doctor of Men and Manners* (1949), pp. 80-2. McGhie received his A.B. and M.D. at Edinburgh, the latter in 1746. He did not receive his appointment to Guy's Hospital until early 1754, and died 7 June 1756. Arthur Sherbo insists that McGhie helped translate some of the mottoes for *The Adventurer*. See *Samuel Johnson, Editor of Shakespeare* (1956), pp. 148-9.

follower of Shaftesbury. For the orthodox Johnson this was cause enough for constant argument. The result was that Johnson 'so often snubbed him' that Barker's attendance at the club 'became less and less frequent'.

The other two members, whom I have left to the last, are the most interesting of the lot. Both were theologians—one an elderly dignitary of the Church of England, the other a young prospective Nonconformist minister.

Samuel Salter was a very tall man, a Cambridge divine who had held a number of church positions.[15] According to Hawkins, a dispute with his children had driven him from his home in Norwich, to come to live in London. Over seventy years old, he was not a remarkable scholar, but he was 'well-bred, courteous, and affable, and enlivened conversation by the relation of a variety of curious facts, of which his memory was the only register'. Evidently Salter was a sitting duck for Johnson's tendency to needle minor representatives of the establishment. Although a Church of England man himself, Johnson loved to argue with church dignitaries lower than a bishop, even at times being a bit 'splenetic and pertinacious', though not 'wanting in civility'. With the much older Salter, Johnson 'took delight in contradicting, and bringing his learning, his judgment, and sometimes his veracity to the test'. Despite the efforts of other members of the club to calm the waters, Johnson refused to be diverted. Why? One can only guess, but Hawkins's own explanation does appear to have some validity.

As someone who had been forced by poverty to leave the university after only thirteen months without a degree, Johnson was jealous of those who had been more fortunate and who had led a softer, more easy life. When someone with what he thought lesser intellectual endowments treated him as an inferior because of his lack of a degree or church position, Johnson naturally boiled. Each time, of course, there must have been other personal factors, but Hawkins's shrewd analysis of Johnson's motivation is fairly convincing. Even when the dignitary was as polite and unruffled as

---

[15] Salter had been prebendary of Norwich and archdeacon of Norfolk. It is claimed that he later retired to a boarding-house kept by Mrs. Hawkesworth in Bromley, Kent (*DNB*). He was living in Bromley, not with the Hawkesworths, in June 1752. We know this from a reference in the diary of John Loveday (information sent to me by Mrs. Sarah Markham).

Salter, Johnson could not resist probing his remarks with insistent scepticism. Fortunately, as Hawkins adds:

Dr. Salter was too much a man of the world to resent this behaviour: 'Study to be quiet' seemed to be his rule; and he might possibly think, that a victory over Johnson in any matter of dispute, could it have been obtained, would have been dearly purchased at the price of peace. It was nevertheless a temerarious act in him to venture into a society, of which such a man was the head.

So far as we can tell, Johnson and Salter apparently remained on friendly terms until the latter's death in 1756.

I have left until last the most intriguing, though perhaps the most controversial, member, young Samuel Dyer, who together with Hawkins also belonged to the later Club.[16] There is sharp disagreement over some of Dyer's qualities. Percy, Malone, Boswell, and other members of the later group praised him highly and defended his character against what they thought were Hawkins's slurs.[17] Yet even if Hawkins were prejudiced, and stressed too much certain of Dyer's traits, if one attempts to describe what he was like one must use Hawkins's account as a base, though always with some scepticism.

The son of a London jeweller who was a dissenter, Dyer was educated first at a private school near Moorfields, then at an academy at Northampton, and at Glasgow, where he studied ethics and metaphysics under Francis Hutcheson, the well-known philosopher. Intended by his father for the dissenting ministry, he was sent to Leyden to complete his 'learned education' and to study Hebrew literature under Albert Schultens, a celebrated professor at the university.[18] After two years he returned to London eminently qualified, so his father must have thought, for his projected calling. 'He was an excellent classical scholar, a great mathematician and natural philosopher, well versed in the Hebrew, and master of the Latin, French and Italian

---

[16] See *Life*, i. 480; iv. 10–11; *The Correspondence and other Papers of James Boswell Relating to the Making of the Life of Johnson*, ed. M. Waingrow (1969), p. 269.

[17] For various information concerning Dyer see *DNB*; Edward Peacock, *Index to English Speaking Students Who Have Graduated at Leyden University* (London, 1883), p. 32; *Letters of Samuel Johnson*, ed. R. W. Chapman (1952), iii. 18 (No. 835.1); James Prior, *Life of Edmond Malone* (1860), pp. 419–26; *Public Advertiser*, 17 Sept. 1772.

[18] Hawkins, pp. 222, 414, etc.

languages.' Moreover, his character was very appealing. 'He was of a temper so mild, and in conversation and demeanour so modest and unassuming, that he engaged the attention and affection of all around him. In all questions of science, Johnson looked up to him.' At the time of the club Dyer was attending a course in chemistry given by Henry Pemberton at Gresham College, and would sometimes entertain the other members of the group by describing various chemical processes, while Johnson would 'listen to them attentively'.

But when his friends pressed young Dyer to begin preaching and teaching so that his talents could be put to some valuable use, he demurred. Apparently he was not yet ready to decide on a profession. At first his friends thought the reason was basically that he was too modest—unwilling to get up and speak before large audiences. Later, as the years wore on, they began to suspect another motivation. Instead of devoting himself to self-sacrificing Christian duties, he found participation in the 'pleasures and enjoyments' of life more appealing.

His company, though he was rather a silent than a talkative man, was courted by many, and he had frequent invitations to dinners, to suppers, and card-parties. By these means he became insensibly a votary of pleasure, and to justify this choice, had reasoned himself into a persuasion that, not only in the moral government of the world but in human manners, through all the changes and fluctuations of fashion and caprice, whatever is, is right.

As a result, he began 'to grow indifferent to the strict practice of religion', and gladly accepted more and more invitations to Sunday parties. To quote Hawkins,

He had an exquisite palate, and had improved his relish for meats and drinks up to such a degree of refinement, that I once found him in a fit of melancholy occasioned by a discovery that he had lost his taste for olives!

Hawkins further described what happened to this young man destined for the ministry:

Having admitted these principles into his mind, he settled into a sober sensualist; in a perfect consistency with which character, he was content to eat the bread of idleness, laying himself open to the invitations of those that kept the best tables, and contracting intimacies with

men not only of opposite parties, but with some who seemed to have
abandoned all principle, whether religious, political or moral. The
houses of many such in succession were his home; and for the gratifica-
tions of a well-spread table, choice wines, variety of company, card-
parties, and a participation in all domestic amusements and recreations,
the owners thought themselves recompensed by his conversation and
the readiness with which he accommodated himself to all about him.

To be sure, Hawkins's description was written long after Dyer's
death and based on observation of his later years. At the time of the
founding of the Ivy Lane Club, when Dyer was only 24 years old,
many of these traits may not have been evident. Most of the
members of the club may still have assumed that Dyer was headed
for the ministry, though, according to Hawkins, 'Johnson suspected that his religious principles, for which at first he honoured him,
were giving way, and it was whispered to me by one who seemed
pleased that he was in the secret, that Mr. Dyer's religion was that
of Socrates.'

When his father died, most of the estate went to his widow and
older brother and sister, leaving very little to Samuel. Could this
have been one way of expressing disapproval at Samuel's shift of
interest? Certainly he did not have sufficient funds to live as
sumptuously as he would have liked. In order for him to earn more,
Johnson and Hawkins urged Dyer to write the life of Erasmus, a
suggestion he refused. Finally he was prevailed on to do a less
arduous task, a revision of the old translations of Plutarch's *Lives*,
and after 'heavy complaints of the labour of his task' it was completed and published in 1758. According to one account, after the
death of his mother and brother, when Samuel inherited the bulk
of their estates, he speculated in annuities on Lord Verney's
estate, on the advice of Johnson, and lost the whole of it.[19] When
Dyer died suddenly at the age of 47 in 1772, it was rumoured that
he had committed suicide, leaving insufficient money even to pay
for his funeral.[20]

During his later years, when he was a regular attendant at The
Club, he became a favourite of Edmund Burke, Thomas Percy,
and others. His keen intelligence was so much admired that it was
even suspected that he was the author of the anonymous letters of

[19] J. Nichols, *Literary Anecdotes*, vi. 266, from a statement by Richard Gough.
[20] Ibid., and account of Dyer in *DNB*.

Junius in 1769–72.[21] Reynolds painted his portrait, and later Johnson secured a mezzotint of it, along with those of Burke and Goldsmith, to hang on his wall.[22] Burke, in a piece written for the newspapers after Dyer's sudden death described him as:

a man of profound and general erudition, and his sagacity and judgment were fully equal to the extent of his learning. His mind was candid, sincere, and benevolent, his friendship disinterested and unalterable. The modest simplicity and sweetness of his manners rendered his conversation as amiable as it was instructive, and endeared him to those few who had the happiness of knowing intimately that valuable and unostentatious man.[23]

Balancing Hawkins's and Burke's opinions, one can see clearly that Samuel Dyer must have been a remarkable person. With all his weaknesses and lack of purpose, his delight in sensual pleasures and an easy existence, which rendered his life largely one of unfulfilled promise, his modesty and polite behaviour, together with his great learning and wide knowledge, clearly rendered him a valuable club member.

What did they talk about on those Tuesday evenings at the King's Head in Ivy Lane? From Hawkins and other accounts we do have an idea. Some of the topics, indeed, were scarcely controversial—recent scientific experiments, new inventions, medical treatments, and similar subjects. When these were brought up Johnson was probably willing merely to sit back and learn. Literature may have been the source of many long discussions, and occasionally they may even have moved into the other arts, though Johnson was largely insensible in this area. As Hawkins makes clear, Johnson had little real interest in music. He was once heard to say that 'It excites in my mind no ideas, and hinders me from contemplating my own.' Of one fine singer, or instrumental performer, he remarked that 'he had the merit of a Canary-bird'.

Moreover, in the visual arts, because of his limited sight in one eye and almost complete blindness in the other, Johnson showed little interest. Of course, Hawkins may give a somewhat one-sided summing-up of Johnson's deficiencies in this area when he says

---

[21] *Notes and Queries*, 2nd ser., ix (1860), 261; Prior, *Life of Edmond Malone*, pp. 419–26; *Life*, iv. 11 n.1.
[22] *Life*, i. 363 n.3.
[23] See account in *DNB*.

that he had little respect for 'symmetry, and harmony of parts and proportions.' For Johnson a 'statue was an unshapen mass, and a sumptuous edifice a quarry of stone.' One evening at the club Hawkins brought with him a small roll of prints (possibly landscapes by Perelle), which he had acquired that afternoon. When Johnson's curiosity made him pick up the roll and examine each print with great attention, he asked Hawkins what sort of pleasure such things could give him.[24] When Hawkins tried to explain how views or rural scenes and landscapes stirred his imagination, Johnson confessed that he was unable to experience the same reaction, for 'in his whole life he was never capable of discerning the least resemblance of any kind between a picture and the subject it was intended to represent'.

For the most part the talk must have concentrated on matters where he could see at least two sides, where there could be sharp disagreement. Once the conversation touched on religion, or philosophy, or politics, his combative spirit was aroused. Then there could be trouble, or at least excitement. Since Johnson, the founding father, was a Tory, and a reputed Jacobite sympathizer, while the majority of the Ivy Lane Club were Whigs, and a good many Nonconformists, it required some constraint on the part of younger members who thought of themselves as Johnson's disciples, but disagreed with what they thought were his prejudices. 'We all saw the prudence of avoiding to call the then late adventurer in Scotland, or his adherents, by those names which others hesitated not to give them.' For the most part, then, one suspects that the club kept off political arguments.

What must have occupied much of their time would have been philosophic matters. When anyone brought up ideas connected with the 'nature of moral obligation' Johnson 'was uniformly tenacious'. He was suspicious of most of the modern 'sects or classes of writers on morality', though he did admire Samuel Clarke. But most of the others drew his withering scorn. 'Little as Johnson liked the notions of lord Shaftesbury, he still less approved those of some later writers, who have pursued the same train of thinking and reasoning, namely, Hutcheson, Dr. Nettleton, and Mr. Harris of Salisbury. . . .' Since Dyer had been Hutcheson's student, he naturally would come to his defence, and

[24] Hawkins, p. 318. The story is not explicitly connected with the meetings of the Ivy Lane Club, but probably occurred then.

others of the group might have been called Shaftesburians. Topics connected with these writers 'were, not unfrequently, the subjects of altercation between Johnson and Dyer'. As Hawkins pointed out, it might be observed of these contests, as Johnson himself once said of two disputants, 'that the one had ball without powder, and the other powder without ball'. Hawkins continues: 'for Dyer, though best skilled in the controversy, was inferior to his adversary in the power of reasoning, and Johnson, who was not always master of the question, was seldom at a loss for such sophistical arguments as the other was unable to answer.'

Hawkins could not resist pointing out that in these discussions:

Johnson made it a rule to talk his best, but that on many subjects he was not uniform in his opinions, contending as often for victory as for truth: at one time *good*, at another *evil* was predominant in the moral constitution of the world. Upon one occasion, he would deplore the non-observance of Good-Friday, and on another deny, that among us of the present age there is any decline of public worship. He would sometimes contradict self-evident propositions, such as, that the luxury of this country has increased with its riches; and that the practice of card-playing is more general than heretofore. At this versatility of temper, none, however, took offence; as Alexander and Cæsar were born for conquest, so was Johnson for the office of symposiarch, to preside in all conversations; and I never yet saw the man who would venture to contest his right.

Let it not, however, be imagined, that the members of this our club met together, with the temper of gladiators, or that there was wanting among us a disposition to yield to each other in all diversities of opinion.

Nor should it be inferred that serious disputation was the chief purpose of their meetings. There was no insistence on keeping discussion to particular topics, and much of the talk was mixed with mirth and humour. Johnson himself 'was a great contributor to the mirth of conversation, by the many witty sayings he uttered, and the many excellent stories which his memory had treasured up, and he would on occasion relate.'

The Ivy Lane Club undoubtedly was a major source of relaxation for Johnson. After he had eaten his supper, so 'solid and substantial' that Hawkins suspected he had had no dinner, he would open up and become the centre of the evening's entertainment. With no other

incentive to hilarity than lemonade, Johnson was, in a short time after

our assembling, transformed into a new creature: his habitual melancholy and lassitude of spirit gave way; his countenance brightened; his
mind was made to expand, and his wit to sparkle: he told excellent
stories; and in his didactic stile of conversation, both instructed and
delighted us.[25]

The club was Johnson's way of getting rid of both professional and
personal problems.

The one special meeting which has often been described came
when Johnson persuaded the club members to celebrate the first
production of a young woman writer named Charlotte Lennox
by holding an all-night party. Hawkins describes the event with
something more than his usual gusto, though unfortunately he
leaves us with a number of difficult problems. All the details do not
seem to fit. Here is the way Hawkins tells the story:

Mrs. Lenox, a lady now well known in the literary world, had written
a novel intitled, 'The life of Harriot Stuart,' which in the spring of 1751,
was ready for publication. One evening at the club, Johnson proposed
to us the celebrating the birth of Mrs. Lenox's first literary child, as he
called her book, by a whole night spent in festivity. Upon his mentioning it to me, I told him I had never sat up a whole night in my life;
but he continuing to press me, and saying, that I should find great
delight in it, I, as did all the rest of our company, consented. The place
appointed was the Devil tavern, and there, about the hour of eight, Mrs.
Lenox and her husband, and a lady of her acquaintance, now living,
as also the club, and friends to the number of near twenty, assembled.
Our supper was elegant, and Johnson had directed that a magnificent
hot apple-pye should make a part of it, and this he would have stuck
with bay-leaves, because, forsooth, Mrs. Lenox was an authoress, and
had written verses; and further, he had prepared for her a crown of
laurel, with which, but not till he had invoked the muses by some
ceremonies of his own invention, he encircled her brows. The night
passed, as must be imagined, in pleasant conversation, and harmless
mirth, intermingled at different periods with the refreshments of
coffee and tea. About five, Johnson's face shone with meridian splendour, though his drink had been only lemonade; but the far greater
part of us had deserted the colours of Bacchus, and were with difficulty
rallied to partake of a second refreshment of coffee, which was scarcely
ended when the day began to dawn. This phenomenon began to put
us in mind of our reckoning; but the waiters were all so overcome with
sleep, that it was two hours before we could get a bill, and it was not

[25] Hawkins, p. 250.

till near eight that the creaking of the street-door gave the signal for our departure.

Hawkins himself had been troubled all evening with a bad toothache, which Dr. Bathurst had tried to alleviate 'by all the topical remedies and palliatives he could think of'. Hawkins later remembered that his conscience troubled him by the resemblance their gathering had to a debauch, but once he had taken a few turns through the Temple grounds and had had breakfast in a neighbouring coffee-house he felt better. While Johnson may have been delighted by this unusual celebration, most of the other members were probably determined not to make it a regular occurrence.

This is the story. But how true is it? For one thing, why did they pick the Devil Tavern? It was certainly famous for all-night debauches. In this old eating-house between Temple Bar and the Middle Temple Gate, nearly opposite St. Dunstan's church, Ben Jonson and his cronies used to dine early in the seventeenth century and make a night of it. Was Johnson merely following the example of his namesake? The sign outside had St. Dunstan pulling the devil by the nose, and naturally the place came to be called the Devil Tavern. It was a resort of booksellers as well as writers.

Even more important, what work of Charlotte Lennox was really being celebrated? And exactly when did the celebration occur? Hawkins says that it was *The Life of Harriot Stuart*, certainly her first published work of fiction, which was brought out on 13 December 1750.[26] Yet in London in December the dawn would not have come shortly after five o'clock. Mrs. Lennox's second work, *The Female Quixote*, her first real success, was completed in the spring of 1751. Could this have been the one being celebrated? *The Female Quixote* could not have been called Charlotte Lennox's 'first literary child', though it was her first good one. Or could the celebration have been arranged when Mrs. Lennox finished writing the first draft of *Harriot Stuart*, perhaps around the beginning of May or late in the summer of 1750? Sunrise in early May would have been about 5.30 a.m. There is even the possibility that Johnson's motive was to stir up interest in publishing the work in John Payne, one of the members of the club.

[26] Duncan Isles, 'The Lennox Collection', *Harvard Library Bulletin*, xviii (1970), 326, 334.

Payne did bring out the novel in December. The fact that he is never mentioned in Hawkins's account might be thought a bit strange if the gathering had been planned to mark the actual appearance in print of Mrs. Lennox's first novel. Or could Hawkins's memory of the time of dawn have been faulty? It may well be that they concluded their all-night conversation about eight o'clock in the morning when the sun was just coming up. All his talk about it taking two hours to wake up the waiters may have been an embellishment for an amusing story. It may have been in December 1750 after all. Obviously we may never know. And really it makes little difference whether the work celebrated was Charlotte Lennox's first or second novel, or whether the gathering occurred in the summer or winter. What is important is the evidence this account gives us as to Johnson's dominance over the Ivy Lane group, of his early enthusiasm for the work of Charlotte Lennox, and of his typical behaviour on such occasions. Even if other club members were never willing again to sit up all night while Johnson imbibed huge quantities of lemonade and placed crowns of laurel on the brows of young authors it undoubtedly happened once and was certainly worth remembering.

Another difficult problem is just when the Ivy Lane Club finally disbanded, and was it later called 'The Rambler's Club'? The evidence is not conclusive. As to the name, some members may always have thought of it as Johnson's club, and after he had become admired in some circles as the author of *The Rambler*, they may have used the term. There is no proof that there really were two clubs. How long it lasted is another matter. One account has it that the club ended about 1753, after only four years; others indicate that it existed until 1756, when it would have been seven years old.[27] Hawkins claims the later date. By then Salter and McGhie were dead, Barker had left the city and moved to Trowbridge, Dyer had gone abroad, and Bathurst was preparing to emigrate to the West Indies. Thus the Ivy Lane Club may gradually have 'petered-out', with fewer and fewer members attending, and finally have come to an end. Again the exact dates really do not matter.

Of one thing we can be certain. For a critical period in Johnson's life, while he was producing the dictionary, and writing some of his best periodical essays, the Ivy Lane Club was an important part

[27] Hawkins, p. 360.

of his life. Here he could relax and discuss at leisure many of the controversial topics which were running through his head. And here he could keep in close touch with the publishing world. Indeed, it appears probable that the first plans for *The Rambler* came out of meetings of the club, and certainly *The Adventurer* was conceived and operated by what Johnson himself called 'the fraternity' made up of members of the Ivy Lane Club.[28]

Perhaps the best short summary of what the club must have meant to its members can be found in an unpublished manuscript in the Osborn collection. Here in a later handwritten account of the career of John Hawkesworth there is the statement that during the early 1750s Hawkesworth 'generally attended the Rambler's weekly club, from which if any ever departed without being wiser or better it certainly must have been his own fault'.[29]

[28] *Letters of Samuel Johnson*, ed. R. W. Chapman, i. 47–8 (No. 46).
[29] From the Hayley Papers, in the James Marshall and Marie-Louise Osborn Collection, Beinecke Rare Book and Manuscript Library, Yale University.

John Black and Montesquieu—
the Search for a Correspondence

ROBERT SHACKLETON

DURING MOST of the time, from 1948 on, that I was working on Montesquieu I was carrying a heavy burden of teaching, even by the exacting standards of Oxford. My research was therefore mainly carried out in vacations or in rare periods of sabbatical leave. The source material I was seeking was usually on the Continent and the distinction between research travel and holiday travel was always vague and most frequently non-existent. Often, when travelling in quest of research material, I filled odd moments by reading in libraries books which were accessible in Oxford but for which no time had been conveniently available.

In this way it happened that, being in Bologna early in July 1954 for the purpose of documenting myself on the background of Montesquieu's visit to the Papal States, I read an article which had long been on my list for study. This was a paper presented in 1857 to the Accademia delle Scienze of Turin by the celebrated Piedmontese jurist Frédéric Sclopis.[1] His writing was elegant and stimulating and I read him with pleasure and profit. At the very end, however, there was a reference to some manuscript letters of Montesquieu which filled me with excitement.

Basing himself on an article by the French critic Villemain, Sclopis spoke of the existence of a collection of letters written by Montesquieu to a Madame Black. These letters were thought to be full of information about Montesquieu's youth, and Lord Brougham was said to have known them. Nothing was said of Madame Black except that she was a 'personne d'un mérite supérieur et d'un esprit aimable'. She was unknown to me. I at once decided that I must find out about her and trace these letters

---

[1] 'Recherches historiques et critiques sur l'*Esprit des lois* de Montesquieu' (Reale Accademia delle Scienze di Torino, *Memorie*, series II, vol. 17 (1858), Scienze morali, storiche e filologiche, pp. 165–270).

which were apparently from the largely undocumented years in Montesquieu's youth. They were going to be important in themselves and in any case I was seeking all the letters I could find for the new edition of Montesquieu which my friend André Masson was preparing, and in which the correspondence was being re-edited by François Gebelin, likewise friend and former librarian in Bordeaux.

I was then about to leave Bologna for Paris, where the investigation could be continued much better than in Bologna, and I could hardly contain my impatience until I was in the familiar reading-room of the Bibliothèque Nationale. I had been working on Montesquieu for six years. How could I have failed to learn of these letters?

The cryptic allusion to Villemain's article in the *Journal des Savants* was quickly elucidated in Paris. The article[2] was in fact a review of four works of Lord Brougham, three of them being his biographical studies of philosophers, men of letters, and statesmen of the time of George III. The relevant work was Brougham's *Lives of Men of Letters and Science who flourished in the Time of George III* (London, 1845). In discussing it, Villemain refers particularly to the article on the Scottish chemist Joseph Black who was a leading figure in the intellectual life of Edinburgh and a friend of David Hume, Adam Smith, and Adam Ferguson. Villemain reports that Black was born at Bordeaux, that his mother was on friendly terms with Montesquieu and exchanged letters with him, and that these letters were preserved as heirlooms in the Black family. In his own words,

Black, né à Bordeaux de parents écossais, avait pour mère une personne d'un mérite supérieur et de l'esprit le plus aimable, qui fut l'objet des assiduités de Montesquieu. Il avait conservé comme titres d'honneur pour sa famille, un grand nombre de lettres du président à cette femme aussi charmante que respectée. Ce dépôt n'a pas péri, sans doute, depuis 1799.

Montesquieu's surviving correspondence, he continues, is slight in volume. How good it would be if we could add to it these letters, '*que lord Brougham paraît avoir connues*' [my italics].[3]

The chase was leading to Brougham, and could best be pursued

---

[2] *Journal des Savants* (Nov. 1855), pp. 653–62.
[3] Ibid., pp. 654–5.

in England. Soon after my return to Oxford I turned to the old biography of Montesquieu by Vian and found that he had heard of Mrs. Black, whom he promoted socially as 'milady Black, aussi charmante que respectable'.[4] I ought to have picked this out on my first reading of Vian, but at this stage I had read him with too little attention, despising him for his many inaccuracies instead of valuing the range of his information.

Meanwhile I read Brougham's memoir. As a student at Edinburgh he had attended one of Joseph Black's last courses of lectures, and wrote of him with sympathy and enthusiasm, and of his father with respect:

Black was born, in 1721, at Bordeaux, where his father, a native of Belfast, was settled as a merchant: he was, however, a Scotchman, and his wife too was of a Scottish family, that of Gordon of Hillhead, in Aberdeenshire, settled like Mr. Black at Bordeaux. The latter was a person of extraordinary virtues, and a most amiable disposition. The celebrated Montesquieu honoured him with his especial regard; and his son preserved, as titles of honour in his family, the many letters of the President to his parent. In one of them he laments the intended removal of the Black family as a thing he could not reconcile himself to, for his greatest pleasure was seeing them often, and living himself in their society.[5]

He alludes later to Montesquieu's praising the thesis of Joseph Black.[6]

Villemain's mention of Mrs. Black is simply a misreading of Brougham's text. 'The latter' in the passage quoted might be held ambiguous; the word 'parent' is of common gender; but 'him' in the third sentence can refer only to Joseph Black's father and Villemain has misread it. From this error arises the story of Mrs. (or *milady*) Black.

It still appeared likely, however, that Brougham had seen the Montesquieu–Black correspondence, and possible that he had owned it. I therefore consulted several scholars who were interested in Brougham: E. G. Collieu, A. Aspinall, C. K. Ogden, A. Cobban. These inquiries led me to the Library of University College, London, where Brougham's surviving papers are held. But nothing resembling, or relating to, the Montesquieu letters

[4] L. Vian, *Histoire de Montesquieu* (Paris, 1878), p. 23.
[5] *Lives of Men of Letters and Science*, p. 325.
[6] Ibid., p. 327.

came to light. The pursuit of Brougham was proving fruitless. I turned instead to Black.

A substantial memoir on the life of Joseph Black is prefixed to his *Lectures on the Elements of Chemistry*, published at Edinburgh in 1803, in two volumes. The author is John Robison, a friend of Black and his colleague at Edinburgh University, best known now for his *Proofs of a Conspiracy against all the Religions and Governments of Europe* (Edinburgh, 1797), in which he denounced what he thought the secret and sinister influence of freemasonry.

All Brougham's information about Black and Montesquieu comes, unacknowledged, from Robison's memoir, and many of Brougham's statements about Black's scientific achievements are based on the same source.[7]

A great part of Robison's information, moreover, is derived from a memoir on Black read by Adam Ferguson to the Royal Society of Edinburgh on 23 April 1801, though not published until 1805, two years after the appearance of Robison's preface to Black's lectures.[8]

Ferguson, after stating that Black was born at Bordeaux in 1728 —Brougham was in error in giving the date as 1721—writes:

While Mr. Black, the father, lived at Bourdeaux, the great Montesquieu, being President of the Parliament or Court of Justice in that province, honoured Mr. Black with a friendship and intimacy, of which his descendents, to this day, are justly proud. They preserve letters, or scraps of correspondence, that passed between the President Montesquieu and their ancestor, as they would titles of honour descending in their race. On a paper wrapped round a bundle of such letters, the following note is found in the handwriting of Joseph Black. 'My father was honoured with President Montesquieu's friendship on account of his good character and virtues.'[9]

The text of the note continues with a eulogy of Black's character.

Robison writes to the same effect, using the same comparison with titles of honour. He continues with a brief account of Mon-

---

[7] For example, the claim by Brougham (pp. 327–8) that Black's *Experiments in Magnesia, Quicklime and other Alkaline Substances* have, methodologically, no equal since Newton's *Optics*, comes straight from Robison (p. xxviii).

[8] 'Minutes of the Life and Character of Joseph Black, M.D., addressed to the Royal Society of Edinburgh' (*Transactions of the Royal Society of Edinburgh*, vol. v (1805), part III, pp. 101–17).

[9] Ibid., p. 102.

tesquieu, and suggests that he may have obtained information about the British Constitution from Black. He goes on:

I am sorry that I did not look more narrowly in the President's correspondence with Mr. Black. I can only recollect the being delighted with the impression which the sight of so much worth and domestic happiness made on this excellent judge of human nature. Dr. Ferguson mentions a letter, written by him, when he heard of Mr. Black's intention to leave Bordeaux. In this letter, among other expressions of kindness, are the following: 'I cannot reconcile myself to the thoughts of your leaving Bordeaux. I lose the most agreeable pleasure that I had, that of seeing you often, and forgetting myself with you.' I remember also another letter, in which were nearly the following words: 'I rejoice to hear of the good health of all your family; and I endeavour to make your satisfaction solace me for the loss of those tranquil hours which I enjoyed in the midst of my friends, contemplating their happiness and their virtues.'[10]

Ferguson does in fact mention the first letter, and gives the French original of the passage quoted.[11] He does not mention the second letter.

Robison—but not Ferguson—refers to the occasion of Joseph Black's taking his degree in medicine:

He sent some copies of his essay to his father in Bordeaux. A copy was given by the old gentleman to his friend the President Montesquieu, who, after a few days, called on Mr. Black and said to him, 'Mr. Black, my very good friend, I rejoice with you; your son will be the honour of your name and of your family.'[12]

This was the sum, so far as I could discover, of published knowledge about John Black and his connection with Montesquieu. It was now necessary to discover the correspondence. I was distracted from this task by heavy academic duties, but as and when I could, I questioned friends and visitors who knew the eighteenth century and were interested in manuscripts. When neither James Osborn nor L. F. Powell could help I began to despair. The National Library of Scotland and the Edinburgh Public Library were willing but unable to help. Miss M. A. Balfour of the latter institution said that all inquiries led back to Robison and to Ferguson, and that Robison was only a rehash of Ferguson.

Dr. Cecil Courtney, now Fellow of Christ's College, Cambridge,

---

[10] Robison, pp. xix–xx.   [11] Ferguson, p. 103.
[12] Robison, pp. xxviii–xxix.

but then a research student working with me, made inquiries in Belfast. His friend Mr. James Vitty, of the Linen Hall Library, suggested writing to Dr. Douglas McKie, of University College, London, later professor of the history and philosophy of science. I wrote to him in June 1957 and began a close friendship which ended only with his death in 1967. He himself was, I discovered to my gratification, working on Joseph Black and had had access to his papers. 'Like you', he wrote on 4 July 1957, 'I had looked forward very much to seeing these "letters and fragments of correspondence" said to have been preserved among the Black papers, but I regret to say that this proved completely disappointing, since there were just none at all.'

This was even more disappointing for me, and I began to think that the letters had disappeared for all time. Before long I was preoccupied with preparing my biography of Montesquieu for the press. On Black I quoted what was said by Ferguson, but had to content myself with a vaguely hopeful statement about what the correspondence might tell us if it could be rediscovered.[13]

After the appearance of my biography in the summer of 1961, my preoccupations moved away, temporarily, from Montesquieu. In April 1962 Douglas McKie wrote to me with much background information about Black. He had discovered that Joseph Black's mother came from a family of devoted Jacobites; that John Black had a house in the Chartrons (the *quai* at Bordeaux where the wine-merchants live to this day) and a country house in the parish of Lormont to the north-east of the city, and that though he left Bordeaux in 1751 he returned for a long visit some years later. But of his correspondence with Montesquieu, not a word. McKie was still hoping, but his health became poor and his research suffered. In 1966 I was appointed to the office of Bodley's Librarian and my own time for research was much reduced. Black now seldom crossed my mind.

In the autumn of 1968 I was in North America on a lecture tour which took me to the west coast. After Los Angeles and Berkeley I went to the University of British Columbia, where I was scheduled to give two lectures, one of them on Montesquieu. On my first evening, which was 31 October, I was invited to dinner by Ian Ross, professor of English and specialist in the Scottish Enlightenment. When he met me he greeted me with the words, 'Some years

---

[13] R. Shackleton, *Montesquieu, a critical biography* (Oxford, 1961), pp. 209–10.

ago you asked me about Montesquieu's correspondence with John Black. Here are xerox copies of the letters.'

The chase had led me from Bologna to Vancouver. The originals of the letters were in Edinburgh University Library.

On 24 February 1967, Air Commodore R. C. Jonas wrote to Mr. E. R. S. Fifoot, Librarian of Edinburgh University, saying that his aunt, Miss E. N. W. Black, had in her possession notebooks and letters that had belonged to Joseph Black, and wished to offer them to Edinburgh University. The gift was readily accepted, and announced in *The Scotsman* for 19 May 1967 in an article signed C.P.F., the initials of C. P. Finlayson, Keeper of Manuscripts in Edinburgh University Library.

Among the letters in the collection is one from Joseph Black to his brother George, in Belfast, dated 7 October 1793, saying:

I now write to ask the favour of you to look among my father's old letters, if you still have them, for some which were wrote to him by the lat celeebrated Baron de Montesquieu, the author of the *Spirit of Laws*, in French. Our father gave me one dated Augst. 1751 & showed me others dated 1749 & 1750. If you can find them & any others I shall be much obliged to you for letting me have them, & I shall return them again if you chuse it.[14]

The reply was unsatisfactory, for on 9 November 1799 Joseph Black writes to George Black junior, his nephew, who is in Belfast:

You need not send me a sight of my father's letters. I am well acquainted with his excellent character & manner of writing. But he had a few French letters from Baron Montesquieu which I desired much to have. They are probably destroyed. Your father to whom I applyed not having been able to find them.[15]

Three letters from Montesquieu to John Black are indeed in the collection. One of them is the original letter while the two others are contemporary copies. They are accompanied by a covering note. I publish them here, with the kind permission of the Librarian of Edinburgh University Library.

The covering note is as follows.[16]

[14] The manuscript is shelfmarked MS. Gen 874/V/64–5.
[15] MS. Gen 874/V/122.
[16] Half-brackets as ⌐ ¬ are used to indicate passages crossed out in the manuscript.

My father was honoured with ⌐Baron⌐ President Montesquieu's Friendship on account of his good character & virtues. He had no ambition to be very rich, but was chearfull & contented, benevolent & liberal minded—he was industrious & prudent in business, of the strictest probity & honour, & very temperate & regular in his manner of living, ⌐A pious protestant but of a chearfull temper and benevolent liberal mind.⌐ He & my mother, who was equally domestic, educated thirteen of their children, eight sons & five daughters, who all grew up to be men & women & were settled in different places.

The Baron addressed his letters to my father as 'Negotiant Anglois'. The French at Bordeaux seldom make any distinction of the British subjects but call them all 'Anglois'.[17]

⌐The occasion of his writing one of these letters was a war[18] between France & England and an order from Court requiring all the British to depart from France except some persons who had been long settled & who might be allowed to remain under certain conditions & engagements.⌐

My Uncle referred to in one of these letters was the then Gordon of Halhead.[19] He had been engaged in the rebellion in Scotland & was living at Bologne. M. Byres[20] supposes that when the Pretender was arrested in the playhouse at Paris[21] my Uncle with others of that party in France were so much offended ⌐as to⌐ & behaved so disrespectfully to the French government that it was thought necessary to check them.

A letter and two copies of letters from the ⌐Baron⌐ President Montesquieu to my Father.

The copies were made by me with my father's permission

The first letter from Montesquieu, written on 22 October 1749, follows. It is a copy in the hand of Joseph Black. There are a

[17] The French tendency to include Scots within the term *Anglais* is not restricted to Bordeaux or to the eighteenth century.

[18] This is a false recollection. Britain and France had been at peace since the Treaty of Aix-la-Chapelle of 1748. The steps taken against British residents in France were directed against suspected Jacobites.

[19] The uncle was George Gordon of Hallhead (Aberdeenshire) whose sister was married to John Black. After the 1745 rebellion in which he had been an active participant, George Gordon (whose father Robert had long been settled at Bordeaux) took refuge in France. In 1749–50 he was at Boulogne. See A. and H. Tayler, *Jacobites of Aberdeenshire and Banffshire in the '45* (Aberdeen, 1928).

[20] Probably Patrick Byres, 'the Jacobite laird', who lived in France after the '45. His aunt Isabel Byres had married Robert Gordon, so that he was a first cousin of John Black.

[21] Prince Charles Edward was arrested at the Paris opera on 10 December 1748.

number of spelling mistakes and the transcription has been modernized. The letter bears the shelfmark MS. Gen.874/IV/2.

Copy of a letter from the Baron de Montesquieu to
Mr. John Black, Merch[t.] Bordeaux.

Monsieur l'abbé Gordon[22] m'a apporté, Monsieur, une lettre de votre part au sujet d'une lettre que vous désirez que j'écrive à Mr de Mirepoix[23] en faveur de Mr votre beau-frère,[24] mais comme il avait aussi une lettre de Mr votre beau-frère contradictoire à la vôtre nous sommes convenus que je n'écrirai ma lettre qu'après des éclaircissements de vous et de lui et je l'ai prié de lui écrire et de lui dire de vous envoyer la lettre qu'il recevrait afin que vous voyiez les nouveaux ordres que vous aurez à me donner.

Mr votre beau-frère a une théologie très rigide et il ne veut pas entendre parler de l'article de votre lettre par laquelle il promettrait de ne rien faire qui pût troubler l'état présent et les choses actuellement établies. Je représentai à Mr l'abbé Gordon qu'il n'était pas proposable de demander une chose et de s'ôter les moyens de la demander, qu'il n'y avait point d'État qui pût recevoir un sujet ou étranger, sans la condition d'y vivre tranquille, que si on ne la demandait pas à des gens non suspects, c'était qu'on la supposait par la confiance qu'on avait en eux, qu'avant d'entreprendre une chose il fallait commencer par être bien d'accord avec soi-même, que si on venait à lui faire la demande et qu'il refusât, sa condition deviendrait pire parce qu'il serait noté pour jamais, qu'il m'exposerait même à des reproches bien aigres de Mr de Mirepoix pour l'avoir commis, et l'avoir fait soupçonner d'avoir par sa protection voulu introduire des gens mal intentionnés; et qu'ainsi il fallait de deux choses l'une, ou rester comme on était, ou bien faire ce qu'il fallait pour être autrement, et qu'il valait mieux être mal que de se mettre dans un état pire; que si un domestique se présentait à un maître et que le maître lui dît, je vous recevrai à condition que vous soyez tranquille dans ma maison, et qu'il dît qu'il ne voulait pas faire

---

[22] The abbé Gordon cannot be identified with certainty. Two Gordons were Catholic priests, both of them being connected with Scots College in Paris. Robert Gordon (1687–1764) is the subject of an article in the *DNB*. He was banished from England in 1745 and took refuge in Flanders and France, until 1749 when he left for Rome. John Gordon (d. 1777) was known to Hume, Boswell, and Adam Smith. He was highly regarded by the Young Pretender. See the note on him in Yale edition of Horace Walpole, vol. xv. I am inclined to select John Gordon as the person referred to, since he was a more firmly established figure in French society. He *may* be related to Robert Gordon of Hallhead, while Robert Gordon came from Kirkhill near Inverness.

[23] The duc de Mirepoix, who was a close friend of Montesquieu, was French ambassador in London from 31 July 1749 to 30 April 1752.

[24] George Gordon of Hallhead.

cette promesse, il n'y a pas de maître qui le reçût. Voilà, Monsieur, mes objections. Mr l'abbé Gordon en a été frappé, m'a dit qu'il lui écrirait avec ordre de vous envoyer la lettre, et pour lors je ferai ce que vous jugerez à propos. Je lui ai même dit que j'avais lieu de croire que Mr de Mirepoix ferait tout ce qu'il pourrait pour me faire plaisir dans cette occasion. Vous êtes prudent et sage. J'attends. Faites-moi le plaisir de me mander si vous avez été payé de Mr de Mirepoix[25] et de Mr l'évêque de Soissons.[26]

Je vous souhaite une bonne santé. Aimez-moi un peu parce que je vous aime beaucoup.

Signed   MONTESQUIEU

A Paris ce 22 8bre 1749.

This letter, which is unusually clumsy in style, provides new evidence of the closeness of Montesquieu's links with the Jacobites.

The second letter is the manuscript original. It is in the hand of Damours, a secretary who served Montesquieu from 1748 to his death. It is reproduced without change, save that capitalization and punctuation have been regularized. It bears the shelfmark MS. Gen.874/IV/3.

J'ay mon cher Monsieur recu de Mr de Saint Sulpice[27] deux cent quatre-vingt quatorze livres trois sols pour le montant de deux bariques de vin blanc que vous luy avez envoiés, et j'ay chargé Madame de Montesquieu de vous les faire remettre et je vous prie de luy en donner un recu. Je suis bien aise Monsieur et tres cher ami que vous aiez de la satisfaction de toute votre famille, elle est si bien née que cela ne peut pas etre autrement. Quand Monsieur le Docteur[28] viendera a Paris je le recomanderay à tous les docteurs de ma connoissance. Mr Smith[29]

---

[25] The payment was undoubtedly for wine. Mme de Mirepoix spoke of introducing the wine of La Brède into England (*Œuvres complètes de Montesquieu* (Paris (Nagel), 1950–5), iii. 1212).

[26] The bishop of Soissons, François de Fitz-James (1709–64), was a son of the Duke of Berwick and a close friend of Montesquieu.

[27] Presumably Jean Dulau Dallemans who was *curé* of the parish of Saint-Sulpice from 1748 to 1777. Montesquieu's Paris apartment was in this parish and the priest was present at his death.

[28] A facetious reference to Joseph Black, then studying medicine.

[29] Since Smith was concerned with the affairs of George Gordon who was then at Boulogne, this is probably Charles Smith, a banker at Boulogne, several times referred to in W. B. Blaikie (ed.), *Origins of the Forty-Five* (Edinburgh, 1916, reprinted 1975). There are two other references to Smith in Montesquieu's correspondence (*Œuvres*, Paris (Nagel), iii. 1455 and 1460); the first of them has gratuitously been assumed to be Adam Smith. Both can probably now be taken as Charles Smith.

que jay vu icy ajant en vüe de suivre l'affaire de Mr Gourdon[30] j'en ay ecrit a Monsieur de Mirepoix, et je desire bien qu'il reusise dans sa negotiation. Je desire bien fort que vous vous portiés bien. Je trouve mon fils et mon petit fils tres heureux de l'amitié que vous leurs accordez, je vous prie de la conserver aussi pour moy et de croire que personne ne vous aime et ne vous estime plus que &c.   MONTESQUIEU

a Paris ce 24 fevrier 1750

A Monsieur
Monsieur Jean Black
Negotiant anglois aux charterons
a Bordeaux

The third letter, of 7 August 1751, is again a copy made by Joseph Black. In the transcription spelling and punctuation have been modernized. It bears the shelfmark MS. Gen.874/IV/4.

From the Baron de Montesquieu
to Mr. John Black, Merch^t· Bordeaux. Copy.
Votre lettre, Monsieur mon très cher ami, m'a extrêmement surpris et je vous avoue que je ne me fais point à l'idée de vous voir quitter Bordeaux. Je perds le plaisir le plus agréable que j'y eusse, qui était de vous voir souvent et de m'oublier avec vous.[31] Je ne perdrais jamais la mémoire, Monsieur et très cher ami, d'une amitié de quarante ans et qui a commencé avec nos pères et qui a toujours été maintenue. Elle sera dans nos enfants comme elle a été entre nous. Vous goûtez, Monsieur, le bonheur de tous ceux qui ont le cœur bien placé, qui est d'avoir beaucoup de gens qui vous aiment. Vous avez des enfants qui ont le meilleur naturel du monde, et le ciel vous les a accordés ainsi paroo que vous aviez un bon naturel vous-même. Je compte vous voir pourtant avant votre départ et il est bien sûr qu'en quelque pays que je sois et en quelque pays que vous soyez que vous aurez un ami et que j'en aurai un.

Permettez-moi d'avoir l'honneur de vous embrasser de tout mon cœur.

MONTESQUIEU
A Montesquieu ce 7 août 1751.

The Black letters contain three other relevant passages. Joseph Black, writing a long letter from Edinburgh to his father in Belfast on 10 March 1753, interjects:

---

[30] Gourdon is a frequent French spelling of Gordon.
[31] The words from 'je ne me fais point' to 'avec vous' were correctly quoted in French by Adam Ferguson (p. 103).

I see the President's extream affection & regard for you extends to all your family & I long to thank him for his kindness. But I now find I cannot see him so soon as I expected. I have so much business on my hands with 5 classes beside the shop & the infirmary that it is impossible for me to write the thesis and prepare for my degree this season . . .[32]

A further letter from Joseph Black is addressed to his father at Blamont, near Bordeaux, on 23 November 1754.

I take this opportunity [he writes] to send you a few copies of my inaugural dissertaion which it is the custom here for the young doctors to distribute very liberally among their freinds and fellow students and this custom obliged me to print off 170 copies—a peice of expence attended with no manner of advantage to me but which could not be avoided.[33]

He suggests to his father that it might be of interest to Jean-Baptiste de Secondat, Montesquieu's son, but says nothing about the father.

John Black had Montesquieu in mind, however. The bundle of books was dispatched on 23 November 1754 and must have reached Bordeaux quickly. Before the end of December Montesquieu left for Paris. Late in January he was attacked by a fever from which many were suffering, and on 10 February he died. John Black had been one of his last visitors in Bordeaux, carrying his son's thesis *De humore acido a cibis orto*.

The last letter we are to note was addressed by Joseph Black on 2 September 1755 to his father, still apparently far from home:

I observed with gratitude how carefull you have been to put my thesis into the hands of all such as you imagined would have any relish for it, but the great name of Montesquieu among these renewed my melancholy. I had already heard of that loss all the world has reason to mourn and it affected me the more sensibly as he was your intimate friend.[34]

The letters are not great letters, but they establish a stronger link than was known to exist between Montesquieu and the

[32] MS. Gen. 874/V/7-8.
[33] MS. Gen. 874/V/9-10.
[34] MS. Gen. 874/V/11.
After this article had gone to the printer I learnt of the existence of a valuable work, A. L. Donovan, *Philosophical Chemistry in the Scottish Enlightenment* (Edinburgh, 1975), which gives useful background information about John Black, derived in part from manuscripts in the Public Record Office of Northern Ireland.

Scottish Enlightenment. They illustrate also Montesquieu's connection with a tightly-knit group of Jacobite exiles. They point, indeed, to the desirability of further research on the intellectual consequences of the Jacobite dispersion in Western Europe, a subject which would have appealed to the imagination of James Marshall Osborn.

William Blackstone and the Legal Chairs at Oxford

LUCY SUTHERLAND

THIS ESSAY is in no way intended to make a contribution to legal knowledge. Any interest it may possess is as an examination of an episode in the history of the University of Oxford in the eighteenth century, and in the career of William Blackstone, one of the University's most distinguished sons. The scholar to whose memory this volume is dedicated always delighted in the by-ways of biography, and (a devoted alumnus of Oxford) often sat in the Codrington Library of All Souls under the shadow of Bacon's towering statue of the author of the *Commentaries*.

Blackstone has received less than his due attention from biographers, partly because of the breakdown of his friends' plans to provide an adequate memoir as a foreword to the posthumous edition of his *Reports*,[1] partly because he left no corpus of correspondence (though the number of his scattered letters known to survive is mounting), but most of all because so much of his life was bound up with his College and University, the eighteenth-century history of which has been woefully neglected. It has been said that 'the years that Blackstone spent mainly at Oxford, 1753–1761, were the most productive of his life'.[2] They were the years in which, abandoning for the time being the ambition to

---

[1] James Clitherow, Blackstone's executor and the editor of the *Reports of Cases Determined in the Several Courts of Westminster Hall Taken and Compiled by the Honourable Sir William Blackstone Knt.*, 2 vols. (London, 1781), tells us that it had been hoped to print a Memoir with them by his old and intimate friend Benjamin Buckler D.D., Fellow of All Souls, an admirable stylist and a man concerned in many of Blackstone's activities, but ill health prevented this, and James Clitherow himself took over. Though he was a former colleague of Blackstone's, and later his brother-in-law and though he was assisted by the advice of friends and 'a short Abstract of every Circumstance of Consequence in his life written by himself with his accustomed accuracy' he proved a singularly unenterprising biographer.

[2] H. Carter, *A History of the University Press* (Oxford, 1975), i. 408.

make a successful career at the Bar, he concentrated on his career at Oxford, and delivered, first as a private venture and then as the first Vinerian Professor of Common Law, the courses of lectures which when published in 1765-9 as the *Commentaries on the Laws of England* won him international fame. During these years he also made his maximum impact on the University and was without doubt the most powerful and enterprising individual in it. As a leading figure in Oxford his career was far longer. It showed at all stages—in the early years of the reorganization of All Souls, as a reformer and leader in the administration and politics of the University, and (when he had given up all formal contacts with it) in his plans for revolutionizing the road-system of the City[3]— great powers of mind and character, a capacity to exercise influence over friends and colleagues, a passion for order and efficiency, and an immense capacity for hard work, which gave him pre-eminence in the small and closely-knit society in which he found himself. It was in the University that these qualifications gave him as a man of action, a personal status which he was never later to assume.

Nevertheless outside the University and a small group of men distinguished in his profession who saw his potentialities, he was little known, and it is not surprising that after his death a number of stories (often apocryphal) began to circulate about the earlier years of his life. One of the best known of these purports to explain the circumstances in which he decided to deliver the lectures which were to make him famous and to illustrate in a dramatic way the political conditions at the time this decision was reached.

The story first appeared in print in J. Holliday's *Life of William late Earl of Mansfield* (London, 1797).[4] No independent contemporary version of it has been found, though it was widely copied, with slight embellishments, by later writers.[5] Holliday, who knew Mansfield well in his later years, had to depend in his account of his earlier life on accessible public sources, the reminiscences of a few surviving contemporaries, and anecdotes in general circulation

---

[3] For this little-known activity of his see E. de Villiers, *Swinford Toll Bridge 1769-1969*, Eynsham History Group (1969) and the Bertie MSS. in the Bodleian.

[4] pp. 88-9.

[5] The best known of them was Lord Campbell, *The Lives of the Chief Justices of England* (1849), ii. 378-9.

—the kind of evidence which is seldom accurate but often contains some basis of fact. The story runs:

A fair occasion offered, about this period of time, for Mr. Murray[6] to manifest his love of his profession, and an ardent desire to lay a better foundation in one of our universities for initiating and training students in legal knowledge by the fostering hand of an able law-professor. The first duke of Newcastle[7] was the warm friend and patron of Mr. Murray. The civil law professorship in the university of Oxford being then vacant, Mr. Murray took the liberty of expostulating with his Grace who was the Chancellor of the university of Cambridge on the appointment of a successor . . . he then expressed an anxious wish, that an able professor of civil law might be sought for and invited to fill the vacant seat. Dr. Jenner was the person thought of by the Duke of Newcastle, yet he paid Mr. Murray the compliment of asking him if he could recommend any gentleman who would fill it with greater ability. Antecedent to the establishment of the Vinerian Professorship, the late Mr. Justice Blackstone, who was then at the bar, and had given proof that he possessed those qualifications which early pointed him out as *the most worthy* to be promoted on this occasion, was by Mr. Murray introduced and warmly commended to the duke of Newcastle, who considered it as part of his duty to probe a little the political principles of the new candidate, by addressing Mr. Blackstone 'Sir, I can rely on your friend Mr. Murray's judgment as to your giving law-lectures in good style, so as to benefit the students; and I dare say, that I may safely rely on you, whenever any thing in the political hemisphere is agitated in that university you will, Sir, exert yourself in our behalf.' The Answer was 'Your Grace may be assured that I will discharge my duty in giving law-lectures to the best of my poor abilities'. 'Aye! Aye!' replied his Grace hastily, 'and your duty in the other branch too'. Unfortunately for the new candidate, he only bowed assent, and a few days afterwards he had the mortification to hear that Dr. Jenner was appointed the civil-law professor.

Holliday goes on to state that this rebuff 'induced Mr. Murray and some other friends of Mr. Blackstone's strongly to recommend and persuade him to sit down at Oxford to read law-lectures to such students as were disposed to attend him, and that his lectures not only had the success which was well-known, but soon afterwards suggested the idea to the mind of Mr. Viner to establish a real law professorship in the university of Oxford.'

[6] William Murray (1705–92) later (1776) 1st Earl of Mansfield; at this time Solicitor-General.

[7] At this time Secretary of State; (1754) 1st Lord of the Treasury.

Holliday did not date his story, though from its position in his book, he apparently attributed it to the late forties. Since it refers to Newcastle's office as Chancellor of the University of Cambridge, it could not have belonged to a time earlier than the end of 1749. In fact, if it occurred, it must be dated some years later. Dr. Henry Brooke, Regius Professor of Civil Law at Oxford, died on 24 November 1752, and (a fact not noticed by some scholars) there was a considerable delay in the appointment of his successor Dr. Robert Jenner, which was not announced until the beginning of April 1754.[8] If Blackstone's interview with Newcastle took place (as the story goes) only a few days before the announcement of Jenner's appointment, it could not have occurred before the latter days of March 1754.

There are several difficulties about accepting this account as it stands. The first is one of interpretation. The reader is obviously intended to assume that Newcastle injected into the question of the appointment the issue of party politics by 'probing' Blackstone's political principles, and that Blackstone was taken aback when he did so. At no date during the vacancy of the Chair would this have been a fair reflection of the position of the two men. The Government and the predominant 'Old Interest' or Tory party in the University had been for years at daggers drawn, and Blackstone, always a staunch supporter of the 'Old Interest' in the University (though never a Jacobite), had since 1750 stood out as perhaps the most powerful leader among the Tory politicians there, a fact of which Newcastle could not fail to be aware, since it was largely through his efforts that the Tory Sir Roger Newdigate (for long to sit for the University in the House of Commons) had been elected in 1751. If Newcastle did at any time sound Blackstone on his political allegiance, it would not have been to discover what it was, but to find out whether he was prepared to abandon it in return for preferment. Still further, though Blackstone may have been disappointed that Murray's personal influence over the Minister did not over-ride political considerations, he would not have been surprised. Under the first two Hanoverians, appointments to the various Regius Chairs were expected to be used for political purposes.[9] Indeed the Regius

---

[8] Such delays were not unusual in royal appointments, but they were apt to suggest that no strong and obvious candidate had presented himself.

[9] After the Chancellor's election in 1759, for instance, Humphrey Sibthorpe

Chairs of Modern History were invented largely for this purpose.[10]

An awkward problem, too, is that of dating. There could be no time less propitious for a deal between Newcastle and this leader of the Oxford Tory opposition than the last days of March 1754, for within a few weeks the country was to go to the polls in the 1754 General Election, including that for the contested election for Oxfordshire, one of the most bitterly fought party conflicts of the century. The centre of the Tory opposition lay in the University[11] and Blackstone was deeply engaged in it. Such a deal would have been too late to affect the County election itself, and would have been seen by the supporters of both parties as the rankest treachery. Chronological difficulties also beset the consequences which were supposed to flow from the choice of Jenner and Blackstone's disappointment thereat. Clearly it cannot be held to have led to Blackstone's decision to return to Oxford and to begin private lectures there, for he had been delivering them already since November 1753, and had announced his intention to do so in the preceding June. Nor can it be held to be the indirect cause of Charles Viner's founding his Professorship in the Common Law (encouraged, it was suggested, by the success of Blackstone's lectures) since, though Viner's last Will was dated December 1755 and was thus drawn up some time after Blackstone had begun his lectures, the benefaction had been planned and incorporated in earlier Wills dating from 1752, well before they were even announced.

Nevertheless, though Holliday's account as a whole can hardly be accepted, many of its constituent parts may well be based on fact. Other contemporary sources refer to the eminent lawyers who backed Blackstone's venture in 1753,[12] and Murray, with whom

---

lost the appointment to the Regius Chair of Medicine, which he had expected, because he had failed to support the Government candidate, and it went to Dr. John Kelly of Christ Church, a very dubious appointment. The Dean of Christ Church thanked Newcastle on behalf of the Whigs as it was, he said, good for them 'at this critical time . . . as it is a strong proof of our being countenanced and attended to . . .' (B.L. Add. MS. 32888, fos. 80 and 128).

[10] N. Sykes, *Edmund Gibson Bishop of London 1669–1748* (Oxford, 1926), pp. 94 f.

[11] See W. R. Ward, *Georgian Oxford. University Politics in the Eighteenth Century* (Oxford, 1958), pp. 192 f.

[12] J. Clitherow in his *Memoir* states that at the Courts he 'contracted an Acquaintance with several of the most eminent Men in that Profession, who saw through the then intervening Cloud, that great Genius, which afterwards broke forth with so much Splendor' (*Reports*, i, p. vii).

Blackstone was to have a long friendship, was very likely to be chief among them. There is no doubt of the close links between Murray and Newcastle, particularly in 1752, at the time the Chair became vacant, when, in addition to their political alliance, Newcastle was deeply beholden to Murray for his help in trying to straighten out his desperately confused personal finances.[13] And, though Holliday links Blackstone's disappointment with the publication of Jenner's success, he might have known that his own hopes had been dashed before the position was offered to anyone else. The trouble in trying to reach conclusions has been that there has been no evidence as to what, if anything, did happen, either in the printed sources such as Blackstone's biography, or the manuscripts in the public collections, such as the correspondence between Newcastle and Murray. In consequence everything concerning the matter long remained in the field of conjecture.

Fortunately, however, evidence has more recently come to light in a private manuscript collection, the large body of papers preserved by Sir Roger Newdigate, now deposited in the Warwickshire County Record Office, which throws a good deal of light on events, though it does not enable us to determine precisely what happened. Its source is unimpeachable, for it is Blackstone himself who is writing in a letter to his friend and patron Sir Roger Newdigate. He writes:

Mr Eyre called upon me some Days ago, with the Papers in Mr Ludford's Cause against You and Lady Newdigate . . . in order to consult with me upon them as You had kindly directed. But I declined meddling with them for Reasons which I then gave him, and which I told him I would myself communicate to You. And this I have now the Honour to do, by informing You that I have taken up a Resolution no longer to attend the Courts at Westminster, but to pursue my Profession in a Way more agreeable to me in all respects, by residing at Oxford. And I have been persuaded to engraft upon this Resolution a Scheme which I am told may be beneficial to the University as well as to myself and of which the enclosed Papers will give you the Particulars . . .[14]

---

[13] He drew up an admirable report on them on 5 November 1752 (R. A. Kelch, *Newcastle, a duke without money* . . ., London, 1974, pp. 143 f.). Murray is hardly likely to have been pushing Oxford Tory candidates on the Administration after the early months of 1753, when he was chiefly concerned with rebutting charges of Jacobitism in his youth, in connection with which Oxford was a liability.

[14] Presumably the printed Advertisement he circulated, dated 23 June 1753.

[here follows some legal advice to Newdigate]
You will wonder perhaps at the sudden Resolution I have taken. Indeed it is not a sudden One: It has been growing upon me for some Years. My Temper, Constitution, Inclinations, and a Thing called Principle, have long quarreled with active Life, at least the active Life of Westminster-Hall, and have assured me I am not made to rise in it. Besides there are certain Qualifications for being a public Speaker, in which I am very sensible of my own Deficiency; and happy that I am sensible so early. I am therefore withdrawing myself from that Branch of the Profession, in which I can promise myself no considerable Success, the bustling practical Part; in order to be the more at Leisure to cultivate another, in which I have better Prospects, the thinking theoretical Part.

As to my Scheme for Lectures, You will imagine, and very justly, that it had its original from the Thoughts I was taught to entertain of the Professorship; for which also I found I wanted *some* Qualifications; as you rightly guessed, at this time twelvemonth. Having by that means begun to think in this train, it was not easy to leave it off, especially as I found a Pleasure in it; and I have the Satisfaction to find my Design meets with the Approbation of Persons of the greatest Eminence and Learning, as well in the Inns of Court as at Oxford; and if those Gentlemen in the Country, whose Opinion I value, entertain the same favourable Sentiments, my utmost Ambition will be satisfied. I was desired to take the civil law into my Scheme; but, as I had been so much talked of for the Professorship, I thought it would argue Resentment, or at least Disappointment, in me; of both of which I declare myself clear. I therefore judged it more decent to leave that Field open to the Professor Regius, when our Governors, in their great Deliberation, shall think proper to send us one.[15]

Several points of interest arise from this letter. In the first place it contains the first proof positive that Blackstone had been considered for the Regius Chair of Civil Law and that he had been rejected. It makes clear that he had been encouraged to stand by people whose opinion he respected, and that he had been 'much talked of' for it. In the second place it is also clear that by July 1753 it was a thing of the past, though we need not take at its face value his denial of resentment or disappointment. (The tone of his letter lacks the cheerful self-confidence normally characteristic of

[15] Letter of 3 July 1753, Warwickshire County Record Office, Newdigate MSS., CR136/B, 1488. A small part of this letter has been printed under the heading 'Blackstone' in the biographical columns of *The History of Parliament, 1745–90*, ed. L. B. Namier and J. Brooke (1964).

his private correspondence.) Still more interesting is the fact which becomes apparent, that his candidature was planned before the death of the holder of the Chair. Blackstone (the most accurate of men) speaks of plans in connection with it, in which Newdigate had a part, twelve months before the date of his letter, and thus some four months before Brooke's death. It should be noted that when the scheme began there was no question of any contact between Murray and the Duke of Newcastle about it. The Duke was in Hanover with the King, and all business had to be transacted in writing. Murray's letters to the Duke survive and contain no reference to this matter. The Duke was not back in England until a few days before Brooke's death. In order to improve his qualifications for the position (at this time rather slight[16]) Blackstone had set to work on the lectures he would expect to deliver if he were appointed. How soon he knew that his efforts were in vain is not known, but there is a slight piece of evidence which suggests that he was not long kept in uncertainty. Writing to a prominent legal friend (who would presumably know of the candidature so much talked of) on 9 January 1753—that is some six weeks after Brooke's death—he adds in a PS. 'What has become of our Professor of Law?'[17] Hardly the query of a candidate still awaiting his own fate.

There is no indication of the cause of his rejection, but it can hardly, given the mediocrity of the man who was ultimately appointed, be other than political. Perhaps the melancholy suggestion that 'a thing called Principle' stood in his way as a practical man may hint at it. But perhaps the most valuable point to emerge from it is that Blackstone's rejection was early enough to affect his decision to return to Oxford to give private lectures, and that it was the first stage of his preparation of the Civil Law lectures he would have given had he been elected which stimulated his taste for this kind of 'thinking theoretical' work.

There is only one subject on which his account of his motives may be less than complete, the reason why he chose to read his

[16] His *Essay on Collateral Consanguinity 1750*, arguing the case against Founders' Kin at All Souls, depended largely on Civil Law comparisons. In 1753 he was made Assessor of the Vice-Chancellor's Court where the procedure was that of the Civil Law, but he had concentrated his interests, when his work for his degree was finished, on the Common Law.

[17] University Archives WP α 22 (1), fo. 9ᵛ. Notes by Blackstone in a reply to R. Wilbraham, dated All Souls, 9 January 1753.

lectures in Common and not in Civil Law. The explanation he gives is a reasonable one, but it is negative not positive. Much has been claimed by later scholars for his originality in introducing the study of the Common Law[18] into the University. But this is to ignore a matter of significance, Viner's proposed benefaction. The fact that in 1752 Charles Viner, a benefactor already in his seventy-fifth year, had completed plans to foster the study of Common Law at Oxford, where it had been completely neglected; that the core of his scheme was the endowment of a well-paid Professorship to be held, on attractive conditions, by a qualified Civilian who was also a barrister-at-law, and that within a year William Blackstone, an able and ambitious young D.C.L. and barrister (who was also a Fellow of All Souls) should present himself to lecture on his own initiative on precisely this neglected topic, is on the face of it a somewhat surprising series of coincidences. It is indeed sufficiently surprising to justify some examination into the possibility that these facts were connected. That some such connection existed seems virtually certain. It was not, as has been suggested a personal link between Viner and Blackstone—of this there is no evidence[19]—but there is every reason to believe that there was a more indirect one.

When the University received the benefaction after Viner's death in 1756, a vociferous party there maintained that the benefactor had intended to limit the teaching responsibilities of his Professor to a solemn (or formal) Lecture once a term.[20] The Delegacy of Convocation who were deputed to draw up the scheme for the use of the benefaction, on the other hand, emphatically denied this, and maintained that Viner had intended his Professor to deliver not only these solemn lectures, but regular lectures to students (provided they were given outside the law terms) as Blackstone had then been doing for some years. At this time a document was circulated, based not only on early copies of Viner's Wills, but on his correspondence with 'a Gentleman of Distinction

[18] e.g. W. B. Odgers, 'Sir William Blackstone', *Yale Law Journal*, xxvii (1918), 604.
[19] See G. H. Hanbury, *The Vinerian Chair and Legal Education* (Oxford, 1967), pp. 11–12.
[20] In the scheme for the Vinerian Endowment the term 'Solemn' Lecture was used in a different sense from that usual in the University, where it was a 'term of art' meaning a lecture proper as distinct from the old cursory lecture, or commentary on texts (Stat vi, § 13). In the Vinerian Scheme it meant something more like a present-day inaugural lecture. The benefactor appears to have used it in this sense. See Vinerian Bundle, University Archives.

in this Place' who had 'permitted his Letters to be made use of upon this Occasion'[21] in support of the views adopted by the Delegacy. Evidence in the University Archives shows that this 'Gentleman of Distinction' was Dr. William King,[22] the well-known Tory Principal of St. Mary Hall; it also shows that the document based on his correspondence was compiled by William Blackstone.[23] Since King and Blackstone were friends and close political associates, since King strongly supported his young friend's candidature when the benefaction came in—even celebrating his success in an 'elegant oration' in Convocation[24]—and since Blackstone claimed the support of eminent persons in the University as well as the Inns of Court for his decision to offer his private lectures in Oxford, it is hard to believe that he was ignorant of Viner's benefaction and of the form it was to take. Still further the advice given to Viner by Dr. King in 1752 so closely resembles what we know of Blackstone's views on the use of the benefaction —sometimes even in wording[25]—that it seems by no means unlikely there was consultation between the two men at the time when Viner's earlier Wills were being drawn up.

In these circumstances it is hard not to believe that, among the considerations which led Blackstone to decide to lecture on the Common Law, was the fact that a benefaction for a Chair in this subject would soon be received, and that an experienced lecturer in the University in this unfamiliar subject would be favourably placed to benefit from it. If this were among the calculations of Blackstone and his friends, they certainly proved correct, and (thanks to the remarkable success of his lectures) more so than his

[21] Two versions of this document were printed, one for the use of the Delegacy, summarizing at the end the points at issue (University Archives, Vinerian Documents (V/3/5/4)), the other, without a conclusion, for general circulation (a copy is in Bodl. Gough Oxf. 96 (15a)).

[22] W. S. Holdsworth, *A History of English Law* (1938), xii. 93, first drew attention to this identification.

[23] The compiler of this document stated that the material for it had been deposited with the Vice-Chancellor. This material can be identified in the bundle of Vinerian Documents in the University Archives, where each item is particularized by a capital letter. They are items V/3/1/2–V/3/1/11. Most of them are endorsed in Blackstone's hand, and they are accompanied by a list, also in his hand (V/3/1/12).

[24] Acta Convocationis, B h 35, p. 50.

[25] Particularly in the arguments for placing Viner's Scholars in a Hall rather than a College. For Blackstone's views see Clitherow (*Reports*, 1, p. xvii) and for King's letter to Viner see University Archives, Vinerian Bundle.

most sanguine supporters could have hoped. When the election
to the Chair came up in 1758, Blackstone did not step into it
without opposition (some of it very heated), but it was his strength
that not even his bitterest enemies could challenge his qualifications
for it, and it is significant that they did not succeed in finding a
candidate to stand against him, though his supporters claimed that
they tried.[26] Nevertheless, if Blackstone himself, then at the height
of his power as a University politician, had not seized control of
the plans for the Foundation, deflecting them by a bold *coup* from
the Hebdomadal Board to Convocation[27]—had not controlled
from without the activities of the Delegacy of Convocation set up
to consider them (on which he could not himself conveniently
serve but of which his most intimate All Souls friend Benjamin
Buckler was the spokesman) and if he had not fought off a short but
ferocious pamphlet campaign by his enemies, the Vinerian Foundation would not have taken the form which it did. The story of
this academic battle is too long to be retailed here; but it was one
of the most intense of Blackstone's career, and when Viner's
estate had been wound up, the Statutes passed, he himself elected
without opposition to the new Chair, and when Dr. King had
delivered his 'elegant oration' of praise, he did what he never did
in any other of the campaigns of these strenuous years—he had
something of a nervous breakdown.

Writing on 12 November 1758 to thank Sir Roger Newdigate
for his congratulations he told him

The late Hurries, and too great a Quantity perhaps of dyed Tea, have
lately put my nervous System a little out of order; (though I assure you
the Report of my Death was groundless) but by Spa Water, Abstinence
from that jentacular[28] Poison, a Sabbath as to mental Employment, and
a regular Use of gentle (very gentle!) Exercise, I am now pretty well

[26] *A View of the Misrepresentations in the Reply to the Examiner* [B. Buckler],
1 July 1758, 'Will all the Managers of the Opposition deny, that Candidates
have been searched for to oppose him?' (Bodl. Gough Oxf. 96 (25)).

[27] The account of the beginning of this campaign is best taken from a note by
Blackstone himself in his *Letter to the Revd. Dr. Randolph*, 21 May 1757 (reprinted by I. G. Philip, 'William Blackstone and the Reform of the University
Press in the Eighteenth Century', *Oxford Bibliographical Society Publications*,
N.S. VII, 1955). The Acta Convocationis (never very satisfactory) broke down
completely at the height of this controversy. The pamphlet material is considerable, but has the disadvantages inherent in its nature.

[28] 'drunk at breakfast'—from the Latin *jentacula*, first meal of the day. The
adjective has not found its way into the Oxford Dictionary.

recovered, and hope to be quite stout in a Week more. Much Writing does not yet agree with me . . .[29]

He could afford to relax, for his election to the Vinerian Chair set the seal on the success of his lectures, and made certain his later fame.

[29] Warwickshire County Record Office, Newdigate MSS., CR136/B, 1496.

New Anecdotes of Lady Mary Wortley Montagu

ROBERT HALSBAND

IN HER own lifetime Lady Mary Wortley Montagu enjoyed and endured a variegated reputation that ranged from fame as a wit, traveller, and letter-writer to notoriety as the repellent character created by Alexander Pope in his satires, and later echoed by Horace Walpole in his letters. Since her death (in 1762) her reputation has brought her ample tribute in the form of fake letters, fake portraits, and fake anecdotes. If imitation is the sincerest form of flattery, counterfeit and fraud are the clearest proof of fame and notoriety.

Lady Mary's genuine Turkish Embassy letters, which she compiled soon after her return from Constantinople in 1718, were published in three small volumes a year after her death. Their popularity was immediate and widespread; and their excellence was trumpeted throughout Europe by no less a herald than Voltaire.[1] Four years later (in 1767) a fourth volume, entitled *Additional Volume To The Letters*, appeared in print. Buttressed by some authentic pieces—a letter, essay, and a few poems, all of them previously published—the volume contains five letters which are spurious. The manuscript sources for these have never been found, and their contents are demonstrably false.[2] Yet these letters, in spite of an editorial warning when they were reprinted in Lady Mary's letters and works, have sometimes been used by careless anthologists and even by a critic as products of Lady Mary's epistolary genius.[3]

---

[1] *Gazette littéraire de l'Europe*, repr. in *Œuvres complètes*, ed. Louis Moland (Paris: Garnier Frères), vol. xxv (1879), p. 163.

[2] For a fuller discussion, see my edition of Lady Mary's *Complete Letters* (Oxford: Clarendon Press, 1965–7), vol. i, p. xviii; and my biography *The Life of Lady Mary Wortley Montagu* (Oxford: Clarendon Press, 1956), p. 289. (Hereafter in these notes LM stands for Lady Mary.)

[3] *The London Book of English Prose*, ed. Herbert Read and Bonamy Dobrée (London: Eyre and Spottiswoode, 1931), pp. 211–16; (New York: Macmillan,

Her reputation as a traveller to the Near East has also been the inspiration for bogus portraits. Art dealers and auctioneers, when confronted by any lady in oriental dress, immediately nominate Lady Mary as the sitter, not because they are in pursuit of historical accuracy but (need it be added?) because they are in pursuit of the highest price-tag. How much more astute to identify the portrait as Lady Montagu (the error in nomenclature is typical) than to label it 'Unknown lady in oriental dress'! Even at best, historical portraiture is fraught with perils. The editor of the blue-stocking Elizabeth Montagu's early correspondence, in seeking a likeness of Lady Mary for an illustration, chose a portrait whose sitter sports an elaborate hairdress in fashion several decades after Lady Mary's death.[4]

In the same manner, Lady Mary's reputation as a wit has led to her being credited with repartee and bons mots that she never uttered. In a recently published essay she is supposed to have replied to someone who told her at the opera that her hands were dirty, 'You should see my feet.'[5] Apart from the fact that this hardly qualifies as wit, one wonders about the anecdote's authenticity. No source for it earlier than the late nineteenth century can be found. A few years ago I was startled to hear exactly the same verbal exchange in a Yiddish joke about a man in a Latvian village who was famous for being terribly dirty. What I surmise has happened is that this anecdote, like a free-floating parasite, attaches itself to any host susceptible to it. Since Lady Mary's reputation for slovenliness, firmly established by Pope and Walpole, has been kept in circulation through the frequent reprinting of their writings, the unsavoury anecdote has been gratuitously attributed to her because it supports that characterization.

A very different kind of fake anecdote is one which has been printed in anthologies of death-bed remarks: that as Lady Mary lay dying, she said, 'It has all been very interesting.'[6] This puzzled me because the only source I could discover for it was the biography

1949), pp. 183–7; William Henry Irving, *The Providence of Wit in the English Letter Writers* (Durham, N.C.: Duke Univ. Press, 1955), pp. 210–11.

[4] Elizabeth Montagu, *Correspondence 1720–1761*, ed. Emily J. Climenson (London: John Murray, 1906), i, facing p. 80.

[5] Louis Kronenberger, *The Republic of Letters* (New York: Knopf, 1955), pp. 67–8.

[6] *Dictionary of Last Words*, compiled by Edward S. Le Comte (New York: Philosophical Library, 1955), p. 152.

by Iris Barry, *Portrait of Lady Mary*, published in 1928.[7] When I met Miss Barry some years ago, I asked her where she had found Lady Mary's death-bed remark. Her reply was that as a girl she had determined that these would be her own last words, but then she thought such a verbal epitaph fitted Lady Mary so well that she used it in the *Portrait*. As I scolded her (gently) for falsifying historical biography she in turn reproved me by asking me to re-read that scene of her book more carefully. I must confess that she proved to be guiltless, for the passage reads: 'Only to herself, as if it were a magic ritual, she [Lady Mary] kept saying firmly: "It has all been very interesting; it has all been very interesting". . . . She tried so hard to give expression to her phrase that she fell asleep.' Here, then, fiction almost masquerades as fact, but not quite.

The discovery of any new anecdotes about Lady Mary more than two hundred years after her death must be greeted with scepticism. That was my attitude when the Osborn Collection acquired the manuscript (printed below) written in an unidentified hand and headed 'Communicated by Sir Francis Hutcheson'. Without any doubt at all I am now convinced that these are authentic, the product of a visit that Hutchinson (as his name is usually spelt) paid to Lady Mary in Venice in 1757. The conversation he related can be corroborated in detail by her own letters and other contemporary sources.

The circumstances of the interview seem to be these. Lady Mary had abandoned England in 1739—for several reasons, mainly for the purpose of living in romantic proximity to Francesco Algarotti, the young Italian littérateur with whom she had become infatuated. She restlessly waited for him in Italy for two years, one of them in Venice. Then after a brief and disillusioning rendezvous with him she moved to Avignon, remaining there until 1746, when she made her way to the province of Brescia. For the next ten years she lived a retired, rural existence, in 'a solitude not unlike that of Robinson Crusoe', she told her daughter.[8] In 1756, to escape the financial importunities of an Italian nobleman with whom she was involved and to enjoy once more the cosmopolitan felicities of Venice, she again settled in that city. Her busy social life embraced Venetian patricians as well as expatriates and

[7] (Indianapolis: Bobbs-Merrill), p. 328.
[8] *Complete Letters*, iii. 32.

travellers on the Grand Tour, to whom she made herself easily accessible.

Although we know a great deal about Lady Mary's life in Venice, very little survives about Francis Hutchinson, who met her there in October 1757. His full name and title on the document make it possible to identify him as an Irish gentleman of County Wicklow. Born in 1726, a son of the Bishop of Killala, he took a B.A. at Trinity College, Dublin, succeeded to his father's estates in 1780, and was created a baronet (in the Irish peerage) in 1782. The next year he served as Sheriff of Wicklow and was elected to the Irish Parliament, where he sat until 1790. He died in Dublin in 1807.[9] As a young gentleman and landed heir (to Castle Sallah) he would normally take the Grand Tour, on which Venice was a customary place to visit. In October 1757 Lady Mary remarked to her daughter on the great number of English visitors there, mentioning by name Fulke Greville, who (these anecdotes tell us) was calling on her at the same time as Hutchinson.

Vivid and trustworthy as these anecdotes are, they also raise some provocative questions: when were they 'communicated' by Sir Francis Hutchinson, as the document's heading states, and for what purpose? Since the document shows the watermark 'BUD-GEN 1804' the anecdotes must have been communicated orally (as their style clearly indicates) half a century after his interview in Venice, between 1804 and 1807 (the year of his death). His precise and specific information and especially his quoting Lady Mary's exact words (including her ribald diction) suggest that he had made careful notes soon after their meeting, and was now repeating them. To whom? No clue remains to identify the scribe—except his autograph.

A different clue, on the outside of the document, is the endorsement: 'Notes for Lady M. W. Montague's letters'. This phrase, which is written in a different hand, could have been jotted on the document at any time subsequent to Hutchinson's dictation of the anecdotes. It is not the hand of James Dallaway (1763–1834), who had been chosen by Lady Mary's grandson in 1803 to edit the first authorized edition of her works, including her correspondence. The next edition, issued in 1817, was probably arranged by Dallaway as well.

And so the challenging puzzle remains; and only future resear-

[9] G. E. Cokayne, *Complete Baronetage*, v (1906), 410–11.

chers can hope to determine who took down Hutchinson's anecdotes and who planned to use them. For the present we must rest content with the rich reward of the anecdotes themselves; they give us, with startling clarity, a fresh glimpse of the irrepressible Lady Mary as an expatriate in Venice.

Communicated by Sir Francis Hutcheson[10]

Was introduced to Lady M. W. Montague at Venice in 1757 by a Venetian Lady, a great friend and intimate of Lady Mary's, which Lady shew'd him a number of letters in French that she received from Lady M. She kept them carefully and had them bound up in a Volume.[11]

The weather being intensely cold, Lady Mary was all cover'd up in [a] great Beaver Cloak. She ask'd him, did she not look like one of the old women that sold roasted Chesnuts at Whitehall, and the Bridges in London.

Mr. Greville was there. She complimented him highly and even flatter'd him on his book, The Maxims. The moment he left the room she laugh'd, and said she was obliged to do so out of common civility, but, to be sure, his book was the saddest stuff she ever met with.[12]

She mention'd the same thing to Sir Francis that she did to Dr. Law;[13] abused Pope, Swift and Bolinbroke.[14] [She] shew'd him her Commode, with false back of books, the works of Pope, Swift and Bolinbroke; said she knew them well. They were the greatest Rascals, but she had the satisfaction of shitting on them every day—

She was a little woman, fair complexion and well enough looking for her age—[15]

---

[10] In transcribing the manuscript I have only expanded abbreviations and adjusted punctuation.

[11] See note 18 below.

[12] Fulke Greville (1717–c. 1805), M.P. 1747–54. His book was *Maxims, Characters, and Reflections, Critical, Satyrical, and Moral* (London: J. & R. Tonson, 1756; 2nd edn. 1757). LM described this 'curious Book' to her daughter, and in ironical vein wrote a verse panegyric on it (*Complete Letters*, iii. 136–7; *Essays and Poems*, ed. Robert Halsband and Isobel Grundy (Oxford: Clarendon Press, 1977), pp. 307–8).

[13] In 1757 LM had seen 'Mr. Law', governor of a Mr. Oliver on the Grand Tour (*Complete Letters*, iii. 139, 150). The scribe's comment suggests that Law had also related to him LM's conversation.

[14] A fierce enemy of all three, LM frequently vented her contempt of them and their writings in her letters and in her verse, which includes a pamphlet against Pope in 1733 and against Swift in 1734. A visitor of LM's in 1757 noticed Bolingbroke's portrait in her library (Anne-Marie du Boccage, *Lettres . . .*, in *Recueil des Œuvres*, Lyons, 1762, iii. 178).

[15] In 1762 both Horace Walpole and Elizabeth Montagu thought that LM had hardly aged in twenty years (Halsband, *Life of LM*, p. 281).

[She] knew Lady Orford at Naples. She was Miss Rolle, married to the second Lord Orford, Sir Robert's eldest son. Mr. Shirley courted and married her for her Estate. He had not liv'd long with her, when he told her one day he found their tempers could not agree, and they had better separate, that he would take care to allow her £700 a Year. She thank'd him for being so gracious; it was just what she design'd for him, and had previously setled her fortune to her sole and separe [*sic*] use.[16] This was Bite the Biter,[17] and every body was rejoiced.

The Venetian Ladies name was Signora Michele. She had been Ambasadress in Spain, her own name, Bragadini; these were two of the 12 Apostle families. This Lady was very clever and accomplished. The letters were in French; [Sir Francis] does not recollect whether any in Italian—[18]

Visited Wortley Montague at Turin. [He] would only talk to him (Sir F.) in French, did not speak English. Told him he was going immediately to Egypt. Je m'en vais a l'Egypt, je veux tacher le debarrasser de ce fatras de miracles que l'on a l'inonde.[19]

[16] Margaret Rolle (1709–81) married Lord Walpole in 1724, and deserted him in 1734 to live on the Continent. LM had seen her often in 1740, but in Florence, not Naples. Sewallis Shirley (1709–65), a son of the 1st Earl Ferrers, had lived with Lady Orford, and married her soon after her husband's death. At the time, LM assumed (correctly) that Shirley had married her for her money, and (incorrectly) that like all her lovers he would not be refused anything. They parted after three years (*Complete Letters*, ii. 213, 486, 487–8).

[17] From Juvenal's *Satires*, 2. 35: *Castigata remordent*, the same phrase used in 1714 as the motto for LM's essay in *The Spectator*, No. 573 (*Essays and Poems*, p. 69).

[18] In 1740 LM had become a friend of Chiara Michiel *or* Michieli (d. 1780), daughter of Daniele Bragadin and wife of Antonio Michiel, Venetian ambassador to Spain 1741 to 1744 (*Complete Letters*, ii. 170, 218 n.6). In 1765 James Boswell witnessed her cleverness and perhaps accomplishments (*Boswell on the Grand Tour . . . 1765–1766*, ed. Frank Brady and Frederick A. Pottle (New York: McGraw-Hill, 1955), pp. 10, 94, 95, 97–9). The surviving correspondence between LM and her, entirely in French, consists of 35 letters from LM and 5 from her.

[19] Edward Wortley Montagu, junior (1713–76), LM's only son, had long since alienated her, and she carefully avoided meeting him. In 1763 he made the first of several extended visits to Egypt, and after converting to Roman Catholicism became and remained a Muslim until his death.

Thomas Percy, *Don Quixote,* and Don Bowle

CLEANTH BROOKS

THOMAS PERCY (1729–1811) and John Bowle (1725–88) have to their credit some remarkable scholarly accomplishments. The century in which they lived was itself a remarkable period in literary scholarship. This was the contention of the late Professor David Nichol Smith, whose course in the history of the growth of English studies James Osborn and I took at Oxford in the 1930s. But Bowle's work has been largely forgotten, and Thomas Percy's general reputation as a scholar has been tarnished by his ill-advised method of editing some of the ballad texts that he printed in his *Reliques of Ancient English Poetry* in 1765. Had Percy's projected edition of *Tottel's Miscellany* been published shortly after the *Reliques*—most of it had in fact been printed off in 1767—instead of perishing years later in a warehouse fire, we would have today a more just estimate of Percy's integrity as a scholar. In any case, we have to remind ourselves that the folk ballad is only one of the literary genres represented in the *Reliques*, and that the *Reliques* itself, for all its fame, is only one of the several important literary works that Percy produced. His was the first translation of a Chinese novel into English; he published *Five Pieces of Runic Poetry*; he produced a translation of the Song of Solomon considered not as Scripture, but as a primitive marriage song, furnishing examples of oriental imagery. Percy also translated Henri Mallet's *Northern Antiquities*, the book which opened to English readers the riches of the Elder Edda and other examples of Norse poetry. These books—plus others that I have not mentioned—all fall into a remarkable decade that stretches from 1761 to 1770.

Yet much nearer to Percy's central concern than Scandinavian or Chinese or Hebrew poetry was the literature of Spain, for his acquaintance with the Romance languages was far from trivial. He had translated his Chinese novel, by the way, not directly from the Chinese but from a Portuguese version. His translation of the *Northern Antiquities* was from the French. Spanish was another Romance language which Percy read with facility and in which he was very much interested.

The *Reliques* contains two poems that Percy translated from the Spanish, but it was not until a few decades ago that the extent of Percy's knowledge of, and concern for, Spanish literature began to unfold. In 1932 important evidence came to light when what remained of Percy's personal collections came to the Bodleian Library through the gift of his great-granddaughter, Miss Constance Meade.

In this collection there turned up proof-sheets of a book entitled *Ancient Songs, Chiefly on Moorish Subjects, translated from the Spanish*. Percy had evidently meant to publish it in 1775, but the book, for reasons at which we can only guess, did not achieve publication in his lifetime—in fact, not until 1932, when the Clarendon Press brought it out in a handsome format with a preface by David Nichol Smith. Percy, quite characteristically, had preserved not only the proof-sheets but the copper plates that had been especially engraved for the title-page and the frontispiece. These, along with several rejected designs—again, on copper plates carefully preserved by Percy—and three drawings for woodcuts, were used in Nichol Smith's edition.

In giving a brief résumé of what the Constance Meade material reveals about Percy's interest in Spanish, I think that I can do no better than to make use of excerpts and summaries from Nichol Smith's excellent preface. He pointed out that the books and papers which the Bodleian Library had recently acquired show that Percy worked hard at French, Spanish, and Portuguese. For example, in 1751, Percy wrote out in his own hand a compendium of French grammar, and in 1756 an abridgement of Italian grammar. A letter of Percy's, dated 21 September 1755, refers to his having received three Spanish books and a Portuguese grammar. This young man—for he was still a young man in the 1750s—had obviously not been content with the usual grounding in Latin and Greek, but had gone on to acquire the Romance languages.

In his preface Nichol Smith quotes two undated drafts of a letter addressed by Percy to an unidentified London bookseller. Percy was attempting to interest the bookseller in a new translation of *Don Quixote*. He writes: 'I find in your New Catalogue . . . four or five Old Spanish Romances &c of that kind which is so ridiculed in *Don Quixote*. . . .' Percy goes on to point out that since the translations of *Don Quixote* never make reference to these romances, 'all the fine ridicule of *Cervantes* must be lost upon [the ordinary reader], and the wittiest passages of all, appear obscure and unintelligible.'[1] Any sound translation of *Don Quixote* ought to make these passages intelligible.

From the early part of his life, Percy tells the bookseller, he has been a great reader of 'Old Books of Chivalry', and has collected 'those old Romances, which *Cervantes* had in his Eye'. But he has not yet managed to acquire all of them. 'I am not yet possessed', he writes, 'of those five mentioned in your Catalogue: and it is in consideration of these Volumes, that I make you the first tender of my Work, which you shall, if you please, be concerned in, upon reasonable Terms: One of which must be your supplying me with whatever books I have occasion to consult. With the assistance of your five Books above mentioned, (which, when I have done with them, may make their appearance again in one of your future Sales), together with what Collections I have by me, & what we may procure from other books: I doubt not that I can throw together materials for a couple of handsome Volumes *octavo* & *12mo* and *one Quarto*. . . .'[2]

The proposal is really rather charming. Percy even suppresses his concern as a collector, for one notes that the five books that he needs can go back, when he is done with them, to the bookseller to be sold. The letter—or rather the draft—ends with a disarming *apologia pro sua vita:*

After all this, it will naturally be a Question, who I am?—to which I answer that I am no Author by profession, tho' literary Persuits constitute the principal part of my amusement, and I am at this time concerned in a Work of some consequence. [The work was probably the *Reliques*.] I am, Sir, a Clergyman, tollerably well provided for, & domestic Chaplain to a noble Lord, with whom I constantly reside. I am beneficed in the County of Northampton, and shall receive any Letter, that you inclose under a Cover for The Right Honorable Henry Earl of Sussex at Easton Maudit (By the Castle Ashby Bag Northamptonshire).[3]

Nichol Smith believed that these drafts were probably written

---

[1] *Ancient Songs*, p. xi.   [2] Ibid., pp. xi–xii.
[3] *Ancient Songs*, pp. xiii–xiv.

some time between 1760 and 1764. The latter date is fixed by a reference in Boswell's *Life of Johnson*: when Johnson paid his visit to Percy in 1764, from 25 June to 18 August, Boswell tells us that he chose 'for his regular reading the old Spanish romance of Felixmarte of Hircania, in folio, which he read quite through'.[4] Felixmarte is one of the five coveted volumes that Percy had noted in his bookseller's catalogue. By 1764 he had evidently secured it, but whether from the bookseller to whom he addressed the letter quoted we do not know.

In the light 'of these two drafts', Nichol Smith observes, a further interest now attaches to the pamphlet which John Bowle published in 1777 entitled *A Letter to the Reverend Dr Percy, concerning a new and classical edition of . . . Don Quixote*. Bowle's *Letter*, which describes the kind of edition that he hoped to publish, and indeed did publish in 1781, tells us, however, nothing very specific about Percy's interest in *Don Quixote*. By addressing his *Letter* to Percy, Bowle showed that he regarded Percy not only as a friend but as a man who had great interest in *Don Quixote*; but there is nothing in the *Letter* and nothing in what Nichol Smith in 1932 referred to as 'the scanty remains of their correspondence' that quite accounts for the handsome terms in which Bowle, at the conclusion of his printed *Letter*, acknowledges his indebtedness to Percy.

Recently, however, the scanty remains of their correspondence have been greatly augmented. Some years ago I learned, through the good offices of Mr. Wilmarth Lewis, of the existence of a packet of the correspondence between Percy and Bowle in the Library of the University of Cape Town. The Library had acquired from a descendant of John Bowle a number of volumes, which included a quarto letter-copy book containing Bowle's copies of the letters that he wrote, and a folio letter-book 'bound in the skin of Bowle's dog', in which Bowle had pasted the letters that he had received. The quarto volume yielded copies of sixteen of Bowle's letters to Percy; the folio volume, originals of thirty-three letters from Percy to Bowle. Bowle's letter of 11 May 1777 was printed long ago on pages 165–6 of the eighth volume of John Nichols's *Illustrations of the Literary History of the Eighteenth Century*,[5] but all the rest of the material still remains unpublished. The letters run from 1767 to 1781, though there are evident gaps in the correspondence. It should be noted that the Bowle side of the

---

[4] Boswell's *Life* (1934), i. 49, 553.   [5] 8 vols., London, 1817–58.

correspondence covers only the period from 1772 to 1780. If Bowle preserved copies of his letters to Percy before 1772, they are not to be found in this collection.

Thus, we now have an opportunity to learn how Percy and Bowle came together, the kind of service that each rendered the other, and the gradual shifting of the *Don Quixote* project from Percy to Bowle. The correspondence begins in 1767 with a letter dated 11 February, which Percy addressed to Bowle before the two men became personally acquainted. Percy writes: 'Calling in at Mr Jackson's shop this morning, he tells me that You were so good as to speak of some curious particulars you had, or could direct me to, relating to the subject of the *Old Minstrels*: I should be much obliged to you, Sir, if you would do me the favour to communicate the same to me, or inform me, where I could have recourse to them. As a New Edition of the *Old Reliques* is coming out,[6] any Information for improving that little work would be thankfully accepted: and a Copy of the Book when published, will be the least acknowledgement you will be intitled to from, Sir, your most humble servant Thomas Percy.'

The bookseller was Andrew Jackson (1695–1778), and Jackson was a thoroughly appropriate intermediary for bringing together these two scholars of our older literature. John Nichols, in his *Literary Anecdotes of the Eighteenth Century*, gives a very engaging account of Jackson. Nichols describes him as 'well known to many dealers in old books, and black letter', remarking that he 'kept a shop for more than forty years in Clare Court, Drury Lane. Here . . . midst dust and cobwebs, he indulged his appetite for reading; legends and romances, history and poetry, were indiscriminately his favourite pursuits. Unlike a contemporary brother of the trade, he did not make the curiosity of his customers a foundation of a collection for his own use, and refuse to part with an article, where he found an eagerness in a purchaser to obtain it. Where [Jackson] met with a rarity, he would retain the same till he had satisfied his own desires in the perusal of it, and then part with it agreeable to his promise.'[7]

Jackson was also something of an eccentric. In 1740 he published

---

[6] The second edition had been printed off by 17 June 1767. See *The Correspondence of Thomas Percy and Richard Farmer*, ed. Cleanth Brooks (Baton Rouge, 1946), p. 138.

[7] *Anecdotes*, iii. 625.

his own rhymed version of the first book of Milton's *Paradise Lost*. He even published four of his catalogues in rhyme—which is surely an instance of a bookseller going beyond the call of duty and perhaps the call of common sense. What does *Paradise Lost* sound like when it wears the fetters of rhyme? Here are Jackson's opening lines:

> Of man's first disobedience, and repast
> On that forbidden fruit, whose mortal taste
> Brought death into the world, and all our woes,
> With loss of Eden, till one greater rose,
> Restored us, and regained the blissful seat,
> Sing heavenly muse. . . .

Jackson would better have written: 'Sing hobbled muse. . . .'

What occasioned Jackson to mention Bowle to Percy as a person able to help him with the *Reliques*? One can make a plausible guess. In 1764 Bowle had published anonymously *Miscellaneous Pieces of Antient English Poesie*. This little volume includes 'The Troublesome Reign of King John, Written by Shakespeare, Extant in no edition of his Writings' (S.T.C. 13646), John Marston's 'The Metamorphosis of Pygmalion's Image' (S.T.C. 17482), and Marston's 'Scourge of Villany' (S.T.C. 17486). It is an unusual— even curious—little collection, and at the least it indicates a lively and intelligent interest in Elizabethan literature.

But whatever Jackson's original reason for recommending Bowle to Percy, Percy's second letter to Bowle, written a month later, shows that he had soon been made aware of Bowle's interest in *Don Quixote*. He writes in a letter of 12 March 1767: 'Inclosed I send a very full Catalogue of *Don Quixote's Library*: [that is, books that Percy was satisfied Don Quixote must have perused]. You will at once see what I have; and what I *want*.—The *latter* articles the more easily to catch your eye are denoted by an Asterisk. . . . *El Verdadero Suceso de Batalla de Roncesvalles* was not long since in your neighbourhood, and perhaps may be unnoticed in some bookseller's shop in Salisbury[8] still:—I should be glad to get it at any Rate.—I must also implore your Assistance as I do that of every Man of Letters, towards completing my *Quixotic Library*. . . .'

---

[8] Salisbury was the nearest town to the village of Idmiston, where Bowle was vicar of the parish.

Here sounds the voice of the enthusiastic collector and scholar. Bowle's now-lost reply to Percy's first letter must have mentioned his interest in *Don Quixote* in such terms as to assure Percy that he was dealing with a brother in the craft. Percy's 'Quixotic Library' was to attain a considerable measure of fame among his friends and associates. In 1772, for example, Boswell notes that Percy 'showed me . . . a collection of all the Spanish Authours mentioned in *Don Quixote*; and he told me that a clergyman down in the country, who has probably more spanish learning than any Spaniard, was assisting him in finding out the various passages mentioned or alluded to, that he may make a kind of key to *Don Quixote.*'[9] The clergyman was, of course, John Bowle.

Percy had soon become convinced that Bowle was an authority on Spanish literature, for a few months later, in a letter dated 25 January 1768, he is addressing Bowle in the following terms: 'I am astonished at your extent of knowledge in relation to Spanish and other Antiquities: I doubt whether there is any Man now in Spain, Who knows so much of the literary and genealogical History of that Nation, as yourself.' In this letter Percy includes a list of nine books in Portuguese and Spanish that had been offered for sale by a country bookseller, about the merit of which he wanted Bowle's opinion. Six weeks later (2 March 1768) Percy writes to tell Bowle that he has found the little volume containing a song that gives the history of the Marqués de Mantua 'so particularly referred [to] in many places of Don Quixote. . . .' Indeed, by this time, Percy informs his friend, 'I want, now, scarce any old Spanish Ballad but that of Verdadero Susceso de la Batalla de Roncesvalles:—and even on this I have got a large Poem in 35 Cantos, written by Nicolas Espinosa, as a 2ᵈ Part to Urrea's Translation of Orlando Furioso.'

In the same letter Percy asks Bowle to note, as he reads *Don Quixote*, 'all our Author's *Allusions*, *References* to, *Quotations* of, and accidental or particular *Mention* of any of the *Old Books of Chivalry*. After that I wish you would read over some of my *Old Books of Chivalry and Romance*, to see what illustration they would afford Cervantes.'

[9] See *Private Papers of James Boswell from Malahide Castle*, ed. G. Scott and F. A. Pottle (Mt. Vernon, New York, 1928–34), ix. 37; and *Boswell for the Defence, 1769–1774*, ed. W. K. Wimsatt and F. A. Pottle (New York, 1960), p. 65.

Why does not Percy do this for himself? How can he justify putting this burden upon Bowle? Because, as he goes on to write, 'You have leisure and retirement: I have neither in my present situation and it will probably be some years before I attain either. Such assistance as this, would encourage me and enable me to bring my Scheme to a much earlier conclusion than I shall ever be able to do otherwise. As I have Duplicates of some of the Romances, you could be reading them in the Country, while I was occasionally examining the Passages, you referred me to, here in Town.—Pray think of this Proposal and oblige me with your sentiments upon it.'

Many of the Percy–Bowle letters have to do with book-buying. For example, Percy writes on 3 April 1771: 'I did not neglect your Commission at Baker's Auction: the following articles I was fortunate enough to secure for you, and I shall have great pleasure in delivering them to you, when you come to Town, which I hope will be soon.' After mentioning several lots among a certain Mr. Webb's books, Percy continues: 'All the other articles were bought out of our hands. . . .' The use of 'our' is significant: in an important sense the *Don Quixote* enterprise had in fact become a joint effort. In a letter dated 13 January 1772, Percy refers to 'our great research'.

Another letter of the same period (6 April 1772) indicates the sort of measures that Percy and Bowle took to keep from bidding against each other at auctions. Percy writes: 'I have received your List, relative to Beighton's Sale, and shall purposely abstain from every book in it, tho' some of them I had marked to bid for, except one which you would very much oblige me, by resigning to me; especially as you shall have the use of it, at all times as much as myself, and it is so necessary to my *Quixote Library* (which I have bought, latterly as much for your use as my own) that it is defective without it. . . .'

The books were indeed shared. Bowle's letter of 2 May 1772 mentions several of Percy's books then on loan to him. He writes: 'Felix Marte, alias Florismarte de Hircania stands unmolested with his two Brother Knights del Febo, and Oliva, Tirante is at a proper distance. All well and kiss your hands.' Even when Percy did not own the book himself he usually managed to secure the use of it for Bowle. He writes, for example, on 2 June 1772: 'I received your kind letter, but could not get *Avellaneda*: there was an unlimited

Commission given and it sold for more than it was worth; which I was the less anxious about, as I am promised a Copy from abroad, and in the mean time have had the Book lent me: which I have also procured leave to have lent to you, and it is here with me ready to be sent you, if you will favour me with a Direction by return of the Post how it can be safely sent.'

On 24 March 1774, Percy sent Bowle proposals for a new version of *Don Quixote*. The edition was to be a mere catchpenny affair, but he thinks the proposals are important as at least showing that 'the Publick is constantly awake to every new proposal relating to our favourite author: which is encouragement to hope that we may make some effort ourselves, with advantage.' Percy's remark continues to point to a joint effort.

The earlier letters indicate that Percy had hoped to do a translation of *Don Quixote*, to which Bowle would supply the index, maps, and notes. It seems likely that Percy tried to persuade Bowle to help with the translation, for in his letter of 31 March 1774 Bowle tells Percy: 'I cannot give over all thoughts of a Classical Edition of this great Work, and should reluctantly make publick in a Translation what the Author perused in the Originals, which should be pointed out.' Bowle then goes on to mark out a division of labours: 'Be mine the Merit hereafter to avail myself of the past drudgery of my Indexes, and *poner las Anotaciones y Acotaciones* in consequence of them, and believe me this has been frequently work enough; Be it yours in due time to give him an English Dress. . . .'

Bowle was to abide by his resolution not to translate. Just when it was that Percy came to realize that he himself would never have time to manage the translation, we do not know. At any rate, Bowle pressed ahead with his plans for his 'Classical Edition', and Percy's letter of 3 February 1777 acknowledged the receipt of the pamphlet addressed to him, the aforementioned *Letter to the Reverend Dr Percy, concerning a new and classical edition of . . . Don Quixote*. It amounts to 68 pages, and describes with detailed illustrations Bowle's notion of what a proper edition ought to be. It even includes sample pages for the index and a map of Spain, 'Acomodada A La Historia de Don Quixote', with an index to the map. The last page of the pamphlet serves notice that 'speedily will be published, proposals for printing by subscription' the new edition.

In a letter of 10 February 1777, Bowle writes to Percy, 'Although upon the whole my Labours will be principally for such as are conversant in both the Spanish and the Italian, yet it may induce several to commence an acquaintance with the Original, as the principal intent of the Annotations will be to facilitate the knowledge of it.' This is to take a high and austere line indeed, and though Percy immediately set about procuring subscriptions from friends like George Steevens and Thomas Tyrwhitt, and Daines Barrington, he had already warned Bowle (in a letter of 3 February 1777) that he feared that the merits of Bowle's edition would be lost upon the general public. I 'am much afraid', he writes to Bowle, that such an edition 'will be Caviar to the Million; and that you must be content to gratify a select number of curious Readers, like myself who admire the excellent Cervantes and endeavour to relish him in his original Language. Should my fears in this respect, (which friendship for you excites) prove groundless, no one will more sincerely rejoice [than I].'

In one of his earlier letters, Bowle uses a rather poignant phrase to characterize the amount of applause that he thought his kind of scholarship was likely to elicit. He writes on 31 March 1774: 'The Solitary Satisfaction of the Philosopher's Ευρηκα is sometimes my case. . . .' One has the impression that such satisfaction was perhaps enough for this scholar who set such formidable standards for most English readers. But Bowle did hope for a favourable reception in Spain. He writes to Percy (10 February 1777) that he has sent copies of his *Letter . . . concerning a new and classical edition* to various authorities in Spain and that if his plan should succeed, he has 'no doubt his edition would be admissible into Spain . . .'. Later (27 October 1777) he was able to report to Percy that he has received very favourable notice from Don Casimiro de Ortega who speaks highly of the Reverend Mr. Bowle's new edition and praises 'la Idea original de imprimir la obra de Cervantes con todos los honores de un Autor Classico . . .'.

By the end of the year 1778, Percy had pretty clearly given up his own hopes for publishing anything on *Don Quixote*. In a letter of 29 August he asks Bowle to 'impart to me from time to time your future Discoveries, as leisure and Opportunity suggest. I am only sorry that I must continue as Idle Spectator of your curious Researches, without being able to advance them.' This letter does not specifically renounce plans for a translation, but it is significant that from this time onward we hear nothing further about it. Bowle, on the other hand, moved steadily on in his preparations for his edition. In his letter to Percy of 12 November 1778, he includes for Percy's reading a letter that he has received from Don Antonio Pellicer of Madrid. It was a letter that Bowle was happy to print in his 1781 edition, for Pellicer was a distinguished Cervantes scholar and was to become the editor of the first of the great editions of *Don Quixote* published in Spain.

Bowle's letter of 28 July 1780 is filled with details concerning the forthcoming edition. He speaks with the cheerful complacency of the confident scholar. He tells Percy: 'I hope I do not impose upon myself when I assert that no one can understand Cervantes fully that does not come to my school. Who can be said to know him well who is unacquainted with his Obligations to the Italian Poets? Who among his numerous readers has any Idea of this? The enclosed sheet has but little of it, but the characters of El Cura, el Oidor, y La Pelea in the 45th Chapter of the first part will appear in double lustre when confronted with the several passages from Ariosto: and the great Genius of Boiardo seems transfused into Cervantes from the happy use he made of him in Sancho's *Perdida del Rucio*, and which he has himself pointed out in the fourth Chapter of the second Part.'

Bowle was certainly entitled to his glow of exhilaration as the work rounded to a close. Parts of it—particularly the index—had been tedious drudgery, and some of the reading that had been required of him had proved wearisome and unrewarding. On one occasion he wrote to Percy (27 October 1777): 'Shall I have fought thro the whole Battle of Roncesvalles, and say nothing of the Event or the Engagement to my respected Friend Dr. Percy? That be far from me. Yes, dear Sir, I have done this. With my accustomed perseverance I have toild and turmoild thro six and thirty as dull and tedious Cantos of El Verdadero Suceso de la Famosa Battalla de Roncesvalles con la muerte de los doze Pares de Francia . . . as ever merited Fire, or perpetual Oblivion. If I have not in many instances traced Cervantes here, yet to make some amends for my drudgery various Illustrations of his text have presented themselves from this Quarter.'

In his letter of 28 July 1780, Bowle, by the way, mentions having had 'two interviews with Dr Johnson, at the first I left with him the whole I had printed with the first sheet of the Anotaciones, to which he expressed some objection, as being separate from the text: but acquiesced at length from its being not practicable to place them in the usual manner. He had heard of my undertaking, was civil and obliging and wished to see me when I came to town again.' So ends Bowle's side of the correspondence. A letter from Percy of 15 July 1781 completes the tally of extant letters. As this letter indicates, the edition of *Don Quixote* had been published, and Percy's comments and queries are mostly concerned with the list of subscribers and with their payments on their subscriptions. But Percy does express the wish that Bowle might add another volume or two 'containing *all the metrical Romances and Epitomes* (at least) of *all the Prose Stories*, which are quoted or referred to, or (at least) necessary to understand our favourite author'.

It may or may not be significant that we have no letters written after the publication of the edition of *Don Quixote*, though Bowle was to live on for another seven years. I have found no hint that any coolness sprang up between the men. Presumably the correspondence did continue, at least in desultory fashion, but if so, the letters have dropped out of sight.

The edition was printed at Salisbury.[10] Bowle, for divers reasons, saw to it that the dedication to the Right Honourable Francis, Earl of Huntingdon was written in English, but everything else in the work is in Spanish, including Bowle's acknowledgement to his friends and helpers. Percy's name heads the list of these and the first sentence of the statement of thanks may be translated: 'It remains only to add my obligations to my benefactors and friends who through their own persons and through their influence have inspired me to proceed with the editing of, and commentary upon, this work. Thanks are owed principally to the Reverend Dr. Thomas Percy, Dean of Carlisle, who from his library of romances having to do with Quixote has given me the use of a great many books necessary to illustrate his history.' Now that so many letters between him and Percy have at last come to light, we can better appreciate the justification of this handsome acknowledgement.

How was Bowle's elaborate edition received? Percy's forecast proved correct. The edition made little impression upon the English

[10] For a detailed description of the first and second printings, see R. M. Cox, *The Rev. John Bowle: the Genesis of Cervantes Criticism* (Chapel Hill: The University of North Carolina Press, 1971), pp. 48–52.

public. I have been able to find very little notice of it in the reviews. The *Monthly Review* for 1783 gives a favourable account, but the difficulties that the edition sets up for the English reader are acknowledged. The writer in The *Monthly Review*—Richard Owen Cambridge, as the late Benjamin Nangle informed me—observes: 'Mr. Bowle has taken such pains in endeavouring to explain the words of the author, that we should have little occasion for a dictionary if he had given the explanations in English, instead of the Spanish language. . . .' But Cambridge praises Bowle for his 'great labour and diversity of reading', qualifications which have enabled him to 'illustrate every passage which time has rendered obscure—particularly allusions to places, men, and books; the memory of which may not survive the work wherein they are recorded'. Bowle managed, however, to irritate the hot-blooded Joseph Baretti who published in 1786 a sharp attack entitled *Tolondron: Speeches to John Bowle about his edition of Don Quixote*.

I do not know just how the quarrel arose, but in his *Letter to the Reverend Dr Percy concerning a new and classical edition of Don Quixote*, Bowle makes a disparaging reference to Baretti. Perhaps this was the spark that ignited the powder train. Bowle heard of derogatory comments that Baretti had written in the margins of a copy of his edition of *Don Quixote*. In 1784 Bowle publicly complained of the conduct of two people—though he did not name them—with regard to his edition of *Don Quixote*, and in 1785 published *Remarks on the Extraordinary Conduct of the Knight of the Ten Stars and his Italian Esquire, to the Editor of Don Quixote: In a Letter to the Rev. J.S.D.D.*[11]

The *Monthly Review* in its account of this publication says: 'We acknowledge ourselves incompetent judges, as to the real ground of the dispute or quarrel which has given rise to these strictures. If Mr. Bowle, to whom the public hath lately been obliged for a valuable edition of Don Quixote, in the original Spanish, hath been ill-treated by Signior Baretti, or others, he hath here, we apprehend, amply avenged himself on his adversary's character and writings.' It was in reply to these 'Remarks on the Extraordinary Conduct' that Baretti issued his *Tolondron*.

Late in 1786, Percy, now Bishop of Dromore in Ireland, wrote to his friend Edmond Malone, requesting a copy of *Tolondron*

[11] For a detailed review of the controversy, see Cox, *The Rev. John Bowle*, pp. 18–26.

'and whatever answer my friend Bowle published in reply'. Whether or not Percy had heard directly from Bowle, we do not know. At any rate, Percy asked Malone to favour him 'with a little insight into that curious controversy'. Malone replied promptly as follows: 'I know nothing of Tolondron, but that it is a reply to an attack make on Baretti in the Gentleman's Magazine, which he chose to ascribe to Mr Bowle, but the Don solemnly assured me he wrote not a line of it. The humour of Tolondron, if any it has, seems to be quite Italian, and not well adapted to the English taste.'[12]

For an estimate of the real merit of Bowle's edition of *Don Quixote* we ought to look to Spain. Bowle's edition was readily accessible only to a Spanish-reading public, and, of course, all but a few of the scholars who could really judge its value were themselves Spaniards. If we submit the book to trial before Spanish judges it comes off most handsomely. The first truly scholarly edition of *Don Quixote* to appear in Spain was that edited by Juan Antonio Pellicer, published at Madrid in 1797, a full sixteen years after Bowle's edition. Indeed, Bowle was the first editor in the whole world to treat *Don Quixote* with the care appropriate to a classical author. Pellicer himself acknowledges as much in his edition. It is 'Don Juan Bowle, pastor de la parroquia de Idmestone' to whom he pays high praise for his full and scholarly notes and his copious index. So much for Bowle's Spanish contemporaries.[13] If one consults the standard work today, the *Bibliographía Crítica de Ediciones del Quijote*, edited by Juan Suñé Benages and Juan Suñé Fonbuena, Barcelona, 1917, one finds Bowle's edition listed among the Castillian editions of *Don Quixote*. The comment upon it may be translated thus: 'One can say without fear of contradiction that the meritorious D[on] Juan Bowle was the first commentator of Quixote and that he contributed materials to the commentaries of Pellicer, Arritea, Clemencin, Bastus, Aribau and other commentators.' Furthermore, in the *Bibliographía* it is stated that to Bowle falls 'the glory of having been the first to interpret and facilitate the understanding of obscure and scabrous passages, of idioms of chivalric phraseology, and of the

[12] *The Correspondence of Thomas Percy and Edmond Malone*, ed. Arthur Tillotson (Baton Rouge, 1944), pp. 48–50.

[13] For a more detailed account of the Spanish reception of Bowle's work, see Cox, *The Rev. John Bowle*, pp. 101–12.

infinitude of words in little use today that one encounters in [*Don Quixote's*] immortal pages.'

Bowle deserves a place, then, among that remarkable group of scholars in eighteenth-century England, a group which includes men like Thomas Tyrwhitt, who laid the foundations of modern Chaucer scholarship, George Steevens and Edmond Malone, who produced the great learned editions of Shakespeare, and Thomas Warton, who wrote the first history of English poetry. Thomas Percy was the friend and associate of these men and he obviously held his friend Bowle in like estimation.

Another close friend of Percy's, Richard Farmer, of Cambridge, convincingly demonstrated in 1767[14] that if one wished to understand Shakespeare's words and allusions, one had to read the books that Shakespeare himself had read. It was just such a principle that Percy had himself invoked several years earlier in his letter to the London bookseller with reference to an edition of Cervantes. Apparently neither Percy nor Bowle had to learn this principle from the other nor from any third person, Both men seem to have arrived at it independently and early in their careers.

The story of the co-operation of Thomas Percy and John Bowle is not an important chapter in the history of English scholarship. But I think that it has its own interest, and I must confess that I find it heartening and even exhilarating. How clearly our scholarly ancestors of two hundred years ago discerned the essential problems, how quickly they devised appropriate methods for dealing with them, and with what zeal and diligence they prosecuted the work.

---

[14] In a short work entitled *An Essay on the Learning of Shakespeare.*

What do we do when two texts differ? *She Stoops to Conquer* and Textual Criticism

Tom Davis and Susan Hamlyn

The answer to the question posed in the title is,[1] we make a subjective decision. The answer in editorial practice has often been,
we pretend we are making an objective choice. Arthur Friedman,
Goldsmith's best editor, in one of the best editions of any
eighteenth-century author, says that textually *She Stoops to
Conquer* 'offers few difficulties'.[2] In other words, there is little
need for subjective editorial decisions. This paper begins with an
attempt, based on new evidence from rather odd sources, to show
that this statement is untrue; it proposes, incidentally, a method of
dealing with such evidence; finally it generalizes from this instance
to a discussion of the central problem of textual criticism: what,
precisely, is an editor doing when he chooses between the readings
of two texts?

We begin with what is known about the text of *She Stoops to
Conquer*. The first draft was written by September 1771. Goldsmith was short of money, and anxious for a success in the theatre:
the mere promise of performance would satisfy his creditors for
the moment, at least. However, the play was a theatrical risk,
because it was (as we might now say), too funny: funny, that is, in
a 'low' manner, and at the expense of the currently fashionable
Sentimental Comedy. The story of how George Colman 'was
prevailed on at last by much solicitation, nay, a kind of force, to
bring it on'[3] is well known. But the textual implications of this

---

[1] The title is based on a remark made by Erasmus: 'What are we to say when
we see that the exemplars of this edition do not agree?' as quoted and translated
by P. Davison in his 'Science, Method, and the Textual Critic', *Studies in Bibliography*, xxv (1972), 28.

[2] Arthur Friedman, ed., *Collected Works of Oliver Goldsmith*, v (1966), 96;
hereafter referred to as 'Friedman'.

[3] Boswell, *Life of Johnson*, ed. Hill–Powell, iii (1934), 320–1. The full story
is well set out in Friedman, v. 87–95.

have not been pointed out. Goldsmith was ready to revise his play heavily, and to have others revise it, for the sake of getting it performed. We know that Joseph Cradock 'altered' the play;[4] we know that Goldsmith wrote to Colman in the following desperate terms: 'Whatever objections you have made or shall make to my play I will endeavour to remove and not argue about them . . . I have as you know a large sum of money to make up shortly; by accepting my play I can readily satisfy my Creditor that way. . . . For God sake take the play and let us make the best of it.'[5] But Goldsmith was in general reluctant to revise or accept revision, as we may deduce from the fact that he had strongly resisted any attempt, five years earlier, to revise his first play *The Good-Natured Man*. Thus we may conclude that *She Stoops to Conquer* went through a series of revisions, some of them at least against Goldsmith's aesthetic judgement, in order to make the play less funny; in order to bring it more into line with canons of taste that its first performance would render obsolete. These revisions are irreversible: we cannot rescue the play from their damage, since the early texts are lost. This is a cause for concern rather than complacency. The instability of the text we have is already evident.

The play was first performed on 15 March 1773. At some point shortly before that a manuscript copy was deposited with the Lord Chamberlain. This copy was produced by a scribe for the purpose of licensing the play, and was, we may assume, based on either the author's manuscript or a prompt-book copy: it presumably represents fairly closely the state of the text on the night of the first performance. Its punctuation is more scanty and erratic than that which we are accustomed to finding in printed books, as is rather common with manuscripts of any period; in this case we should remember that the play was as yet primarily an oral artefact, its true punctuation being realized by the actors' delivery; so the punctuation of this text cannot, strictly, be said to be defective. The manuscript is now in the Larpent Collection at the Huntington Library: it is the earliest extant text of the play.[6]

---

[4] *Literary and Miscellaneous Memoirs*, i (1828), 225.

[5] Goldsmith, *Collected Letters*, ed. K. C. Balderston (1928), pp. 116–17. It was denied later (*Morning Chronicle*, 29 Mar. 1773) that any of Colman's alterations were in fact made to the play.

[6] The Larpent MS. has been described, and its variants from the first edition of the play listed in full, by Coleman O. Parsons in 'Textual Variations in a Manuscript of *She Stoops to Conquer*', *Modern Philology*, xl (1942), 57–69.

Ten days after the first performance, while the play was still running, it was published in printed form: at four o'clock on 25 March. This was apparently something of a rush job, produced for sale in the theatre, and printed, it is thought, in two printing shops.[7] The punctuation and spelling are normalized to the conventions of print, but there is an odd quirk in this: the compositorial styling of the part printed in the second shop is different— much looser, more inconsistent, and more careless—than that of the remainder. The play went very quickly through a further five impressions from standing type; for the second, the styling was normalized, so that the inconsistencies of the second part were made to conform with the greater regularity of the first. It is worth noting that we have no evidence to suggest that Goldsmith was remotely connected with any of these three states of punctuation: what evidence we have, from his extant autograph manuscripts, suggests that his own pointing was erratic and scanty in the extreme. This set of anomalies is perhaps not important in itself —though in view of the obsession of current textual criticism with these so-called 'accidentals' it is not negligible[8]—but it serves to reinforce the fact that the work now existed in two versions: one a playhouse text that the audience would see enacted, and the other a printed text that they might have bought from the orange-sellers who hawked it in the theatre. Each with its own conventions: one with the richness of spoken and enacted discourse, the other with the considerably more limited conventions of print. It is important to this discussion that it should be accepted that this distinction is not one of context, but of text; not one text and two contexts, but two texts.

In terms of actual physical documents we have two substantive texts of the play extant, the earlier, Larpent, text, and the slightly later printed edition, which we will call *1773*. Apart from the variation in styling between these two versions mentioned earlier there are a number of variants in the words of the play, some 91 in all. These variants present the editor with a problem, though not,

---

[7] See W. B. Todd, 'The First Editions of *The Good Natur'd Man* and *She Stoops to Conquer*', *Studies in Bibliography*, xi (1958), 133–42.

[8] It is, for instance, worth noting that Friedman is forced by his adherence to the Greg–Bowers rule of copy-text to use the punctuation of the first impression as the basis of his edition. Thus he carefully preserves the idiosyncrasies of a text that contains two noticeably different and inconsistent styles, neither of which is likely to be authorial.

apparently, a very difficult one: which version should he prefer in his production of the single text that convention forces upon him? The most obvious hypothesis offers a ready solution: that the later, printed, text preserves a later version of the play, and that the Larpent manuscript therefore shows only (as Friedman remarks) 'the state of the play before Goldsmith made his final revisions' (v. 96). That the revisions are authorial can, of course, only be assumed. These assumptions offer material that can be shown in stemma form, the central line representing the manuscript prompt-book.

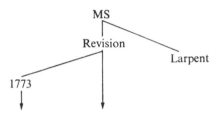

This stemma apparently makes the editor's task simple: he should use *1773* as the basis for his text, and emend it in favour of *Larpent* only when the latter preserves a 'good' reading that shows up a printer's error in *1773*.

There is, however, another set of texts of the play. They have hitherto been ignored, as being hopelessly too late to have any trace of an author's hand: Goldsmith died in 1774; all but one of these were published after 1790. The subsequent textual history of the play is that two more editions were produced under the imprint initiated by John Newbery, Goldsmith's patron and friend —in 1785 and 1786. There were also two Dublin editions, that appear to derive their text from *1773*. But there is also another kind of publication: a set of collected plays, in numerous volumes, by different authors, containing *She Stoops to Conquer* among them. This kind of publishing venture did not, of course, begin in 1791, and it is still no doubt a viable commercial proposition now.[9] But what distinguished most of those published between the first appearance of Goldsmith's play in this form and 1825, an arbit-

---

[9] For instance there is a collected text published as early as 1774—in Altenberg, for some reason. It does not, however, have the distinct title-page reference to the playhouse text, or any of the distinguishing textual characteristics that isolate the corpus we are about to discuss.

rarily chosen terminal date, is that on the title-pages either of the play, or of the volume containing the play, is some form of the words 'Regulated from the prompt-books' (*Bell's British Theatre*, 1791) or 'printed under the authority of the managers, from the prompt book . . . as performed at the Theatres Royal, London' (*Dolby's British Theatre*, 1823).[10]

It seemed for this reason that these odd and commercial volumes were at least worth looking at, and as a beginning a text of 1806, 'with remarks by Mrs. Inchbald', was collated against *1773*. The results were very curious: this late text was found to preserve a number of the readings of the Larpent manuscript, that had hitherto been thought to have been superseded by the printed text of 1773. It is an axiom of textual criticism that if two texts agree significantly against a third, the third text cannot be intermediate between the other two. Thus the usual explanation of the relationship between *Larpent* and *1773* was cast into considerable doubt, and an improved hypothesis suggests itself: that some of the variants in *Larpent* remained in the theatrical tradition, were thus in existence at the same time as the printed variants, and were of equal, and not less, authority. That Goldsmith intended (or acquiesced in) two, and not one, versions of his play: one printed and the other performed, and that these differed in wording as well as in the inevitable differences between spoken and written language.

To test and elaborate this, it was necessary to examine the other collected texts of the play, and to attempt to construct a revised stemma that would incorporate the new evidence. Fifteen of the collected versions were collated, and it was found that in all some twenty-five of the 91 *Larpent* variants from *1773* had survived. Some of the texts had some variants, some others, in no immediately apparent pattern. To make some sense of the evidence, it was necessary to borrow some of the techniques of the textual criticism of manuscripts, stemmatics. A necessary first step was to ignore those readings in which, while a late text agreed with *Larpent* against *1773*, the agreement could have occurred through

---

[10] A complete short-title check-list of these texts is appended; any reference on the title-pages to the source of the copy is given in full. It cannot be claimed that all of the texts of the play up to 1825 have been examined, but all of those to be found in the British Library have been collated; this must represent a textually adequate sampling.

coincidence: technically, these are termed *reversible* variants.[11]
These are not unimportant *textually*, since the editor must make
his choice between one or the other, but are insignificant *stemmatically*, since they cannot be held to be evidential for the con-
struction of the textual map. Thus for instance at 111.3–4,[12] *1773*
has 'What a quantity of superfluous silk has thou got about thee'.
Larpent has 'hast', and so do the later texts, but it is clear that this
need only mean that later compositors relied on common sense,
rather than that they required a text with the *Larpent* reading to
inform them of the obvious. On the other hand, at 159.17, *1773*
has 'made my blood freeze again'. *Larpent* has 'froze me to
death', and so do three of the later editions. It is hard to imagine
that they can have conceived of this variant without having derived
it from a text related to *Larpent*, so this is a non-reversible or
divergent reading: one, that is, which indicates a line of descent for
all those texts which contain it which is distinct from all that do
not.

   This analysis furnished us with twelve test-variants of this kind,
in all of which some or all of the later texts agreed with *Larpent*
against *1773*. Analysis of the relationship between them on the
basis of these variants provided us with two groupings. The first is
deducible from a set of variants in which all of the collected texts
tended to agree with *Larpent* against *1773*. These are as follows;
five in all. We use the accepted symbol Σ to indicate 'all other
texts'. The variant is italicized.

1. 132.15–
   16   puts me in mind of the Duke of Marlborough, when
          we went to besiege Denain *1773*: . . . when *he*
          went. . . . Σ

2. 135.8   a *great* deal *1773 Dolby*: a *good* deal Σ

3. 151.12   all I can say will *never* argue down a single button
            from his cloaths *1773*: . . . will argue *L* . . . will *not*
            argue Σ. This in fact is expressed by the formula

----

[11] The methodology proposed here is based (loosely) on W. W. Greg's classic
Calculus of Variants (1927). The fact that all but one of the texts used are printed,
and all are datable, and that no attempt at a precise stemma is made, removes
most of the otherwise devastating objections to stemmata made by George Kane
in his edition of *Piers Plowman* (*A text*) (1960).

[12] For convenience, references to *She Stoops to Conquer* are keyed to Friedman's accessible edition (v. 99–217), by page- and line-number. The spelling
and punctuation of quotations from *1773* are taken from that text; similarly for
Larpent readings. Quotations from the mass of collected texts, whose styling
varies freely, are modernized.

1773:L:Σ; but it strongly suggests that the reading of the collected texts is based on a text that supplied the manifest lacuna in *Larpent* differently from the way in which *1773* did; thus the variant shows textual divergence.

4. 173.3   Mrs. *Langhorns 1773*: Mrs *Longhorns* Σ.
5. 215.25–   *Constance* Neville *1773: Constantia* Neville Σ.
   216.1

This grouping is hardly completely satisfactory. The variants are apparently not as stemmatically significant as one would wish. Dolby's edition of as late as 1823 can reverse the 'great/good' variant, and texts not connected with the tradition we are attempting to define have individually come up with two of the distinguishing variants, by coincidence or editorial perspicacity: the Dublin edition of 1774 has 'he' at 132.15–16, and the two texts published outside England, in Altenberg (1774) and Copenhagen (1812), both come up with the reading 'Longhorns' (though we believe the later text to have derived its readings from the earlier). Individually, then, some of these readings could have arisen without the copyist having seen a text connected with *Larpent*. Whether all five of them could have done so is debatable.

The second grouping is much clearer, and does not admit doubt. In this, *Larpent* agrees with only three of the collected versions: the ?1806 *Inchbald* (*I*), the second edition of *Inchbald* (*I2*, ?1816), and *Dolby's British Theatre* of 1823 (*Do*). A formula for this relationship may be expressed as *L I I2 Do:Σ*.

6. 121.20–1   you *understand me 1773* Σ: you *know I, I I2 Do*
7. 138.4–11   *1773* and Σ have as follows:
              MARLOW. (*Reading*) For the first course at the top, a *pig*, and pruin sauce. HASTINGS. Damn your *pig*, I say . . . HARDCASTLE. And yet, gentlemen, to men that are hungry, *pig*, with pruin sauce, is very good eating.
              Larpent has '*Pig's face*' for each of the occurrences of *pig. I, I2, Do* have only the first of these substitutions: that is, they print '*pig's face*' in the first instance only and '*pig*' in the rest.
8. 146.21–2   Who could ever suppose this *fellow* impudent upon some occasions. *1773* Σ: . . . *Gentleman . . . L I I2 Do*.

9. 152.14   *Mrs.* Niece *1773* Σ: *my* niece *L I I2 Do.*

10. 159.17   made my blood freeze again *1773* Σ: froze me to death *L I I2 Do.*

11. 159.26–7 when I was *in my best story of the Duke of Marlborough and Prince Eugene, he asked 1773* Σ: when I was *talking of my Friend Bruce, ask'd me L*: when I was *talking of the Duke of Marlborough and my friend Bruce, he asked I I2 Do.*

Strictly this expresses the relationship Σ:*L*:*I I2 Do*, but the reference to 'Bruce' incontestably supports a grouping with *L*.

12. 160.16–17 we don't meet many such at a horse race in the country *1773* Σ: he has a very passable complexion *L I I2 Do.*

No one, we suppose, will deny that these variants are divergent, and indicate manifest links with the *Larpent* text.

There is one further piece of evidence to take into account. The earliest text to contain our five readings that may indicate the separate tradition is not, in fact, the earliest collected text we looked at, but, rather confusingly, the last (1786) text published by Newbery. When we came to collate these texts against *1773* we found that they preserved the *1773* text uncontaminated by *Larpent* readings up to and including the second Newbery edition of 1785. *1786*, however, has all five of the readings that we used to distinguish our first major grouping, and is the earliest of all texts of this play to have them. There is, moreover, a gratifyingly neat bibliographical proof that this text and no other is the ancestor of this tradition. At 130.10–11 Marlowe says he cannot bring himself 'to blurt out the broad staring question, of, *madam will you marry me?*' (italics as in *1773*). This is the version in the Newbery texts from *1773* up to *1785*, and in *Larpent*. Seven of the collected texts have the curious and manifestly erroneous reading 'star-question' for 'staring question'. Five more make a poor attempt to make sense of this by reading 'start-question'. The remaining three hit on the correct reading, but apparently by the native wit of the editor or compositor rather than through consultation of the early Newbery texts, since one of them, the earliest, *The British Drama* of 1804, prints 'staring-question'—still, that is, influenced by the error. This error indubitably originates in *1786*, since that text prints 'star-[line break]question'. Obviously the compositor broke the word 'star-ing' at the end of the line, but forgot to finish it on the next line.

All of this suggests the following hypothesis. The *1773* version of the play coexisted with, and did not supersede, another, distinct, version, that contained at least some of the *Larpent* readings. This source was neglected by printers for thirteen years, but may have been tapped by the editor of the *1786* Newbery edition, and was certainly tapped again, more thoroughly, for the 1806 *Inchbald* text. Its capacity for survival without the preservation of print is remarkable. Where did it survive? It is hard to believe that the Larpent MS. itself was the source. This manuscript was thirteen years old in 1786, and thirty-three in 1806; and it had been deposited in the Licenser's office. The title-pages of these editions almost unanimously attest an interest in contemporaneity; the antiquarian instincts of the textual editor are not theirs. The earliest texts of the play must have been manuscript: Goldsmith's holograph, and the manuscript scribal copies that constituted the prompt-book and the actors' own texts; *1773* was not published until ten days after the first performance. We may deduce that one of these texts was consulted, at least in 1806, as being the source of a contemporary theatrical text, and a printed text based on *1786* was marked up to include its readings. If this is so, then the original manuscript prompt-book and perhaps the actors' copies were still in use in the theatre. In other words, there was from the beginning an acting text and a reading text of the play, both at least tacitly authorized by Goldsmith.

F. W. Bateson concluded, over thirty years ago, after an examination of late and manuscript texts of Sheridan, that 'the fact must be faced, with all its potential complications, that Sheridan was capable of drawing a distinction between the acting and the reading versions of his plays'.[13] The same is evidently true of Goldsmith, and the same complications must be faced.

There is further evidence that Goldsmith entertained the

[13] 'Notes on the Text of Two Sheridan Plays', *Review of English Studies*, xvi (1940), 316–17. This conclusion was amply endorsed and augmented by Cecil Price in his authoritative edition of Sheridan's plays (i (1973), 24 ff.). Philip Gaskell has provided further evidence of this kind of situation in a valuable chapter in his *From Writer to Reader*, 1978, where he analyses the differences between reading and acting texts of Tom Stoppard's *Travesties*. The present discussion is in part stimulated by a reading of this essay, which we were privileged to see in typescript.

possibility of two such versions. After the first night he was the
object of resentment from one Rachael Lloyd, flippantly referred
to in the play as a member of the 'Ladies Club' (172.19, 173.3).
Horace Walpole wrote to the Countess of Upper Ossory (27
March 1773) that 'Miss Loyd is in the new play by the name of
Rachael Buckskin, though he [Goldsmith] has altered it in the
printed copies'.[14] And in fact the *Larpent* text has 'old Miss
Rachael Buckskin', while *1773* has 'Biddy' for 'Rachael'. Thus we
have a fragment of external and direct evidence supporting the
view that (in this case, for rather obvious reasons) Goldsmith
could contemplate the simultaneous existence both of an acting
and a reading text of the play.

Where, then, are the attendant complications? Firstly, two
specific and rather alarming ones for *She Stoops to Conquer*. We
know from Walpole's letter that in this case the *Larpent* reading
was not superseded by the reading text but coexisted in an acting
text. It is not, however, to be found in any of our later collected
texts. So at least one of the *Larpent* readings has authorial sanction
but did not survive in the acting version that persisted until at
least 1806. Moreover our textual analysis has enabled us, not to
reconstruct an acting text, but to point out at least one, possibly
two, waves of revision of a reading text (the reading text of 1786)
by means of *consultation* with an acting version: a partial consultation. Both these points indicate that some—all?—of the variants
known only in *Larpent* may have coexisted in time and authority
with the *1773* reading version and its successors. Thus the first
conclusion is that *all* of the 91 readings that distinguish the *Larpent*
from the *1773* versions acquire at least a possible authority, and
must be consulted by any editor of the play, as representing an
alternative *and authoritative* tradition.

Secondly, we may deduce from internal evidence that Goldsmith revised for the reading version of 1773, though we cannot
know the extent of his revision; but after that, he left it alone. As
Friedman remarks, with some definiteness, 'Goldsmith quite
certainly did not revise the printed text of the play' (v.96). But
there is some evidence that Goldsmith was prepared to revise the
acting version. 'Conversation' Cooke relates that this was the only
means that could be found to induce him to go into the theatre on
the first night: 'it was on the remonstrance of a friend, who told

[14] Quoted in Friedman, v. 173.

him, 'how useful his presence might be in making some sudden alterations, which might be found necessary in the piece' that he was prevailed upon to go to the theatre.'[15]

Goldsmith died in April 1774, but *She Stoops to Conquer* was revived three times before the end of 1773. Given the possibility, at least, of authorial revision of the acting version, and given the fact that our corpus of late texts preserves authoritative early readings, we must accept that some, and therefore any, of their readings—in addition, that is, to the *Larpent* ones—have this authority. Thus an entire, and rather large, range of variants from *1773* is brought into play: we are forced to the conclusion that any of the readings in the two texts (*1786*, and the 1806 *Inchbald*) that apparently first introduce the two waves of revision, have at least a possible authority.

In addition, the new information suggests more general considerations. The first point is that it highlights a theoretical oversimplification in the rationale for editing any play. The model that an editor of plays usually appears to have in mind is as follows. An author will produce initially a written version of the play. This he passes on to actors and director, who will translate the work from, as it were, the two dimensions of print to the three dimensions of theatrical presentation. Just as spoken discourse is considerably more informative than written discourse, because it is assisted by intonation and gesture, so this third dimension will add very greatly to the range of meanings that the play has to offer. Furthermore any production will also alter, as well as add to, the written version. Thus there will be cuts, radical variation in intonation and emphasis, 'business', and even alteration or expansion of the wording preserved in the written version. But all of this is regarded as free variation, non-authoritative and somehow superficial, while the written text remains reassuringly stable and unitary. The editor seeks to recover as accurately as possible this basic text, so that he, like the author in the first place, may present it to directors and actors to do with as they will; and to readers, who will also produce and direct it, in the three dimensions of their mental stage.

The existence of two apparently authoritative versions of *She Stoops to Conquer*, which we have called acting and reading texts, immediately upsets this notion. The written text is no longer a

[15] 'Memoirs of Dr Goldsmith', *European Magazine*, Sept. 1793, p. 173.

single and sole source of authority: it may be conflated with an acting version, tapping this alternative, equally valid, but much less fixed text of the play. That for this or any play there should be two equally authoritative texts disturbs the essential rationale of textual criticism: that in choosing between variants the choice is either between error and correctness, or between early and late, unrevised and revised, readings. Secondly it points out that the unitary notion of 'author' embodied in the term 'authoritative' is a fiction. Plays are manifestly collaborative. They are written to be acted, usually, and since authors plainly cannot act all the parts themselves this collaboration is inevitable. The distinction outlined above between what actors and directors do, and what authors do, is not in practice a real one, because the two sets of people talk to each other: they collaborate. When Goldsmith came back into the theatre on the first night of *She Stoops to Conquer* he came to alter the play, presumably in consultation with George Colman and the actors. When the results of this collaboration are fed back into the (no longer stable) written version, our unitary notion of author is threatened, and the textual critic, in order to save it, is forced back into adopting the criterion of authorial approval: a 'true' reading becomes that which the author either generated, or, if someone else produced it, liked or accepted. But if there are two versions, coexisting in time and neither obviously a revision that supersedes the other, even this (already tenuous) anchor is lost.

A route to reassurance is offered by the notion that these two versions may be 'acting' and 'reading' texts respectively. This act of classification liberates us (apparently) into deciding either (since editing must be a unitary, singling-out activity) to print as our edited text the one we prefer on aesthetic grounds, or to take a harder line and treat the acting version as something that is specific to a period and place, of historical interest, but to be the object of study of members of the Department of Drama rather than the Department of English.

The distinction between the two is, however, less convenient than this suggests: authors, actors, and publishers are not at all solicitous of providing patterns that suit the restrictions by which a textual editor is bound. In the case of our revised pattern for *She Stoops to Conquer* this is well exemplified. The written text was clearly thought of in two ways: as a version of the play designed to be read, and as a summary of what went on on the stage. Even the first edition of *1773* has, on the title-page, 'as it is acted at the Theatre-Royal in Covent-Garden'. Thus the written text has both an independent existence, and a secondary one. In that it is secondary, it can be revised to bring it more into line with the theatre text, which by its nature is transitory, considerably subject to change, and only very partially recordable. Authors have not necessarily thought of the two texts as being as distinct as the convenience of a textual editor would dictate.

None the less, the editor is forced to print only one text. The economics of publishing, and the needs of his readers (no one *wants* to read two or more texts of *She Stoops to Conquer*) impose this upon him. Thus he must on occasion choose between two equally authoritative variants. He can only do so on the basis of subjective and aesthetic judgement: there may be no possible objective rationale or scrap of external evidence to relieve him of this responsibility.

It is here that the general and exemplary importance of this textual conundrum may be seen. Subjectivism of this kind has tended to be feared and avoided by editors, not only of plays, but of any kind of text. The choice between two equally authoritative texts is an unpalatable one, and some rule of thumb is generally sought as a substitute for this kind of decision. Thus for instance the choice between readings in two texts, one revised by an author and the other in an earlier, unrevised state, is usually referred to a rule of thumb propounded by W. W. Greg,[16] to the effect that the revised reading should be preferred.[17] Or, even more revealingly, supposing (as frequently happens in the editing of novels) an editor is faced with the choice of copy-text between two texts, one a holograph manuscript, the other a carefully proof-read first edition. The styling of each will be different: the manuscript will be punctuated by the author, but perhaps inadequately; the book will be styled by the copy-editor or compositor, but perhaps in a way that has been expected and acquiesced in by the author.

---

[16] In his famous 'Rationale of Copy-text' first printed in *Studies in Bibliography*, iii (1950–1), 19–36. It is appropriate to note in the context of the present collection that this classic paper, indisputably the foundation of the textual criticism of modern literary texts, first saw the light when it was read to the English Institute, on 8 September 1949, in the absence of Greg, by James M. Osborn.

[17] Thus Friedman, as was mentioned above, believing the *Larpent* readings to be earlier, largely ignores them.

Clearly here we have two authoritative substantive texts: the choice between them, as in the case of our play, can only be aesthetic.[18]

The urge to avoid this choice is based on a misconception. It must be recognized as fundamental that a given literary work is not, and has never been, an existent entity. It has always been a subjective construct, any physical manifestation being an approximation. The province of textual criticism 'has the strange, striking characteristic of not having entities that are perceptible at the outset and yet of not permitting us to doubt that they exist and that their functioning constitutes it'. The analogy that this quotation suggests—it is from Saussure's *Course in General Linguistics*,[19] and is one of his attempts to point the distinction between language and its physical manifestations: *langue* and *parole*—is more liberating and reassuring than its paradoxical content would suggest. At another point, on the same distinction, he remarks that 'Language [*langue*] is comparable to a symphony in that what the symphony actually is stands completely apart from how it is performed; the mistakes that musicians make in playing the symphony do not compromise this fact' (p. 18).[20] This is a precise—and, in fact, specific—evocation of the problems of textual criticism. The symphony—the play—does not exist wholly in any of its performances or published forms, but none the less only by them is it known. Once this rather vertiginous fact is grasped, the paradoxes are resolved. The editor reproduces, not *the* text, but *a* text. To do this he consults all the physical evidence to hand. He is engaged in the production of a construct, and this new text will, like any previous text, be unlike any other that has previously been. In order to make this construct he is bound by the evidence at hand—evidence, for instance, as to the

---

[18] The best discussion we have seen of this particular problem may be found in Gaskell's *From Writer to Reader*, on editorial problems in Dickens and Hawthorne. For a contrary view to his, and ours, see for instance, G. T. Tanselle's 'Problems and Accomplishments in the Editing of the Novel', *Studies in the Novel*, vii (1975), 344–50.

[19] Ed. Charles Bally and Albert Sechehaye, transl. Wade Baskin, revised edition, 1974, p. 107.

[20] We are grateful to Miss Deirdre Burton, of the Department of English Language and Literature, Birmingham University, for pointing out the appropriateness of this quotation; and in general for the opportunity to discuss these opinions in a seminar on Text led and instituted by J. McH. Sinclair, Professor of English Language in that Department.

ultimately unknowable author's intention—but what he must do is construct a text from this that represents his subjective perception of the work itself. His task in this is—not analogous with, but identical to—that of the literary critic, who characteristically reconstructs a work by a process of paraphrase, and asks that his readers should recognize his reading of it in their own. Thus by consulting his own intuitions the textual critic is making potentially objective statements: 'every man, said Imlac, may, by examining his own mind, guess what passes in the mind of others'; only in this kind of collective consensus, which can itself only be perceived by the subjective guesswork of individuals, can the literary work, like *langue*, be said to exist at all. The textual critic's isolated guesses at objectivity are necessary: they are necessitated by the kind of object that a literary work *is*.

Let us, finally, return—rather sharply—to *She Stoops to Conquer* for an instance of this process in action. At the end of the fourth act, Tony Lumpkin hits on the idea which will (but it won't) resolve the problems of two of the lovers. He says 'Meet me two hours hence at the bottom of the garden; and if you don't find Tony Lumpkin a more good-natur'd fellow than you thought for, I'll give you leave to take my best horse and Bet Bouncer into the bargain. Come along. My boots, ho' (195.21–5). And the curtain falls. Thus in *1773* and the *textus receptus*. In the *Larpent* version he gives them leave, instead, to 'run me through the Guts with a shoulder of mutton'. The evidence adduced by this paper suggests that both these readings are of equal authority, though the printed variant may be deliberately less 'low' than the theatre variant preserved in *Larpent*. Which is the 'right' reading? It seems appropriate to leave the exercise of choice to the reader; but please reflect as to what, precisely, you are doing when you choose.

TEXTS

In chronological order, with: information from title-pages of the book and section of the book, if relevant; the two separated by a solidus thus /; date; place of publication; editor/publisher; cue-title used in this paper. An asterisk denotes texts belonging to the corpus we have attempted to distinguish.

*1. Larpent MS. of *She stoops to conquer*. 1773 [*Larpent; L*].

2. [First edition.] She stoops to conquer: or, the mistakes of a night

. . . as it is acted at the Theatre-Royal in Covent-Garden . . . London: printed for F. Newbery . . . MDCCLXXIII [1773].

3. A collection of new plays by several hands vol. I. Altenburgh. Printed for Gottl. Eman. Richter. MDCCLXXIV/The mistakes of a night.

*4. She stoops to conquer: or, the mistakes of a night . . . as it is acted at the Theatre-Royal, in Covent-Garden . . . London: printed for E. Newbery . . . MDCCLXXXVI [*1786*].

*5. She stoops to conquer; or, the mistakes of a night . . . adapted for theatrical representation, as performed at the Theatres-Royal, Drury-Lane and Covent-Garden. Regulated from the prompt-books, by permission of the managers . . . London: printed for the proprietors, under the direction of John Bell, British Library, Strand . . . MDCCCXCI [*Bell's British Theatre*].

*6. She stoops to conquer; or, the mistakes of a night . . . adapted for theatrical representation, as performed at the Theatres-Royal, Drury-Lane and Covent-Garden. Regulated from the prompt-books, by permission of the managers . . . Dublin . . . for William Jones . . . MDCCXCII [there was a reissue of this edition in 1795, with a volume title-page reading 'Jones's British theatre . . . vol. III . . . 1795' The title-page and text of *She Stoops* are identical].

*7. The British drama . . . comedies. Vol. II—Part II. London, published by William Miller . . . 1804 [there is no title-page for *She Stoops*, which is on pp. 939–65].

*8. Sharpe's British theatre . . . vol. IV/ She stoops to conquer; or the mistakes of a night . . . London . . . 1804.

*9. She stoops to conquer . . . as performed in the Theatres Royal, Drury Lane and Covent Garden. Printed under the authority of the managers from the prompt book. With remarks by Mrs. Inchbald. London [n.d.; the B.L. Catalogue[21] suggests 1806. *Inchbald; I*].

*10. The modern British drama. In five volumes. Volume fourth. Comedies. London: printed for William Miller . . . 1811 [there is no title-page for *She Stoops*, which is on pp. 538–63].

11. Collection of English plays with explanatory notes in the Danish language by Fredk. Schneider . . . vol. II. Copenhagen, 1812./The mistakes of a night [this text probably derives from the Altenberg text of 1774].

*12. The London theatre . . . volume IV/She stoops to conquer; or, the mistakes of a night . . . correctly given, from copies used in the theatres, by Thomas Dibdin . . . prompter of the Theatre Royal, Drury Lane . . . London. 1814.

---

[21] That is, the catalogue residing in the Reading Room. The published version differs considerably.

*13. The British theatre . . . with biographical and critical remarks, by Mrs. Inchbald . . . Vol. XVII . . . London . . . 1808/She stoops to conquer . . . as performed at the Theatres Royal, Drury Lane and Covent Garden. Printed under the authority of the managers from the prompt-book . . . London [n.d.; the B.L. catalogue dates this at 1816. It also states that it is a reissue of the first Inchbald text. It is in fact a new edition. *I2*].

*14. Comedy of she stoops to conquer; or, the mistakes of a night . . . adapted for theatrical representation, as performed at the Theatres-Royal Covent-Garden and Drury-Lane. Regulated from the prompt books, by permission of the managers . . . by R. Cumberland, Esq. . . . London [1817; date from volume-title].

*15. The new English drama . . . by W. Oxberry, comedian. Volume fourth./She stoops to conquer . . . the only edition which is faithfully marked with the stage business and stage directions, as it is performed at the Theatres Royal . . . London . . . 1818.

*16. Oxberry's edition. She stoops to conquer . . . the only edition existing which is faithfully marked with the stage business, and stage directions. As it is performed at the Theatres Royal. By W. Oxberry, comedian. London . . . 1820 [this is not a reprint or reissue of 12].

*17. Dolby's British theatre./She stoops to conquer . . . printed under the authority of the managers, from the prompt book . . . also, an authentic description of the costume, and the general stage business, as performed at the Theatres Royal, London . . . London . . . 1823 [*Dolby; Do*].

*18. She stoops to conquer . . . as performed at the Theatres-Royal, Drury-Lane and Covent-Garden. Printed under the authority of the managers from the prompt book. With remarks by Mrs. Inchbald. London [n.d.; the B.L. catalogue suggests 1823].

*19. The London stage . . . accurately printed from acting copies, as performed at the Theatres Royal, and carefully collated and revised. Vol. I. London [n.d.; B.L. catalogue suggests 1824. No title-page for *She Stoops*].

*20. She stoops to conquer, or the mistakes of a night . . . correctly given, as performed at the Theatres Royal . . . New York . . . 1824.

Dr. Burney, 'Joel Collier', and Sabrina

ROGER LONSDALE

I

THE LATE summer of 1774 was an unhappy period for Dr. Charles Burney. His expeditions to the Continent in 1770 and 1772 in search of musical materials had been followed by the successful publication of accounts of his travels.[1] Now he had to settle down to the much more arduous task of producing the scholarly *History of Music* to which the musical tours had been merely preliminaries. For a busy and often harassed music-teacher the *History* was in itself to be an exhausting preoccupation for the next fifteen years. What particularly disturbed Burney's concentration in August 1774 was the collapse of an ambitious scheme which he had devised with Felice Giardini, the violinist and composer, of establishing a Music School in the Foundling Hospital, where Giardini was already the musical director.

Burney's aim was both altruistic and patriotic: that of giving a musical education to poor but talented children, of raising the standard of musical education in England, and of making the importation of expensive foreign singers unnecessary. At the same time it may be noted that the elaborate 'Plan', which Burney drew up for the inspection of the Governors of the Foundling Hospital in July 1774, included the appointment of himself and Giardini as the two 'principal Masters' of the Music School at a salary of £200 a year each. The Governors eventually approved the 'Plan' and the Music School was actually opened on 28 July. To Burney's horror, another meeting of the Governors on 3 August ordered the School to be closed, on the grounds that the Act of Parliament which had established the Foundling Hospital did not sanction

---

[1] *The Present State of Music in France and Italy* (1771); *The Present State of Music in Germany, the Netherlands, and the United Provinces*, 2 vols. (1773).

such a use of the institution. Burney was to remain embittered about what he considered to have been the sabotage of his ambitious scheme for many years.[2]

Worse humiliation was to follow. Joseph Cradock later recalled a meeting between Burney and Lord Sandwich, First Lord of the Admiralty and a notable music-lover, which must have taken place at this time: 'An awkward embarrassment once occurred, from Lord Sandwich's asking Dr. Burney (not knowing it was a ridicule), whether he had read some new musical travels by Mr. Collyer, as advertised in the papers. These were the ludicrous travels by Joel Collyer. . . .'[3] The work which caused Burney so much embarrassment was published by George Kearsley on 20 August 1774,[4] little more than two weeks after the collapse of the Music School at the Foundling Hospital. Lord Sandwich's error was understandable for, as the advertisements explained, the *Musical Travels through England* by 'Joel Collier, Organist' was 'printed on a proper Size to be bound up with the celebrated Musical Tours to France, Italy, Germany, Netherlands, and United Provinces, to which it is intended as a Supplement'. The book was widely advertised well into September and extracts appeared in various newspapers and periodicals.

On 23 August, for example, the *London Chronicle* devoted more than a page to quotations from it. A copy of this newspaper reached William Bewley, a close friend of Burney's years as a teacher in King's Lynn, who was staying with Lord Orford at Houghton. Although Lord Orford concluded from the extracts that the work was 'only a harmless though extravagant parody' of Burney's own *Musical Tours*, the loyal Bewley 'raved & even foamed at the mouth'. A regular contributor of scientific articles to Ralph Griffiths's *Monthly Review*, Bewley immediately 'bespoke the Review of this production, least it should fall into the hands

[2] For a more detailed account of Burney's scheme and its collapse, see my *Dr. Charles Burney: A Literary Biography* (Oxford, 1965), pp. 149–53, where the existence in the Osborn Collection of two manuscript versions of Burney's 'Plan' was revealed. A full text has since been printed by Jamie C. Kassler, 'Burney's *Sketch of a Plan for a Public Music-School*', *Musical Quarterly*, lviii (1972) 210–34.

[3] *Literary Memoirs and Correspondence*, 4 vols. (1828), iv. 168.

[4] *Public Advertiser*, 20 Aug. 1774. Some newspapers and periodicals described the parody as by 'Joseph Collyer', no doubt through a confusion with Joseph Collyer (d. 1776), a compiler whose *History of England*, 14 vols. (1774–5), was also being advertised at this time.

of a less competent judge'.[5] His indignant attack on 'Joel Collier'
for 'mimicking his betters—talking gross bawdy—and . . . f—ting
in the face of his audience, by way of humour' duly appeared in
the *Monthly Review* for September 1774.[6] Elsewhere, however,
the parody of Burney's books was received more favourably. The
London Magazine admitted in October that its humour was often
'too low' and that its treatment of Burney was 'justly reprehens-
ible', but admired the 'satirical address to the governors of the
Foundling Hospital'.[7]

Although Fanny d'Arblay seems to have succeeded in suppress-
ing all direct evidence of her father's own response to 'Joel
Collier', it can easily be deduced from letters written to him by
Bewley and by his other loyal friend and adviser, Thomas Twining
of Fordham, who was later to contribute so much to the *History of
Music*. Like Lord Sandwich, Twining had at first been misled by
the advertisements into assuming that 'Joel Collier' was intended
as a serious supplement to Burney's own books. Twining's misapprehension had soon been removed by a letter from Burney in
which he had threatened to abandon his *History of Music*, such
was his distress at the ribald parody. With characteristic good
sense, Twining, who had not yet read the parody, urged Burney
not to be so foolish: 'If there was the least *shade* of seriousness in
your *shill-I-shall-I* about going on with your work, you deserve to
be threshed. Shall the envy & illnature of such a fellow be allowed
to weigh a grain against the general approbation your introductory
little works have met with?'[8] The parody, so Twining argued, was
an indirect tribute to the fame of Burney's own *Musical Tours*.

Burney evidently found little comfort in such arguments. By
mid-October 1774 Twining had read 'Joel Collier', admitted that
it was 'perfectly blackguard, & . . . *sub-beastical*', but rejoiced that
the anonymous critic in the *Monthly Review* had 'treated him
properly'. He ended with another serious warning to Burney: 'If
you would give one farthing to annihilate the book, & all memory

---

[5] Bewley to Burney, 5 Sept. 1774 (Osborn Collection).

[6] li (1774), 242.

[7] xliii (1774), 499–500. Other reviews or extracts appeared in the *St. James's
Magazine*, i (Aug. 1774), 302–4; *Scots Magazine*, xxxvi (Sept. 1774), 491;
Weekly Miscellany (5 Sept. 1774), ii. 535–40.

[8] Twining to Burney, 17 Sept. 1774, copy (British Library, Add. MS. 39933,
fos. 114–15).

of it, you are a vain man.'[9] Twining's comment seems to substantiate an assertion made many years later by J. T. Smith: 'The Doctor was rendered uncomfortable beyond measure, by the publication of a small work, in which he was ridiculed under the appellation of "Joel Collyer." Upon this squib, he, according to calculations, expended full two hundred pounds in buying up copies wherever they were offered for sale.'[10] F. J. Fétis later explained the rarity of the parody with a similar story,[11] which, given Burney's concern for his reputation and dignity, is far from impossible. Yet any such attempt to suppress a book could have only one result. A letter from William Bewley early in May 1775 reveals that, at Burney's insistence, he had read a second edition of 'Joel Collier', which contained some 'execrable . . . Additions', including a 'mortally stupid' reply to his own review, and he had already seen an advertisement for a third edition, which was to be further enlarged. Even Bewley now began to think that Burney was being far too sensitive about the parody: 'How could you be so serious about that Joel Collier!'[12] After the success of the first volume of his *History of Music* in the following year, Burney could no doubt afford to forget, or at least ignore, 'Joel Collier'. The author of the parody was evidently not, as Bewley had at first assumed, some easily identifiable '*personal* enemy'. According to Fanny d'Arblay in 1832, her father 'imagined it . . . the work of some stranger, excited solely by the desire of making money from his own risible ideas; without caring whom they might harass, or how they might irritate. . . .' That the parody was simply as opportunist as Fanny suggested is unlikely, as will become clear, nor was she correct in her comfortable assertion that the parody had few readers and was never reprinted.[13] After its first appearance in 1774, there was a second edition before the end of the year, a third in 1775, a fourth in 1776, a 'new edition' in 1785, and a somewhat renovated version, *Joel Collier Redivivus*, in 1818.

---

[9] Twining to Burney, 13 Oct. 1774, copy (British Library, Add. MS. 39933, fos. 116–17).
[10] *Nollekens and his Times*, 2 vols. (1828), i. 196.
[11] *Biographie universelle des musiciens* (2nd edn., Paris, 1860–5), ii. 336.
[12] Bewley to Burney, 1 May 1775 (Osborn Collection).
[13] *Memoirs of Doctor Burney*, 3 vols. (1832), i. 258–60.

II

The author of Joel Collier's *Musical Travels Through England* has never been finally identified,[14] although nine names have been suggested at various times, several of which will still be found unpredictably or in bewildering combinations in library catalogues and reference works. Before the claims of the various candidates are considered, some account of the parody itself should be given.

The Dedication of the first edition, addressed 'To The Governors of the Hospital for the Maintenance and Education of exposed and deserted young Children', at once suggests that this is no opportunistic piece of hack-work. 'Collier' had considered dedicating his book to Burney himself, as 'the original inventor of this species of composition, and the first musical traveller of our nation, to whom I stand so much indebted for the plan, and conduct of my book' (p. iii). But the recent attempt by Burney and Giardini to establish a Music School in the Foundling Hospital had persuaded the author to address his *Travels* with heavy sarcasm to the Governors of the Hospital. (The Dedication was written before the failure of Burney's Plan on 3 August.) In prose which has at times considerable satiric edge, the Dedication expresses the attitudes which animate the rest of the book, most notably a profound suspicion of the corruption of manly English virtues by decadent foreign sophistication. Burney is ridiculed not so much personally as for his enthusiasm for Italian music and for his plan, symbolic of the decadence feared by the parodist, of converting the Foundling Hospital into a Music School modelled on the Italian *conservatorios* Burney had seen and admired in Italy in 1770. Such a plan marked, for 'Joel Collier', 'the dawn of an *Augustan* era', although he admitted that

men of narrow and contracted minds, who have neither *ear*, nor *voice*, nor *hand*, will still imagine, that it might prove of more national utility, to breed these adopted children of the public, to *Husbandry*, *Navigation*, &c. the objects of their original destinations; than to convert one of the noblest of our public charities into a nursery for the supply of musical performers at our Theatres, gardens, and hops.—But this is a vulgar prejudice . . . when we have rivalled the *Italians* in music, it will be time

---

[14] In my biography of Burney in 1965 I stated my conclusions about the authorship without any exposition of the evidence assembled here. Percy Scholes, *The Great Doctor Burney*, 2 vols. (1948), i. 272–5, mentioned only four editions of the parody and reached no conclusions about its authorship.

to think of our navy, and our agriculture. We have already (to our shame be it spoken) better sailors than fidlers, and more farmers than *contrapuntists*. (p. vi)

Collier's musical journey is a coarse, spirited, and often amusing burlesque of Burney's accounts of his travels on the Continent. He first describes his childhood in the village of Gotham[15] and his (truly) 'uncommon musical propensities'. Some personal knowledge of Burney's provincial origins and years in Norfolk may lie behind Collier's statement that he has been 'well inform'd that the infancy, and indeed the riper years of the great Mus.D. or musical Doctor (whom I call, *par excellence*, DR. MUS) passed in much the same manner' (pp. 4-5). Before setting out on his own musical journey, he decided to change his name 'from *Collier* to *Coglioni* or *Collioni*, as more euphonious' (p. 5). The parodist's intention in naming his hero with the Italian word for testicles is explained by Burney's preoccupation during his visit to Italy with the problem of the source of supply of *castrati*. The figure of the *castrato* is a recurrent topic of humour throughout the parody, representative of the threatened emasculation of English virtues by a taste for foreign music.

Collier's travels take him to Lincoln, Sheffield, York, Darlington, Durham, Carlisle, and Bristol, with extravagant comic interludes at each place. In imitation of Burney's interviews with musical celebrities on the Continent, Collier visits Dr. Dilletanti at Lincoln, who eats, drinks, and, indeed, performs all bodily functions, including 'conjugal endearments', in strict musical time; Dr. Hiccup at York, a musical 'enthusiast', who imitates that 'great and devout musician, King *David*' by dancing half-naked with a harp, and whose daily life is recorded by Collier with a bathetic detail which parodies Burney's accounts of the domestic habits of Gluck and other composers; Mr. Eccho of Durham, who conversed only by means of his violin; and Mr. Quaver of Carlisle, who aimed at recovering prelapsarian musical harmony by ingeniously devising concerts of animals, which include a singing she-ass, and a duet between a cat and a raven. (The leading performer, a counter-tenor pig, was indisposed after 'rolling too long upon an unaired dunghill'.)[16]

---

[15] There may be an allusion to the musical satire in Charles Churchill's *Gotham. A Poem* (1764), i. 117-58.

[16] In his copy of the parody (see note 32 below), Francis Douce noted several

Stylistically, Burney is parodied by the use or misuse of his musical jargon and of his more pretentious or quaint phrases in ludicrous contexts. Some more precise details of his *Tours* are mocked. Lord Sandwich's assistance is glanced at when Collier declares that 'I was neither patronized, nor franked on my tour by any Dillettante Lord' (p. 6). Collier's journey by sea from Carlisle to Bristol is a travesty of Burney's intrepid voyage down the Danube by raft, Collier remarking that he lacked 'Dr. MUS's lousy blanket' (p. 36). The most offensive personal reflection on Burney occurs at the end of Collier's journey, when a young lady of Bristol, anxious to persuade him that he would be much happier if emasculated, 'advised me by all means to undergo the operation as the Doctor had done in *Italy*, tho' his excess of modesty prevented him from boasting of it in his excellent treatise' (pp. 45–6).

Collier is indeed finally castrated by an enraged barber with whose wife he is discovered *in flagrante* and thus painfully attains his ambition to become a *castrato* ('I . . . found my powers wonderfully improved, and my execution delicate, interesting, and full of effects'—p. 53.) There is a final return to the sarcasm of the opening:

If they [his *Travels*] tend in any shape to promote the study and practice of music in this country, and by that means lessen our national reproach of being *The savages of Europe*, immersed in politics, philosophy, metaphysics, mathematics, and other sour and abstruse speculations, I shall have gained my end, and shall congratulate myself on having in some humble degree assisted the generous efforts of the great musical Doctor, and the governors of the *Foundling Hospital*, to polish and *Italianize* the genius, taste, and manners of the *English* nation. (pp. 58–9)

A second edition of the parody was published less than four months later (in mid-December 1774,[17] but with '1775' on the title-page). The text received careful stylistic revision and fifty-

examples of a tradition of 'animal concerts' on the Continent from the early sixteenth century. Closer to home, however, is an amusing 'letter from Mrs. Mary Midnight to the Royal Society, containing some new and curious Improvements upon the Cat-Organ' in Christopher Smart's *The Midwife*, i (1750), 98–103.

[17] The *Public Advertiser*, Sat. 10 Dec. 1774, announced its publication on the following Monday, but the copy for 12 Dec. is missing from the Bodleian file. It was advertised as 'published' for the rest of the week.

three pages were added to the original fifty-nine, Collier's voyage from Carlisle to Bristol being replaced by a land-route which takes him to Lancaster, Liverpool, Chester, Wolverhampton, Birmingham, and Worcester. Although Collier's new adventures are of very much the same order as in the first edition,[18] the purpose of the satire is clarified in various ways. Burney is now referred to directly instead of as 'Dr. MUS', and the title-page depicts a cat playing a fiddle and sitting upon rifles laid over a drum which bears the royal initials, suggesting the triumph of musical triviality over England's manlier qualities. This theme remains the dominant preoccupation of the book, as the ingenuous Collier, earnestly aping the jargon and manners of an Italian musician, or of an Englishman (like Burney) obsessed with a taste for foreign music, is subjected to repeated abuse and beatings. His efforts to perform on his favourite bassoon are usually greeted with derision, his consolation being that

in former times *Romulus* and *Alfred*, and in the present Signior *Giardini*, and Dr. *Burney*, have met with similar treatment; though the first pair introduced arts and civilization into their respective countries, and the second have attempted a greater action, that of castrating the children of the Foundling Hospital. (p. 70)

A number of additional footnotes in the second edition make explicit the parallels with Burney's own *Tours* and give the source of quotations from them. Burney's own opinions are at times cited to support the satirist. Burney himself had not been insensitive to the harsh contrast between the 'affluence and luxury' of the musical German courts he had visited and the poverty of the common people, and Collier quotes one such passage to support his own statement that 'the wild notes of liberty, and the quaverings of Italian airs, can never be heard together in concert' (p. 87). Another long note replies directly to Bewley's abusive review of the first edition. The anonymous reviewer is in fact introduced in person as a villainous character in the additional narrative, but the footnote contains a passage of full seriousness, which denies that any personal malice against Burney had been intended and argues

---

[18] The satirist does, however, include some miscellaneous material which had come to his attention recently. Collier's visit to Beverley (pp. 21–5) is added primarily to comment on corruption among the trustees of a charitable foundation in Yorkshire, which had been described in the *Gentleman's Magazine*, xliv (Sept. 1774), 490.

that criticism or burlesque of any voluntarily published work is justifiable (p. 78 n.). The parodist appears to have been genuinely angry that his book should have been dismissed simply as malicious personal abuse. The note trails off, however, into an attack on reviewers in general and on Lord Chesterfield. Elsewhere Burney's patron, Lord Sandwich, receives some extra attention, particularly in his aspirations as a drummer (p. 6 n.).[19] The combination in Sandwich of a reputedly corrupt government minister and a prominent musical dilettante exemplified precisely what most offended the satirist. A less predictable new object of mockery is 'Mr. Garrick's celebrated *Ode on Shakespeare*', which Garrick had recited at the Shakespeare Jubilee at Stratford in 1769 (pp. 45–6).

The third edition, which appeared on 28 April 1775,[20] consists of sheets of the second edition with a new title-page and the addition of a 28-page Appendix, 'Containing An Authentic Account Of the Author's Last Illness and Death. By Nat. Collier, School-Master'. References in this additional narrative to a Dr. Hipps indicate that an incidental target of the satire is Dr. William Hawes's pamphlet narrative of the last illness of Oliver Goldsmith, which was attracting attention at this time.[21] But in general the style of this account of Joel Collier's death, supposedly by his cousin, is noticeably more earnest and severe than the main burlesque narrative and suggests the possibility that the Appendix is the work of another hand. After a late conversion to Methodism, Collier had come to condemn 'the levities of his former life' in a manner which, as his cousin notes, was unlike his 'usual conversation . . . both in stile and sentiment' (p. 12). Not only Italianate music but all fashionable accomplishments are now derided. Dancing-schools 'were seminaries of debauchery; and . . . all amusements of the same kind, though more fashionable and polite, were liable to the same imputation' (pp. 3–4). There is a new concern with the inadequacies of female education: 'to destroy all natural delicacy, and to impart an artificial sensibility, both to

[19] For Sandwich as a drummer see Cradock, *Literary and Miscellaneous Memoirs* (1828), i. 117, 122, iv. 172, and Laetitia M. Hawkins *Memoirs, Anecdotes, Facts and Opinions* (1824), i. 307–8 n.

[20] *Public Advertiser*, 28 Apr. 1775. The second edition of Burney's *German Tour* had been published on 4 March 1775. The 'Appendix' could be obtained separately and is therefore sometimes to be found bound up with copies of the first and second editions of the parody.

[21] *An Account of the Late Dr. Goldsmith's Illness* (1774; three editions).

mind and body, is the avowed end of all present female education'
(p. 6). Eventually the complete degeneration of English society is
envisaged:

our noblemen are become fiddlers instead of statesmen, and their wives
and daughters have exchanged the modest and amiable qualities which
once adorned them, for meretricious airs, and a meretricious conduct . . .
libertinism is increased at the expence of honourable love, domestic
discord invades the peace of families, fiddlers, opera-dancers, and hair-
dressers stain the bed of nobles; and every disorder which is the sure
forerunner of national destruction extends its ravages in this devoted
country. (pp. 10–11)

In such a context, Burney himself is merely symptomatic of
larger ills when the satirist describes the decline of modern
literature from earlier strenuous ideals:

Is some fiddler weary of officiating at boarding-schools, and directing
the vibrations of young ladies' fingers?—he commences writer, deluges
us with music, and fills large volumes with pompous anecdotes of
superannuated castrati. (p. 21)

Such comedy as remains in the narrative of Collier's last days
tends to be submerged beneath harsh irony and denunciations of a
degenerate society. Lord Chesterfield and Patrick Brydone's *Tour
Through Sicily and Malta* (1773) receive similar treatment in the
'Appendix', which finally returns, however, to Joel Collier's
original model and hero:

when this nation shall cease to be formidable by its fleets and armies;
when commerce, and honesty, and liberty, shall have abandoned us;
when our statesmen and patriots alike shall be changed into pimps and
fiddlers; and the whole science of government shall have become the
art of extorting money from a corrupt and miserable people: even at that
period, so immensely distant, (if one may judge from the present happy
and contrary state of things) shall the name of COLLIER survive, and
share the admiration of posterity with those of GUADAGNI and Doctor BURNEY. (p. 28)

The fourth edition of the parody appeared in 1776, perhaps in
response to the publication of the first volume of Burney's *History*.
Apart from further careful stylistic revision and some minor
expansion, various notes are added (supposedly by Nat. Collier).
The most significant addition is a footnote on the issues of slavery

and American independence, introduced rather irrelevantly through an account of Collier's father, who is said to have been transported to America for fourteen years and to have returned ardent for liberty. The added footnote dwells on the contradiction between American treatment of Negro slaves and their 'rage for Liberty and Independence' (pp. 4–5 n.). The 'new' (fifth) edition of Collier's *Musical Travels*, which appeared in a smaller format and with an unaltered text in 1785, may have been reissued to greet the publication of Burney's *Account of the Commemoration of Handel* in that year. The parody's final appearance as *Joel Collier Redivivus* in 1818 almost certainly has little relevance to the present investigation. The original text is retained in an abridged form, the more indelicate passages (notably Collier's castration) are omitted, and most of the references to Burney removed, and the original footnotes are replaced by new notes adapting the satire rather awkwardly to John Bernard Logier (1777–1846), a music-teacher whose controversial techniques of teaching the piano aroused considerable controversy at that time.[22] It is hard to believe that, forty-four years after the first appearance of 'Joel Collier', the original author had clumsily revised his parody of Burney merely to mock a minor musician.

III

In a letter to Burney of 18 May 1776 Thomas Twining commented: 'Well, but your letter—voyons—Joel Collier in the Fleet! I always understood it was Kenrick himself. Pray tell me who.'[23] No subsequent explanation of Burney's hint has survived. Twining had identified 'Joel Collier' as William Kenrick (1725–1779), who at various times had attacked several members of the Johnson Circle in print. The only feasible explanation of Burney's phrase 'in the Fleet' is that he believed that his parodist was Archibald Campbell (1726?–80). Described by Boswell as 'a Scotch purser in the navy', Campbell had published two satires

---

[22] Logier's main 'innovations' were the 'gamut board' and the 'Chiroplast', a contrivance which was claimed to facilitate piano-teaching. The *Quarterly Musical Magazine and Review*, i (1818), 111–39, summarizes and reviews six pamphlets published in response to Logier's claims, and there were several others, including *The Musical Tour of Dr. Minim* (1818), an apparent imitation of 'Joel Collier'.

[23] British Library, Add. MS. 39933, fo. 96.

on Johnson's style in 1767, *Lexiphanes* and *The Sale of Authors*.[24]
Always a reverent admirer of Johnson, Burney may merely have
been seeking consolation in the possibility that he had been satir-
ized by the same writer as his idol.

No more substance appears to lie behind other early attributions.
The name of George Steevens, the formidable Shakespeare
scholar to whom malicious literary attacks were regularly (often
erroneously) ascribed, was inevitably mentioned.[25] Lord Sandwich
and Dr. Johnson, both incidental targets in the parody, at first
believed that Soame Jenyns, the poet and wit, was the culprit.
'Ha! (said Johnson) I thought I had given *him* enough of it',
Boswell records; but Boswell goes on to describe the parody
confidently as 'the late Mr. Bicknell's humorous performance'.[26]
J. T. Smith in 1828 was equally confident about its authorship:
'after the death of Mr. Bicknell, it was discovered among that
gentleman's papers, that he wrote it.'[27] But which Mr. Bicknell?
In the mid-nineteenth century, F. J. Fétis vaguely attributed the
early editions of 'Joel Collier' to 'un musicien nommé *Bicknell*',
but, with much more conviction and probably definite evidence,
identified *Joel Collier Redivivus* of 1818 as the work of 'M. Georges
Veal, alto de l'orchestre de l'opéra italien, à Londres'.[28] From
Fétis derives the strangely garbled article by Edward Heron-Allen
in the *Dictionary of National Biography* (iv.803), which ascribes *all*
editions of the parody to the mysterious George Veal, an attribution still followed in many library catalogues. Other catalogues
and reference works identify 'Mr. Bicknell' as Alexander Bicknell,
a miscellaneous writer of the period, sometimes in combination
with Peter Beckford, the author of the once-popular *Thoughts on
Hunting* (1781).[29]

---

[24] *Life of Johnson*, ed. G. B. Hill and L. F. Powell, 6 vols. (Oxford, 1934–50),
ii.44 and n. Hawkins, in his *Life of Johnson* (1787), had first ascribed *Lexiphanes*
to Kenrick and then in the second edition (p. 347) to Campbell, who 'as well for
the malignancy of his heart as his terrific countenance, was called horrible
Campbell'.

[25] Smith, *Nollekens and his Times*, ii. 196–7.

[26] Cradock, *Literary Memoirs and Correspondence*, iv. 168; Hill–Powell, i.
315. The references to Johnson occur in the Appendix to the third edition of the
parody.

[27] See note 25 above.

[28] See note 11 above. A T. G. Veal published *Oswald, a Tale; with other Poems*
in 1818.

[29] S. A. Allibone, *A Critical Dictionary of English Literature*, 3 vols. 1877), i.

Since Alexander Bicknell did not die until 1796, Boswell must have had someone else in mind when he referred in 1791 to 'the late Mr. Bicknell'. Precisely who, is clear from an entry in the *European Magazine*, which recorded the death on 27 March 1787 of 'John Bicknell, esq. Barrister at Law, author of the Musical Travels of Joel Collyer, and the Dying Negro, a Poem'.[30] This attribution may well have been made by William Seward the anecdotist, a close friend of Bicknell and later a frequent contributor to the *European Magazine*. Seward had introduced Boswell to Bicknell on 18 November 1786, four months before Bicknell's death,[31] and Boswell's later confident identification of the parodist would hardly have been made without Seward's authority.

The attribution of the parody to John Bicknell is strengthened, if also complicated, by a series of notes made by the antiquarian Francis Douce in his copy of 'Joel Collier'.[32] Beneath an inserted portrait of Thomas Day, Douce wrote: 'He is said to have written Joel Collier in conjunction with J. B. Esq.^{e}' Another note records that 'Thomas Day has been mentioned as the joint author of Joel Collier; but I have been informed that Mr Beckford wrote it in conjunction with John Bicknell.' Bicknell's is the name which recurs in these ascriptions and it may be assumed that he is the subject of yet another note by Douce, which refers to 'The pleasant and ingenious author of Joel Collier's travels, of whom I had some knowledge before his untimely death', especially as both Douce and Bicknell were members of the legal profession and Bicknell had died in his early forties.

If Douce's notes confirm Bicknell's involvement in the parody, they also add to our perplexity. There is nothing in the career of Peter Beckford, a wealthy music-lover who had spent several years in Italy in the 1760s, to suggest a motive for an attack on Burney

---

410. Allibone's source for this attribution may have been the anonymous *Fly Leaves; or, Scraps and Sketches, Literary, Bibliographical, and Miscellaneous . . . Second Series* (1855), pp. 71–2, to which Mr. Michael Kassler drew my attention.

[30] *European Magazine*, xi (1787), 296.

[31] *Private Papers of James Boswell*, ed. G. Scott and F. A. Pottle, 18 vols. (New York, 1928–34), xvii. 10.

[32] Douce's copy of the second edition is in the Bodleian Library. A copy of the fourth edition in the Bodleian has a manuscript attribution to Bicknell, probably transcribed directly from the *European Magazine*.

or his love of Italian music.[33] And why should the high-minded Thomas Day, author of *Sandford and Merton*, a famous early book for children, have been involved in a parody of Burney? What becomes clear is that it is impossible to pursue the shadowy figure of John Bicknell without encountering the uncompromising Thomas Day at every turn, and the following curious narrative will attempt to provide the circumstantial evidence that they collaborated in the parody.

IV

John Bicknell (1746?–87)[34] was the closest friend of Thomas Day (1748–89) during their school-days at Charterhouse in the late 1750s and early 1760s, when William Seward was a fellow-pupil.[35] Thereafter their paths separated for a time. Bicknell was admitted to the Middle Temple, while Day went to Corpus Christi College, Oxford, in 1764. Day quickly became a staunch admirer of Rousseau's educational theories and a somewhat priggish believer in a severe simplicity of dress and manners. In a letter of 1769 to Richard Lovell Edgeworth, like Day a Corpus man and an admirer of Rousseau, Day declared that 'Were all the books in the world to be destroyed . . . the second book I should wish to save, after the Bible, would be Rousseau's *Emilius*.'[36] Anna Seward, the Swan of Lichfield, who came to know Day well, described him at this period as 'a rigid moralist, who proudly imposed on himself cold abstinence, even from the most innocent pleasures. . . . For that mass of human character which constitutes polished society, he avowed a sovereign contempt. . . .'

After a tentative and unsuccessful courtship of Edgeworth's sister, Day blamed his rejection on 'the modern plans of female education, attributing to their influence the fickleness which had stung him'. He remained intent on marriage, but equally determined that his wife should accommodate herself to his own rigor-

[33] See A. Henry Higginson, *Peter Beckford Esquire: Sportsman, Traveller, Man of Letters* (1937), pp. 82–6.

[34] A. S. Bicknell, *Five Pedigrees* (1912), pp. 20–1, 26–7.

[35] The story of Thomas Day and Sabrina Sidney has been told many times. The fullest and most reliable account is G. W. Gignilliat, *The Author of Sandford and Merton* (New York, 1932). The following narrative is based, however, on the original sources.

[36] *Memoirs of Richard Lovell Edgeworth, Esq. Begun by Himself and Concluded by his Daughter, Maria Edgeworth*, 2 vols. (1820), i. 236.

ously 'systematic ideas'. She was to be sufficiently educated to be a fit companion for his intended seclusion from a corrupt world and to train his children 'to stubborn virtue and high exertion'. In addition, she was to be 'simple as a mountain girl, in her dress, her diet, and her manners; fearless and intrepid as the Spartan wives and Roman heroines'. Since Day was unlikely to find many volunteers for this self-sacrificing role, he decided to select and train a girl to be his wife according to his own specifications. The most promising material for his purpose would be an orphan, uncorrupted by sophisticated education, whose training could be accomplished without parental interference.[37]

Day came to London and entered the Middle Temple in the summer of 1769, the year in which he became twenty-one and gained control of the considerable estate left him by his father. He lived at this period, 'on terms of intimate friendship', with John Bicknell, who agreed to help Day's scheme. The youthful Day was not obviously the most suitable guardian for a female child, but Bicknell, slightly older and 'of taintless reputation', was prepared to vouch for his friend's integrity. Edgeworth, a married man, assisted less voluntarily. Before the end of the year he discovered that he had acquired as a nominal apprentice a pretty twelve-year-old girl, whom the bachelors Day and Bicknell had selected from the branch of the Foundling Hospital established at Shrewsbury and whom Day had decided to name Sabrina Sidney. To make doubly sure of the success of the scheme, Day and Bicknell also visited the Foundling Hospital in London and chose an eleven-year-old blonde, whom Day called Lucretia, as a companion for Sabrina.[38] If the apparent ease with which Day was able to take charge of the two girls has always seemed surprising, it should be remembered that the main aim of the Foundling Hospital was to apprentice the children in its care (though usually in a more conventional manner), that fairly strict conditions had to be complied with, and that at precisely this period the Governors of the Hospital were concerned about the much larger number of girls than of boys in the institution. (In 1769 there were 428 boys and 1,038 girls.) As a further gesture, on 27 December 1769,

[37] Anna Seward, *Memoirs of the Life of Dr. Darwin* (1804), pp. 33–5; cf. James Keir, *An Account of the Life and Writings of Thomas Day, Esq.* (1791), pp. 27–9.

[38] Seward, pp. 35–7; Edgeworth, i. 214–16.

'Thomas Day, Esq.' of Barehill, near Maidenhead, Berks., became a Governor of the Foundling Hospital, no doubt on payment of a handsome subscription.[39]

Day felt that he could begin the education of the girls most easily outside England and set off at once for France. According to Anna Seward, he soon found that the girls were unresponsive to his severe and idealistic schemes of instruction. He also found France distasteful and wrote scornfully to Edgeworth about French attachment to exteriors and lack of 'manliness of sentiment and strength of reason'. Day had returned to England by the spring of 1770. He had found Lucretia unpromising material for his purpose and she was accordingly placed with 'a chamber milliner', eventually married, and so disappeared from Day's life. Sabrina was sent temporarily to stay in the country with Bicknell's mother but re-joined Day in the summer of 1770 at Lichfield, where he took a house until the following year and became friendly with a circle which included Anna Seward, Erasmus Darwin, Edgeworth, and other local intellectuals. Day continued Sabrina's 'education', which included various ordeals to test her fortitude, such as firing pistols by her ears and dropping melted sealing-wax on her arms.

By 1771, however, Day decided that Sabrina was too old to remain with propriety in his house and he 'put her to a very respectable boarding-school at Sutton Coldfield'. His views on education had not changed: 'Here it was intended, that she should improve in reading, writing and arithmetic, and in all the useful species of accomplishments. To make a musician or a dancer of his pupil was far from his wish.' Day's attention turned meanwhile to Miss Honora Sneyd, a young lady whom he had met at Lichfield. His courtship ended painfully when Honora refused to adapt herself to the 'plan of life' upon which Day insisted for his wife. He then turned to her sister, Elizabeth Sneyd, his attachment to whom eventually overcame his deep-rooted horror of polite manners and accomplishments. Elizabeth objected to Day's 'austere singularities of air, habit and address' and, accompanied by Edgeworth, Day gallantly resolved, against all his principles, to go to Paris for a year, and commit himself to dancing and fencing masters. He did so; stood daily an hour or two in frames, to screw back

[39] R. H. Nichols and F. A. Wray, *The History of the Foundling Hospital* (1935), pp. 175–7, 182, 191. 382.

his shoulders, and point his feet; he practised the military gait, the fashionable bow, minuets, and cotillions; but it was too late; habits, so long fixed, could no more than *partially* be overcome.

The result was worse than ever. On his return to England late in 1772, Elizabeth Sneyd found the grotesquely half-polished Day even less appealing than his ungainly former self. Day was wretchedly disappointed: after the humiliation of surrendering his principles and of submitting to the follies and tortures of French dancing-masters, his rejection left him obsessively convinced of the stupidity of contemporary female education and deeply suspicious of the foreign sophistication which he had so conspicuously failed to acquire. His pain was not eased by Honora Sneyd's marriage in the summer of 1773 to his close friend R. L. Edgeworth, who would also in due course marry the other object of Day's admiration, her sister Elizabeth.[40]

In 1773 Day returned to the Middle Temple, where Bicknell was pursuing an easy-going life as a barrister and minor writer. Edgeworth, who had come to know Bicknell through Day, considered him 'a man of uncommon abilities', 'a man of nice discrimination, sound judgement, and various conversation'.[41] In the summer of 1773 Bicknell was working on a poem, based on a true incident, entitled *The Dying Negro*, supposedly written by a Negro separated from his intended wife by enslavement. The subject appealed to Day in his particular emotional state and he wrote an extensive addition to the poem: the evidence suggests that Bicknell wrote 161 lines and Day 146 of the final version. Apart from depicting the pangs of frustrated love, *The Dying Negro* describes the innocent, noble, and manly Africans trapped and enslaved by arrogant, avaricious, degenerate, if supposedly 'civilized', Europeans. Published by July 1773, *The Dying Negro* was one of the first and most successful poems on what would become a familiar theme before the end of the century.[42]

Day's thoughts had meanwhile turned back to Sabrina, now an attractive girl of sixteen, and he resumed his plan of marrying her.

[40] The preceding two paragraphs are based on Seward, pp. 37–45 and Edgeworth, i. 223–4, 240–73. See also *The Life of Mary Anne Schimmel Penninck*, ed. C. C. Hankin, 2 vols. (1858), i. 12.

[41] Edgeworth, i. 187. For satirical paragraphs in newspapers written (according to William Seward) by Bicknell and erroneously attributed at the time to George Steevens, see *Gentleman's Magazine*, lxx (1800), 180.

[42] For the composition of the poem see Gignilliat, pp. 102–10.

All went well until a trivial failure on her part to obey one of his
severe injunctions as to simplicity of dress convinced him of her
lack of attachment and 'want of strength of mind', and he 'quitted
her for ever'. This parting probably occurred early in 1774.
Sabrina was sent away with a female companion to live on an
allowance of £50 a year, boarding first at Birmingham and later in
Shropshire, though still visiting her friends in Lichfield from time
to time.[43]

Day returned to London, eventually purchasing chambers in the
Temple. Enough will have been said to illustrate his hatred of
decadent sophistication, superficial refinements, and polite accomplishments, which was no mere Rousseauistic idealism, but an
obsessive conviction born of cruel humiliation under the dancing-
masters of France and the mocking laughter of the young women
he had courted and lost. Day rationalized his personal failings into
a harsh condemnation of contemporary education, especially that
of females, although, as his later career showed, he also had a
genuine concern for the poor and under-privileged. It can hardly
be doubted that so dominating and dogmatic a figure would have
had a strong influence on his close friend, John Bicknell, an
intelligent but lazy lawyer, who amused himself by writing poetry
and letters to the press. *The Dying Negro* itself is sufficient evidence
of such similarity of outlook.

Thomas Day was also a Governor of the Foundling Hospital.
The Plan for establishing a Music School on the Italian model in
the Hospital was offered to the Governors by Burney and Giardini on 20 July 1774 and finally rejected on 3 August. On 20 August
the *Musical Travels* of Joel Collier appeared, sharply attacking the
Governors for their original acceptance of the Plan, coarsely mocking Burney, and depicting this imitation of degenerate foreign
taste as a last step in the degradation and emasculation of England.
It would be convenient if it could be demonstrated that Day was
present at any of the meetings of Governors, particularly that of
3 August, at which he would no doubt have enjoyed hearing what
Burney later deplored as 'the Cant of Music Corrupting the
Morals of a people'. A letter of 10 August, however, reveals that
by then Day was in Holland engaged in a three-week tour of that
country. At about the same time, he wrote to Bicknell about the
second edition of *The Dying Negro*, but without any reference to

[43] Edgeworth, i. 337-40; Keir, p. 29; Seward, p. 50.

events at the Foundling Hospital (at least in the available extract).[44] It remains possible that, as one of the Governors, Day had known of Burney's scheme before leaving England and had urged Bicknell to attack it as vigorously as possible, but this is mere speculation. What seems perfectly understandable is that Bicknell, imbued with Day's ideas but with his own fondness for robust comedy, should have written the first version of Collier's *Travels*.

In August, Day expected to remain abroad until October and may have returned briefly to England then, but was in Brussels early in 1775. It seems certain that the expanded second edition of Collier's *Travels*, published in mid-December 1774, was still entirely the work of Bicknell. Day was brought back to England in February 1775 by news of the illness of his friend Dr. William Small of Birmingham, who died on 25 February a few hours before Day's arrival.[45] Greatly upset by Small's death at the age of forty, Day returned to the Middle Temple to try to lose his grief in legal work. He was called to the Bar on 14 May 1775. In the previous March he had written to a friend of Small's, 'Steal from disagreeable reflection by whatever means fortune suggests'.[46] Late in April 1775 the third edition of 'Joel Collier' was published, expanded by the addition of an Appendix. As has already been suggested, Joel Collier's conversion to Methodism and the persona of his cousin Nat. Collier permit a new style in the Appendix, which drives home the main but more scattered points of the earlier editions of the parody with an unexpectedly intense irony and earnestness. In these attacks, not merely on degenerate musical taste but on dancing-schools and the follies of female education, the more rigorous and even obsessive contribution of Thomas Day is to be detected.

Not long after the publication of the third edition of 'Joel Collier', Day and Bicknell brought out a third edition of *The Dying Negro*, to which they had added a dedication to Rousseau. The hand of Day is clearly visible in the sharp attack on modern decadence:

Let the present age enjoy the boldest panegyrics its admirers can bestow. But if our boasted improvements, and frivolous politeness, be

[44] Thomas Lowndes, *Tracts in Prose and Verse*, 2 vols. (1827), ii. 3–6; J. J. C. Timaeus, *Thomas Day, Esqr; Das Leben eines der edelsten Männer unser Jahrhunderts* (Leipzig, [1798]), p. 185.
[45] Gignilliat, p. 120.   [46] Ibid., pp. 121–2.

well acquired by the loss of manly firmness and independence, if in order to feel as men it be necessary to adopt the manners of women, let us at least be consistent, nor mingle the excesses of barbarism with the weaknesses of civilisation. (pp. vii–viii)

A later passage exposed the contradiction between the practice of slavery and growing American demands for liberty:

Yet, such is the inconsistency of mankind! these are the men whose clamours for liberty and independence are heard across the Atlantic Ocean!... Let the wild inconsistent claims of America prevail, when they shall be unmixed with the clank of chains, and the groans of anguish. (p. ix)

The most significant addition to the fourth edition of 'Joel Collier' in 1776, as has been recorded above, is a long note on America, similarly objecting to

that rage for Liberty and Independence which has been for full ten years past the characteristic of that country; and which Mr. Burke in his last printed speech very ingeniously attributes to that Elevation of Sentiment which he says is only to be acquired by flogging negro-slaves. (p. 5 n.)

Once the War of Independence had begun, Day's attitude changed to whole-hearted support for the American cause.[47] During 1776 he published several works on the subject, one of them, a poem called *The Devoted Legions*, being an attack on the war with America addressed to the commanders of the British forces. Day's idiosyncratic and slightly archaic use of the word 'devoted', to mean 'doomed' or 'cursed', in his title recalls a passage in the Appendix to 'Joel Collier', which refers to 'this devoted country' (p. 11).

Both Bicknell and Day died at relatively early ages and the rest of the story can be quickly summarized. Day at last married in August 1778, having found in Esther Milnes a young woman who was fully prepared to adapt herself to his rigorous demands and whose only shortcoming in his eyes was her wealth. In particular, she was required to give up the accomplishments acquired during her 'polite' education: 'Music, in which she was a distinguished

---

[47] During the 1770s there were many Americans in the Middle Temple, one of whom, John Laurens, became a close friend of Bicknell and Day. Bicknell named his elder son after Laurens, who died fighting the British in 1782. See Keir, pp. 114–17.

proficient, was deemed trivial. She banished her harpsichord and music-books.'[48] Miss Milnes had been educated during the 1760s at a large boarding-school for girls in Queen Square in London, almost certainly the same boarding-school at which Burney taught from the early 1760s until 1776, so that, ironically, he may well have been responsible for the musical proficiency of which her husband disapproved.[49]

After his marriage Day increasingly devoted himself to agriculture, philanthropy, and political reform, his political activities continuing until 1785, with the familiar theme of 'singing, fiddling, Frenchified Britain' often to be found in his writings.[50] By then he had already started publishing *Sandford and Merton* (3 vols., 1783-9), a children's book which remained extremely popular to the end of the nineteenth century. Even Dr. Burney thought highly of the story, and the copies which he presented to his daughter Fanny have survived, with the cheerful recommendatory verses which he sent with the second volume (dated 18 April 1786) still affixed.[51] Burney may not have read the story with close attention, however, for Day's dislike of music and musicians is evident in *Sandford and Merton*, often closely linked with his views on female education:

As to music, though Miss Simmons had a very agreeable voice, and could sing several simple songs in a pleasing manner, she was entirely ignorant of it; her uncle used to say that human life is not long enough to throw away so much time upon the science of making a noise . . . I have never seen any good, would he say, from the importation of foreign manners . . . to what purpose should I labour to take off the difficulty of conversing with foreigners, and to promote her intercourse with barbers, valets, dancing-masters, and adventurers of every description, that are continually doing us the honour to come amongst us.

We encourage a vicious indolence and inactivity, which we falsely call delicacy; instead of hardening their minds by the severer principle of reason and philosophy, we breed them to useless arts, which terminate in vanity and sensuality. In most of the countries which I had visited,

[48] Seward, p. 48.

[49] Thomas Lowndes, *Select Miscellaneous Productions, of Mrs. Day and Thomas Day, Esq. In Verse and Prose* (1805), pp. 31, 129; Lonsdale, *Dr. Charles Burney* (1965), pp. 54, 227.

[50] *Reflections upon England and America* (5th edn., 1783), p. 27.

[51] Yale University Library. 'See, see! my dear Fan,/Here comes, spick & span/Little Sandford & Merton/Without stain or dirt on. . . .'

they are taught nothing of a higher nature than a few modifications of
the voice, or useless postures of the body . . .[52]

These and similar passages make it unnecessary to try to evoke
Day's reaction to a scheme to turn foundling girls into Italianate
singers. Suffice it to say that James Keir in 1791 described the
story's purpose as 'to guard the rising generations against the
infection of the ostentatious luxury and effeminacy of the age'.[53]

Day died in September 1789, after a fall from his horse. John
Bicknell meanwhile had continued his career as a lawyer. Maria
Edgeworth tells us that

He lived in London, partly engaged by pleasure, and partly pursuing
his profession of the law. . . . But he had some of the too usual faults of
a man of genius; he detested the drudgery of business. He is said to
have kept briefs an unconscionable time in his pocket, or on his table,
unnoticed. Attorneys complained, but still he consoled himself with wit,
literature, and pleasure, till health as well as attorneys began to fail.[54]

In the early 1780s, as his health deteriorated, Bicknell remembered
Sabrina Sidney, the girl whom he had helped Day to choose from
the Foundling Hospital at Shrewsbury some fifteen years earlier
and who had since been leading a secluded life in the country.
Bicknell visited Sabrina, now aged about twenty-five, fell in love
and married her, probably in 1784. Thomas Day seems not to
have approved of the match but handed over to his friend the £500
dowry which he had formerly agreed to allow Sabrina in the event
of her marriage.[55] Bicknell's health did not improve and he died
a few years later in March 1787, leaving Sabrina to support their
two infant sons, Henry Edgeworth Bicknell and John Laurens
Bicknell. Thomas Day made Sabrina a small allowance, which his
wife continued after his death, and Richard Lovell Edgeworth also
apparently made an annual contribution.[56] But Bicknell had left

---

[52] *Sandford and Merton, The Original Edition Unabridged* [1890], pp. 238–9,
371. The phrase, 'the science of making a noise', in the first quotation recalls
phrases in the dedication to the second edition of 'Joel Collier': the children of
the Founding Hospital will be given 'an opportunity of making a *noise* in the
world' by Burney's 'Plan' and will study 'the science of sound' (p. iv).

[53] Keir, p. 80.

[54] Edgeworth, ii. 110–11.

[55] Seward, pp. 51–2; Edgeworth, ii. 113. William Seward printed an undated
letter from Day to Bicknell on the subject of the latter's ill health in the *European
Magazine*, xxviii (1795), 21–2.

[56] Seward, pp. 53–4; *Cornhill Magazine*, lxiii (1927), 676.

Sabrina in a difficult financial position, which forced her 'to labour for her daily bread, in a situation scarce above that of a common servant'. Eventually the legal profession raised some £800 for her support. Anna Seward was active in urging George Hardinge, the eminent lawyer, to collect this money, as a series of her letters in 1788 and 1789 reveals, one of them also throwing unexpected light on the character of John Bicknell himself. She wrote to Hardinge in March 1789,

> The evidence you bring of Mr. B——'s bachelor voluptuousness, is irresistibly strong. I suppose Mr. Day knew it not, or, with his general abhorrence of sensuality, he had spared to mention him with so much esteem:—but, Lord! what a pale, maidenish-looking animal for a voluptuary!—so reserved as were his manners!—and his countenance!—a very tablet, upon which the ten commandments seemed written.[57]

Such information about Bicknell would have possible relevance only if it were to be doubted that a close friend of Thomas Day— Day himself being, according to Edgeworth, 'the most virtuous human being whom I have ever known . . . I never knew him swerve from the strictest morality in words or action'[58]— could have written a somewhat scurrilous satire on the respectable Dr. Burney.

V

It must be emphasized that the purpose of the preceding investigation has not been to propose a new identification of the author of Joel Collier's *Musical Travels* but to provide evidence to substantiate a perfectly sound and early attribution, which has simply been submerged by the number of other candidates. That Bicknell wrote the parody is irrefutable, and the striking coincidences between the content and purpose of the parody, especially its Appendix, and the known views of Thomas Day, his connection with the Foundling Hospital, his hatred of foreign sophistication, and his attitude to America, make his involvement in the parody at a late stage extremely likely.

With the deaths of Bicknell and Day it might seem that this

---

[57] *Letters of Anna Seward*, 6 vols. (Edinburgh, 1811), ii. 250; see also ii. 176, 195, 234–5, and her *Life of Darwin*, pp. 52–3.

[58] Edgeworth, i. 182. An obituary notice of Day from an unidentified newspaper, inserted in Douce's copy of the parody, states that Day 'attained, as near as is given to humanity, the summit of virtue'.

narrative of so many curious events had reached its conclusion. Yet a postscript must be added, in which further ironies will emerge. Among the former friends of John Bicknell who concerned themselves about the fate of the widowed Sabrina and her two infant sons was William Seward, and he it was who was responsible for bringing Sabrina's predicament to the attention of another old Carthusian, Dr. Burney's second son, Charles Burney, the Greek scholar and schoolmaster.[59] Two months after her husband's death, Sabrina wrote to Charles Burney to offer her 'ardent & most greatful thanks' for his offer to take her elder son into his boarding-school, then at Hammersmith. Although John Laurens Bicknell was still too young, she hoped that the offer might be accepted later:

I assure you good Sir I shall have the most perfect satisfaction in his being under your care & I am well convinced if he is so disposed, he may receive from you impressions that will tend to his future welfare and happiness. I do not presume to say this from my own judgement, but from a far superior one, that of my dear dear lost friend, whome [sic] I have often heard express great regard & respect for you & your abilities.[60]

Nothing is known about Charles Burney's earlier acquaintance with John Bicknell, apart from the fact that, like Day, Bicknell, and Seward, he had been educated at Charterhouse, which he entered in 1768. There is no reason why he should have been aware that Bicknell had written the ribald parody of his father's *Musical Tours*, which had caused the elder Burney so much distress. Yet Charles, like his father, would certainly notice Boswell's attribution of the parody to Bicknell when they assiduously read their copies of the *Life of Johnson* in 1791. By then, however, or within at the most a month or two, Sabrina Bicknell had become a member of the younger Burney's household and remained in it when the school moved to Greenwich in 1793. In 1804 Anna Seward concluded her narrative of Thomas Day and Sabrina by relating that

That excellent woman has lived many years, and yet lives with the good

---

[59] This is one of the 'hard' facts to emerge from Madame d'Arblay's highly imaginative narrative of Day and Sabrina in her French Exercise Book I, quoted in her *Journals and Letters*, ed. Joyce Hemlow *et al.*, v (Oxford, 1975), 6 n.

[60] Sabrina Bicknell to Charles Burney, Junior, 16 May 1787 (Osborn Collection).

Dr. Burney of Greenwich, as his housekeeper, and assistant in the cares of his academy. She is treated by him, and his friends, with every mark of esteem and respect due to a gentlewoman, and one whose virtues entitle her to universal approbation.[61]

The Burney papers provide plenty of evidence of Sabrina's popularity. Fanny rarely wrote at any length to her brother after 1791 without a respectful inquiry about Mrs. Bicknell, as did many of Charles's friends and former pupils of his school. When the school passed to Dr. Charles Parr Burney, after his father's death in 1817, Mrs. Bicknell remained, and, some forty years after entering the household of the second Dr. Burney, she was still serving the third. She died at Greenwich on 8 September 1843, some seventy-four years after Thomas Day and John Bicknell had chosen her from the orphanage at Shrewsbury.[62]

As for the first Dr. Burney, who had undoubtedly learned in 1791, if not earlier, that John Bicknell had been his parodist, there is no evidence about his attitude to Sabrina's presence in his son's household. Sensitive to the end of his life to all the affronts and disappointments of his long career, he may nevertheless have been able to forget the mockery of Joel Collier when, as must often have been the case, he met Mrs. Bicknell at his son's house.

John Laurens Bicknell (1785/6–1845), the elder son, was educated at Charles Burney's school and, like many members of the family, followed a highly respectable legal career, became a F.R.S. and F.S.A., solicitor to Chelsea and Greenwich Hospitals, one of the founders of the Westminster Bank, and a trustee of Sir John Soane's Museum. Although he can hardly have remembered him, he seems to have been acutely conscious of his father. When Anna Seward told something like the full story of Thomas Day and Sabrina for the first time in her *Memoirs of Dr. Darwin* in 1804, young Bicknell, then aged eighteen or nineteen, was deeply shocked to learn about his mother's origins and sent Miss Seward

---

[61] Seward, *Life of Darwin*, pp. 53–4.

[62] In the possession of Mr. Michael Burney-Cumming is a receipt, dated 1 Nov. 1843 and signed by Sabrina's executors (including her sons Henry and John), for the sum of £3,290 0s. 7¼d. owed to her estate by Dr. Burney's grandson, Charles Parr Burney. Apparently the Burneys had been saving part of Sabrina's salary for her throughout her long period in their service. This is suggested by Madame d'Arblay's description of her brother, at an early stage of Sabrina's employment, as 'un bienfaicteur pour sa fortune': see note 59 above.

an outraged letter of protest, which greatly upset her.[63] Maria
Edgeworth may have heard about the violent correspondence
which followed. She had already given a fictionalized version of
the Day–Sabrina story in her novel *Belinda* (1801).[64] When, after
her father's death, she was preparing to publish his *Memoirs*, in
which the fullest account yet of the strange narrative was told, she
took the precaution of consulting Mrs. Bicknell.

Miss Edgeworth visited Sabrina at Greenwich on 15 October
1818 and they went through the relevant sections of the manuscript of the *Memoirs* together. Mrs. Bicknell asked for some
blurring of the events connecting her with the Foundling Hospital, 'on account of her sons', especially John Laurens Bicknell:

He was dreadfully shocked a few years ago by meeting with his origin
or his mother's origin in Miss Sewards life of Darwin. He was just then
in weak health. He had never heard the circumstances before. . . . He
came to his mother in such a state of irritation as she could not describe.
He has high spirit and was violently enraged with Miss Seward. They
had a furious paper war.

Miss Edgeworth was surprised to find Mrs. Bicknell 'a stirring
housekeeper', without any of the 'softness and timidity' Thomas
Day had formerly complained of. 'She spoke . . . of Mr. Day as
having made her miserable—*a slave* &c! It was a very painful visit
to me.'[65]

At some point John Laurens Bicknell learned about his father's
authorship of the parody of Dr. Burney and was no doubt torn
between loyalty to his father and his sense of indebtedness to the
Burneys. Like his father he was a minor and very miscellaneous
writer with a satiric bent. In 1820 he published a collection entitled
Original Miscellanies, in Prose and Verse, which was dedicated to
his school-fellow Charles Parr Burney 'and other members of the
Burney Club', which Charles Burney seems to have established
for former members of his school. Bicknell includes a long and
glowing tribute to 'our late excellent friend and master', who had
died three years earlier. The collection includes a continuation of

---

[63] *Journals and Correspondence of Thomas Sedgewick Whalley*, ed. Hill Wick-
ham, 2 vols. (1863), ii. 263–4.
[64] Marilyn Butler, *Maria Edgeworth: a Literary Biography* (Oxford, 1972),
p. 243.
[65] Maria Edgeworth, *Letters from England 1813–1844*, ed. Christina Colvin
(Oxford, 1971), pp. 109, 121–2. Cf. *Memoirs of R. L. Edgeworth*, ii. 114.

his father's poem *The Dying Negro* and, most interestingly, 'Sarah Lloyd; A Burlesque Novel'. At first sight, it might appear rash to insist on any significant connection between this satire and 'Joel Collier', for similarities of tone and method could be explained away merely as burlesque conventions. There is some mockery of the fondness for minutiae found in travel books, which recalls a passage in 'Joel Collier', and some fun is made of fashionable music, but hardly enough to constitute an imitation of his father. The most surprising feature of 'Sarah Lloyd' is an open—though apologetic—parody of an episode from Fanny Burney's *Cecilia* (1782).[66] In the circumstances this was surely a dangerous joke, and at least one contemporary was quick to note the resemblance between 'Sarah Lloyd' and 'Joel Collier'. A writer in *Blackwood's Magazine* in February 1820 described the burlesque novel as 'something in the style of "The Musical Travels of Joel Collier", written by the author's father'.[67] Fascination with his father's offensive parody perhaps compelled John Laurens Bicknell to return to the approximate scene of the paternal crime.

The evidence that J. L. Bicknell knew of his father's authorship of the parody is provided by the musicologist William Ayrton (1777–1858). In a note, dated 12 October 1842, in his copy of the third edition of 'Joel Collier', Ayrton stated that the younger Bicknell had admitted to him that his father wrote the parody but had 'expressed his regret that the work was ever published, adding, that he had bought up every copy he could find—often at an exorbitant price—and had invariably destroyed all that he had purchased'.[68] It seems likely that F. J. Fétis had heard a similar story, possibly from Ayrton himself, to support his explanation of the rarity of a book which had enjoyed five editions in eleven years: 'Les familles de Burney et de Bicknell en ont fait disparaître un grand nombre'.[69] In view of the close involvement

---

[66] 'Sarah Lloyd', pp. 20, 24–5 n., 121–2.

[67] vi. 584. I am indebted for this reference to Mrs. Jamie Kassler. This passage provides more evidence, if more is needed, for the ascription to John Bicknell of the original parody of Dr. Burney.

[68] Ayrton's copy appears as item 332 in the sale of his library by Puttick and Simpson on 3 July 1858. It is described (with minor variants in the passages quoted) in Catalogues 21 (1966; item 1075) and 45 (1974; item 216) issued by Messrs. T. and L. Hannas of Bromley, Kent. I have been unable to trace the present location of this book.

[69] See note 11 above.

of Mrs. Bicknell and her sons with the Burneys, and their indebtedness to them, the explanation makes perfect sense.

This narrative, with its many unpredictable ramifications, must at last reach a conclusion, resisting such tempting avenues of inquiry as the fact that John Bicknell's niece Maria became, after an arduous courtship, the wife of John Constable the painter. Little has been said, it must be admitted, about *Joel Collier Redivivus*, George Veal's adaptation of the satire aimed at J. B. Logier's 'Chiroplast', a controversial mechanism for teaching the piano. New and strange ironic vistas seemed about to open up with the discovery that the Minutes of the Foundling Hospital for August 1818 record an offer from 'A M. Logier . . . to take four girls as apprentices for three years in order to send them out as "Teachers of a New Method of Musical Tuition to Ladies' Schools in the Country"'.[70] Fortunately, the story had not come full circle, for Logier's application was not accepted.

Two hundred years, therefore, after Day and Bicknell reported the death of Joel Collier, that remarkable musical traveller, buffoon, bassoonist, castrato, and Methodist convert, can perhaps be decently laid to rest—if not, as he himself had modestly suggested on his death-bed, should Parliament so decree, 'in Westminster-abbey, near the tomb of *Handel*'.

[70] Nichols and Wray, *History of the Foundling Hospital*, p. 198.

Pursuing Sheridan

Cecil Price

In 1951 I received a letter from the representative of a well-known firm of general publishers, saying that he had read a note I had published in *The Library* on the suppressed Edinburgh edition of Chesterfield's *Letters to his Son* and would like to have a chat with me about it when he next came to Aberystwyth. He had an excellent knowledge of eighteenth-century bibliography so I expected nothing more than agreeable conversation on our common interests, though I probably hoped he would want something written on Chesterfield. The meeting proved to be a pleasant one: we had tea, walked along the promenade, talked of this and that; then, just before he caught his train, he mentioned that his firm had in hand a new series of books for students, and asked if I would be willing to write one on either Fielding or Sheridan. He gave me time to think over a decision and I turned towards Sheridan because I already had in hand some unpublished material concerning him.

At that time I was preparing a doctoral thesis on a totally different period so my progress with the short book was fitful, but I found some opportunities of checking the standard works and was surprised to find more errors, omissions, and wrong interpretations than I recalled from my earlier reading. I gradually became convinced that a basic re-assessment was necessary and, once the thesis was out of the way, decided to try and compile an edition of Sheridan's letters. I reasoned that by this means I would get to know the man thoroughly and would be well able to understand his writing habits, based as these usually are on certain traits of character. From this I might go on to a biography, an edition of the dramatic works, and, eventually a short book for students distilling all I had learned. I did not realize then that the best short book for students is often written by the man who does not know too much about the subject.

My first task was to discover how many letters were available. A personal search at the British Museum and very kind responses from William Van Lennep at Harvard and Charles Beecher Hogan at Yale, revealed that at least four hundred might be used if their custodians would release them. The British Museum required me to obtain the permission of the owner of copyright but could offer me no help in identifying him or her, and this became quite a piece of research in itself. In due course microfilm copies began to arrive and the edition to take shape.

At this stage I first heard from Jim Osborn. He wrote: 'It is good news to hear that you are preparing an edition of the letters of Sheridan. Such an undertaking has long been desirable, though it will try your soul before you finally see it in print.' The year was 1955 and my soul was to undergo eleven years' trial and be found wanting. He was equally far-sighted when he advised me to establish the status of the edition: 'Most collectors like to feel that their property is going into the definitive edition, so it is best to make use of the assurance, when obtained.' He sent me details of the eleven letters by Sheridan that he possessed and, as the years went by, consulted me from time to time about Sheridan correspondence that came on the market. He did not believe in throwing money away and liked to feel that the price paid was a reasonable one. By the time my edition appeared in print, he owned the best collection of Sheridan letters in private hands, and had shown in their acquisition that combination of common sense and astuteness I had learned to associate with him. He had the endearing habit of making his correspondent feel a generous collaborator in building up a monument to scholarship, when all the time the kindness and helpfulness lay entirely on his side. He took such a keen personal interest in the progress of the edition that I could not do less than dedicate it to him.

I was fortunate in looking for material at a time when several important collections came up for auction at Sotheby's. In 1952, Miss M. J. M. Grubbe disposed of a series of letters between Sheridan and her ancestor, John Grubb, concerning the financial affairs of Drury Lane Theatre between 1795 and 1799. They were bought by the Harvard Theatre Collection, but Miss Grubbe still had others in her possession and was most generous in lending them to me. In 1954, Lady Wavertree's collection of her ancestor's works and correspondence was brought from New Zealand to be sold in London. In 1955 and 1957, the Comtesse de Renéville parted with some excellent letters by Sheridan and other members of the family circle. Another thirty letters came up in 1957 as 'the property of a gentleman'. I set about finding the names of their new owners and was frequently gratified to learn that the material had become the property of collectors who had already shown themselves to be very well disposed towards my edition.

The search became exciting in itself. Hardly a week passed without some new information coming my way. My inquiries sent to librarians abroad and visits to libraries and record offices in Britain proved to be very profitable, and my debts of gratitude mounted daily. Goodwill was apparent, even though there were a few people who did not reply to my letters and not even to the fourth epistle. There came a day, too, when I was working in the National Library of Wales and a colleague, John Williams, asked me if I had seen the Sheridan letter there. I had to admit that I knew nothing of it: my inquiries had gone around the world but I had missed a source close at hand. There is the usual moral in this, I suppose.

When the letters had been located, they had to be transcribed. This was not always easy. Writing to the Prince Regent or to some aristocratic friend, Sheridan's hand is—once it is known—quite legible and even elegant, but in the day-to-day press of engagements at Drury Lane or St. Stephen's, or the kind of evening at the Shakespeare Tavern when he wrote 'about thirty letters, which he tied up in a handkerchief, and then resigned himself to conversation', too many of the missives had the appearance of being written with a skewer.

Once they had yielded up their secrets, an even more onerous task presented itself. Over thirteen hundred letters were eventually printed, wholly or in summary, but four-fifths of them bore no date or docketing to indicate the time when they were written. Placing them in sequence became the most difficult part of the editing. Sometimes a date was found in the countermark and was of some use, but usually the sole clues were in allusions scattered about the letters. I came to the conclusion that the only course open to me was to read as widely as possible in the correspondence of the period and to go through the parliamentary and theatrical records as thoroughly as I could. This meant working through many magazines and newspapers as well as the microfilm of *The Times* for the appropriate years. When my eyes began to rebel, I projected the film on to a white wall and took in the words in greater comfort.

Sometimes the puzzles solved themselves. One example of this comes back to my memory without prompting because its reference to 'Mr Budd's Pall-Mall' baffled me for a long time. The Historical Society of Pennsylvania had provided me with a photograph of this hasty letter written by Sheridan and saying that Mr. Budd was welcome to print the pamphlet on the India Bills but that the dramatist could not lend him a copy. At first sight it seemed likely to belong to three or four years after 1788 when the pamphlet, *A Comparative Statement*, appeared. Eventually, however, I came upon a passage in Francis Horner's *Memoirs* stating that in September 1804, Horner put his name down 'in the list of a new club to which Fox, Windham, Sheridan, etc. belong . . . this club meets at Budd's in Pall Mall.' This was just what I wanted.

A couple of very satisfying dates came from *The Times*. One of them settled several questions concerning a Yale letter with a watermark of 1802 and the heading 'Sunday night'. On this occasion, Sheridan had written to his second wife mentioning a Carlton House dinner at which his epigrams were appreciated by the Prince. He added, 'I think "My Trunk" might amuse your Mother and Henry and the Epigrams too.' Thomas Moore had printed 'My Trunk' in his biography of Sheridan, but had not dated it, so I had to wait until I read *The Times* of 4 February 1811 before I understood the circumstances: 'A few evenings since, as Mrs. Sheridan was coming to town in her carriage from Barnes to her house in Queen Street, Mayfair, a portmanteau, containing lace, silk, and valuable articles to a considerable amount, was cut from behind the carriage, with which the robbers made their escape.' The verses of 'My Trunk' then appear as a lamentation by Mrs. Sheridan at its loss. With this clue it was easy to discover from the *Diaries of Sylvester Douglas* that the Prince and his friends had dined together at Carlton House on 27 January 1811, and to find that the three epigrams by Sheridan had been printed in the *British Press*, 30 January 1811, over the signature 'No Toad Eater'.

The other date was connected with a letter written on 'Sunday' and to a 'Most recreant Major'. References to Byng at Brentford brought me eventually to *The Times* of 1807, and in the issue of 15 June there were allusions that made much of the letter comprehensible, once we allow for Sheridan's sense of humour. The Major was William Augustus Downs, who had organized a subscription fund for the purpose of scrutinizing votes in the Brentford election, but had then paid out cheques to Guy Fawkes, the Drury Lane Society of performers on the marrow-bone and cleavers, as well as other unworthy characters. It was now possible to date the letter with certainty '17 May 1807'.

Unfortunately it was not possible to be equally sure of the accuracy of the text. When I had collated the passage printed in the Morrison Catalogue with that given by Messrs Maggs in one of theirs, I had found several variants and had written to the booksellers to ask if the letter were still for sale. As always, they were very obliging but had to say that it had been recently disposed of and that they could give me the purchaser's name but not his address. The name was not one I knew, but six or eight months later it appeared again in The *Times Literary Supplement* as that of the author of a book being reviewed. The subject had no connection with the theatre but I took the chance of writing to the author care of his publishers and I received a helpful reply. He happened to be a friend of Laurence Harvey and had given the letter to him as a birthday present. I duly wrote to the actor and my letter found him in San Francisco. He replied saying that I should see the text as soon as he returned. When time went by and I wrote again, he answered rather ruefully that a change had taken place in his domestic circumstances and he had mislaid the letter. It never came to light, so I printed the text and indicated the variants. No doubt the original will come to hand again one day and it will be possible to judge, once and for all, between the versions.

By these far from direct paths I plodded on towards my goal. Fortunately I had been encouraged by the Clarendon Press to go on with the project and had learned that an early result was not expected. I guessed that the work would take me three years and was counselled to allow five. By the summer of 1960 I had before me an annotated typescript of all the letters I had found.

Many of the texts were based on photographs and the time had come to check them against the originals in the United States. At this point I was fortunate enough to be awarded a fellowship at the Folger Shakespeare Library, then under the forceful direction of Louis B. Wright. It contained an immense amount of background material of interest to me as well as the Drury Lane Theatre account books for the period of Sheridan's management. I was soon able to place more accurate dates on some of the most difficult letters. Dorothy Mason was particularly helpful for she was able to lay a finger instantly on whatever was likely to help me in those plagues of the researcher, unindexed extra-illustrated volumes.

I also paid briefer visits to the other great libraries of the north-eastern states, and marvelled at the richness of their eighteenth-century material. At Yale, Jim Osborn was delighted to show me his new acquisitions and to suggest new sources of information. I returned home with the highest possible respect for American scholarship in my field and for the generosity of American curators and collectors.

My delight at having made such splendid progress in a few months was increased in an unusual way. I discovered that the photographer of one of the letters in a microfilm sent to me had forgotten to photograph the docket, and that this now revealed a date that tallied exactly with the one I had tentatively placed on the letter. This gave me an access of confidence and made me feel equal to completing my task without further delay.

I have now learned to distrust that feeling because in my experi-ence things rarely work out so conveniently. For one reason or another—and all of them good—I did not make any real progress for another fifteen months. The typescript finally went to the Press in late 1963.

Twelve months later, when proofs were fairly advanced, a very long letter by Sheridan was offered for sale. It was unpublished and was most interesting because it expressed in forthright terms his personal indignation at certain proposals made by Garrick. Harvard Theatre Collection bought it at a high figure but very generously made it available to me for publication. It had been in the possession of an elderly lady who had written to me many years earlier to say that she owned nothing of importance. I had accepted her word but now it dawned on me that however well disposed elderly people may be towards a request, they do not always recall what they own.

My edition of the letters was published on 7 July 1966, exactly 150 years from the day of Sheridan's death, but I was glad to find that the publicity given it in reviews brought to the surface very few new letters. For the time being there was a lull.

I hoped this would continue indefinitely, but five years later the estate of Clare Sheridan came up for auction and it included quite a number of letters not in my edition. I had written to her, too, many years before, and she had immediately responded by saying that the 'half-dozen' letters she possessed she had given to another member of the family. I saw these, but knew nothing of the treasures that had slipped out of her memory. Her forgetfulness was not at all surprising: the letters had been collected by, or had come down to, her husband, Wilfred Sheridan, and had been lost sight of after he had been killed in battle in 1915. Mrs. Sheridan's later career had been nomadic and eventful.

The cache included manuscripts of sections of Sheridan's plays, a mass of paper dealing with his management of Drury Lane Theatre, some very interesting letters to his second wife, and eleven to John Hosier, a trustee of the playhouse. There was much else, and I felt some chagrin at the thought that such a good collection had eluded me. Fortunately many of the letters fell into the hands of benevolent people or well-disposed institutions, and I have been able to make copies of a considerable number.[1]

Many of them had also appeared in typescript copies in Lady Wavertree's collection and (silently correcting obvious typing errors) I had already used them as the source of my text. Now that I had the opportunity of collating them with the originals, I found few errors of much importance, though proper names, as usual, had sometimes been misread. Sheridan's letter to his brother on 2 April 1782 illustrates what I mean. At one point, neither the Wavertree version nor Fraser Rae's makes good sense: Wavertree read 'now France'; Rae, 'man Foine'. This merely demonstrates again the difficulties presented by Sheridan's handwriting, for guessing does not help much. The letter is now in the possession of William LeFanu, who has kindly informed me that the words are 'mon Frère'.

A number of other letters have come slowly into the auction rooms. Many concern that intractable and rather tedious subject, money; others seek posts for relatives and acquaintances. The affairs (and particularly the debts) of Drury Lane Theatre are frequently mentioned. Political opinions are aired, and political events described. There are others that are peculiarly personal in character and that hold our attention even when they are almost baffling. Four of them I should have dearly liked to quote in my

[1] See, for example, C. Price, 'The Clare Sheridan MSS. in the British Theatre Museum', *Theatre Notebook*, xxix (1975), 51–6.

edition, however I now have the consolation of printing them here. I have not solved all the puzzles, but I can at least suggest some rather interesting possibilities.

The first one is the simplest. Only a brief catalogue entry concerning it appeared in my edition (Letter no. 41), but now we have it in full, though without the name of the recipient. The letter is in Robert H. Taylor's collection, and is full of the jaunty self-confidence of the young dramatist:

My dear Sir,
     As I have at Present a great deal of scrib[b]ling on my Hands I won't lose time in attacking, as I should otherwise do, your doubtful manner of asking me for so trifling a Thing as a Prologue.—I shall set about it immediately, and shall be very happy if I can produce any thing on the Hint you give, if not you must be content with what comes/Yours very sincerely/R B Sheridan

Jan. 15th: 76

G[reat] Queen-Street.

The letter contains a note on the verso that reads, 'Richd. Brinsley Sheridan promising a Prologue, which of course never was written.'

The next letter is also from Mr. Taylor's collection, but is not so easily dated:

My dear Sir,
     I thank you very sincerely for your Letter—but am sorry to say I have not title to the word congratulate—Mrs. Sheridan has lately thought herself so safe that she was perswaded not to observe the caution she has used for some time past of not going into a carriage—the consequence is that she was yesterday taken ill and an infant not six months old brought into the world to live an hour!—Nothing could be more distressing to me at any time—but I shall certainly be attentive to the Point you mention as I assure you my Feelings as an Author are at present very much absorbed in my apprehension for her.—/I am, dear Sir,/yours sincerely/and affect[ionately]/R B Sheridan

Wednesday

Elizabeth Sheridan had a number of miscarriages, but on Tuesday, 6 May 1777, gave birth to a still-born child that may possibly be the same as the one described by her husband. If the letter were written next day, Sheridan's 'Feelings as an Author' would have been concerned with the imminent first performance of *The School for Scandal* on the Thursday of that week. The tone of the letter is rather like that of his later correspondence with David Garrick, and the great actor himself wrote on the following Monday to inquire about Mrs. Sheridan's health and to say that he was 'mad about the *School*'.[2] If this seems flippant after Sheridan's serious tone, we should recall that the *General Evening Post*, 10–13 May 1777, reported that 'Mrs. Sheridan, who on Friday last was thought to be in imminent danger, is so much better that the gentlemen of the faculty who attend her give it as their opinion, that she is safe, and in a fair way of recovery.' My interpretation is conjectural, but in default of more plausible facts, it may be acceptable.

The next letter is in the Osborn Collection; it bears the date 'Dec. 29th:' in Sheridan's hand, and '1792' in that of a contemporary. To my knowledge it has never been mentioned before, and it gives us an insight into Sheridan's puzzling behaviour in the six months after Elizabeth's death.

Early in that year she had given birth to a child, this time by Lord Edward Fitzgerald. In June tuberculosis had caused her death. Sheridan was overcome by grief but, some months later, fell in love with Pamela, the nineteen-year-old beauty who was said to be the daughter of Madame de Silléry[3] by Philippe Égalité. They stayed with Sheridan at his house in Isleworth and, at the end of November, he, his son Tom, and a friend named George Reid, accompanied them to Dover. After five days' delay caused by contrary winds, Sheridan and Tom saw Reid and the ladies off on the packet-boat. Madame de Silléry says that Sheridan 'would have crossed with us, but that some indispensable duty, at that moment, required his presence in England'.[4] It is not difficult to understand what kept him behind: the Whigs were squabbling among themselves and rumours of changes in the administration were heard. *The Times*, 1 December 1792, said that it was possible that in a new government Sheridan would become Secretary in Ireland.

In its issue of 26 December, it printed a paragraph that was

---

[2] *The Letters of David Garrick*, ed. D. M. Little and G. M. Kahrl (Cambridge, Mass., 1963), iii. 1163.

[3] Earlier and better known as Madame de Genlis.

[4] T. Moore, *Memoirs of . . . Sheridan* (2nd edn., 1825), ii. 196.

altogether more personal: 'It is said that a treaty of marriage is on the tapis between Richard Brinsley Sheridan, Esq., and Miss Pamela, a near relation of Philippe Egalité, and the companion of Mademoiselle d'Orleans.' Lord Edward Fitzgerald now met Pamela in France and was instantly reminded of Elizabeth. Madame de Silléry completes the story: 'Nous arrivâmes à Tournay dans les premiers jours de Décembre de cette même année, 1792. Trois semaines après j'eus le bonheur de marier ma fille d'adoption, l'angélique Paméla, à Lord Edouard Fitzgérald.'[5]

Sheridan makes no reference to this development in his letter of 29 December, and it is unlikely he knew about it until four days later, when Lord Edward and his bride arrived in London. The letter is, as so often, a collection of excuses, but it raises an important question: to whom is it addressed? Possibly George Reid was the recipient, though we should have expected him to stop in Paris rather than go on to Tournai. Could it have been sent to Pamela? The tone is far from passionate, but it is delicately deferential and we are bound to wonder why about eight lines are missing from the manuscript. The letter (which may well be a draft) reads:

This moment I receive your Letter and I must write but one Line or I shall lose the opportunity of sending this: I give you my word of Honor that I have never received a single Line from Mad. S. since that from Calais—and I have been in the greatest suspense and anxiety in consequence because the moment I found that I must delay my coming to Paris, which I meant however to delay only to the present time when Parliament will adjourn for three weeks, I wrote a very very *long Letter* to Mad. S. I know that it is impossible that she could have received it. I am sure she would have replied to it if she had.—that they have open'd here all letters to or from France I have known for some time— but there has been a fatality in their with[h]olding Letters which could answer no Purpose to them. how inconsistent and unfeeling you must have thought me and now when I hoped to have surprised you at Tournay War and Public Folly are raising new Obstacles.

I admit my Friend that from appearances you ought to have reproach'd me still more—but have I no claim in my turn

[*about 4 lines missing*]

. . . least interest?

Pray tell me however by what conveyance your Letter was sent—it was not by the Post and it has been nearly three weeks coming to me.

[5] T. Moore, *The Life and Death of Lord Edward Fitzgerald* (2nd edn., 1831), i. 179.

I must not now stop to tell you the rage I have been in at the ungrateful Decrees which I hope however will be heard no more of. adieu I will write to Mad. S. by the next Post. Mr Rose[6] is at my request now in search of you, for I really began to fear the Autho[rity?] had seized you all
[*about 4 lines missing*]
Tom is with me and I will make him write for himself.
I shall be most impatient to hear from you./R B Sheridan

London
Dec. 29th:

As far as I am aware, the letter has never been mentioned by any writer on Sheridan, but it is striking because it belongs to a period of his life when comparatively little is known about him, one in which he seemed about to be gratified with rich rewards of a political and an emotional kind but was vouchsafed neither.

The last letter I shall quote also needs interpretation. It seems to concern Reynolds's portrait of Elizabeth Sheridan as St. Cecilia, exhibited at the Royal Academy in 1775 and owned by Sheridan. Eventually it came into the hands of Henry Burgess, the dramatist's solicitor, but the tone suggests that the letter was sent to some other possible purchaser. Since Sir William Beechey had made a copy of the picture for Sheridan, I take it that Beechey had also given advice on the value of the original.

Saville-Row
Thursday Evening Novr: 23d [1815]

Private
My Dear Sir
My friend P. Moore undertook to call on you from me to Day—I shall part from this Picture as from Drops of my Hearts blood, and therefore it is that I now think S[i]r W Beechey's advice right that the advance upon it should be it's fair estimated value, and by regular Purchase. I enclose you a line of introduction to S[i]r William. I have only to add, what I am not ashamed to own to YOU, that an IMMEDIATE accommodation will be the service and accommodation conferr'd on ME. —with respect to the more important object we discuss'd yesterday you shall hear from me in a few Days—/very truly your's/R B Sheridan.

The letter is now in the Manuscript Division of the Australian National Library, Canberra.

[6] Probably John Hurford Stone, who had given Sheridan his French address as ' "Rose, Huissier", under cover of the President of the National Convention'.

These letters indicate Sheridan's protean character, but there are still sides of his nature that are not revealed in any great detail. His confidence in his ability to produce a prologue without difficulty seems, in the above instance at least, not to have been justified, and it would be useful if new letters could be found that provided us with more information about his creative powers and methods. His bond with his first wife is well illustrated in the example I have already given, but only one fragment of a letter to her is extant. Their relationship in his creative period was so important that it is greatly to be hoped that vaults and archives will soon yield up their secrets. Sheridan was at his best when writing to women and we would welcome more notes to Lady Bessborough in the playful, witty tone of the only one that is extant. So the pursuit goes on in the hope that we may put together eventually a speaking likeness of one of the most distinguished figures in our theatrical and political history.[7]

[7] I am greatly obliged to the late James M. Osborn and to Mr. Robert H. Taylor as well as to the Yale University Library and the Australian National Library for permission to print these unpublished letters, and am also grateful to Dr. Stephen Parks for kind assistance.

The Application of Thought to an Eighteenth-Century Text: *The School for Scandal*

F. W. BATESON

I

IN AN exuberant moment Fredson Bowers once described the editing of eighteenth-century English literature as 'a field that has usually been one of the disgraces of scholarship'. No evidence was provided to justify the insulting generalization—which will be found on page 24 of Bowers's *Textual and Literary Criticism* (Cambridge, 1959) and has, of course, no basis whatever in fact— and it might be thought charitable to overlook this *lapsus linguae* by a scholar we all respect. But the invocation of 'scholarship', by which Bowers meant textual expertise, raises central problems of editorial procedure not confined to the eighteenth century that are still unresolved. Even at the merely textual level W. W. Greg and R. B. McKerrow, and their vocal followers on both sides of the Atlantic, have only opened a debate—sometimes far too dogmatically. Why, for example, should the accidentals of a first edition be preferred, as Bowers has done in his edition of Dekker's plays, to the spelling system evident in an author's autograph manuscripts?[1] And in any case what information of literary significance is obtainable from the occasional authorial spellings that slip through the compositors' normalizations? All right. Shakespeare did prefer the spelling *scilens*, as Pope preferred the spelling *shew*. So what?

The most serious methodological objection that can be made to what Bowers has called 'biblio-textual' research is that, though it may enable us to correct a *misprint* (a term in which I include any miscopying, even to the careless omission of a letter or word

---

[1] I have elaborated this objection in my *Essays in Critical Dissent* (1972), pp. 26–7.

in the author's own 'foul papers'), it is helpless before authorial *revision*. An editor's ambition, among his many other duties, is to establish a definitive text of whatever the work of literature is on which he is engaged. And this means that he must not only correct misprints but also from time to time decide whether in a particular passage the original reading should stand or he should substitute a revision (or one of several revisions) that is clearly by the author. The preferred reading will then be incorporated into the text, those that have been rejected being tucked away either in small print at the bottom of the page or in a special textual appendix at the end of the explanatory notes. Whichever method is used for recording the rejected readings, only one reader probably in a hundred will realize that the passage exists in an alternative form that is often quite as authentic as that sanctified in the text. And only one reader in a thousand will know that between the preferred form and those rejected the choice has often had to be made on totally irrational grounds. The text would sometimes have been better if the editor had just tossed up a coin. Heads, for example, *sullied* (in the first line of Hamlet's first soliloquy), of which the *sallied* of Q1 and Q2 is presumably a misprint; tails *solid* as in F1.

Greg's ruling on the matter, which he modestly agrees is 'frankly subjective', will be found in 'The Rationale of Copy-Text' (*Collected Papers*, p. 387):

Granting that the fact of revision (or correction) is established, an editor should in every case of variation ask himself (1) whether the original reading is one that can reasonably be attributed to the author, and (2) whether the later reading is one that the author can reasonably be supposed to have substituted for the former. If the answer to the first question is negative, then the later reading should be accepted as at least possibly an authoritative correction (unless, of course, it is itself incredible). If the answer to (1) is affirmative and the answer to (2) is negative, the original reading should be retained. If the answers to both questions are affirmative, then the later reading should be presumed to be due to revision and admitted into the text, whether the editor himself considers it an improvement or not.

That Greg meant by that last interdiction exactly what the words say is confirmed by the example he gives to illustrate the principle. In Jonson's *Masque of Gipsies* a gipsy is said in the original version to *maund*, a word familiar in gipsy cant, perhaps indeed derived from the Romany, meaning to beg; in the revised version of the masque, Jonson substituted the more commonplace *stalk*. The revision, Greg concludes, 'must be allowed to pass as (at least possibly) a correction [i.e. revision], though no reasonable critic would *prefer* it to the original' (p. 388).

Greg, an essentially humane man, was doing his best here not to be too dogmatic, but the principle that emerges is still what Bowers has called 'the last-edition-in-the-author's-life-time formula'.[2] A correction, still more a revision, that can be shown to be probably authorial *must* be preferred, even if a competent editor knows in his bones that the earlier reading is really superior. The author, that is to say, must be allowed, literally, the last word.

Must he? This, I suggest, is to confuse the external logic of the corrected misprint (using the term in all its wider senses) with the internal logic of the revision. Once a misprint is corrected it will be expected to stay corrected in later reprints or editions. Its original imperfection was a by-product of current systems of publication over which an author's control is never complete, though his degree of helplessness varies very considerably from period to period and genre to genre. A revision, on the other hand, may stay or go or revert to its original form as the author decides —on the inexplicable spur of the moment, or in the light perhaps of the passage's immediate context, or reconsidered to conform to the general pattern of the work or his writings generally (or even his life).

I attribute Greg's mechanical ruling in the matter of authorial revisions primarily to his special interest in Elizabethan drama, where both printing and publishing are to be seen at their most primitive and the scholar is consequently more often concerned with the emendation of a corrupt reading than with authorial revisions. Thus the *sallied, sullied, solid* controversy revolves around the external evidence for a single archetypal word—as variously heard (in the 'reported' Q1 which the printers of Q2 are thought to have consulted when puzzled by Shakespeare's handwriting) or spelt or misprinted. In such cases emendation is often necessary—and underlying it therefore the history of the text's transmission, an area in which both Greg and Bowers have often speculated usefully. The question, however, 'Which is the *best* reading, the original one or the author's later revision?' did not often arise for them, or if it did it was dismissed as irrelevant.

---

[2] *Textual and Literary Criticism*, p. 24.

Where it insists on an answer, as with Donne's poems, a clear-cut one is rarely possible in terms of textual transmission, partly because none of them seem to survive in Donne's own hand-writing.

Such textual philistinism as Greg's may be ultimately social in its origin. Greg was a rich man. Now the possession of wealth naturally encourages an undue interest in property and with it a special if unconscious sympathy with other property-holders. Greg's editorial assumption would seem to have been that the *Masque of Gipsies* was the private property of Ben Jonson and that as such he was entitled to do what he liked with it, right or wrong. And, a more pernicious deduction, that future generations of editors must condone and become accomplices in an author's 'correction' that 'no reasonable critic would *prefer*'.

The *a priori* objection to such perversities is clear. A work claiming to be literature depends in the long run upon the agree-ment of readers and critics—and their academic hangers-on—that it *is* literature. Every single one of the particular work's particular words and word-order may not be, all things considered, the very best words and word-order available to the author, but most of them must be expected to be. And whenever an author has offered more than one version of a passage a responsible editor will be expected to provide in the text whatever after due consideration he (the editor) believes the best authorial version to be, whether it happens to be early, middle-period, or last.

I can see no escape from this eclectic conclusion. And a method-ological conclusion follows from it. Since the text is eclectic—one in which the conscientious editor has to plump for one reading rather than another—his collation or array of textual notes cannot be limited to a tabulation of the possible substantive alternatives. A short summary is also necessary of the *reasons* why one reading is incorporated into the text and its rival or rivals are excluded. Not to do so is to commit the sin of irresponsible eclecticism. The good editor is responsibly eclectic. To be such the cards must be face up on the table.

To the sceptic, however, I now offer a detailed illustration from an analysis of an eighteenth-century dramatic masterpiece which has survived in at least twenty different versions, some half of which have corrections in the author's own hand.

II

Sheridan, I once wrote (almost exactly fifty years ago),[3] was afflicted by the *cacoethes corrigendi*. No author, except perhaps Henry James, has fussed so nervously and continuously over minute problems of *le mot juste*—which in his case was not only what would read best but in the first place what would act best. As the Manager of Drury Lane Theatre from 1776 to 1809 his words were required to exploit to the full the talents and looks of the principal actors on the Drury Lane pay-roll *before* they reached a reading public. A certain contradiction between the expectations of his two audiences may well have been one of the reasons why he did not ever publish *The School for Scandal*, though characteristically he kept dangling a final text before various publishers. And friends were allowed manuscript copies, often with revisions in them in his own hand.

Some of the revisions were simply quite long cuts,[4] but most of the variant readings recorded in Cecil Price's *The Dramatic Works of Richard Brinsley Sheridan* (2 vols., Oxford, 1973)—a model incidentally of recent eighteenth-century scholarship, readable, reliable, and comprehensive—are of single sentences, phrases, or words. An example of his surgical methods which is not recorded by Price is the following passage.[5] It occurs early in the famous 'screen' scene (IV.iii) immediately before Joseph Surface parades his casuistical logic of seduction before Lady Teazle. Its subject is the wealthy heiress Maria whom Joseph is hoping to marry, as Lady Teazle is beginning to suspect, though for the moment he is still able to allay her suspicions. I quote *verbatim et literatim*; I have enclosed the first seven words in square brackets because they were not crossed out like the rest of the passage and in fact survive in all the later texts:

---

[3] *TLS*, 28 Nov. 1929, p. 998, in an article on the text of *The Rivals*, entitled 'The Text of Sheridan'.

[4] The cuts are most drastic in the Lady Sneerwell scenes. The newspapers' comments on the first performance almost all condemn the play's excessive length. See Price, ii. 312 ff.

[5] This deleted passage, not in Sheridan's hand, is clearly a survival from an early draft of the play, and appears in print only in W. Fraser Rae's edition, *Sheridan's Plays . . . as he wrote them* (1902), p. 193.

L:Teazle
[Well, well I'm inclin'd to believe you]—besides I really never could perceive why she should have so many admirers.

Surface
O for her fortune—nothing else.

L:Teazle
I believe so—for tho' she is certainly very pretty—yet she has no Conversation in the world, and is so grave and so reserv'd, that I declare, I think she'd have made an excellent wife for Sir Peter.

Surface
So she would.

L:Teazle
Then one never hears her speak ill of any body, which you know is mighty dull.

Surface
Yet she doesn't want understanding.

L:Teazle
No more she does—yet one is always disappointed when one hears her speak. For tho' her Eyes have no kind of meaning in them—she very seldom talks Nonsense.

Surface
Nay, nay, surely she has very fine Eyes.

L:Teazle
Why so she has tho' sometimes one fancies there's a little sort of a Squint.

Surface
A Squint O fie—Lady Teazle—

L:Teazle
Yes, yes, I vow now—come there is a left-handed Cupid in one eye—that's the Truth on't.

Surface
Well—his aim is very direct however—but Lady Sneerwell has quite corrupted you.

L. Teazle

No indeed I have not opinion enough of her to be
taught by her, and I know that she has lately rais'd
many scandalous hints of me, which you know one
always hears again from one common friend or other.

Surface

Why to say truth I believe you are not more oblig'd to
her than others of her acquaintance.

Sheridan may have decided to cancel the passage when 'Perdita'
Robinson, for whom he had intended the part of Maria and whose
fine eyes were to attract the Prince of Wales the following year,
became *enceinte* and had to surrender the part to Priscilla Hopkins,
the Drury Lane prompter's daughter and a far less glamorous
figure. But the passage has a psychological interest in the glimpse
it gives us of a chivalrous element in Joseph, which might interest
the reader of the play, though on the stage it would merely delay
the accumulating melodramatic action.

In any case Greg's notion that the transmission of texts was the
beginning if not the end of all textual criticism receives no support
from this passage. It is unquestionably authentic, and survives in
only two manuscripts—the 'Frampton Court MS.' in the Collection
of Robert H. Taylor of Princeton, and that in the Victoria and
Albert Museum which Price has called 'Spunge' because this was
the name originally given in them to Charles Surface's man-servant
Trip. The passage does not, as far as I am aware, occur in any other
manuscript or early edition. Textually, then, if textual criticism
is primarily the study of the transmission of texts, as Greg maintained more than once, it is meaningless. Nevertheless it exists.

The truth is, of course, that an authorial revision is an anomaly
in the science or pseudo-science of textual criticism in so far as
that is limited to the 'stemmatic' or genealogical methods which
Greg had learnt from Lachmann and his classical successors. The
basic stemmatic assumption is a textual archetype, reproducing or
approaching the author's original intentions, which can be
reconstructed from an orderly ('genealogical') tabulation of errors
or non-authorial forms in early manuscripts or editions. As applied
to *misprints*, in the wide sense of external interference I have given
the term, the collection of textual 'families' has its uses. It has been
especially successful in restoring the texts of the Greek and Roman

classics—largely perhaps because the authors' 'foul copies' were drafted on wax tablets which were erased as the final fair copy emerged for transcription on papyrus or vellum. Some degree of *revision* is in any case a built-in element or stage in the process of all literary composition and a definitive text calls for its recognition as such, if only in a bare textual note.

An example of the embarrassments a revision can create is Sheridan's substitution of 'novel' for 'sermon' in Act II, scene i. Sir Peter and Lady Teazle, for once in agreement, are interchanging recollections of her salad days in the country. As the daughter of the manor-house she had had to submit to various tedious indignities. One that she particularly resented was to have to read aloud to her aunt a 'novel' (in the Crewe and Scott MSS.), but a 'sermon' in all the other manuscripts and early editions. What then was Aunt Deborah's favourite form of literature most likely to have been? The delightful passage in which she occurs is a late example of the comic Augustan topos of the horrors of country life for the daughters of the squirearchy. Its masterpiece is Dorimant's final surrender to Harriet in *The Man of Mode*, which she celebrates in a mocking invitation to him to 'a great rambling lone house, that looks as it were not inhabited, the family's so small; there you'l find my Mother, an old lame Aunt, and myself, Sir, perch'd up on Chairs at a distance in a large parlour; sitting moping like three or four Melancholy Birds in a spacious vollary.' Another familiar specimen is Pope's 'Epistle to Miss Blount on her leaving the Town after the Coronation'. It was a convention into which the reading of sermons to an aunt naturally entered; I cannot recall a single instance of the reading of novels being the alternative drudgery. As it happens, one of the very few literary judgements in Sheridan's *Letters* expresses his own distaste for novels. 'I hate Novels', he wrote to Thomas Grenville on 30 October 1772, 'and love Romances. The Praise of the best of the former, their being *natural*, as it is called, is to me their greatest Demerit. Thus it is with Fielding's, Smollet's etc.' Price does not comment on either the almost uniqueness of the textual reading or the improbability of the sentiment. Lady Teazle, the sentimental heroine without a name of her own, could not possibly have committed such an offence against literary decorum. For Sheridan to allow his own distaste for novels to penetrate into his revision of the text was an error of authorial judgement.

Why, then, does every modern edition that I possess of *The School for Scandal*, including those of the judicious Price, read 'novel' instead of 'sermon'? The answer, I am afraid, has nothing to do with the respective merits—as literature, or even as comedy —of the two readings. It is a relic of the last-therefore-best formula to which Greg reluctantly succumbed in 'The Rationale of Copy-Text'. The 'novel' is preferred for a merely mechanical reason: it is found in the Crewe MS., which Moore described in his *Memoirs of the Life of Sheridan* (i. 260 of the two-volume edition, London, 1825) as 'the last, I believe, ever revised by himself'. Moore, as the official biographer, had been allowed access to whatever manuscripts the Sheridan family possessed, and his comments with the corrections from the Crewe MS. in a copy[6] of the Dublin edition of 1799 (whose own text, though authentic, is probably earlier than that of the first performance at Drury Lane, 8 May 1777) make it clear that, apart from the Crewe MS., he was unfamiliar with any manuscripts of the play not owned by the family. Here are some representative specimens:'not in MS.—but *is* in an earlier', 'Is in the early MS.', '. . . as it is in the other MS. copies', 'In one of the MSS. instead of "Maid" here, there had been originally put "Madam Scovack" [misreading of "Maid Servant"]'.

All in all Moore's tentative 'I believe' has in my opinion been taken too literally. If the Crewe MS. was actually the last version of the play to be revised by Sheridan, why is it (i) that all the evidence, external and internal, points to it being fairly early, and (ii) that there are at least three important texts that must be much later? The Crewe MS. was a presentation copy to the beautiful, clever, immoral Frances Anne Crewe ('. . . From the Author/R.B. Sheridan') and it is impossible not to connect it with the ecstatic Popian couplets he sent her with a copy of the play a month or two after the first performance in 1777 that he called 'A Portrait', though the extant Crewe MS.—now at Georgetown University, Washington—is more likely really to be a second Crewe MS. In the competition for her bed Sheridan had in an inscribed copy of his brilliant unpublished comedy—much the most immediately successful of any Restoration or post-Restoration play—a gift to offer her that none of his wealthy aristocratic rivals could equal. Mrs. Crewe, to do her justice, was essentially an intellectual, her

[6] This copy of the 1799 edition is now in the Irish Academy (Dublin).

mother being the all-accomplished Frances Greville, to whom
Sheridan dedicated the first edition of *The Critic*, and the author of
the brilliant 'Prayer for Indifference'.

A *terminus ad quem* for the Crewe MSS.—Price thinks there may
have been three[7]—is suggested by a letter from Sheridan's sister
Elizabeth to their elder sister Alicia, now married and in distant
Dublin. 'You know also', Elizabeth reported on 27 November
1788, 'that Mrs. Crewe among other lovers (favoure'd ones I
mean) has had our Brother in her train . . . but her charms have
diminished, and passion is no longer the tie between them.'[8]
Walter Sichel, the most detailed of Sheridan's biographers, thought
the 'infatuation' ended in 1784—and with its end presumably the
incentive to give specially revised presentation copies.

That Sheridan was prepared to make public as early as 1781 the
revised text of the play he had prepared for Mrs. Crewe's private
eye is suggested by two advertisements that have hitherto escaped
notice. In its issue of 20–22 June 1781 *Lloyd's Evening Post* carried
the following notice: 'In a few Days will be published, The
School for Scandal . . . By R. B. Sheridan . . . for J. Murray, No.
32, Fleet-Street.' This J. Murray was the founder of the great
publishing house of John Murray. But nothing came of this
promise and it was not until 1823 that John Murray II, Byron's
publisher and Moore's, was able to bring out a Murray edition of
The School for Scandal. (It was in fact a mere reprint of the play
from the *Works* of 1821.) On 25 October 1781, however, a second
advertisement followed. The publisher this time was Thomas
Beckett, who had just brought out *The Critic* ('Corrected and
Revised by the Author'), his third edition of which being announced in the *Morning Herald and Daily Advertiser*, 25 October,
by Beckett 'By whom will be speedily published, The School for
Scandal . . . by R. B. Sheridan'.

I suspect that the version of the play which Sheridan dangled
successively before both Murray and Beckett, perhaps obtaining

---

[7] 'The Second Crewe MS. of "The School for Scandal" ', *Papers of the
Bibliographical Society of America*, lxi (1967), 356.

[8] Cited by both W. Fraser Rae, *Sheridan. A Biography* (2 vols., 1896), and
R. Crompton Rhodes, *Harlequin Sheridan* (Oxford, 1933), from the Lefanu
Papers. It was all over two years earlier, if Sheridan meant what he said when he
told the Duchess of Devonshire in October 1786 that his heart was 'shut against'
Mrs. Crewe (Walter Sichel, *Sheridan*, 2 vols., London, 1909). The Crewe
family do not permit access to his letters to her (*Letters*, ed. Price, 1966, vol. i,
p. xxii), and the 'affair' is still obscure.

an advance from each, was essentially the Georgetown text. But his compulsive search for stylistic perfection undoubtedly continued unabated. Price (ii.323) has found a notice in *The World* (15 October 1787) which, while acknowledging the play's general supremacy ('perhaps in all but tendency, the best in the language'), deplored some recent changes in it 'not for the better'. Nothing more is heard of publishing until 1799 when James Ridgway, the publisher of Sheridan's *Pizarro*, inserted the following dramatic announcement in the fifteenth edition of that successful but now unreadable melodrama:

SCHOOL FOR SCANDAL
A genuine Edition from the Original Copy,
By R. B. SHERIDAN, Esq.
Is in the Press, and will be published on *Monday*,
30th Sept. instant, 1799.

JAMES RIDGWAY having purchased the Copyright of the above celebrated Comedy, gives Notice, that the Venders of the *Spurious Copies* which have been attempted to be imposed on the Public, will be prosecuted as the Law directs.

But Monday, 30 September 1799, came and went—and Sheridan's final revision was still unobtainable, except in the 'bad quartos' (more often octavos or duodecimos) of an early text issued in great numbers by Dublin and American pirates, who were safe from Ridgway's threats of prosecution. According to what Ridgway told Moore some twenty years later he (Ridgway) 'expostulated pretty strongly' over this delay. Sheridan's impudent but no doubt honest answer was, 'The fact is, Mr. R., I have been nineteen years endeavouring to satisfy my own taste in this play, and have not yet succeeded.' Moore has recorded Ridgway's recollection of this curious conversation in his *Journal* (5 May 1819) and he repeats its gist in the *Memoirs*.

The conversation rings true to me. But why *nineteen* years? The figure is curiously specific—and the interval that divides the negotiations with Beckett and those with Ridgway *was* exactly nineteen years. The implication of Sheridan's excuse is that throughout all those nineteen years he had continually returned to *The School for Scandal* in the hope that he could at last achieve its ultimate polish, as Congreve, for example, and Pope had obtained theirs by constant revision.

At least two other revised manuscripts seem to belong to Sheridan's later life. One is Act I of the 'Spunge' MS. which is unique in the number of new readings it introduces in Sheridan's own hand, though few of them can be considered changes for the better.[9] The Powell MS. of *c.* 1809 is more conservative, but its Act I shares a number of readings with the text of the play published in the 1821 *Works*—after Sheridan's death—which has a far better claim than the Crewe MS. to constitute Sheridan's last revision of his comedy.[10] A detail of the external evidence that suggests a late date is that Crabtree no longer jokes about Charles Surface's popularity with the Jews as causing prayers for his life to be read 'at the Synagogue'; it is now 'at the synagogues'. In the eighteenth century the Great Synagogue, abutting on Duke's Place in the City, was the only one generally known to London's West End Gentiles, but the number of synagogues multiplied in the early nineteenth century as the wealth and social status of Jews improved.[11]

The moral of this much too short summary of the history of some of the principal texts of *The School for Scandal* is simple, and, I suggest, irrefutable. If textual 'Last' is automatically textual 'Best' the determination of textual finality becomes impossibly precarious—and if ever obtained it will commit us to some very unattractive readings. Is the game worth the candle?

III

Housman ended his lecture on 'The Application of Thought to Textual Criticism' with what was, for him, unusual blandness: 'Knowledge is good, method is good, but one thing beyond all others is necessary: and that is to have a head, not a pumpkin, on your shoulders, and brains, not pudding, in your head.'

The concession that method is good is the narrow loophole through which an unthinking editor may hope to escape from the problem of the 'indifferent' reading. Many of the variants in *The School for Scandal*, as indeed in all the texts of the greatest English

[9] They are printed by Price, iii. 851–2. He omits the nine passages already printed by Rae (*Sheridan. A Biography*, i. 332), but they are included in his collation of the play.

[10] I have discussed the claim more fully in 'The School for Scandal', *TLS*, 5 Dec. 1929, p. 1029.

[11] See Cecil Roth, *A History of the Jews in England* (1941) and *The Great Synagogue* (1950).

classics, are superficially of this type. It is part of the penalty we suffer from having abandoned an inflected for a primarily uninflected language in which gender is no longer grammatical. Should Snake be allowed to say (in I.i) 'here is company coming' (Licenser's copy), or is 'here's company coming' (Crewe MS.) really preferable? In a theatrical text such as a prompt-book, from which the actors' parts are or used generally to be copied, such minutiae are perhaps genuinely indifferent, because they are at the particular actor's discretion. But in a reading version the reader will need the author's guidance. The Crewe MSS., both the first layer prepared by a Drury Lane copyist and the second layer consisting of Sheridan's own corrections and revisions, are noticeably careful in providing colloquial abbreviations at the right time and in the right mouths. (Mrs. Candour's inflections tend to be colloquial, whereas Joseph, except when nature breaks in or he is talking to himself, prefers the more formal alternative.)

Sheridan compels an editor to think such issues out for himself. A blind confidence in the Georgetown manuscript is laboursaving, but it is not a rationally respectable behaviour. Whether the dogmatic umbrella is the Last Edition doctrine or the Best Edition doctrine (a variant of the former to which the same objections apply), how can an editor hope to explain or defend every single authorial reading in any one text? Shakespeare may be beyond our question, but Sheridan certainly is not. Like Wordsworth he was continually questioning himself—and very often coming up with the wrong answer! Price prudently deserts the Georgetown text on a number of occasions, but he has a general preference for it that amounts to favouritism. For him it tends to be both the Best Text and the Last Text. A decision that I particularly regret in Price's generally sensible and informative edition of the *Dramatic Works*—of which *The School for Scandal* occupies less than a quarter if measured by pages—is his neglect of the text in the *Works* (1821). R. Crompton Rhodes states that John Murray 'bought the copyright from Ridgway' (*The Plays and Poems*, Oxford, 1928, ii. 162), but I suspect that this is just a guess. That Murray had a special interest in the play, perhaps inherited from his father's possibly burnt fingers, is clear from his being the sole publisher of the 1823 reprint of it from the *Works* (which were published jointly by Murray, Ridgway, and Wilkie), though where Murray got the manuscript from is not known. (My own guess would be the banker-poet Samuel Rogers.[12]) However, the authenticity of the revisions in it does not depend upon external evidence.

Here are some specimen readings, all from the play's first scene, that are to be found in Murray and that I venture to think superior—more genuinely Sheridanian—than any they displace (page- and line-references to Price's edition):

p. 362, l. 12. Snake has just been rallying [arraigning *all MSS.*] me on our mutual attachment. [Snake is not accusing Lady Sneerwell but enquiring with a polite surprise.]

p. 363, l. 24. I slipped out and ran [run *all MSS. except 'second' Crewe*] hither. [The form *run* in the past tense only survived in dialect (perhaps an Irishism).]

p. 362, l. 5. I confess [own *all MSS.*], madam. [Maria is superficially apologizing to Lady Sneerwell, her hostess and elder, for dissenting from her.]

p. 365, l. 5. Indeed [*om. all MSS.*] I am very sorry ma'am, the town is not better employed [has so little to do]. [Within the limits of drawing-room politeness Maria wishes to rebuke Mrs. Candour for her deplorable inquisitiveness about Charles.]

p. 365, l. 22. I'll answer for't there are no grounds for that [the *all MSS.*] report. [Maria adds emphasis to her denial of the gossip about her friend Miss Prim.]

p. 366, l. 26. Lady Sneerwell, I kiss your hand [hands *all MSS.*]. [Even Crabtree would not offend so grossly against propriety as to kiss both his hostess's hands upon entering. With the hat fashionably under the left arm, it would anyhow have been almost physically impossible.]

p. 367, l. 18. a neat rivulet of text shall meander [murmur *all MSS.*] through a meadow of margin. [Sir Benjamin is promising Maria some love-elegies in quarto. James Hammond's immensely popular *Love Elegies* (1743) have four lines in each verse, the second and fourth lines indented and so producing a visual effect resembling the windings of the Phrygian river Maeander.]

Price justifies his neglect of the *Works* text on two grounds:[1]

---

[12] Sheridan's letter to his second wife of 15 Oct. 1814 (Price, *Letters*, ii. 202) and a letter from Lady Holland to Lord Grey of 4 Feb. 1816 (see note in *Letters*, iii. 243–4) show that Rogers, supported by Byron, was doing his best to get a collected edition of Sheridan's writings published before he died.

[13] i. 348.

(i) Moore 'had no hand in its editing' (true, but Moore was in France at the time of its preparation and publication—in hiding from his creditors); (ii) the 1821 text is 'based on an early manuscript that was corrected in the nineteenth century—but almost certainly not by Sheridan'. It is true that like most of the principal manuscripts it has two layers, but there is absolutely no evidence that Sheridan was not responsible for the later and probably nineteenth-century layer. And 'A Portrait' is published here in full for the first time. Rogers or the Sheridan family—even perhaps Lady Crewe (as she had now become and with whom Sheridan never actually quarrelled)—must clearly have found a copy of it for John Murray to use. Its appearance *guarantees* the edition some degree of authoritativeness.

The critical editor, faced by the challenge of variants of the type listed above (which continue to the end of the play), none of which appear in the manuscripts, will reply with Bentley *ratio et res ipsa centum codicibus potiores sunt*.[14] Most of the readings are, I suggest, unquestionably *better* (in their context)—considered as meaning, good English, good literature—than those they displace. The exact circumstances surrounding this 1821 edition are obscure (we must leave them to future literary detectives to clear up), but in some of its readings—not all by any means—I believe Sheridan did finally succeed in satisfying his own taste. I am not saying that that taste was impeccable. There was a certain ineradicable vulgarity or immaturity in Sheridan from which Congreve, his principal model, was almost always free. And the Murray edition is, of course, not without its own quota of misprints, corruptions, and deplorable revisions or failures to revise.   1975

---

[14] On Horace, *Odes*, III. xxvii. 15. Bentley's confident aphorism is quoted by the German classical scholar Paul Maas (*Textual Criticism*, trans. Barbara, 1958, p. 41). Maas adds: 'This remark has always tempted some scholars to misuse it, and it will always continue to do so; but it is true.'

The Term 'Conceit' in Johnson's Literary Criticism

DONALD GREENE

ASTONISHED AT a theory advanced by a fellow historian, which a glance at the primary sources of evidence at once demolished, that great scholar F. W. Maitland speculated that 'the Canon's armchair was comfortable, and the statute books and the journals of Parliament stood just beyond his reach. . . . We are sinners, all of us. The guess-working spirit is so willing; the verifying flesh is often weary.'[1]

Comfortable armchairs have not been absent during the study of Samuel Johnson's criticism. His 'distrust of imagination'[2] in literature has often been asserted, in spite of the occurrence of that word and its cognates 'image' and 'imagery' dozens, perhaps hundreds, of times in his criticism; the deep concern for effective poetic imagery reflected in that frequent use; and the vivid imagery which makes so much of his own writing and talk memorable—'A woman's preaching is like a dog's walking on his hinder legs', 'Hell is paved with good intentions', and the like. He has been called 'the most advanced abstractionist of his time'; 'in *Rasselas*, as we know, he lays down, like Reynolds,[3] that the

---

[1] *Selected Historical Essays of F. W. Maitland*, ed. Helen M. Cam (Boston: Beacon Press, 1962), p. 256.

[2] The notion probably springs from, or is reinforced by, a misapprehension of the chapter title in *Rasselas*, 'The Dangerous Prevalence of Imagination'. True, Johnson believed, and few would disagree, that it is dangerous when an individual's imagination that he controls the movements of the heavenly bodies, or is Napoleon Bonaparte, prevails over his contact with reality. But to go on to deduce from this that Johnson also thought it dangerous to use imagery in poetry seems itself a fairly wild flight of imagination.

[3] Reynolds is also in process of being rescued from this imputation. Cf. Harvey D. Goldstein, '*Ut Poesis Pictura*: Reynolds on Imitation and Imagination', *Eighteenth-Century Studies*, i (1968), 213–35. Again, much of the trouble seems to spring from a small but widespread misunderstanding. Blake's famous 'To generalize is to be an idiot' was a comment, not, as is often thought and stated, on something said or written by Reynolds, but on a remark attributed by Malone to Burke. In any case, generalization is not the same as abstraction.

business of art and poetry is to be abstract.' Yet the word 'abstract' occurs nowhere in his writings, so far as I can tell, as a term of literary criticism. The word in Chapter X of *Rasselas* which seems to have been equated with 'abstract' is 'general', a term which he does often use in his criticism. But if one bothers to examine the many places where it occurs, one finds that he uses it more often as a term of censure than one of praise, a fact that should cause students to examine its semantics carefully. Recent students have proved more willing to abandon such *idées reçues* in favour of a closer look at what Johnson actually wrote.[4] One misconception, however, remains stubbornly current, and it may be well to examine it here.

In the second edition (1957), of *A Glossary of Literary Terms*,[5] a work that for decades has been the vade-mecum of students and teachers of literature, M. H. Abrams, under the heading 'Conceit', writes,

Originally meaning simply an idea or image, 'conceit' has come to be applied to a figure of speech which establishes a striking parallel— usually an elaborate parallel—between two apparently dissimilar things or situations (see *simile* and *metaphor* under *Figurative language*). The term was once derogatory, but it is now best employed as a neutral way of identifying a literary device. Two species of conceits are often distinguished. [An account of 'the Petrarchan conceit' follows.] The *metaphysical conceit* is a characteristic kind of figure in the poems of John Donne and his followers (see *Metaphysical poets*). It was described by Dr. Johnson, in a famous passage, as 'a kind of *discordia concors*, a combination of dissimilar images, or discovery of occult resemblances in things apparently unlike.'

If one takes the trouble to turn to the source of this quotation,

---

[4] For example, Oliver Sigworth, 'Johnson's *Lycidas*: The End of Renaissance Criticism', *Eighteenth-Century Studies*, i (1967), 159–68; the essays by Hoyt Trowbridge, Lionel Basney, David W. Tarbet, and Howard D. Weinbrot in a special number of *Eighteenth-Century Studies*, v (1971); Arthur H. Scouten, 'Dr. Johnson and Imlac', *Eighteenth-Century Studies*, vi (1973), 506–8. I have discussed some of these matters, as well as the subject of this essay, in '"Pictures to the Mind": Johnson and Imagery', in *Johnson, Boswell, and Their Circle: Essays Presented to L. F. Powell*, ed. Mary Lascelles et al. (Oxford: Clarendon Press, 1965), pp. 137–58, and in *Samuel Johnson* (New York: Twayne Publishers, 1970), pp. 200–5.

[5] New York: Holt, Rinehart, and Winston, also the publishers of the third edition, 1971. The first edition, 1941, is New York: Farrar and Rinehart.

the 'Life of Cowley', one finds that Johnson did no such thing. The 'famous passage' reads 'But Wit, abstracted from its effects upon the hearer, may be more rigorously and philosophically considered [than in Pope's "What oft was thought, but ne'er so well expressed"] as a kind of *discordia concors*. . . .'[6] Nowhere in the passage, or its immediate context, does the word 'conceit' occur.

Perhaps this discrepancy was called to Professor Abrams's attention, for in his third edition of the *Glossary* (1971), the one in use as this is written, the passage becomes

The *metaphysical conceit* is a characteristic figure in John Donne and other *metaphysical poets* of the seventeenth century. It was described by Dr. Johnson, in a famed passage in his 'Life of Cowley,' as wit which is

a kind of *discordia concors*, a combination of dissimilar images, or discovery of occult resemblances in things apparently unlike. . . . [Ellipsis in the *Glossary*.] The most heterogeneous ideas are yoked by violence together.

This is no improvement on the second edition. Johnson does not describe 'conceit' or 'metaphysical conceit' as 'wit which is' anything. The sentence omitted from the quotation reads, 'Of wit, thus defined, they [the "metaphysical poets"] have more than enough.' Its omission disguises the fact that Johnson here is not talking about 'conceit' at all.

The equation of the term 'conceit' in literary criticism with 'extended metaphor', 'elaborate image', or the like seems to have been a product of the 1930s or 1940s, the heyday of 'New Criticism', when the chief concern of critics of poetry was imagery.[7] In the first edition (1941) of the *Glossary*, by Dan S. Norton and Peters Rushton—Abrams was not then associated with it—the article 'Conceit' stresses imagery:

---

[6] Johnson, *Lives of the Poets*, ed. G. B. Hill (Oxford: Clarendon Press, 1905), i, 20 (para. 56). All citations from the 'Life of Cowley' will be from this edition, with paragraph number given there.

[7] T. S. Eliot's review (1921) of Sir Herbert Grierson's selection, *Metaphysical Lyrics and Poems of the Seventeenth Century*, reprinted in Eliot's *Selected Essays* (1932) as 'The Metaphysical Poets', gave a strong impetus to the study of the imagery of the 'Metaphysicals', although its thesis of 'dissociation of sensibility' is now discredited. Eliot, as always, is respectful and just to Johnson. His comment 'A degree of heterogeneity of material compelled into unity by the operation of the poet's mind is omnipresent in poetry' Johnson would certainly have agreed with; as Eliot says, 'We may find it in some of the best lines of Johnson himself.'

Toward the end of the seventeenth century . . . critics limited the meaning of conceit to farfetched fancies and artificial, merely ingenious
images as they were often contrived by the Metaphysical Poets of the
earlier years of the century. The Metaphysical Poets . . . were actually
very often ingenious in their images. . . . [Apropos of Donne's 'Valediction', with its image of compass legs] He had made what the seven-
teenth- and eighteenth-century critics called a conceit. These critics
meant, of course, that the image had become overdone and had lost its
force of meaning in becoming only intricate. The meaning which they
gave to the word 'conceit' has remained with it, even though latter-day
critics would disagree with them in a good many of their specific
examples.

Here we see the pattern, which was to become familiar, of
mentioning older critics' alleged definition of 'conceit' and following it with the suggestion that those critics were often blind to its
potential excellences. Interestingly, Johnson is not saddled here
with the responsibility of defining 'conceit' as a form of imagery,
though it might be argued that he is strongly implied (what other
'seventeenth- and eighteenth-century critics' could be meant?). I
do not know whether Professor Abrams was the first to charge
Johnson with that responsibility, but later such guides have
enthusiastically followed his lead, and the 'fact' of Johnson's
responsibility is much used as evidence of his critical limitations.
From the glossaries in two recent anthologies of poetry for college
students:

Conceit: an extended comparison of unlike things. . . . The Metaphysical
poets, and particularly John Donne, overturned the conventionality of
the Petrarchan conceit by finding obscure and unexpected comparisons.
As Dr. Samuel Johnson wrote of the Metaphysicals' conceits: 'The
most heterogeneous ideas are yoked by violence together; nature and
art are ransacked for illustrations, comparisons, and allusions.'[8]

The last three stanzas [of Donne's 'Valediction'] make up a *metaphysical
conceit*. It is an extended simile . . . it may be said to be metaphorical in
effect. Such extended similes and metaphors were attacked in the
eighteenth century by Samuel Johnson, who felt that they were strained
and overwrought; when he applied the term metaphysical conceit to the
devices of certain seventeenth-century poets, including Donne, he
intended to deride their excessive playing with philosophy and the over-

[8] *Poetry Past and Present*, ed. Frank Brady and Martin Price (New York:
Harcourt, Brace, and Jovanovich, 1974), p. 504.

ingenuity of their figurative analogies. But modern readers have found much to admire in the poetry of Donne and his colleagues. . . .[9]

A competing handbook of literary terminology reads,

A *conceit* may be a brief METAPHOR but it may also form the framework of a complete poem. . . . [In] the METAPHYSICAL CONCEIT . . . complex, startling, and highly intellectual analogies are made. In the eighteenth and nineteenth centuries, the term was used in a derogatory sense, the *conceit* being considered strained, arbitrary, and false. Dr. Johnson was particularly devastating on the METAPHYSICAL CONCEIT. . . . In contemporary verse the *conceit* is again a respected vehicle for the expression of witty perceptions and telling analogies. It is used with great effect by Emily Dickinson [contemporary?], T. S. Eliot, Allen Tate, and John Crowe Ransom—[10]

whose poetry poor obtuse Johnson would presumably have been unable to appreciate.

Surprising as it may seem after all this authoritative assurance, one will search the 'Life of Cowley' in vain for any definition by Johnson of 'conceit'. Far from 'applying the term metaphysical conceit to the devices of certain seventeenth-century poets', he never uses the expression 'metaphysical conceit' at all. It may also surprise students to find that the definition of 'conceit' as 'extended metaphor', 'elaborate image', or the like did not make its way into standard English dictionaries until around 1960. Until that time, lexicographical practice fairly closely followed Johnson's own treatment of the word in his last revised edition of his *Dictionary* (1773), of which a condensed version follows:

CONCEIT, n.s.
1. Conception; thought; idea; image in the mind. . . .
2. Understanding; readiness of apprehension. . . .
3. Opinion, generally in a sense of contempt; fancy; imagination; fantastical notion. . . . 'Malbranche has an odd *conceit*/As ever entered Frenchman's pate.' *Prior*
4. Opinion, in a neutral sense. . . .
5. Pleasant fancy; gaiety of imagination; acuteness.[11] 'His wit is as

---

[9] *Poetry: Points of Departure*, ed. Henry Taylor (Cambridge, Mass.: Winthrop Publishers, 1974), p. 26.
[10] C. Hugh Holman, *A Handbook to Literature*, rev. W. F. Thrall and A. Hibbard (3rd edn.; Indianapolis: Odyssey Press, 1972), p. 116.
[11] The first edition (1755) gives only 'A pleasant fancy'.

thick as Tewkesbury mustard; there is no more *conceit* in him than is in a mallet.' *Shakspeare*
6. Sentiment, as distinguished from imagery. 'Some to *conceit* alone their works confine,/And glitt'ring thoughts struck out at ev'ry line.' *Pope*
7. Fondness; favorable opinion; opinionative pride. . . .
8. *Out of conceit with.* No longer fond of. . . .

Webster's Second New International Dictionary (1934) gave the following significations applicable to literature, clearly indebted to Johnson's senses 3, 5, and 6:

3.a. A fanciful, odd, or extravagant notion; variously: a quaint, artificial or affected conception, or a witty thought or turn of expression; a whim, quip, or trick. 'Tasso is full of *conceits* . . . which are not only below the dignity of heroic verse, but contrary to its nature.' *Dryden*
b. Use or presence of such conceits as an element of style. 'Some to *conceit* alone their taste confine.' *Pope*
4. Imagination or fancy as a faculty or trait; active fancy. [Same quotation as in Johnson's 5.][12]

Webster's Third New International (1961) however, telescopes these and introduces the new signification 2.b.:

2. [tr. of *It concetto*] a. a whimsically or fancifully ingenious idea. b. an elaborate, startling, extravagant, or strained metaphor. c. the use or presence of such conceits as an element of poetry [why not of prose, one wonders].

The shorter 'college' dictionaries of about the same time make the same innovation. Such significations as '2.b: an elaborate or

[12] The *Oxford English Dictionary* likewise follows Johnson closely:

III. 8. A fanciful, ingenious, or witty notion or expression; now applied disparagingly to a strained or far-fetched turn of thought, figure, etc., an affectation of thought or style; = CONCETTO. . . . c. (without *pl.*) The use of conceits as a quality of literary taste or style; 'sentiment, as distinguished from imagery' (J.). . . . 1709. POPE *Ess. Crit.* 291 Some to conceit alone their taste confine . . . d. 'Gaiety of imagination' (J.), wit. [Same quotation as in Johnson's 5.]

Neither the 1933 nor the 1975 Supplement to the *OED* has a further entry for 'conceit'. The *Concise Oxford Dictionary* (6th edn., 1976), however, includes 'far-fetched comparison' among its definitions of the word. An earlier edition of the *COD*, interestingly, adds 'or euphuism', which certainly does include 'elaborate similes and parallels' (Abrams, 2nd edn., s.v.).

strained metaphor', in *Webster's Seventh New Collegiate Dictionary* (1963), and '5. an elaborate, fanciful metaphor, esp. of a strained or far-fetched nature', *Random House Dictionary of the English Language (College Edition)* (1968) will not be found in their predecessors, the older *Webster's Collegiate Dictionary* and the *American College Dictionary* (1947).

As Johnson says, 'Critical remarks are not easily understood without examples,' and I have appended to this article a number of quotations from the 'Life of Cowley' and the Shakespeare edition which seem to me to form a representative selection of his use of the word 'conceit'; I refer to them below by the letters placed before them in the appendix. A longer, even a complete listing of the occurrences of the word in Johnson's criticism would of course be desirable. Space for such a listing is not available here, but I do not think I have omitted any instance of a use that would seriously weaken my thesis, that, whatever else 'conceit' meant to Johnson, he did *not* equate it with 'metaphorical language'. For that signification, he had another, quite adequate term, which he used whenever he needed it—'image' (or 'imagery'). Indeed, it must be stressed that, in his *Dictionary* definition 6, and in quotations A and C he insists that 'conceit', in a context of literary criticism, is *opposed* to 'imagery'—to 'pictures in the mind'. Rather, it involves 'sentiment' (*Dictionary*: 'Thought: notion; opinion') and 'inferences' (*Dictionary:* 'Conclusion drawn from previous arguments'); as we should now say, 'cerebration', a mental, or verbal, activity, as contrasted with a sensory one. Conceits are 'unaffecting' (K), emotionally 'frigid' (D), counteracting the 'pathetick' (D, K, N) (*Dictionary:* 'Affection: 2. Passion of any kind'; 'Pathetick: Affecting the passions; passionate: moving'), interrupting what is 'agitated', 'perturbed', 'issuing from the heart' (M). 'The power of Cowley', the arch-constructor of conceits, 'is not so much to move the affections, as to exercise the understanding' (para. 108).

That this is how Johnson used the word is not unexpected: the noun 'conceit', cognate with 'concept' and 'conception', and, like them, implying an act of conscious cerebration, goes back at least to Chaucer. As a literary term, some dictionaries, though not Johnson's, point out, it may derive from Italian *concetto*, and was used in a derogatory sense long before Johnson. One of its most

striking occurrences is in Ben Jonson's *Bartholomew Fair*, where
Littlewit opens the play with the exclamation 'A pretty conceit,
and worth the finding!'—namely, his discovery that a man named
Bartholomew is to be married on 24 August, St. Bartholomew's
Day, thus enabling Littlewit to say, 'Bartholomew upon Bartholomew!' Johnson remembered and enjoyed this (I, N).[13] The
derogatory overtones of the word also surely have something to do
with its use in the sense of excessive self-esteem, 'opinionative
pride' (Johnson's definition 7), itself deriving from Proverbs 26:
12, 'Seest thou a man wise in his own conceit? There is more hope
of a fool than of him', which Johnson quotes under his definition
4.

'Bartholomew upon Bartholomew', though a conceit for both
Jonson and Johnson, is not imagery: no 'pictures in the mind' are
conjured up. It is simply elementary word-play—the conjunction
of the two Bartholomews seems to Littlewit an amusing and clever
discovery. The image-associating power remains, for both writers,
wit, of which Locke's account, quoted in *Dictionary* definition 2,
'Imagination; quickness of fancy', was surely the one most
influential with Johnson: 'Wit lying most in the assemblage of
ideas, and putting these together with quickness and variety
wherein can be found any resemblance or congruity, thereby to
make up pleasant pictures in the fancy.' The importance here of
'ideas'—deriving from the Greek verb for 'to see', cognate with
Latin *video*—or 'pictures', not words, 'in the fancy' can hardly be
overstressed. But Johnson's 'conceits' include verbal, non-
imagistic quips like 'Bartholomew upon Bartholomew', 'Hero
and hero' (F), and 'Percy and pierce' (H), and no doubt E, with
its rather puzzling objection to 'free from comeliness'.

As quotation B indicates, Johnson relies heavily in his use of
'wit' and 'conceit' on the discussion in *Spectator* 62, where Addison
distinguishes the categories of true, false, and mixed wit. True wit,
says Addison, relying in turn on Locke, consists in resemblance
of *ideas*. False wit, however, consists in the resemblances of words,
and includes such games as equivokes, puns, quibbles, verbal
echoes, doggerel rhymes, acrostics, rebuses, *bouts rimés*. Since the
only 'resemblance' detectable in 'Bartholomew upon Bartholomew'

---

[13] 'A conceit left in his misery, a miserable conceit' seems to be an addition
or adaptation by Dryden, in his Preface to *Fables, Ancient and Modern* (*Essays
of John Dryden*, ed. W. P. Ker (Oxford: Clarendon Press, 1926), ii. 256).

is a verbal one, it is presumably false wit—or, strictly speaking, no wit.

According to Johnson's discussion in B, the principal vehicle of at least Cowley's conceits is 'mixed wit', which consists, Addison says, partly in the resemblance of words and partly in the resemblance of ideas. Johnson revises this to 'thoughts true in one sense of the expression and false in the other'—in the example given, talk about figurative (false) fire as though it were true fire. We begin with the metaphorical expression, 'I am on fire with love', and then ring the changes on literal flames, combustion, ashes, extinction of the flames by tears, and so on. As Johnson says, Sannazaro did it earlier: the speaker says he is both Etna and the Nile at the same time, since he is both in love (figurative fire) and weeping (literal water).

In modern terminology what we seem to have here is a dead or almost dead metaphor ('on fire with love') unexpectedly and laboriously brought to life again; and certainly this is often what Johnson means by a conceit. This is the case in quotation G— when one talks about a dead man embracing the earth ('biting the dust'), one does not normally think of the action so concretely as Shakespeare here represents it. Likewise with Warburton's use of 'conceit' in I: when we use 'fraction' in arithmetic, we do not normally have a picture of literal breaking in our minds. Johnson, however, denies that the arithmetical metaphor enters into it: 'fraction' in Shakespeare's time could still mean a literal breaking or breaking off; since only the literal meaning is involved, there is no conceit. Likewise K, beginning with the near-dead metaphor of 'My heart is dried with grief'; likewise with L—when one says 'gall', meaning bitterness, one does not usually think of either the animal or the vegetable substance; likewise M— 'the guise of the world' does not normally suggest literal clothing.[14]

For Johnson, then, a conceit may take the form of word-play pure and simple (false wit), or of playing with both the (weakened) metaphorical sense of a word and its literal sense (mixed wit).[15] It is true, however, that from time to time he discovers 'conceit' in a collocation of genuine images (true, if here ineffective, wit). In

[14] Or perhaps the conceit is the feeble epigram 'Less without, and more within'.

[15] I also give an example (J) of Johnson's using 'conceit' in the neutral sense of 'thought' (definition 1 or 4 in his *Dictionary*).

quotation A, Donne speaks of midnight as 'Time's dead low-water', and compares the deep sleep of the ordinary mortal at that hour to the sleep of the grave, and so on. But it is not the extent and complication of the imagery in themselves that bothers Johnson. Pope's comparison in the *Essay on Criticism*, ll. 219–32, of the scholar to a mountain climber, which Johnson thought 'perhaps the best [comparison] that English poetry can shew' is as long, elaborate, and detailed as anything in Donne. So, for that matter, is Johnson's own description of the scholar's life in *The Vanity of Human Wishes*, ll. 135–56. It is that, instead of impressing on the reader vividly and concretely the picture of night, as Dryden does, it presents him with a series of intellectual puzzles. (Why is the sleep of the grave 'scarce a type' of the labourer's sleep in bed? Because it is 'subject to change'—i.e. presumably, rudely interrupted by the last trumpet.)

It is not extension of metaphor or elaboration of imagery that Johnson objects to in his long series of quotations from Donne, Cowley, and Cleveland (paragraphs 64 to 101 in the 'Life of Cowley'). It is the intrusion into them of various inappropriate products of what he thinks to be conscious cerebration and the desire to impress the reader with the author's cleverness, which seem to him to interrupt or destroy the emotional atmosphere the poem is trying to create. He catalogues these carefully: (1) 'They sometimes drew their conceits from recesses of learning not very much frequented by common readers of poetry'—the 'tree of Porphyry', rabbinical lore, abstruse points of geographical and medicinal knowledge. Johnson believes poetry should be comprehensible by a wider audience than specialists in such matters.[16] (2) 'They use "enormous and disgusting hyperboles".' (3) 'Their

---

[16] 'As they were wholly employed on something unexpected and surprising, they had no regard to that uniformity of sentiment, which enables us to conceive and to excite the pains and the pleasure of other minds': 'Life of Cowley', para. 57. In *Rambler* 60 Johnson stresses the fundamental importance for him in literature of what we call 'empathy'. Johnson's own imagery tends to be drawn much more from familiar, even homely, matters than from learning (cf. my 'Pictures to the Mind', p. 144 n. 1). Two of Johnson's own uses of imagery in the 'Life of Cowley' are worth noticing: one from real estate matters, 'Pope has some epitaphs without names; which are therefore epitaphs to be let, occupied indeed for the present, but hardly appropriated' (para. 103); and one which is surely 'mixed wit': 'If their conceits were far-fetched, they were often worth the carriage' (para. 60). There seems no reason why these witticisms should themselves not be classified as 'conceits'—except that they 'come off', their humour seems spontaneous and unforced.

fictions were often violent and unnatural'—fish crowd around a
beautiful woman bathing as they would around a fisherman's night
light; her beauty illuminates the water as though the sun itself set
there. (4) 'Their conceits were sometimes slight and trifling'—
e.g. the hackneyed contrast of April showers and May flowers.
(5) 'As they sought only for novelty they did not much enquire
whether their allusions were to things high or low, elegant or
gross'—whether the emotional connotation of the vehicle is in
keeping with that of the tenor: Cleveland calls the sun a 'coal-pit
rampant': Cowley compares a lover's heart to a hand grenade. (6)
Their choice of diction is likewise inappropriate to the subject:
'They were in little care to clothe their notions with elegance of
dress . . . they were sometimes indelicate and disgusting . . . their
expressions sometimes raise horror, when they intend perhaps to
be pathetick', as in Cowley's 'As men in hell are from diseases
free,/So from all other ills am I.' (7) 'They were not always strictly
curious whether the opinions from which they drew their illustrations were true', such as the notion that a 'Venice-glass' would
break if poison were poured into it. Presumably the reader's
inability to take such folklore seriously would interfere with his
emotional response to the poem. One feels sure that it is not only
in the poetry of the 'Metaphysicals' that Johnson believes such
faults to occur. Indeed, objections similar to each of these can be
found in his criticisms of Shakespeare and of post-'Metaphysical'
poetry.

   To sum up. The sense of the term 'conceit' in Johnson's literary
criticism is still close to its origin in French *concevoir* or Latin
conceptus—something too obviously intellectually contrived, *voulu*,
organically unrelated to the poetic occasion. It may manifest itself
in word-play, in a combination of word-play and imagery, or even
in a true combination of images when those images are so 'heterogeneous' or so 'violently yoked together' that the reader's response
is intellectual rather than emotional. Or, as far as that goes, when
a trite and banal image (showery April and flowery May) is
mechanically used.[17] Perhaps the closest synonym of the term in

---

[17] Or perhaps, though he does not use the term 'conceit', in 'The artifice of
inversion, by which the established order of words is changed, or of innovation,
by which new words or new meanings of words are introduced, [which] is
practised, not by those who talk to be understood, but by those who write to be
admired' (para. 117). It is interesting that, though they have nothing to do with
the 'Metaphysicals'—indeed, Cowley is praised for eschewing them—Johnson

current English is 'gimmick', defined in the *Concise Oxford Dictionary* (6th edn., 1976) as 'Tricky device, esp. one adopted for the purpose of attracting attention or publicity.'[18]

It may well be that Johnson's fulminations against the obviously cerebral and contrived in poetry—is the position very distant from Wordsworth's 'All good poetry is the spontaneous overflow of powerful feelings'?[19]—are not of much practical value so far as the judgement of excellence in poetry is concerned. The 'intellectuality' of Donne's metaphors does not inhibit the emotional response of the modern reader: though, it must be granted, for him so to respond, as for the poet so to write, 'It is at least necessary to read and think', as Johnson remarked. It must also be granted that not many of the excerpts from Donne which Johnson holds up for dispraise would be selected by modern readers for inclusion in an anthology of 'The Best of Donne'. And, ironically, Victorian and later critics were to make the same charge against the poetry of Dryden and Pope, which Johnson admired—that it is too 'cerebral' and not 'emotional' enough; though here again, modern readers who take the trouble to acquaint themselves with the 'intellectual' content find it adequately 'affecting'.

However all this may be, if modern critics wish to invent a term, 'metaphysical conceit', and to define it as 'extended metaphor' or 'elaborate image', it is certainly their privilege to do so. But it is an error to think that Johnson was responsible for this new usage. He firmly asserts (quotation B) that the 'conceits' he censures in the poetry of Cowley are also to be found in classical Greek and Latin poetry, in the poetry of Renaissance Italy, and, certainly, they are to be found in Shakespeare. They are not something peculiar to the 'Metaphysicals'. For Johnson there is no such thing as a 'metaphysical conceit'. There are only 'conceits': poetic—we may extend it to artistic—gimmickry, which is not of an age, but, alas, for all time.

---

cannot resist mentioning in this context those *bêtes noires* of his, which he so roundly condemns as affectation in Gray and Collins.

[18] A recent edition of *Bartholomew Fair*, annotating Littlewit's 'Bartholomew upon Bartholomew! there's the device!' (Littlewit has earlier called it 'a pretty conceit'), glosses 'device' as 'gimmick': *Drama of the English Renaissance*, ed. Russell A. Fraser and Norman Rabkin (New York: Macmillan, 1976), ii. 196 n. 1.

[19] Johnson's praise of spontaneity in quotation M might be noted.

APPENDIX

Quotations from the 'Life of Cowley' are identified by 'C.' followed by the number of the paragraph(s) in Volume I of *The Lives of the Poets*, ed. G. B. Hill (1905). 'S.' followed by a number indicates the page in *Johnson on Shakespeare*, ed. Arthur Sherbo (1968), The Yale Edition of the Works of Samuel Johnson, vols. vii, viii (paged continuously). I am indebted to Professor Sherbo for assistance with these. To save space I have printed quoted poetry in 'run on' form. I have italicized 'conceit(s)' and some other significant terms.

A. C.98. In forming descriptions they looked out not for *images*, but for *conceits*. Night has been a common subject, which poets have contended to adorn. Dryden's *Night* is well known; Donne's is as follows: 'Thou seest me here at midnight; now all rest,/Time's dead low-water; when all minds divest/To-morrow's business; when the labourers have/ Such rest in bed, that their last church-yard grave,/Subject to change, will scarce be a type of this./Now when the client, whose last hearing is/To-morrow, sleeps; when the condemned man—/Who when he opes his eyes must shut them then/Again by death—although sad watch he keep,/Doth practise dying by a little sleep;/Thou at this midnight seest me.' [The Dryden reference seems to be to *The Indian Emperor*, III. 2: 'All things are hush'd, as Nature's self lay dead,/The mountains seem to nod their drowsy head;/The little birds in dreams their songs repeat,/And sleeping flow'rs beneath the night-dew sweat. . . .']

B. C.120–1. The principal artifice by which *The Mistress* is filled with *conceits* is very copiously displayed by Addison. Love is by Cowley as by other poets expressed metaphorically by flame and fire; and that which is true of real fire is said of love, or figurative fire, the same word in the same sentence retaining both significations. Thus, 'observing the cold regard of his mistress's eyes, and at the same time their power of producing love in him, he considers them as burning-glasses made of ice. Finding himself able to live in the greatest extremities of love he concludes the torrid zone to be habitable. Upon the dying of a tree, on which he had cut his loves, he observes that his flames had burnt up and withered the tree.'

These *conceits* Addison calls mixed wit, that is, wit which consists of thoughts true in one sense of the expression, and false in the other. Addison's representation is sufficiently indulgent: that confusion of images may entertain for a moment, but being unnatural it soon grows wearisome. Cowley delighted in it, as much as if he had invented it; but, not to mention the ancients, he might have found it full-blown in modern Italy. 'Aspice quam variis distringar, Lesbia, curis,/Uror, et heu! nostro manat ab igne liquor;/Sum Nilus, sumque Ætna simul; restringite flammas/O lacrimæ, aut lacrimas ebibe flamma meas.'

C. C.154, 159, 167–8. One of the great sources of poetical delight is description, or the power of presenting pictures to the mind. Cowley gives *inferences* instead of *images*, and shews not what may be supposed to have been seen, but what thoughts the sight might have suggested. When Virgil describes the stone which Turnus lifted against Æneas, he fixes the attention on its bulk and weight. . . . Cowley says of the stone with which Cain slew his brother, 'I saw him fling the stone, as if he meant/At once his murther and his monument.' . . . Whatever he writes is always polluted with some *conceit*: 'Where the sun's fruitful beams give metals birth,/Where he the growth of fatal gold does see,/Gold, which alone more influence has than he.' . . . Rymer has declared the *Davideis* superior to the *Jerusalem* of Tasso. . . . [In the description of heaven] the different manner of the two writers is sufficiently discernible. Cowley's is scarcely description, unless it be possible to describe by negatives; for he tells us only what there is not in heaven. Tasso endeavours to represent the splendours and pleasures of the regions of happiness. Tasso affords *images*, and Cowley *sentiments*.

D. S.74. He is not long soft and *pathetick* without some idle *conceit*, or contemptible equivocation. He no sooner begins to *move*, than he counteracts himself; and *terrour* and *pity*, as they are rising in the mind, are checked and blasted by sudden *frigidity*.

E. S.198. To wish 'that men were as free from faults, as faults are free from comeliness' (instead of 'void of comeliness') is a very poor *conceit*.

F. S.370. '*Claudio*. O Hero! what a Hero hadst thou been.' I am afraid here is intended a poor *conceit* upon the word 'hero.'

G. S.412. '. . . many a widow's husband groveling lies,/Coldly embracing the discolour'd earth.' This speech is very poetical and smooth, and except the *conceit* of the 'widow's husband' embracing 'the earth,' is just and beautiful.

H. S.487–8. '*Falstaff*. If Percy be alive, I'll pierce him.' I rather take the *conceit* to be this. To 'pierce a vessel' is to 'tap' it. Falstaff takes up his bottle which the Prince had tossed at his head, and being about to animate himself with a draught, cries, 'if Percy be alive I'll pierce him,' and so draws the cork. I do not propose this with much confidence.

I. S.720. 'After distasteful looks, and these hard fractions,/With certain half-caps, and cold moving nods,/They froze me into silence.' [*Warburton: hard fractions.* An equivocal allusion to fractions in decimal arithmetic. So Flavius had, like Littlewit, in *Bartholomew-Fair, a conceit left in his misery*.] There is, I think, no *conceit* in the head of Flavius, who, by *fractions*, means *broken* hints, *interrupted* sentences, *abrupt* remarks. [I have given a fuller quotation from this passage than Sherbo. D.G.]

J. S.805. '[He] is content/To spend his time to end it.' I know not whether my *conceit* will be approved, but I cannot forbear to think that our authour wrote thus . . . 'To spend his time, to spend it.'

K. S.862. 'Throw my heart/Against the flint and hardness of my fault,/Which, being dried with grief, will break to powder,/And finish all foul thoughts.' The *pathetick* of Shakespeare too often ends in the ridiculous. It is painful to find the gloomy dignity of this noble scene destroyed by the intrusion of a *conceit* so far-fetched and *unaffecting*.

L. S.876. 'And with mine eyes I'll drink the words you send,/ Though ink be made of gall.' Shakespeare, even in this poor *conceit*, has confounded the vegetable 'galls' used in ink, with the animal 'gall,' supposed to be bitter.

M. S.901–2. 'I'll disrobe me/Of these Italian weeds, and suit myself/ As does a Briton peasant. . . . Let me make men know/More valour in me, than my habits show . . . To shame the guise o' th' world, I will begin/The fashion. Less without, and more within.' This is a soliloquy of nature, uttered when the effervescence of a mind *agitated* and *perturbed spontaneously* and inadvertently discharges itself in words. The speech, throughout all its tenour, if the last *conceit* be excepted, seems to issue *warm from the heart*. [A detailed psychological analysis of the speech follows.]

N. S.957. His comick scenes are happily wrought, but his *pathetick* strains are always polluted with some unexpected depravations. His persons, however distressed, 'have a *conceit* left them in their misery, a miserable *conceit*.'

Edmond Malone, Horace Walpole, and Shakespeare

Wilmarth S. Lewis

One of the victims of our present postal discontents was my invitation to contribute to this Festschrift. I understand that it was sent in the middle of 1975, but it never reached me. Fortunately, Mr. Wellek's reminder that my contribution was due by the end of the year did get through in time and so I am of the company, after all, honoured and pleased to be so.

My subject has been inspired by Walpole's letter to Malone written from Berkeley Square, 11 February 1785: 'Mr Walpole is very sorry he cannot answer the favour of Mr Malone's obliging letter with his own hand having had two relapses of the gout, and being still much out of order. Mr Walpole knows he has notes on several of the characters of Shakespeare, but they are at Strawberry Hill, and till he can go thither they cannot be got at, but as soon as he has recovered enough to go there, he will certainly look them out, and will send them to Mr Malone, and hopes they will not be too late for his edition.' Malone knew that Walpole was a dedicated Shakespearian. We know from Walpole's letters that he regarded Shakespeare as 'our first of men'. Doubtless he talked about him with the same ardour.

The 'notes on several characters in Shakespeare' that he refers to are, I think, those in his 'Books of Materials', which he kept under lock and key in the Glass Closet at Strawberry Hill. He began them in 1759 and 1771 and added a 'Miscellany' in 1786 that he kept up until 1795. The notes on Shakespeare that he sent Malone in March 1785 were not from them, but were apparently his marginalia in a copy of Rowe's edition of the plays, which has unfortunately disappeared. Walpole's Second Folio, Pope's, Hanmer's, and Malone's editions of the plays are at Farmington, but have disappointingly few marginalia. Why Walpole did not send Malone his 'notes on several characters of Shakespeare' from his 'Books of Materials' is a mystery, for they are much fuller and richer than those he sent in March.

While the 'Books of Materials' were at the Folger Library, J. Q. Adams kindly let me print privately in 1940, 100 copies of the notes on Shakespeare for the Sixteenth Number of my *Miscellaneous Antiquities*. I gave them all away except the two that I kept for my wife and myself. The 'Books of Materials' have since migrated to Farmington and I am now offering their Shakespearian notes again, this time as a tribute to Malone's historian who wrote a contribution to my Festschrift in 1967, 'Horace Walpole and Edmond Malone'. So this chapter becomes a postscript to his, an instance of gratitude perhaps unprecedented in the history of Festschriften.

In Shakespeare's Henry 8th where he makes Wolsey deliver to the King by mistake an inventory of his personal estate, is a great instance of the poet's art. The fact which he applies to Wolsey was true of Ruthall Bishop of Durham, and Wolsey who hated the latter, took occasion to tell his master that he now knew where to have money when he wanted it. See the account in Bishop [Francis] Godwin de Presulibus Angliae [1616].

It was not necessary that Shakespeare should be an exact genealogist. He was not, and yet he had looked so far into our histories, that he sometimes observed the connections between his personages, tho not minutely. I had long been puzzled with a passage in Richd 2d, where mentioning the persons that landed with Bolinbroke, he names the Archbishop and calls him Henry's brother. I thought there might be a line wanting; but I have found at last, that Thomas Fitzalan Archbishop of Canterbury was brother to the mother of Henry's first wife, consequently his uncle by marriage. Richard Fitzalan Earl of Arundel among other children had the following, which will explain the relation:

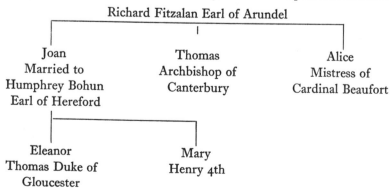

Richard Fitzalan Earl of Arundel

Joan	Thomas	Alice
Married to	Archbishop of	Mistress of
Humphrey Bohun	Canterbury	Cardinal Beaufort
Earl of Hereford		

Eleanor	Mary
Thomas Duke of	Henry 4th
Gloucester	

There is a greater difficulty in Scene 8, Act 5, of the same play. Bolinbroke or Henry 4th calls the Abbot of Westminster, who conspired against him, his trusty *brother-in-law*. To call a religious, Father or Brother, is common: but Shakespeare had certainly some grounds for stiling him the King's *brother-in-law*. Yet I cannot discover the reason. Dart, at the end of his Antiquities of Westminster says this abbot's name was Richard Harounden: tho he owns that the confusions of times have left it uncertain.

In the same play of Richard 2d, last act, there is a scene between the Duke and Duchess of York. The poet has taken a very allowable liberty of supposing that the Duchess was mother of Aumerle, and that the Duke had no other children. But his second son Richard Earl of Cambridge makes a considerable figure in our author's Henry 5th. Duke Edmund had likewise a daughter; but all his children were by his first wife, not by the second, who was his wife at the time of Aumerle's conspiracy. Shakespeare has made a stronger anachronism by drawing Richard's 2d Queen Isabel as a woman, who was a child at his death and never consummated her marriage with him.

Stowe, in his account of the proceedings in Wales previous to the deposition of Richard 2d, calls Sir Stephen Scrope his author, who was with the King at that time. It is pity Scrope's own narrative is not known. Hollingshed seems to confirm the same. Hollingshed calls the Abbot of Westminster William, and says he died of an apoplexy.

Addison in some of his Spectators approaches nearest to Shakespeare's natural humour, that is character. When each are most excellent, it is the wit of humour: their personages have the wit that results merely from their peculiar character. Sir Roger de Coverley is the best drawn character next to Falstaff: but Falstaff has not only more wit, but whereas Sir Roger is a character that has or may have been seen, there cannot be another Falstaff without being an imitation. Falstaff and Caliban are not only created characters, but talk a language that would suit no other being but themselves.

When Lord Northington was dying and the women cried in his room, he said, turn out all the bitches but Bridget—his favourite daughter. The character given of Kent by one of Lear's daughters, of being an interested knave that passed off bluntness for honesty, is exactly Lord Northington's. Mr. Hardinge.[1]

In 1773. Mr Garrick produced his Hamlet altered, in which he had omitted the scene of the grave diggers, from injudicious complaisance to French critics, and their cold regularity, which cramps genius.

---

[1] That is, this observation was made by George Hardinge (1743–1816), Walpole's correspondent and the Jefferies Hardsman of Byron's *Don Juan*.

Objections made to that admirable scene of nature, is, that it is burlesque, unheroic, and destroys and interrupts the interest of the action, and diverts Hamlet from his purpose on which he ought only to think, the vengeance due to the murder of his father. Not one of these objections are true. If Garrick had really been an intelligent manager, he would have corrected the vicious buffoonery which lay in his actors, not in the play. The parts of the grave-diggers have long been played by the most comic and buffoon actors in the company, who always endeavoured to raise a laughter from the galleries by absurd mirth and gesticulations. The parts ought to be given [to them] who could best represent low nature seriously, and at most the jokes between the men themselves previous to Hamlet's entry might have been shortened, tho those very jests are natural and moral, for they show that habit can bring men to be cheerful even in the midst of the most melancholy exercise of their profession. That the scene is not unheroic, tho in prose, is from the serious remarks it draws from Hamlet. Is every low character inconsistent with heroic tragedy? What has so pathetic effect as the fool in Lear? in how many Greek and modern tragedies are the nurse, a shepherd, a messenger, essential to the plot? Mirth itself, especially in the hands of such a genius as Shakespeare, may excite tears not laughter, and ought to do so. The grave-digger's account of Yorick's ludicrous behaviour is precisely an instance of that exquisite and matchless art, and furnishes an answer too to the last objection, that the humour of the grave-digger interrupts the interest of the action and weakens the purpose of Hamlet. Directly the contrary; the skull of Yorick and the account of his jests could have no effect but to recall fresh to the Prince's mind the happy days of his childhood, and the court of the King his father, and thence make him [see] his uncle's reign in a comparative view that must have rendered the latter odious to him, and consequently the scene serves to whet his *almost blunted purpose.* Not to mention that the grave before him was destined to his love Ophelia—what incident in this scene but tends to work on his passions?—O ignorance of nature, when the union of nature and art can make critics wish for art only!

Is it not amazing that as all rules are drawn from the *conduct* of great genius's, not from their *directions*, nobody should have thought of drawing up rules from Shakespeare's plays, rather than of wishing they had been written from rules collected from such subaltern genius's as Euripides and Sophocles? I maintain that it was likely we should have had finer tragedies, if Shakespeare's daring had been laid down for a rule of venturing, than by pointing out his irregularities as faults. Let me add, that the Witches in Macbeth, are by the folly of the actors, not by the fault of Shakespeare, represented in a buffoon light. They are dressed with black hats and blue aprons, like basket women and soldiers' trulls, which must make the people not consider them as beings endowed with supernatural powers.

Addison is a glaring proof that pedantry and servility to rules could dishabilitate a man of genius. Compare his Cato and Shakespeare's Julius Caesar. There is as much difference as between the soul of Julius and the timidity of Addison. A school boy of parts might by 19 have written Cato. The other was written by a master of human nature, and by a genius so quick and so intuitive, so penetrating, that Shakespeare from the dregs and obstacles of vile translations, has drawn finer portraits of Caesar, Brutus, Cassius, Antony and Casca than Cicero himself has done who lived with and knew the men. Why? because Cicero thought of what he should say of them; Shakespeare, of what they would have said themselves.

But Shakespeare has not only improved on Cicero, but on the founders of his art, Euripides and Sophocles, for he has done, what they did not, he has introduced a chorus properly and speaking and acting in character. The Roman mob before whom Brutus and Antony plead, is just. They did plead before the Roman mob, and the mob is made by Shakespeare to display the effect that eloquence has on vulgar minds. Shakespeare does not make Brutus and Cassius disclose their plot to the Roman people—That would not have been a stroke of nature or of art, but of absurdity. Shakespeare never introduces a chorus but with peculiar propriety. Fluellin &c in Henry 5th are in effect a chorus: But they are not a parcel of mutes unconcerned in the action, who by the mouth of one representative draw moral and common place reflections from the incidents of the piece. A chorus was the first idea; to incorporate the chorus in the body of the drama, was an improvement wanting. Instead of observing that Shakespeare's enlightened mind had made that improvement, we have had men so absurd as to revert to the original imperfection—just as some men have wished to revive the feudal system—for some men cannot perceive the discrimination between original principles and original usages.

The Bishop of Poitiers going to excommunicate William 9th Comte de Poitou, the Count threatened to kill him if he did not absolve him. The Bishop begged a respite, and having obtained it, pronounced the anathema, and then cried, 'Now strike, I am prepared!' 'No,' said the Count, 'I don't love you well enough to send you directly to Paradise.' Shakespeare seems to have imitated this passage in the Hamlet, when he will not kill the King at his prayers. Hist. des Troub[adours]. Vol. 1, p. 5.

Shakespeare in that most beautiful scene between Northumberland and Lady Percy in the second part of Henry 4th makes Lady Percy in her fond description of her husband Hotspur, say,

And speaking thick, which nature made *his* blemish,
Became the accents of the valiant.

Perhaps our marvelous poet took the hint from this character of Sir
James Douglas in an old Scottish poet,

His bodie well made and laurie,
As they that saw him said to me.
When he was blythe, he was lovely,
And meek and sweet in company;
But who in battle might him see,
Another countenance had he,
And in his speech he lispt some deal,
But that set him right wonder well.

Barbour, in the notes to Sir David Dalrymple's Annals of Scotl. Vol. 2.
p.137.—Shakespeare, who looked into all nature, knew that what was
graceful in a hero, tho a defect, would be mimicked by the apes and
coxcombs of the age. There is a pretty simplicity in the older bard; in
our countryman that slight sketch is worked up by the hand of a master
into a portrait of human nature. It is a picture that exhibits mankind,
as well as the likeness of a single character. They are those strokes that
raise Shakespeare above all authors who ever wrote. Many copyists
have imitated his language—if they did aim at his intuition into nature,
they miscarried so entirely, that we cannot trace their attempts. The
inimitable scene I have mentioned is never acted, because no principal
actress will condescend to speak but two speeches; tho it would be
sufficient fame for any actress that ever existed, to pronounce those two
speeches with all the pathetic tenderness and enthusiasm with which
they ought to be spoken. The scene of the grave-diggers in Hamlet, the
finest piece of moral pathos that can be imagined, was sillily omitted by
Garrick, because it had been generally acted in a buffoon manner, and
because French critics, who did not understand it, condemned it as low.
I have seen old Johnson[2] play the first grave-digger in the very spirit in
which Shakespeare wrote it: He jested slightly with his companion
before Hamlet entered, marking the insensibility that habitude produces
in men accustomed to sights that shock or impress with melancholy
those not broken to them—but when the Prince entered, Johnson
resumed his seriousness to a certain degree, yet not so much as to
destroy the stronger emotions of Hamlet. It was natural to a grave-
digger to recall the wantonness of a young merry courtier, and recount
it as he felt it—but to the Prince, it brought back reflection on the happy
hours of his childhood, which he could not but compare with the dismal
scenes that had ensued, and with his own present melancholy situation.

[2] Benjamin Johnson (1665?–1742) of the company at Drury Lane.

In this just light the skull of his father's jester roused the indignation of Hamlet and egged him on to the justice he meditated on his uncle; and thus that rejected scene hastened on the catastrophe of the tragedy, and more naturally than the most pompous exhortation would have done from the mouth of Horatio. A spark falling on combustible matter may light up a conflagration. A great master produces important events from a trifle naturally introduced. A piddling critic would waste his time in describing the torch with dignity that set fire to the combustion. Compare Ben Johnson's Catiline with Hamlet. The former is al pedantry and bombast. Are the royal dignities of the Ghost, of the Queen or of Hamlet lowered by the variety of familiar incidents taken from common life that are introduced into the tragedy? The rules of Aristotle, of Bossu, are ridiculous and senseless, if they prohibit such conduct and operations of the passions. Is there an incident in all Racine, Corneille, Voltaire, Addison or Otway, so natural, so pathetic, so sublime, as Prince Arthur's reprimanding Hubert of his having bound a handkerchief wrought by a princess on the jailor's temples? It is that contrast between royalty and the keeper of a prison that exalts both, and augments the compassion for Arthur. Dr Johnson has dared to say that when Shakespeare aimed at being sublime he was bombast; that is, Johnson had no idea of sublimity but in the pomp of diction, and he himself in his common conversation is always hyperbolic and pedantic. He talks like ancient Pistol, and is the very thing he condemns. Is there no sublimity in ennobling a vulgar image or expression? Voltaire did not know there is, any more than Johnson. The Frenchman condemns Hamlet's expression *of a bare bodkin*; every Englishman of taste feels the happy energy of the phrase. I do not doubt but we lose many beauties in the ancients from not understanding the whole force of their language and allusions: but it would be the extremity of folly to sacrifice our glory, Shakespeare, to French critics, who undoubtedly cannot comprehend half his merit. Will Dr Johnson or Voltaire reject this passage

> When your own Percy, when my heart—dear Harry,
> Threw many a northward look to see his Father
> Bring up his powers—but he did look in vain!
> Who then persuaded you to stay at home!
> There were two honours lost, yours and your son's.

No words can be more trite, more vulgar, less laboured, less selected— *my heart—dear Harry* would suit the mouth of Mrs. Quickly—yet how tender when wrung from the lips of a wife, who felt the loss of her domestic happiness, and was not considering herself as the partner of a hero of a conspiracy!

Who then persuaded you to stay at home.

Would not that line be ridiculously bad, and familiar, if not ennobled by distress and sentiment? Is not the cadence of the whole passage harmonious, tender, and accented by grief! In short, let Dr Johnson translate these five lines into his decompounds of Greek frenchified— aye, let him put them into any words but those simple ones employed by Shakespeare, and see if they will be improved. O Shakespeare, thou first of men, I am happy to possess that language in which thou didst write, that not one of thy excellencies are lost on me!

I purposely forbore to quote the lines that follow, because they rise to genuine poetry, in proportion as the enthusiasm of the speaker rose. Shakespeare's exquisite taste knew how to distribute simple language to grief and argument, and exalted diction to enthusiastic love. Raise the expression in the first five lines, and you would destroy the musical energy of the succeeding. Pope's Epistle of Eloisa is one continued strain of poetic love, laboured and polished to the highest perfection— but is Eloisa as natural as Lady Percy? There is another merit in the latter, of which there is not the smallest trace in the former. The images of Eloisa might be those of any popish age, nay are too gorgeous for those in which she lived—whereas Lady Percy exhibits the image of the plain wives of our old barons in that savage age. She regrets the enjoyments of domestic life, recalls the honours paid to her husband, but does not drop a hint of any luxury she had tasted but in him. Constance in King John is precisely such a mother, as Lady Percy is a widow.— They dwell on no ideas that are foreign to their grief—but there would be no end to a comment on Shakespeare's beauties—He has faults enough to glut the critics—but let them not dare to meddle with his excellencies, which no other mortal ever could attain. How would Voltaire or the greatest genius of any nation have been puzzled if proposed to them to specify in tragedy that their hero stammered, or to call him by a nickname! Yet how beautiful is the description of Hotspur's speaking thick, and calling him my heart—dear *Harry!*

Walpole made these last three entries in his final notebook, the 'Miscellany'. *They have been edited by Lars E. Troide in his* Horace Walpole's Miscellany, 1786–95, *Yale University Press, 1978.*

Richard 2d, says Froissart, had a favourite greyhound called Matt who shocked him by fawning on his successor. Gough's Sepulchral Monuments. cxxiv. How beautifully has Shakespeare introduced and dignified this anecdote by applying it to the horse on which Bolinbroke rode to his coronation, and which had belonged to poor Richard. The name of Roan Barbary, instead of Matt, shows how well Shakespeare knew how to improve and exalt little circumstances, when he borrowed them from circumstantial or vulgar historians.[3]

His reviving Richard's Queen Anne, in the place of his second wife Isabel, who was an infant, is another instance of his judgment to move our sensibility. When Shakespeare copied chroniclers verbatim, it was because he knew they were good enough for his audiences. In a more polished age he who could so move our passions, could surely have performed the easier task of satisfying our taste.

Dr Farmer's elucidation of the sources whence Shakespeare drew the subjects and circumstances of many of his plays, put an end to the fantastic discussions on his supposed learning. But the best comment on the marvellous powers of his genius in drawing and discriminating characters is contained in Mr Whateley's *remarks on some of the Characters* of Shakespeare [viz, Macbeth and Richard 3d] printed for Payne, in a thin octavo pamphlet, 1785. It ought to be prefixed to every edition of Shakespeare as a preface, and will tend more to give a just idea of that matchless genius than all the notes and criticisms on his works. It would teach men to study and discover new magic in his works, instead of settling the text of many scenes that are not worth being understood. When he wrote carelessly and ill and only to please the mob, it signifies not whether he used one silly word or another. To show how perfectly he possessed the knowledge of human nature, might hint to future authors that plot, rules, nor even poetry, are not half so great beauties in tragedy or comedy as a just imitation of nature, of character, of the passions and their operations in diversified situations. How inadequate would Voltaire or Racine appear to their office, were the characters in their tragedies to be scrutinized and compared like those of Macbeth and Richard!

Ramus sentoit trop les beautès des anciens pour en admirer les defaults. *Tableaux des revelations de la literature*, 1786, p. 190.—so ought we to judge of Shakespeare.

There are gleams of sense in that book that make one wonder the author did not make a better book on so fruitful a subject. He gives the French the superiority in eloquence, in which they are vastly inferior to our orators: and in taste—but their taste is too timid to be true taste—or is but half taste. Their authors are more afraid of offending delicacy and rules, than ambitious of sublimity. Shakespeare, with an improved education and in a more enlightened age might easily have attained the

---

[3] Thomas Davies, *Dramatic Miscellanies*, 1784, i. 191, says of the Roan Barbary passage: 'This is one of those scenes which disgrace the tragedy of a great king.' Walpole has noted beneath this in his copy of the book (now WSL): 'yet this is one of those exquisite and affecting touches of nature, in which Shakespeare excelled all mankind. To criticize it is being as tasteless as Voltaire.'

purity and correction of Racine; but nothing leads one to suppose that Racine in a barbarous age would have attained the grandeur, force and nature of Shakespeare. Racine had been taught by Corneille to avoid all the faults of their predecessors, and was taught by his own judgment and by that of his friend Boileau, to avoid the faults of Corneille. The latter was inspired with majesty by Roman authors and Roman spirit; Racine with delicacy by the polished Court of Louis 14. Shakespeare had no tutors but nature and genius. He caught his faults from the bad taste of his cotemporaries. In an age still less civilized Shakespeare might have been wilder, but would not have been vulgar. Had he drawn absolute Savages instead of Clowns, perhaps we should have had as beautiful delineations of a state of nature, as he has given in his pictures of the passions in a corrupted state of society, I mean, in his Macbeth, Othello, Richard 3d—in short, in all his best scenes. Now he [who] invented such a compound as Falstaff, and could make every picture of such a fictitious character perfectly natural, could not have failed in painting simple natures.

The Apotheosis of Voltaire

BERNARD N. SCHILLING

CARLYLE NEVER ceases to repeat that all popular uprisings including the French Revolution have the same cause. After enduring generations of imposture, misgovernment, betrayal, injustice—the French people could go on no longer. They rose up against their false heroes, cast them out in asserting the everlasting human need for manful guidance and truly heroic leadership.

If Carlyle was so far right, it was still not enough for the people to destroy those who had betrayed their interests. They naturally sought in turn to honour the men who in their judgement had served them well, had indeed prepared the way for freedom. The revolutionary government set up the 'Pantheon of Great Men' in the church of Sainte-Geneviève where due honour was to be done at last to those who had earned the people's reverence. Among these new heroes was Voltaire, a great soldier in the cause of freedom and justice. During life and at his death, Voltaire had been the victim of that very tyranny against which the revolution was a protest. It was especially appropriate that his contribution to the new era should be magnificently recognized in a ceremony which has come to be known as the 'Apotheosis of Voltaire'.

A review of Condorcet's *Vie de Voltaire* set the tone of the French nation's gratitude, soon to take so spectacular a form. Voltaire was the original author of the revolution, since he first undermined the most formidable of all the supports of despotism, religious and priestly power.[1] Over a period of fifty years, men of letters had been preparing the human spirit for its day of regeneration; Voltaire more than any other had influenced his contemporaries, had dared to lift the veil and give truth the power to overcome prejudice.[2] It was therefore appropriate that *La Société de 1789*, Condorcet's organization, should discuss ways of honouring his remains. Well over a year before the actual ceremony, the

[1] *Mercure de France*, vii (1790), 27–8.
[2] *Révolutions de Paris*, viii (1791), 446.

agitation was begun, aided with special energy by Charles Villette whose eloquent letter proposed a formal tribute to Voltaire's body as if it had become a religious relic.[3] Such a tribute would simply acknowledge that 'notre glorieuse révolution est le fruit de ses ouvrages',[4] and would attempt to pay a debt which had come down from the preceding generation.[5]

By the anniversary of Voltaire's death, 30 May 1791, even the National Assembly had become concerned. It was considered appropriate that some mark of public distinction should be given to Voltaire's remains, now to be moved from the Abbey of Sellières as ecclesiastical property was confiscated.[6] The Assembly had been reminded of the nation's debt by a letter from M. Charon, municipal officer of Paris, pointing out that on 30 May 1778, intolerance and fanaticism had exercised their fury against Voltaire in refusing a decent burial to his body.[7] This wrong ought to be rectified by a grateful nation. M. Gossin, reporting on the plans for honouring Voltaire, declared that the French nation itself had suffered the outrage done to a great man, and that being at length free, it should 'faire amende honorable'. Actually the nation was so eager to honour Voltaire that three cities—Paris, Troyes, and Romilly—contended for the remains which once had been unwanted. One city went so far as to suggest that what was left of the body should be divided among them. The entire matter was not settled without weighty discussion, so that Voltaire's friends were able to announce again and again the nation's debt to him. Voltaire's own prediction of the revolution was recalled. It was asserted that he had sown the seeds of French regeneration, and that without him France would never have dared to destroy that feudal serfdom which had dominated the preceding age. The influence of this man of genius upon the revolution was primary and essential; his remains be-

---

[3] Charles Villette, *Lettres choisies* . . . (Paris, 1792), 62–8; *Actes de la Commune de Paris* . . . 2nd Series, i (9 Nov. 1790), 209, 232–3 and n.; ibid. iii (7 Mar. 1791), 95–6.   [4] *Chronique de Paris*, ii (1790), 1262.

[5] 'Translation de Voltaire . . .', *Department of the Seine: Administration* (Paris, 1791), 2.

[6] Jean F. Robinet, *Le Mouvement religieux à Paris pendant la Révolution* (Paris, 1896), i. 531. Mme Du Deffand had told Horace Walpole of the burial of Voltaire, which had been refused at Paris, in the Abbey of Sellières. See *Horace Walpole's Correspondence with Mme Du Deffand* (New Haven, 1939), v. 48.

[7] This and other references to the discussion of Voltaire in the National Assembly are taken from *Archives parlementaires* (1791), xxv. 661; xxvi. 610–11; xxviii. 72.

longed therefore to the entire nation now liberated through his efforts; no division of Voltaire's body should be allowed. The remains should be placed in the Pantheon, after receiving due honour.

Three weeks before the anniversary of Voltaire's death his body had been solemnly exhumed at the Abbey of Sellières by the citizens of Romilly. They had conducted the now sacred relics with great pomp and ceremony to Romilly and deposited them in the parish church of the town.[8] Rumour had it that little was left of the great infidel beyond the original dust, since he was supposed to have desired the complete destruction of his body. A report reached England that Voltaire had ordered quicklime to be put into the coffin at his burial; when the coffin was opened at Romilly, the body was found to be entirely consumed. Yet the French shut up the case 'and reported the poet in excellent preservation'.[9] This seems to have been mere evil talk, now long disposed of.[10] While it was apparently true that on exposure to the air when the coffin was opened, Voltaire's body changed its aspect,[11] yet it was remarkable in what state of preservation the corpse had been found. M. Favreau, Mayor of Romilly, was especially indignant over certain aspersions cast upon the genuineness of Voltaire's remains. He was present at the original delivery of the body to Sellières and had seen its actual burial. Then on authorization of the assembly, the body was exhumed and exposed in the presence of officials from neighbouring cities and of more than two thousand citizens. The same man who had buried Voltaire in the Mayor's presence now assisted in his exposure; they all recognized Voltaire. When M. Charon made the official 'reconnaissance du corps' in the presence of several thousand persons, the Mayor and his associates again recognized the poet.[12] The truth was that when the coffin was opened, 'the features were found to be unmarred, scarcely more ghastly than in life'.[13]

[8] *Révolutions de Paris*, xiii (21 May, 1791), 297–8.

[9] *Critical Review*, v (1792), 95–6, quoting Stephen Weston, 'Letters from Paris during the Summer of 1791' (1792).

[10] See H. Monin, 'La Translation de Voltaire au Panthéon: a-t-elle été un Simulacre?', *La Révolution Française*, xxx (1896), 193–7.

[11] *Heroes, Philosophers, and Courtiers of the Time of Louis XVI* (1863), ii. 373.

[12] *Le Courrier des 83 Départemens* . . ., xxvi (28 July 1791), 450; 'Translation de Voltaire à Paris', 8 n.

[13] William M. Sloane, *The French Revolution and Religious Reform* (New York, 1901), 174.

The coffin remained at Romilly until a day had been set for the celebration in Paris. Delay was feared because of the excitement attending the flight of Louis XVI to Varennes and his recapture, the possibility of conflict with other events, the enormous complexity and scope of the preparations necessary for so vast and spectacular a celebration, and, later on, the inclement weather. It seemed likely too that fanatical supporters of the old era might cause trouble and try to disrupt the ceremony. But at last M. Charon was sent to Romilly and charged with the task of receiving officially the remains of Voltaire and conducting them to Paris.[14]

On his arrival, Charon was met by the efficient Mayor and a crowd of excited citizens. His first days were spent in receiving delegations from neighbouring cities, sent to do homage to the poet-philosopher Voltaire. Charon also had to arrange for the raising of the sarcophagus and its transportation. At last all was in readiness for the departure to Paris. Charon, made an honorary citizen of Romilly, delivered a touching and appropriate discourse. The ceremonies were so impressive that it was six in the evening

[14] *Le Courrier des 83 Départemens* . . ., xxvi (July 1791), 31, 49, 178. The account of the apotheosis of Voltaire which follows is taken mostly from French periodicals for the month of July 1791. Since these accounts largely repeat themselves, it seems hardly necessary to refer directly to the volume and page for the various statements made about the ceremony. This will be an exercise in description and narration rendered into English from French materials which are abundant and easily accessible. Besides the periodical *Le Courrier des 83 Départemens* . . . referred to above, the following have been useful: *Le Courrier français*, xii; *Le Moniteur universel*, iv; *Le Point du jour*, xxiv; *Révolutions de Paris*, viii–ix; *Chronique de Paris*, III. Charles Villette, *Lettres choisies* . . . *sur les principaux événemens de la Révolution* (Paris, 1792), contains a good account by an active participant in the apotheosis. In *Collection complète des tableaux historiques de la Révolution Française* (Paris, 1804), i. 217, is a large picture called 'Triomphe de Voltaire' along with a good brief description of the ceremony. The 'Translation de Voltaire à Paris . . .', gives a good account of the plans before the actual ceremony took place. See also *Actes de la Commune de Paris* . . . 2nd series, iii; 'Ordre et Marche de la Translation de Voltaire à Paris . . .' (Paris, 1791), in *Bibliothèque historique de la Révolution: Fêtes funèbres;* and Karl Frenzel, 'Voltaire's Triumph und Tod', *Rokoko. Büsten und Bilder* (Berlin, 1895), 294–351; Gustave Desnoiresterres, *Voltaire et la société française au XVIIIe siecle*, viii (1871–6), 479–501; Theodore Child, 'A Museum of the History of Paris', *Harper's New Monthly Magazine*, lxvii (1888), 833–5 gives a brief account of the apotheosis in connection with several relics of that occasion. I am obliged to Dr. Clara Marburg Kirk for bringing this article to my attention. The best modern account in English of the apotheosis is that in William Sloane, *The French Revolution and Religious Reform* (New York, 1901), 173–5. The last chapter of George Brandes's *Voltaire* (1930) is entitled 'Apotheosis', and describes the ceremony of 1791.

before the cortège finally got under way, led by the Mayor and a deputation from Romilly. The vehicle bearing the sarcophagus was an enormous and brilliantly decorated oblong chariot, with four columns of white marble at the corners, draped in violet and decorated with roses and garlands of other flowers. It was drawn by four black horses clad in draperies of violet bordered in white. Atop the marble columns was a canopy flying the national colours. Amid the garlands of flowers was placed a crown of immortal laurel while branches of cypress, oak, and other trees shaded the vehicle on its way. On the front of the chariot were the inevitable verses paying tribute to Voltaire's great services in the cause of liberty. The whole proceeded majestically to the accompaniment of solemn music, soon to be succeeded by airs the most joyous and triumphant, as Voltaire began to approach the city of Paris.

The tribute paid to the procession suggests the universality of feeling for Voltaire. There is no reason to suppose that any other part of France would have been less enthusiastic. In the towns and villages along the way, the great procession received the most distinguished honours. Thousands of lamps and torches were placed along the route as a vast throng of people flocked from everywhere. Even the country priests prayed and said masses for one who after all had attacked only fanaticism and superstition, not true religion. The procession moved through a shower of blossoms and garlands thrown by enthusiastic citizens. Scenes of the most touching emotion were common. Mothers lifted little children in their arms so that they might see and have impressed on their memories this glorious spectacle. Old men of slow step followed the cortège with their eyes, raised their hands and blessed Heaven that they had been permitted to live so long as to witness this beautiful sight. People of all ages and all classes of society joined in the tribute of respect and veneration for this great man, because all of them without exception had profited from his labours in the cause of liberty.

Most impressive and ironical was the semi-religious aspect of the procession. Voltaire's remains were regarded as something like the relics of a saint. Pilgrims by the thousand flocked from far and near. Women touched the sarcophagus with their handkerchiefs and then devoutly kissed the fabric which had become a sacred thing to be cherished as a keepsake. And the smile of Voltaire, that instrument of such colossal power in the fight against these very practices in life, may now have expressed pleasure in this new irony, may indeed have rejoiced at so great a satisfaction to his vanity. Who shall say that he would not have been touched by the respect and care of the deputies sent from Troyes who, sometimes sitting, sometimes standing, sometimes on their knees, steadied the sarcophagus with their reverent hands as if it were the holy grail, lest it be too violently agitated along the way?

By 10 p.m. the cortège had arrived at Nogent, lighted by torches and lamps. Here the mayor received the procession with great solemnity, on behalf of the town and all of the soldiers, citizens, and national guards who were present to pay their tribute to the ashes of this friend of humanity. Charon delivered a touching speech and was in turn moved by the replies of the townspeople. The flowers and garlands of the morning were replaced by new offerings as the cortège moved on. The night of 6 July was spent at Provins where a crowd had been most impatient for Voltaire's appearance. All available bells were rung to greet the procession when it came into view. A special path had been cleared, decorated with leafy and flowery arches of triumph. At Nangis all night was spent in making garlands and crowns of laurel and myrtle. At Mormans the display was touching. Immediately on the arrival of the hearse, groups of young girls dressed in white, bearing crowns and baskets of flowers, let fall a rain of roses and jasmin, and then began to dance around the sarcophagus amid the tearful emotions of the spectators.

Only at Guignes was the general triumph marred by untoward incidents. The procession was to spend the night there, and Charon, used to being received with royal generosity en route, was embarrassed by a suggestion from his hostess, Mme Nouet, that he pay for his lodging. This he refused to do and repaired to an inn, the only public resort in which he spent the night while conducting Voltaire's body to Paris. Not only this, but the whole enterprise was received with irreverent ridicule in some quarters at Guignes whose citizens made things worse by their quarrelsome and unruly behaviour. One man tried to use his sword on a curate who was among the deputies accompanying the procession. Others had tried to dislodge six of the national guardsmen from Romilly and to deprive them of their places in the march. The curate tried to calm the disturbance in vain, and Charon threatened to leave this unruly town at once. He was mollified by M. Nouet, husband of his practical hostess, and by other honest citizens who made up for the disturbance by a thousand services. The chariot was then more brilliantly decorated than ever when it left Guignes.

After a brief pause at Coubert for refreshments which had been prepared in advance by the inhabitants, the procession arrived at Brie-Comte-Robert. The reception here was distinguished by the homage offered by priests to the saint of reason, taste, and the muses. A solemn mass was celebrated at which the entire town assisted, some overflowing outside the church. As the procession moved on, its impressiveness was heightened by brilliant music and the acclamations of the people. At Creteil, it was met by M. Pastoret, the Procureur-général to whom Charon once more addressed a discourse. He had taken possession of the precious dust of Voltaire by official authorization. The citizens of Romilly had groaned over the loss of the sacred remains but had rejoiced at the honours soon to be rendered them. Charon now gave his charge to the Procureur-général, deeply sensible as he did so of the honour of participating in so glorious an episode. After more fulsome words, M. Pastoret in his turn attempted to reply but the tears poured from his eyes and he was unable to utter a single word.

The great procession was now made ready for entry into Paris itself. Led by MM. Pastoret and Charon, the chariot advanced between rows of soldier-citizens, their hats and muskets bearing the usual floral decorations. Presently the Mayor of Paris met the procession with a large detachment of cavalry. The city of Paris had been burning with eagerness to receive back the remains of Voltaire so ignominiously refused burial there by the forces of ignorance and fanaticism. The procession entered at the Faubourg Saint-Antoine which was lined with enthusiastically cheering throngs, crying out for joy as if they were receiving the return of some god.

Following the plan already agreed upon, the procession made its way to the Bastille where the sarcophagus was to remain until the final parade to the Pantheon. Thus did Voltaire's body make a dramatic return to the prison where despotism had twice confined him during life. He had prepared for the overthrow of this symbol of tyranny and was now to be honoured upon the very ruins which had fallen only with the aid of his preparation. At first it seemed that this hope might be frustrated, since the chariot itself could not advance on the irregular surface around the

Bastille. But suddenly a crowd of people seized the sarcophagus itself, and lifted by a thousand hands and arms above a thousand heads, the precious object was carried down a passage beautifully adorned for the occasion and placed upon a platform over the ruins of the tower in which Voltaire himself had been imprisoned. Ravishing music now replaced the clanking chains of despotism; the groans of those unjustly imprisoned gave way to the applause of a vast throng of spectators. The thrilling scene was exquisitely lighted and disclosed beautiful flowers among the ruined stones of the prison, the gorgeous flags and draperies surrounding the elevated sarcophagus. On one of the rocks piled up to make a platform for Voltaire's body, this sign was to be seen: 'Reçois en ce lieu, où t'enchaîna le despotisme, Voltaire, les honneurs que te rend la Patrie.'

It was hardly to be expected that amid all the extravagant enthusiasm showered upon Voltaire, there should be no protest from the undying forces of envy, intrigue, religious fanaticism, superstition, and stupidity. Eight days before the apotheosis, numerous clergy and other reactionary forces began to agitate against it. There was some evidence that a sum of money had been set aside to bribe certain malcontents to disrupt the ceremonies. A petition was also drawn up denouncing Voltaire as unworthy of such an honour; it condemned the apotheosis on the grounds of religion, economy, charity, and public unrest, and was signed by some hundred Jansenists, imbeciles, nay-sayers, Paris curates, and others. Copies of this document were handed out in the streets; it was supplemented by widely distributed posters and placards denouncing the expense of the celebration, which would come to 800,000 livres, and demanding that the money be spent for charity. But the forces of liberty were not to be denied. The petition was indignantly repudiated; copies of it and the fanatical posters were burned or thrown into latrines. Some of the original signers of the petition now regretted their action, and were sorry to have lent their names to so insolent, perfidious, and absurd a document. In a public letter Charles Villette defended the expense which was divided among the interested friends of Voltaire; the city would not have to spend more than 18,000 livres and the whole affair would be excellent for business anyway, in view of the many strangers who would be attracted to Paris for the occasion. The petitioners were overwhelmed by the scornful indignation of those devoted to Voltaire, who were tempted to stage the apotheosis on Sunday in order to create the maximum annoyance to fanaticism. It was even suggested that representatives of royal and clerical despotism be chained to Voltaire's car of triumph, so as to emphasize more fully the meaning of this celebration.

Yet the petitioners and other friends of the old order were not to be denied their final gesture against this, to them, blasphemous enterprise. A priest and others from the petitioners had welcomed the rain on the day of Voltaire's entry into Paris, saying that by this rain God himself was declaring his opposition to so impious a festival, or that a saddened nation was weeping over a great sacrilege. During the evening ceremonies at the Bastille a priest was heard to cry out this sinister warning: 'Dieu! tu seras vengé!' And later in the night an attempt was made by force to steal the body of Voltaire itself and so make the apotheosis impossible. But a guard had been set for the night, consisting of 1,200 Voltairians devoted to his memory and his cause, so that the attempt to destroy this sign of the coming of their evil day failed for the enemies of philosophy.

On Monday, 11 July 1791, the procession was to have begun at eight in the morning. But the weather was unfavourable, the rain persistent. At first an order of postponement was issued, but many of those who were to participate in the ceremony as well as the enthusiastic and expectant populace refused to be denied. After a certain amount of delay in so vast an undertaking, an order was given to begin the parade, and the huge procession got under way somewhat after three o'clock in the afternoon. No sooner had the march begun than the rain stopped, the sun broke through the clouds, and with this evident interposition of the gods themselves, the great festival proceeded to its conclusion. Enormous crowds were waiting along the boulevards. Since the march had been announced for eight in the morning, vast throngs had already appeared by six o'clock in order to be sure of a place of vantage. Now it was estimated that a crowd of 600,000 people had gathered along the way to see a parade which itself was said to number 100,000 participants. Forty-eight masters of ceremony were chosen to help the national guard to direct the march. The official order of progress contained twenty-eight different units, including representatives from all important walks of life, especially from the world of art, letters, and the theatre over which Voltaire had exercised so enormous an influence. Numerous ambassadors from the courts of Europe were said also to have been present, along with abundant delegations from military, diplomatic, and official French life under the revolutionary regime.

The procession began with a detachment of national cavalry leading the way, followed by members of various clubs bearing flags inscribed with patriotic mottoes. At intervals groups of musicians were scattered throughout the parade, since no single musical corps could have provided the beat for so vast a march. Following a deputation of the national guard, came an enormously complicated and elaborate unit centred around an image of the Bastille. This section of the parade was itself divided into twelve different parts, including deputations from various patriotic clubs, a company of men bearing pikes, a group of citizens who had taken part in the fall of the Bastille, together with their wives, widows of those who had died in the attack on the hated fortress, and a crowd of apostles of liberty who had paid homage to models of the Bastille in the various departments. The Bastille image itself was carried by uniformed guards and citizens of the Faubourg Saint-Antoine. It was followed by portraits of Mirabeau, Desilles, Rousseau, and Voltaire, scattered among members of the families of Calas, Mirabeau, and Desilles. Among other objects carried in this Bastille section was a tattered flag which had been seized from the hands of De Launey when the fortress was captured. Among the widows of those who had died in the fall of the Bastille was one who brandished a sabre and marched along in spite of her advanced pregnancy. After the Bastille section came a detachment of 100 Swiss, followed by miscellaneous groups of soldiers, electors, deputies, and other citizens. The eleventh unit of the parade was a deputation of artists and representatives of the theatre, preceding a statue of Voltaire crowned with laurels and borne aloft by men dressed in antique costume. Then came groups of students of painting and architecture, also in ancient classical dress, carrying standards with the names of Voltaire's principal works. Distinguished men of letters and members of Voltaire's family and of learned academies accompanied the golden chest containing his complete works. Beaumarchais had given a complete set of seventy volumes to the Bibliothèque Nationale, as his contribution to the nation-wide tribute to Voltaire, and now in the grand procession another seventy-volume set took its proper place. The sixteenth unit of the parade was a 'grand corps de la musique instrumentale et vocale, exécutant les marches et des chœurs'.

Then came the great chariot carrying the sarcophagus of Voltaire. The catafalque itself was magnificently conceived in a combination of modern and antique styles. It had been executed by distinguished French artists, including David himself, official designer and master of ceremonies for revolutionary pageantry. MM. Célérier and Bien-Aimé had also collaborated in producing the triumphal chariot of Voltaire to which all the arts made their appropriate contributions. It was drawn by twelve superb white horses—harnessed in sky-blue reins spiked with stars—and was sustained on four bronze wheels. The decoration of the whole, which rose high above the level of the street, was carried out in eclectic imitation of ancient pageantry and modern French and Italian models. From the spokes of the wheels to the very top of the entire structure a complex scheme of symbolic and ornate decoration had been worked out. The floral ornaments were gorgeous and profuse. Among other symbolical structures was a chimerical dragon, in turn decorated and ornamented 'avec beaucoup de goût'. Three distinct levels were placed one on top of the other before the actual figure of Voltaire was reached high above all. Over the second platform was a sarcophagus of oriental granite, this time of a severely simple design, such as one might see in many Italian monuments. On its sides were typical inscriptions like those through the entire procession. They paid tribute to Voltaire's war upon intolerance and fanaticism, his contributions to liberty and the enlargement of the human spirit, his great defences of Calas, La Barre, Sirven, and Montbailly, and everrepeated, the debt of the revolution itself to his labours. Among the numerous poems, hymns, songs of various kinds sung, recited, or merely carried on placards throughout the apotheosis was the repeated assertion by the French Revolution itself that Voltaire was the father of this new liberty, that he had in fact made the revolution what it was, that 'il a fait prendre un grand essor à l'esprit humain, et nous a préparés à devenir libres'. At the four corners of the sarcophagus were four masques decorated by garlands of laurel. Here was also a drapery of beautiful blue, sprinkled with golden stars. Atop the sarcophagus lay the figure of Voltaire, as if stretched on his death-bed. At the corners of this bed were vases from which blazed the flames of exquisite incense and perfume. Over the reclining head a figure of Immortality, in the form of a beautiful young girl, held a crown of stars.

Such was the actual vehicle bearing the sacred remains of the revolution's father. The remainder of the procession consisted of various officials, the commissioner in charge of the entire parade, the deputation of fifteen members from the Assembly, judges, and others. A battalion of veterans followed by a corps of cavalry brought up the rear. The route to be followed by this gigantic cavalcade had been carefully worked out, beginning from the Boulevard Saint-Antoine down certain designated streets and boulevards including the Pont-Royal and the Quai Voltaire until final arrival at the Pantheon. The original plan called for three official stops: the Opera, the house of Charles Villette where Voltaire died, and the National Theatre.

The Opera had planned carefully for the arrival of Voltaire's remains, it being in his debt for a number of works. The façade was decked in garlands and festoons of flowers and branches of oak. Amid elaborate draperies was a bust of Voltaire placed upon an antique altar. To this came actors prepared for the spectacle. They all bore crowns in hand which they shook animatedly before the statue. Mme Ponteuil, presenting a crown to the head of Voltaire, was carried away with emotion, and forgetting that she was in the presence of an inanimate image, she kissed the lips of the statue. Tears flowed from the eyes of the throng of spectators at this touching exhibition. After the singing of selections from *Samson* and Chénier's *Hymne*, a deputation of members of the Opera in theatrical costume placed themselves before the actual chariot and joined the march.

The cortège came at length to the Quai des Tuileries and found itself before the Pavillon de Flore. Here an unofficial and unplanned stop was made. The spectators were reminded now of the portentous contrast between this triumphant return of Voltaire to Paris and the recent ignominious flight of Louis XVI, his recapture and forced return to Paris under quite different conditions. This man was nothing more than a king and it rankled in the popular breast that his mean-spirited cowardice had been the means of postponing the return of a truly great man. Louis was now held captive in his own palace by his indignant sovereign, the people. The palace windows were open and crowded with servants of the king, curious and eager to see the procession. Only one window was closed, behind which, seeing without being seen, Louis XVI and Marie Antoinette stood in terror watching the spectacle passing before them and knowing that this tribute to Voltaire was a sign of defeat for the forces which they represented. They may well have heard in the triumphal march the accent of their coming doom and have trembled lest even now they should be forced to join the cavalcade in honour of their enemy. When the chariot itself arrived opposite the Pavillon de Flore, thousands of voices called for the chorus from *Samson*:

> . . . Peuple, éveille-toi, romps tes fers
> La liberté t'appelle
> Peuple fier, tu naquis pour elle;
> Peuple, éveille-toi, romps tes fers.

It was sung and called for a second time and sung again, echoing and re-echoing through the vast throng with a thrilling demand for liberty in the presence of one who symbolized the tyranny here repudiated.

The cortège now followed the Quai Voltaire, whose name had only recently been changed at the suggestion of Charles Villette. An enormous crowd had gathered near Villette's house, overflowing from the street on to the bridges and *quais*. In this house Voltaire had died and here his heart reposed in a mysterious sanctuary, beside his image. Over the entrance to the house, Voltaire's adopted daughter and her husband Villette had placed an inscription reading, 'Son esprit est partout, et son cœur est ici.' The scene had been decorated profusely with flowers, suggesting that every bloom that had come to maturity in the neighbourhood of Paris was being used for the apotheosis. A kind of amphitheatre had been erected before the house on which were seated women and young girls dressed in white, holding crowns of roses, and each bearing a crown on her head. A sash of blue with a figure of the triumphal chariot encircled each waist. Voltaire's adopted daughter herself, the exquisite 'Belle et Bonne', was dressed in white crêpe with a long veil. Her own daughter was before her, and on either side were the two daughters of Calas dressed in mourning. As the procession gradually drew up before the house, its various divisions were fraternally saluted by the throng until Voltaire's statue by Houdon appeared. This was greeted by a rain of flowers and garlands. 'Belle et Bonne' descended to the statue and bowed in religious reverence before it. Then amid the plaudits of the crowd she embraced the image of her foster-father and covered it with kisses. Holding forth her own child in her arms toward the statue of Voltaire, Mme Villette devoutly consecrated the little girl to Philosophy, Reason, and Liberty which had inspired the soul of Voltaire himself. As the head of the statue was crowned by Mme Villette, the crowd of spectators wept unashamedly.

The great chariot itself was now drawn up to the accompaniment of solemn and dolorous music, recalling that Voltaire himself was no more. But the scene demanded a hymn of joy as well, since the apotheosis was a sign of the triumph of Voltaire's message. Joyously a thousand voices now took up an ode written for the occasion, with music by M. Gossec. Once more the greatness of Voltaire was chanted and his contribution to liberty praised, inspiring the hearts of all who sang or heard with a love of liberty. Amid renewed cheers and applause, 'Belle et Bonne', her child, the two Calas daughters and other women stepped down from the amphitheatre and joined the march. Villette himself tried to go on, but overcome by emotion and the great strain of the festival, he could walk but forty paces before his knees gave way. He was taken to a neighbouring house where he was allowed to relieve his feelings by copious tears.

With great stateliness and in perfect order the procession advanced until at nightfall it arrived at the National Theatre. The usual floral decorations and elaborate ornamentation were once more seen before the theatre. While still alive in 1778 Voltaire had already been honoured here, in a kind of 'apotheosis' preliminary to this greater festival. His tragedy *Irène* was being played, and when Voltaire appeared in the theatre he was received with intoxicated enthusiasm. The actors came to his box and crowned him with laurel amid the plaudits of the audience. Shortly after, at Versailles, an ex-Jesuit had denounced this tribute as scandalous,[15] but now in 1791 the forces of reaction were silenced as the National Theatre's tribute was offered to Voltaire. His bust was placed on the stage, and crowned amid redoubled enthusiasm. Amid other decorations on the outside of the theatre were medallions bearing the names and giving inscriptions from Voltaire's various plays. As the procession paused, the draperies before the entrance to the

[15] D'Alembert, 'Particulars respecting the last illness of . . . Voltaire . . .', *Repository*, ii (1789), 96.

theatre opened to disclose once again a statue of Voltaire. The lights were ingeniously placed to shine directly upon the head of the image which symbolically reflected them back with renewed brilliance. Actors and actresses presented Voltaire with crowns of laurel and flowers once more. Kisses were again offered with the roses, music was again performed, including the chorus to liberty from *Samson*, while 'Belle et Bonne' and her companions paid their final tribute to Voltaire's image.

It was now 9.30 on a dark night, and the rain which had so considerately held off during the afternoon, began to fall rapidly. The cortège made its way to Sainte-Geneviève, and to the sound of all the musical instruments in unison and lighted by a thousand torches, the remains of Voltaire made their final entry into the Pantheon of great men. The sarcophagus with the figure of Immortality holding its crown of stars was raised onto a tablet of Egyptian granite placed in the middle of this temple dedicated by revolutionary France to her greatest men. After the extravagant triumph of its journey from the Bastille, the sarcophagus lay at peace in Sainte-Geneviève. The people might there behold the receptacle of that very body which only thirteen years before had sought vainly for a place in the earth of Paris.

In spite of the final visitation of bad weather, the friends of Voltaire were pleased with the results of the festival. It is true that the populace had applauded the procession more vigorously than those inhabiting the best hotels and houses along the route. Yet it was truly a national celebration. One had seen everywhere the busts of Voltaire with their crowns; inscriptions from his works had been widely posted and passages were heard on all sides. An enormous crowd had lined the streets, filled the windows, and covered the roof-tops and trees along the way. Villette was sure that the apotheosis of Voltaire was the most sublime tribute ever paid to a mortal man, a phenomenon unique among the festivals of history, no less extraordinary than he who had been its hero. There could be no doubt that the apotheosis had accomplished its purpose, that it was a symbol of the triumph of what the revolution stood for and the defeat of what France had now cast away. It was a blow to fanaticism, ignorance, error, tyranny, prejudice, and intolerance; it was a promise of freedom, of reason, patriotism, of dignity, and of a noble resolution to sacrifice all in the cause of liberty.

Byron's Songs of Innocence:
The Poems to 'Thyrza'

JEAN H. HAGSTRUM

THE PUBLISHED poems which are the subject of this paper number approximately seventeen. They were written over a ten-year period (1806–16), four before and the rest after the death of the person addressed. The *pre-mortem* poems all appeared in 1806–7 in miscellaneous places. At least five stanzas in *Childe Harold's Pilgrimage* are addressed to the memory of the departed friend, and six separate poems either were once part of the first or second edition of *Childe Harold* or bore some relation to that long poem. The three or four poems that close the canon include one in 1815, which appeared in *Hebrew Melodies*, and also two or three poems of 1815–16 which bear the title 'Stanzas for Music', an appropriate denomination, as we shall see.[1] Although the name 'Thyrza'[2] is

---

[1] For a list of poems Leslie Marchand regards as belonging to this series, see *Byron: A Biography*, 3 vols. (New York, 1957), i. 108 n.6; 308; 313 n.5. My list is somewhat longer, adding poems from 1816, in which I hear echoes of the Edleston relation. Texts of poems are quoted from *The Works of Lord Byron. Poetry*, ed. Ernest Hartley Coleridge (London, 1898–1904).

Some months after writing this paper, I came across Bernard Blackstone's brief but sensitive discussions of the Thyrza poems in *Byron: A Survey* (London: Longman, 1975), esp. pp. 74–6, 97–8, 104–5. Professor Blackstone believes that 'Dear object of defeated care!' (a two-stanza poem, dated Athens, January, 1811; see *Works*, iii. 19 and n.) belongs to the canon. I tend to agree; but I do not find either that the poem is *unmistakably* a part of the series or that it contributes much to the imagery and the mood of Thyrza poetry. My chief disagreement with Blackstone is that he finds that Edleston takes many different shapes and enters a whole series of 'nostalgic-erotic-mystic-guilty-exultant experiences' (p. 76). I find 'Thyrza' to be kept individual and set apart, an oasis of ideality and innocence, as it were. And, as my discussion is intended to show, I do not discover evidence of guilty or ambivalent feelings in Byron about this relationship, though of course Hobhouse may have had them on Byron's behalf.

[2] 'I took the name of Thyrza from Gesner. She was Abel's wife.' Quoted in *Works*, iii. 30 n.2. There is nothing in Solomon Gessner's *Death of Abel* (1761; tr. by Mrs. Mary Collyer in 1818) that is relevant to this series but much that would interest the reader of Byron's *Cain* and *Manfred*.

not used in all or even most of these poems, it becomes clear after study that the primary bond of union between them is that the same person is being addressed. The poems themselves are all characterized by an unrelieved seriousness of tone in which musical imagery and musical effects tend to predominate. The stanzaic forms, the metres, the rhythms, and the rhymes are extremely simple and obvious, coming very close to the ballad metre, usually being some variant of that poetic form. The manner of address is sincere and direct, the vocabulary severe and spare. And the verse embodies qualities not always characteristic of Byron, an almost total absence of histrionics and a total lack of hysteria. Nor is the mood darkened by what we have come to know as Byronism, guilt-obsessed loneliness. These poems are indeed what our title calls them, songs of innocence, singularly free of any sense of physical filthiness, irrevocable damnation, or human alienation. One must concede at the outset that the poems are uneven in quality: some, especially the earlier ones, are flat and conventional, while others can stand among the best lyrics Byron ever wrote. When read in roughly chronological order, the poems reveal growth in depth and power, providing insights into the way deeply felt experience becomes embodied in the permanent forms of art.

Who Thyrza actually was—or whether the person addressed was an imaginary being—has been much discussed; and many earlier editions of the poems of Byron inform the reader that the poet was successful in keeping the secret during his lifetime, eluding the curiosity of readers and the research of scholars. But all that is now changed, thanks largely to a manuscript note by Ernest Hartley Coleridge, which appears in the copy of Thomas Moore's life of Byron now in the Osborn Collection at Yale. The note corrects Lord Lovelace: he, along with many others, believed Thyrza was a girl who died about the time Byron landed in England in 1811 and whose tresses he continued to wear. These, it was thought, he showed to Lady Byron, who understood that they belonged to the female subject of the lyrics. E. H. Coleridge's clarifying and definitive comment is as follows:

Lord Lovelace's rambling and meaningless Thyrza-note was designed to Combat a theory of mine (and the Athenæum's long ago)—obviously the true one—that Thyrza and Edleston were one and the same person. I maintained and maintain that Byron's feelings on this point were entirely to his credit, and that Lord Lovelace wilfully or stupidly misunderstood the whole incident. E.H.C.[3]

All scholars now accept this identification.

We are not without information regarding the person identified. John Edleston was a boy two years the poet's junior who sang in the choir of Trinity College, Cambridge, and whom Byron met in October 1805, soon after he arrived at the university. The young man was of humble birth; he presented, in January 1806 or later, a cornelian to the poet, perhaps as a token of gratitude for having been saved by Byron from drowning. Some evidence suggests that the poet helped the young man financially to such an extent that he was led into deep debt—a fact that may account for the sombre cast of his mood at that time. But sombre or not, the poet's feelings developed into what he called love—a 'violent, though *pure*, love and passion'. So intimate did the affair become that Byron on 23 February 1807 had to 'keep the subject of my "Cornelian" a *Secret*'. Byron was attracted by the young man's voice, countenance, manner—and deeply sympathized with his financial needs. Their almost constant association seems to have led to dalliance as well as discussion of Edleston's future as a partner in a London mercantile house, in which Byron decided to support him. The most striking quality of the friendship was its rapturous release from psychological pain. When the two were together, Byron felt joy in the intimacy; when they separated, his mind became 'a *Chaos* of *hope* & *Sorrow*'.[4]

But separate they did and must. Byron embarked on a two-year tour of the Continent—travels that bore such voluminous and revolutionary literary fruit and that did not bring him back to England until June 1811. He returned from considerable suffering abroad—as well as from exhilarating adventure; but the deep gloom that now depressed his spirits was quite unlike anything he had known before. In his homeland he suffered the loss of five friends and a mother. Although all these friends had been beloved, Byron grieved for none more deeply than John Edleston, about whose death he had heard from the boy's sister some months after it had occurred in May 1811. The grief overwhelmed his spirits at

[3] Quoted in Marchand, i. 296 n. 3.

[4] For the facts and the quotations of this paragraph, see Marchand, i. 107–8; *Byron's Letters and Journals*, ed. L. A. Marchand, Vol. I: *In My Hot Youth* (London, 1973), pp. 88, 110, 122–5.

first and then, along with recollections of the living intimacy, entered deep into his psyche, where it became a kind of Byronic spot of time. It was, when conscious and perhaps also when unconscious, a focused centre not of mystical exaltation but of combined friendship and loss, of combined love and purity—a kind of passionate innocence not easily come by and never again recovered or repeated.[5]

Leslie Marchand is quite right in calling the attachment to Edleston 'probably the deepest, sincerest, and most unqualified of any in his life'.[6] The two-year separation during Byron's travels had not dimmed the memories of the intimate ecstasies, and now the premature death stirred the poet into a series of poetic utterances that exceed in number and quality those made during the young man's lifetime.

Professor Marchand has also said that the Thyrza poems have never been considered as a whole or been accorded the evaluative criticism they deserve.[7] It is to that challenge that the present paper attempts to rise—an attempt that cannot be separated from a study of the poet's sensibility, which for Byron was always the immediate and effectual cause of the verse. Since he looked into his heart and wrote, and since interior experience was always clamouring to get out in the form of verbal expression, no interpreter of his lyrics can ignore his life and his feeling.

On 22 June 1813, Byron wrote to Thomas Moore, 'I don't know what to say about "friendship." I never was in friendship but once, in my nineteenth year, and then it gave me as much trouble as love.'[8] The poet unquestionably refers to the Edleston affair. And since, as we have said, we are concerned with 'sincere' poems, we necessarily turn to the sensibility that stimulated their coming into being. What, then, was the state of Byron's spirits when he first met the young chorister at Cambridge? It cannot be too strongly emphasized that he was already sexually experienced, having been titillated by a wanton maidservant (who combined Scottish piety and low habits) to an unconscionably early and perhaps sordid loss of sexual innocence. It is also true—and we are now on an entirely

---

[5] *Byron's Letters and Journals*, Vol. II: *Famous in My Time* (London, 1973), pp. 110, 114, 117, 119–20, 163–4.

[6] *Byron's Poetry* (Cambridge, Mass.: Harvard Univ. Press, 1968), p. 118.

[7] Ibid.

[8] *Byron's Letters and Journals*, Vol. III: *Alas! the Love of Women!* (London, 1974), p. 67.

different plane—that he had been in love with his beautiful cousin, Margaret Parker, whose early death he mourned, and that at eighteen he had loved Mary Chaworth, who married another— a loss that he mourned long and embodied in his intermittently ardent and beautiful poem of 1816 entitled 'The Dream' ('Our life is Twofold . . .'). Two emotions may have early emerged from his *affaires de cœur* (and *de corps*): physical disgust at Shelleyan nympholepsy, revulsion at whoredom, and a striving after unattainable purity. At Harrow he had added the dimension of 'passionate friendship' and 'affectionate camaraderie'. But about these last there is no evidence of an accompanying sense of evil or shame, a sense that seems to have been reserved for some kinds of heterosexual love. The evidence of the Thyrza poems seems to enforce the view that Byron carried to his Cambridge friendship an aura of sweet and lingering innocence, a gentle contrast to the heartier and headier dissipations of the bottle and the brothel, which also continued at Cambridge. Such venereal and bacchic pleasures— with perhaps laudanum thrown in for good measure—were not allowed to poison the male friendships, including the most passionate—perhaps the only passionate one. It may be hard for some to believe that an ecstatic friendship which apparently involved some physical contact (though how much we of course do not know) could breathe an odour of angelic sanctity. But apparently for the experienced Byron, whom contemporary morality would have called degenerate, precisely that was the case. Flitting from girl to girl in transient affairs smelt of corruption. The friendship with Edleston represented moral nobility and emotions as close as Byron ever came to religious exaltation.[9]

When on 30 June 1809 Byron sailed from Falmouth for the memorable *Wanderjahre* on the Continent, he was 'tolerably sick of vice which I have tried in its agreeable varieties'.[10] On his return he was doubtless even sicker of heterosexual dissoluteness and carnality. And when, after his return, he confronted the loss of his mother and of several dear school companions he thought with especial poignance about the loss of Edleston and began idealizing a friendship that had been at once passionate and pure. Surely one reason Byron came to believe—and there is a long tradition behind

<hr />

[9] Marchand, *Byron: A Biography*, i. 57–8, 62, 78, 90 and n. 2, 118 and n. 5, 122; *Letters and Journals*, i. 103 ff, 165.

[10] *Letters and Journals*, i. 241.

such a view—that friendship was superior to love was that it could not result in marriage. Between men there was no way of kneading 'two virtuous souls for life/Into that moral centaur, man and wife'.[11] But though the relations with Edleston did not result in a waste of shame, they did cost an expense of spirit. Byron had to turn, as was his wont, to poetry for mental and spiritual relief— the only reason, he once said, that he ever wrote.

When we confront the poems, we must provide for each of them —or at least for each appropriate grouping of them—the proper literary ambience. Before he wrote his first Thyrza poem, Byron had had a short but prolific career as a teen-age poet. Many poems from 1802 on are dedicated to girls and concern the subject of love. They are heavily and obviously rhythmic, flat and one-dimensional in meaning; and their range of mood spans cynicism and sentiment, conventional attitudes about death and a few anticipations of the Byronic humour that is to come. These anticipations strike one with greater force than the somewhat surprising recollection of Crashaw in one of the poems 'To Caroline'. Byronic verse tends to yield easily to the lilt of feminine rhymes and literary allusion—

> Why should you weep, like *Lydia Languish*,
> And fret with self-created anguish?
> ('To a Lady': 'These locks, which fondly . . .')

The only reason for pausing to notice the invasion of the early love-poetry by the mercurial lightness of the *Don Juan* tone is that this quality is so conspicuously—and, one would guess, so purposefully—absent from the Thyrza series, which is governed by the unrelenting seriousness that may have characterized Byron's mood during his friendship with Edleston.

Although it has a few feminine rhymes, the first poem to Edleston ('The Cornelian': 'No specious splendour . . .'), so entitled because of the boy's gift of a heart-shaped stone to the poet, is a sentimental poem—in both important eighteenth-century meanings of that adjective. The tear dropped on the blushing gem sanctifies both stone and tear—'And, ever since, *I've lov'd a tear.*' But besides the fashionable and saccharine appeal to the *cœur sensible*, the poem is sentimental in the sense of expressing moral sentence—here the Romantic notion that flowers raised in 'Nature's wild luxuriance' bloom with greater beauty than sheltered plants.

[11] *Don Juan*, v. clviii.

The poem is flawed, particularly in its excessively conceited last stanza. But containing at least two lines of extreme Wordsworthian simplicity, it represents an advance over what Byron had been doing—an advance continued in *Pignus Amoris* ('As by the fix'd decrees . . .'), the next Thyrza poem, which refers to that pledge of love, the cornelian, and expresses, in simple octosyllabic lines rhymed *abab*, the ideal of sincere, open, and innocent love. Without a trace of coyness or false adulation—the poet celebrates the joy of being loved for oneself alone—love here stands naked and even a touch selfish, without Petrarchan excrescence of any kind, virtually without imagery, and certainly with no trace of the dark tensions of guilt. Indeed, the pleasure is unalloyed with baseness, life is without crime, and 'Innocence resides with Joy'—sentiments that scarcely justify G. Wilson Knight[12] in his suggestion that the homoerotic passion expressed in these poems was regarded as sinful.

The 'Form', the 'Voice', and the 'Blushes' join with the 'Seraph Choir' to make of 'Stanzas to Jessy' ('There is a mystic thread . . .') a Thyrza poem—for this complex of imagery is the kind that the Edleston magnet draws to itself. The poem ends platonically as two souls flow into one. But before that conventional climax is reached, the poem comes close to suggesting that the relationship, though guiltless, has not been entirely Platonic: lip is pressed to lip and bosoms pillow aching heads. But the spirit of innocence is not evaporated in this preliminary, boyish, unconsummated kind of dalliance that strikingly recalls the delicate eroticism of the enormously influential Rousseau. If the 'Jessy' poem ends platonically, 'The Adieu' ('Adieu, thou Hill!') ends religiously, as if to enforce upon us the realization that the Thyrza sensibility is never far from religious hope, here expressed by one who believes he will soon die. Byron, about to travel, bids farewell to more than his Cambridge 'Friend' and the 'gentle love' he embodies. In fact, only the seventh stanza is directly addressed to Edleston—a verse that takes on a special quality of purity of body and mind when placed in the context of the young Byron's already turbulent eroticism:

> And thou, my Friend! whose gentle love
> Yet thrills my bosom's chords,
> How much thy friendship was above
> Description's power of words!

[12] *Lord Byron's Marriage* (New York: Macmillan, 1951), p. 14.

> Still near my breast thy gift I wear
> Which sparkled once with Feeling's tear,
>   Of Love the pure, the sacred gem:
> Our souls were equal, and our lot
> In that dear moment quite forgot;
>   Let Pride alone condemn!

The sentiments of equality, purity, tenderness, and gentleness in love make this poem the farewell of a Man of Feeling. Such was the contemporary idiom in which Byron first couched the most heart-penetrating friendship he was ever to know.

Then Thyrza died, and oh! the difference to Byron. The loss represented a fall from what we have described as passionate innocence or sensual chastity, a love enjoyed that may never have been consummated. Without abandoning the ideal of severe simplicity that had hitherto guided him in these poems, Byron now darkens and deepens the tonality and produces poetry of more compelling urgency. But not at once. When Thyrza, the 'more than friend', enters some five stanzas of *Childe Harold*,[13] he inspires rhetoric rather than art, albeit a rhetoric that remains straightforward and heartfelt. The stanzas have biographical and psychological interest, suggesting that of all the friends Byron had lost in so short a space (and one must include his mother) only Thyrza remains an unsullied—perhaps even untouchable—recollection of pure devotion and love. Edleston, entering the deepest mind of the poet, is beginning to glow with an idealism against which the world's slow stains and rapid sins can be for ever contrasted. Thyrza has become a haven of calm, subsisting at the heart of endless agitation.

A cluster of poems, the earliest written in 1811 and all published in the first or second editions of *Childe Harold* in 1812, may be said to spring from grief that is still green. The octosyllabic lines, the prevailing *abab* rhymes, the simple imagery of voice and form, the cornelian (that *pignus amoris*), and 'refined and guiltless' emotions —all these link this cluster with the poems written at Cambridge. Except that now all is lost, and perhaps for the first time Byron is truly *bent* in grief. Loss and a growing sense of the world's evil moved Blake to sing Songs of Experience; Byron continues to sing Songs of Innocence. The first of these, directly addressed 'To Thyrza' ('Without a stone to mark the spot'), ends in a mood of

[13] II. ix, xcv–xcviii.

quiet—even quietistic—submission and prayer. Agitation about the world is implicit ('I would not wish thee here again') but subdued. But agitation replaces calm in 'Away, Away, ye Notes of Woe' as pain clamorously drowns out prayer. The reader's interest quickens because Byron, the world-weary traveller, becomes a presence, though not an overwhelming one, in the poetry. Self-contemplation becomes unbearable to him, and his personal anguish has cosmic overtones, because a mysterious 'Heaven is veiled in wrath'. This shift from the recollected Edleston (a singer who has produced aural imagery in the verse) to the cosmically deserted Byron is exquisitely accompanied by a shift to visual imagery. Thyrza is now

> A Star that trembled o'er the deep.

But as the imagery shifts, the doom is mitigated by the recollection that the star beamed tenderness, the very image and sentiment Byron has expressed for an innocent heterosexual love that he had lost when Mary Chaworth married another ('The Dream': 'Our life is twofold').

Three poems ('One struggle more', 'Euthanasia', and 'And thou art dead') should be considered together, even though one of them may technically not belong to the series. All are concerned with death, two somewhat conventionally, the third in a moving though extremely chaste climax. In 'One struggle more, and I am free', the poet refers to the cornelian that had played such an important symbolic role in the relation of the loving friends. But Byron feels it necessary to conceal his beloved's sex by referring to '*her* grave'. This bit of evasion, fully justified in many poetical circumstances, here tends to veil the naked sincerity we have come to expect in these lyrics. It takes its toll in this particular utterance, which becomes conventionally Anacreontic, as the poet calls for the wine of forgetfulness. But the poem does have two redeeming lines, among the most piercing that Byron ever wrote: 'Though Pleasure fires the maddening soul,/The Heart,—the Heart is lonely still!'

'Euthanasia' ('When Time, or soon or late'), which is not a Thyrza poem in topic, tone, or imagery, is closely related because it envisages the poet's own death, perhaps a response to the continuing contemplation of his friend's. It begins by longing for death's 'dreamless sleep' and ends by asserting, '"Tis something better not to be.' The gentle nihilism here expressed faintly recalls

Swift contemplating his own death and includes a flick at women that is untypical of the series to Thyrza—however much anti-feminism there may be elsewhere in Byron.

In 'And thou art dead, as young and fair' the series reaches its emotional climax. The gentle self-regarding nihilism of 'Euthanasia' is now richer, and the poet has, as in the tradition of the pastoral elegy, achieved a kind of reconciliation to his loss. Above life and even above death, above change and even above immortality, the choir-boy is now, as it were, a dreamless Nothing. In a poem that is metrically and stanzaically the most complex of the series, Byron gives us a memorable phrase in referring to Edleston's as 'thy buried love'. But the word *buried* can also refer to the poet's own recollection, which is sinking deeper and deeper into the unconscious mind. Though the living years are best, they are gone, and one must inevitably turn to what lies underneath earthly and psychological surfaces. Such is Byron's unadorned way of telling us that general *Angst* has now replaced living love and of invoking, without any touches of self-glorification or self-pity, that tortured and alienated spirit of his. This poem is, metrically and thematically, a climactic literary response to the poet's great grief. Art is in the process of taking over, and a chastened and controlled poetry is becoming the correlative of a 'love where Death has set his seal'.

In one sense the series may now be said to have ended. But there remains an artistic after-glow—the emotion being recollected in a harmonious kind of tranquillity like distant music on waters or like broken fragments of a once-loved reality. 'If sometimes in the haunts of men' presents two choices—that of gradual forgetting (the haunts of men can be drowned in the bowl of forgetfulness) or that of loving recollection now made tender with irretrievable loss. Byron chooses the latter—a selection of solitary life and thought over social dissipation. That choice he makes because Thyrza had been the one and only person really to love him—a theme of the earliest utterance and undoubtedly a reality of the relationship that made it unique for Byron. In a slight two-stanza poem 'On a Cornelian Heart Which was Broken' ('Ill-fated Heart!') Byron still is haunted by the gift given him by Edleston, that pledge of love that had been the theme of more than one of the *pre-mortem* poems. And one of the *Hebrew Melodies* ('Oh! snatched away in beauty's bloom') is an exquisite classical elegy, showing that aesthetic distance is setting in. He modifies, with controlled grace, a commonplace used by Dryden in one of his most moving but also most controlled classical imitations, as he hopes that a rose-bearing turf and not a heavy tomb will rest on the remains of his beloved.[14]

Thyrza usually invoked musical imagery, and it is fitting that three of the four poems entitled 'Stanzas for Music' belong to what we have referred to as the poetic after-glow of the loss. Since they are not obviously a part of the main series, something of subjective judgement inevitably enters our relating them to the Thyrza sequence. But without them—or so it seems to one interpreter—a rich delicacy would be lost: indeed, one of the climaxes —the artistic one—would be missed entirely. The poem beginning 'There's not a joy the world can give' is inspired by the Duke of Dorset, another friend of Byron's Harrow years who had died. But unless the ear is entirely deceptive—and if our sensitivity to Thyrza tone and imagery can be trusted—it is the Cambridge choir-boy's all but invisible presence that adds to this poem the warmth and originality that the other poems to Dorset lack. A septenary line is here preserved from lilt and lullaby in order to express genuine pathos. When Byron writes, ''Tis not on Youth's smooth cheek the blush alone, which fades so fast', one thinks of Edleston, not Dorset; and the unadorned cry of the closing stanza invokes the overwhelming Thyrza experience:

> Oh, could I feel as I have felt,—or be what I have been,
> Or weep as I could once have wept, o'er many a vanished scene.

[14] Byron: On thee shall press no ponderous tomb;
  But on thy turf shall roses rear
  Their leaves . . .

Tibullus: Et 'bene' discedens dicet 'placideque quiescas,
  Terraque securae sit super ossa levis'.
  (*Elegia*, II. iv. 49–50)

Dryden: The Sacred Poets first shall hear the Sound,
  And formost from the Tomb shall bound:
  For they are cover'd with the lightest Ground
  ('To the Pious Memory of . . . Anne Killigrew', ll. 188–90).

On a possible relation between the *Hebrew Melodies* and the Thyrza series, Thomas L. Ashton, the editor of *Byron's Hebrew Melodies* (London: Routledge & Kegan Paul, 1972) comments: 'Edleston's voice had made a particularly lasting impression on Byron. Hearing Nathan rehearse his sacred songs perhaps awakened feelings in Byron that made his collaboration with the musician possible' (p. 18).

Another of the 'Stanzas for Music' embodies in its first lines a recollection more appropriate to Thyrza than to any one else:

> Bright be the place of thy soul!
> No lovelier spirit than thine.

The conventional 'Light be the turf of thy tomb!' is here repeated and slightly varied, though somehow its present association with religious optimism and vague, somewhat sentimental theology makes it less impressive. Still, the lightening delicacy of the tone shows us a diminished suffering. The poet is apparently escaping a continuing involvement of spirit that would have left less room for disciplined elegiac art.

Such art is attained in the last of the 'Stanzas for Music' (written on 28 March 1816). No external fact and no internal image compellingly links this utterance of haunting poetic beauty with the Thyrza series. But critical intuition does, leading one to believe that it is the Thyrza friendship which indeed transcends the magic of all of 'Beauty's daughters' and that the sweet voice now heard on the waters is a transmutation of the Cambridge chorister's voice heard at Trinity College. If this instinct is to be trusted, then in this poem a deeply felt experience and an even more deeply felt loss are translated first into nature's nocturnal round and then into a lyric expression as delicate and lovely as anything Byron ever wrote. Since it is difficult to think of an early life experience that more surely deserves such a climax than the affair with Edleston, one hopes that the Thyrza canon closes with this short, two-stanza poem:

> 1.
> There be none of Beauty's daughters
>   With a magic like thee;
> And like music on the waters
>   Is thy sweet voice to me:
> When, as if its sound were causing
> The charméd Ocean's pausing,
> The waves lie still and gleaming,
> And the lulled winds seem dreaming:

> 2.
> And the midnight Moon is weaving
>   Her bright chain o'er the deep;
> Whose breast is gently heaving,
>   As an infant's asleep:

> So the spirit bows before thee,
> To listen and adore thee;
> With a full but soft emotion,
> Like the swell of Summer's ocean.

Everyone agrees that Byron's poetry, whether calm or anguished, was self-expressive, written for the relief of suffering or even of excessively painful joy. The canon of work so abundant and varied as Byron's shows that at different times and for different purposes he was guided by a variety of poetical models and ideals. What ideal governed the Thyrza poems? It could not have consisted of the criteria that Northrop Frye invokes in censuring the Byronic lyric for lacking ambiguity, irony, intensity, and vividness—'the words and images being vague to the point of abstraction'.[15] At his weakest the lyricist deserves Frye's lash. But at his best he ought to be judged by other standards than those requiring many-layered richness; in fact his achievement ought to be measured against the ideal he set for himself in the amorous lyrics. Early in his career he wrote:

> Fictions and dreams inspire the bard,
>   Who rolls the epic song;
> Friendship and truth be my reward—
>   To me no bays belong . . .
> Simple and young, I dare not feign;
> Mine be the rude yet heartfelt strain . . .

('L'Amitié est l'Amour sans Ailes': 'Why should my anxious breast')

That ideal of unfeigned simplicity persists—even as late as the fifth canto of *Don Juan*, where the first two stanzas are devoted to 'amatory poets' and their 'liquid lines mellifluously bland' and to a rejection of the Ovidian, Petrarchan, and Platonic traditions in amorous verse. (He calls Petrarch 'the Platonic pimp of all posterity'—and so fells two of his poetic enemies with one blow.)

> I therefore do denounce all amorous writing,
>   Except in such a way as not to attract;
> Plain—simple—short, and by no means inviting,
>   But with a moral to each error tacked,
> Formed rather for instructing than delighting,
>   And with all passions in their turn attacked.   (v. ii)

One cannot take too seriously the moral profession; but 'plain—

---

[15] *Fables of Identity* (New York: Harcourt, Brace and World, 1963), p. 174.

simple—short' are adjectives that summarize the Byronic manner in the Thyrza poems. They also describe the neoclassical ideal for short lyrical verse, exemplified in the dicta of Dryden, Dennis, Fielding, Hume, and Johnson, who provides what could have been a motto for Byron, 'He that professes love ought to feel its power.'[16]

About Byron's lyrics in general, T. S. Eliot is abruptly dismissive: 'With most of his shorter poems, one feels that he was doing something that Tom Moore could do as well or better.'[17] Using a criterion of impersonality for the lyric that he was later to disown by writing highly confessional religious poetry, and perhaps anticipating Frye's requirements of multivalent richness, Eliot has reached for the wrong critical tools. But his mention of Moore does raise a name which belongs in the Byronic context, however much the Irish bard may have been surpassed by the English peer. In the volume of melodious amatory verse Moore pretended to have collected, *The Poetical Works of the late Thomas Little*, the use of the octosyllabic line, the tender and sentimental themes, the simple rhyme scheme, the relatively few allusions (and these often religious), and now and then the sweet lilt of the feminine rhymes —all these qualities do anticipate Thyrza lyrics.[18] But in assessing poetic values Eliot's quick equation of Moore and Byron is simply unjust to the Edleston verses: the easy, gentle Moore lacks the authentic and serious personal emotion that suffuses the chaste and inevitable simplicity of Byron's lyrical voice.

It is not surprising that poems so simple and personal as Byron's to Thyrza should tend to elude the critical grasp. Judged, as they most certainly should be, by the ideal of lyrical simplicity, they must be allowed to escape the censure that they lack richness of

[16] For a discussion of sincerity in love poetry, see Jean H. Hagstrum, *Samuel Johnson's Literary Criticism* (Univ. of Chicago Press, 1967), pp. 45–6. For a discussion of Byron's ideal of sincerity in *Hours of Idleness* and its immediate antecedents, see Jerome J. McGann's excellent discussion in *Fiery Dust: Byron's Poetic Development* (Univ. of Chicago Press, 1968), pp. 10–27. McGann's point—that it is not sincerity so much as an illusion of sincerity that governs and that illusion is related to poetry conceived of as 'a self-dramatizing vehicle' (p. 26)—seems applicable to the *Hours* as a whole and to Byron in general. In my view the less sophisticated neoclassical ideal of direct sincerity is more applicable to the Thyrza poems, which tend to lack variety, self-dramatization, wit, extravagance, and posturing.

[17] *On Poetry and Poets* (1937), quoted in M. H. Abrams, *English Romantic Poets* (New York: Oxford Univ. Press, 1960), p. 197.

[18] See McGann, pp. 9–12, for a description of Moore's poetry and for a sensitive appreciation of how the young Byron absorbed it.

resonance and the complexity of ambiguity. Sincerity, directness, depth of feeling, piercing lines and stanzas, and growing subtlety and strength they do possess. But they lack the variety of metrical and verbal nuance which Wordsworth's comparable poems to Lucy possess, nor do they reach Wordsworthian depths of psychological desire, controlling philosophical naturalism, or over-arching mystery—qualities that make of Lucy an authentic Coleridgean symbol. Somewhat below, then, the greatest of the shorter Romantic lyrics, Byron's series remains well above the conventional flatness to which Eliot wished to reduce Byronic lyricism. The Thyrza poems do not possess what Goethe isolated as *Manfred's* great quality—'the gloomy heat of an unbounded and exuberant despair'.[19] But they can be said to have achieved the less paradoxical and less ambiguous virtues this paper has invoked. Any worthy and ample anthology of shorter Romantic lyrics would contain many of them, and a good anthology of shorter English lyrics selected from all periods would include four or five of those written after the death of Edleston, when Byron's feelings took on a distance congenial to echoing beauty. One animating life runs through all these poems, even the less successful ones. Something unique in tone, imagery, or form will tell the reader he is in the presence of the acute sensibility that Edleston aroused in Byron. And that impression of unifying energy attests both to the authenticity of the feeling and the authority of the art.

[19] Cited in *The Oxford Anthology of English Literature* (*Romantic Poetry and Prose*), ed. Harold Bloom and Lionel Trilling, 3 vols. (New York, 1973), ii. 316 n.

A List of the Published Writings
of James Marshall Osborn

ALVARO RIBEIRO

1935

1. 'Johnson on the Sanctity of an Author's Text', *PMLA* i (Sept.), 928–9.

1937

2. 'Edmond Malone and the Dryden Almanac Story', *PQ* xvi (Oct.), 412–14 [see also no. 3].

1938

3. 'Edmond Malone and the Dryden Almanac Story', *PQ* xvii (Jan.), 84–6 [see also no. 2].

4. 'William Oldys', *TLS*, 9 Apr., 256 [letter].

5. 'Lord Hailes and Dr. Johnson: "The Lives of the Poets"', *TLS*, 16 Apr., 262.

6. 'Hailes and Johnson', *TLS*, 23 Apr., 280 [letter].

7. *Compilation of: Work in Progress, 1938, in the Modern Humanities.* Modern Humanities Research Association, *Bulletin* No. 16A (May).

8. 'Thomas Birch and the *General Dictionary* (1734–41)', *MP* xxxvi (Aug.), 25–46.

1939

9. *Compilation of:* [with R. G. Sawyer], *Work in Progress, 1939, in the Modern Humanities.* Modern Humanities Research Association, *Bulletin* No. 17A (May).

EDITOR'S NOTE

Abbreviated journal-titles are:

MP	*Modern Philology*
NQ	*Notes and Queries*
PMLA	*Publications of the Modern Language Association of America*
PQ	*Philological Quarterly*
RES	*The Review of English Studies*
TLS	*The Times Literary Supplement.*

1940

10. *John Dryden: Some Biographical Facts and Problems.* New York: Columbia University Press [see also no. 49].

11. 'The Search for English Literary Documents', in: C. Brown, ed., *English Institute Annual, 1939* (New York, 1940), 31–55 [reprinted in: R. C. Boys, ed., *Studies in the Literature of the Augustan Age: Essays Collected in Honor of Arthur Ellicott Case* (Ann Arbor, 1952; and New York, 1966), 232–57; revised in: W. K. Wimsatt, ed., *Literary Criticism, Idea and Act: The English Institute, 1939–1972, Selected Essays* (Berkeley, Los Angeles, and London, 1974), 15–31 (no. 78 below)].

12. '[Bibliography of:] Literary Historians and Antiquaries', in: F. W. Bateson, ed., *The Cambridge Bibliography of English Literature* (Cambridge), ii. 892–932.

13. *Review Article:* 'Joseph Ritson, Scholar at Odds', *MP* xxxvii (May), 419–29 [a review of: B. H. Bronson, *Joseph Ritson, Scholar-at-Arms*, 2 vols. (Berkeley, 1938)].

14. *Compilation of:* [with D. R. Kerr], *Work in Progress, 1940, in the Modern Humanities: A Supplement to the 1939 Issue.* Modern Humanities Research Association, *Bulletin* No. 18A (May).

1941

15. *Compilation of:* [with D. R. Kerr], *Work in Progress, 1941, in the Modern Humanities: A Cumulative Supplement to the 1939 Issue.* Modern Humanities Research Association, *Bulletin* No. 19A (May).

16. *Review Article:* 'Macdonald's Bibliography of Dryden: An Annotated Check List of Selected American Libraries', *MP* xxxix (Aug.), 69–98; (Nov.), 197–212; (Feb. 1942), 313–19 [a review of H. Macdonald, *John Dryden: A Bibliography of Early Editions and of Drydeniana* (Oxford, 1939). Reprinted for private circulation from *MP* xxxix paginated in the sequence 313–19, 69–98, 197–212; pp. 313–19 reprinted as 'Macdonald's Bibliography of Dryden', in: H. T. Swedenberg, Jr., ed., *Essential Articles for the study of John Dryden* (Hamden, Connecticut, 1966), 54–62].

1942

17. *Compilation of:* [with Patricia M. Withner], *Work in Progress, 1942, in the Modern Humanities.* Modern Humanities Research Association, *Bulletin* No. 20A (May).

1942–46

18. *Originator and Editor of: The Seventeenth Century Newsletter.*

1945

19. 'Edmond Malone and "Baratariana"', *NQ*, 27 Jan., 35.

20. *Review of:* A. Tillotson, ed., *The Correspondence of Thomas Percy & Edmond Malone* (Baton Rouge, 1944), in: *PQ* xxiv (Apr.), 150–2.

1949

21. 'The First History of English Poetry', in: J. L. Clifford and L. A. Landa, eds., *Pope and His Contemporaries: Essays Presented to George Sherburn* (Oxford), 230–50.

1951

22. *Review of:* A. Wright, *Joseph Spence: A Critical Biography* (Chicago, 1950), in: *MP* xlviii (Feb.), 215–16.

23. *Review of:* S. H. Monk, *John Dryden: A List of Critical Studies Published from 1895 to 1948* (Minneapolis, 1950), in: *PQ* xxx (July), 267–8.

1953

24. 'Dr. Johnson's "Intimate Friend"', *TLS*, 9 Oct., 652.

1954

25. *Dr. Johnson and the Contrary Converts.* Privately printed for The Johnsonians, 18 Sept. [revised in: F. W. Hilles, ed., *New Light on Dr. Johnson: Essays on the Occasion of His 250th Birthday* (New Haven, 1959), 297–317 (no. 32 below)].

1955

26. 'Pope, the Byzantine Empress, and Walpole's Whore', *RES*, n.s. vi (Oct.), 372–82.

1957

27. 'Ben Jonson and the Eccentric Lord Stanhope', *TLS*, 4 Jan., 16.

28. 'Reflections on Narcissus Luttrell (1657–1732)', *The Book Collector*, vi (Spring), 15–27 [reprinted for private circulation with pagination [1]–15].

29. *Review of:* E. N. Hooker and H. T. Swedenberg, Jr., *et al.*, eds., *The Works of John Dryden*, vol. i: *Poems, 1649–1680* (Berkeley and Los Angeles, 1956), in: *PQ* xxxvi (July), 358–61.

1958

30. 'Thomas Stanley's Lost "Register of Friends"', *Yale University Library Gazette*, xxxii (Apr.), 122–47 [reprinted for private circulation with pagination 1–26].

31. 'Benedick's Song in "Much Ado"', *The Times*, 17 Nov., 11.

1959

32. 'Dr. Johnson and the Contrary Converts', in: F. W. Hilles, ed.,

New Light on Dr. Johnson: Essays on the Occasion of His 250th Birthday (New Haven), 297–317 [see also no. 25].

1960

33. *The Beginnings of Autobiography in England: A Paper Delivered by James M. Osborn at the Fifth Clark Library Seminar, 8 August 1959.* Los Angeles: William Andrews Clark Memorial Library, University of California, Los Angeles.

34. *Edition:* [with an Introduction by Sir John Neale], *The Quenes Maiesties Passage through the Citie of London to Westminster the Day before her Coronacion.* The Elizabethan Club Series, no. 1. New Haven: Yale University Press; London: Oxford University Press.

1961

35. *The Autobiography of Thomas Whythorne.* Oxford: Clarendon Press.

1962

36. *The Autobiography of Thomas Whythorne.* Modern spelling edition. London: Oxford University Press.

37. '"That on Whiston" by John Gay', *Papers of the Bibliographical Society of America*, lvi (First quarter), 73–8.

38. *Review of:* T. A. Birrell, 'John Dryden's Purchases at Two Book Auctions, 1680 and 1682', *English Studies*, xlii (1961), 193–217, in: *PQ* xli (July), 580.

39. *Review of:* C. E. Ward, *The Life of John Dryden* (Chapel Hill, 1961), in: *PQ* xli (July), 585–6.

1963

40. 'Addison's Tavern Companion and Pope's "Umbra"', *PQ* xlii (Apr.), 217–25.

41. 'Travel Literature and the Rise of Neo-Hellenism in England', *Bulletin of The New York Public Library*, lxvii (May), 279–300 [reprinted in: W. G. Rice, introd., *Literature as a Mode of Travel: Five Essays and a Postscript* (New York: NYPL), 31–52].

42. 'On the Growth Factor', *Kenyon Alumni Bulletin*, xxi (July–Sept.), 12–16.

43. '"Renewed" Instructions to a Painter', in: G. deF. Lord, ed., *Some Poems Composed on the Occasion of the Publication of the First Volume of Poems on Affairs of State: Augustan Satirical Verse, 1660–1714* (New Haven, 21 Nov.).

1964

44. 'Edmond Malone: Scholar-Collector', *The Library*, 5th ser., xix.

11–37 [reprinted as a separate monograph for The Bibliographical Society (1968)].

45. *Edition:* [with L. L. Martz and E. M. Waith], *Shakespeare's Poems: A Facsimile of the Earliest Editions*. The Elizabethan Club Series, no. 3. New Haven and London: Yale University Press.

46. *'By Appointment to His Majesty Biographer of Samuel Johnson, L.L.D.'* Privately printed for The Johnsonians, 18 Sept.

47. 'A New Traherne Manuscript', *TLS*, 8 Oct., 928.

48. 'Johnson to Taylor No. 90', *TLS*, 24 Dec., 1171 [letter].

1965

49. *John Dryden: Some Biographical Facts and Problems*. Revised edition. Gainesville: University of Florida Press [see also no. 10].

50. 'Edmond Malone and Dr. Johnson', in: Mary M. Lascelles, *et al.*, eds., *Johnson, Boswell and Their Circle: Essays Presented to Lawrence Fitzroy Powell in Honour of His Eighty-Fourth Birthday* (Oxford), 1–20.

1966

51. *Joseph Spence. Observations, Anecdotes, and Characters of Books and Men, Collected from Conversation*. 2 vols. Oxford: Clarendon Press.

52. 'Spence, Natural Genius and Pope', *PQ* xlv (Jan.), 123–44.

53. *Review of:* B. Grebanier, *The Great Shakespeare Forgery* (New York, 1965), in: *PQ* xlv (July), 566.

54. 'New Poems by Sir John Denham', *TLS*, 1 Sept., 788.

1967

55. 'Horace Walpole and Edmond Malone', in: W. H. Smith, ed., *Horace Walpole, Writer, Politician, and Connoisseur: Essays on the 250th Anniversary of Walpole's Birth* (New Haven and London), 299–324.

56. 'Swiftiana in the Osborn Collection at Yale', *University Review* (Organ of the Graduates Association of the National University of Ireland), iv (Spring), 72–83.

1968

57. 'Joseph Spence's "Collections Relating to The Lives of the Poets"', *Harvard Library Bulletin*, xvi (Apr.), 129–38.

1969

58. *Review of:* P. Quennell, *Alexander Pope: The Education of a Genius, 1688–1723* (London and New York, 1968), in: *PQ* xlviii (July), 380–2.

1970

59. 'Edmond Malone and Oxford', in: W. H. Bond, ed., *Eighteenth-Century Studies in Honor of Donald F. Hyde* (New York), 323–38.

60. 'New Light on Sir Philip Sidney', *TLS*, 30 Apr., 487–8.

61. *Review of:* J. Sutherland, *English Literature of the Late Seventeenth Century* (Oxford, 1969), in: *PQ* xlix (July), 319–21.

62. *Review of:* G. Cannon, ed., *The Letters of Sir William Jones* (Oxford), in: *Johnsonian News Letter*, xxx (Sept.), 4–5.

1971

63. 'Mica Mica Parva Stella: Sidney's Horoscope', *TLS*, 1 Jan., 17–18.

64. *Review of:* S. Schoenbaum, *Shakespeare's Lives* (Oxford, 1970), in: *PQ* l (July), 396–7.

65. 'Sidney and Pietro Bizari', *Renaissance Quarterly*, xxiv (Autumn), 344–54.

66. *Review of:* T. R. Forbes, *Chronicle from Aldgate: Life and Death in Shakespeare's London* (New Haven and London), in: *American Scientist*, lix (Nov.–Dec.), 777.

67. *Review of:* J. H. Middendorf, ed., *English Writers of the Eighteenth Century* (New York and London), in: *Johnsonian News Letter*, xxxi (Dec.), 4.

1972

68. *Young Philip Sidney, 1572–1577.* The Elizabethan Club Series, no. 5. New Haven and London: Yale University Press.

69. 'Fingerprinting Poems', *Books and Libraries at the University of Kansas*, ix (Apr.), 1–6, 11–13.

70. 'Neo-Philobiblon', *Library Chronicle of the University of Texas at Austin*, N.S. v (Sept.), 14–29 [published as a separate monograph (no. 75 below)].

71. *Boswell's Verses on The Club.* Privately printed for The Johnsonians, 15 Sept.

72. 'Pope, the "Apollo of the Arts," and His Countess', in: H. T. Swedenberg, Jr., ed., *England in the Restoration and Early Eighteenth Century: Essays on Culture and Society* (Berkeley, Los Angeles, and London), 101–43.

73. 'General Introduction', to D. Wing, ed., *Short-Title Catalogue ... 1641–1700*, 2nd edn. (New York), vol. i, p. v.

74. 'Wing's STC', *TLS*, 23 Mar., 325 [letter].

75. *Neo-Philobiblon: Ruminations on Manuscript Collecting.* Humanities Research Center, University of Texas at Austin. Bibliographical Monograph Series, no. 7 (Mar.) [see also no. 70].

76. 'A Lost Portrait of John Dryden', *Huntington Library Quarterly*, xxxvi (Aug.), 341–5.

77. 'Ruminations on Method in Literary Research', *MHRA: Annual*

Bulletin of the Modern Humanities Research Association, xlv (Nov.), 20–9.

1974

78. 'The Search for English Literary Documents', in: W. K. Wimsatt, ed., *Literary Criticism, Idea and Act: The English Institute, 1939–1972, Selected Essays* (Berkeley, Los Angeles, and London), 15–31 [see also no. 11].

79. 'Wing via King's', *TLS*, 19 Apr., 418 [letter].

80. 'The Osborn Collection, 1934–1974', *Yale University Library Gazette*, xlix (Oct.), 154–70.

81. 'George Steevens's Mother and Sylvanus Urban', *Eighteenth-Century Life*, i (Dec.), 27–30.

1975

82. 'Thomas Rymer as Rhymer', in: W. Kupersmith, ed., *From Chaucer to Gibbon: Essays in Memory of Curt A. Zimansky* (Iowa City), 152–77 [a special issue of *PQ* liv (Winter); reprinted for private circulation with pagination 1–26].

1976

83. 'In the Hebrides', in: *Our Friend L. F.: Recollections of Lawrence Fitzroy Powell*. Privately printed for The Johnsonians, 17 Sept.

1977

84. 'Some Experiences of a Scholar-Collector', in: *Building Book Collections: Two Variations on a Theme: Papers read at a Clark Library Seminar, February 7, 1976* (Los Angeles), 1–16.

1978

85. 'Thomas Traherne: Revelations in Meditation', in: I. I. Martz and A. Williams, eds., *The Author in His Work: Essays on a Problem in Criticism* (New Haven and London), 213–28.

86. 'Dryden, Shadwell, and "a late fall'n Poet" ', in: *John Dryden II: Papers read at Clark Library Seminars, February 1 and March 1, 1974* (Los Angeles), 27–52.

FORTHCOMING PUBLICATIONS

—*Boswell's Correspondence with Burke, Garrick, and Malone*. Edition of the Boswell–Malone correspondence. The Yale Editions of the Private Papers of James Boswell. The Research Edition.

—*The Club: The Founders' Era* [with Ardelle C. Short].

—'Thomas Whythorne', in: S. Sadie, ed., *The New Grove Dictionary of Music and Musicians*.

—'The Document as Premise', in: a volume of essays to be edited by J. W. Johnson.

MISCELLANEOUS WRITINGS

For Wesleyan University:
—*Editor of: The Wesleyan Wasp*, vols. ix–x (1927–8).
—*Editor of: The Wesleyan Argoose*, 7 June 1968.

Dairy Cattle Breeding:
—*Editor of: The New England Holstein Bulletin* (1944–6).
—*The Holstein Handbook.* Brattleboro, Vermont: Holstein–Friesian Association of America, 1947.
—'The Beltsville Experiment in Cross Breeding', in: *Report of the Proceedings of the Sixty-Sixth Annual Convention of the Connecticut Dairymen's Association, January 21–22, 1947* (Meriden, Connecticut, 1947), pp. 119–31.
—[*Catalogue of*] *Whirlwind Hill Farm Dispersal.* Wallingford, Connecticut, 28 May 1959.
—'Whirlhill Kingpin, His "Reason for Being" as Related by His Breeder', *Holstein–Friesian World*, lxx (10 Feb. 1973), 36, 38.

Index

Abrams, M. H., 338–40
Adams, C. K., 191
Adams, J. Q., 354
Addison, Charlotte, 174
Addison, Joseph, 174, 192, 344–5, 349, 355, 357, 359, 398; *Cato*, 357
Adventurer, The, 201, 213
Agnew & Sons. *See* Thos. Agnew & Sons
Aix-la-Chapelle, Treaty of, 222 n.
Alais, W. J., 190
Alexander the Great, 128–9
Algarotti, Francesco, 243
Allen, Ralph, 155
Allestree Hall, Derbyshire, 127
Ambulator, The, 148–9
American College Dictionary, 343
Andrade, Philip, 147
Andrade Ltd. *See* Reg. & Muriel Andrade Ltd.
Appleby, Arthur, 131
Appleby Bros. Ltd., London, 131
Arblay, Fanny (Burney) d', 160, 199, 283–4, 301, 304 n., 305, 307
Arbuthnot, George, 155
Argyll, John Campbell, 4th Duke of, 137
Ariosto, Lodovico, 257
Aristotle, 91; *Poetics*, 46–7
Arnold, George Henry, 134
Arnold, Lumley, 134–5
Arnold, Matthew, 45, 61
Ashby Lodge, Ashby St. Legers, Northamptonshire, 134–6
Asinius Pollio, 182
Aspinall, A., 217
Astley, Thomas, 167–9
Aston Hall, Birmingham, 148
Aubrey, John, 183
Audubon, J. J. L., 126
Australian National Library, Canberra, 319
Ayris, Samuel, 167–9

Ayrton, William, 307

Babbe, Mr., 31
Babington, Percy L., 67
Bacon, Catherine, 150
Bacon, Francis, 150
Bacon, John, 150, 229
Baker, George, 134–5, 159
Baker, Henry, 170
Baker, Sophia (Defoe), 170
Bald, R. C., 29–31, 40
Bale, John, xx
Balfour, M. A., 219
Barber, Charles, 26
Barber Institute of Fine Arts, Birmingham, 144
Baretti, Joseph, 259–60
Baring-Gould, Sabine, 3, 5
Barker, Dr. Edmund, 199, 202–3, 212
Barnard, Christopher Vane, 10th Baron, 127; collection of, at Raby Castle, Durham, 192
Barrington, Daines, 256
Barrow, Mrs. S., 144
Barry, Iris, 243
Barry, James, 161–2
Baskett, John, 139, 143, 144
Bateson, F. W., vii, 271
Bath, Guild Hall at, 141
Bathurst Collection, Cirencester, 191–192
Bathurst, Dr. Richard, 201–2, 211–212
Baxter, David, 140
Beaumarchais, Pierre-Augustin Caron de, 372
Beaumont, Francis, 194
Beckett, R. B., 190, 195
Beckett, Thomas, 330–1
Beckford, Peter, 292–3
Bedford, Lucy (Harington) Russell, Countess of, 43
Beechey, Sir William, 319
Belden, H. M., 67